AF559577

The Impact of Television Journalism

The Impact of Television Journalism

Sanoj Singh

RANDOM PUBLICATIONS
NEW DELHI (INDIA)

The Impact of Television Journalism

ISBN 978-93-5111-926-5

Published in 2016 in India by

RANDOM PUBLICATIONS

4376-A/4B, Gali Murari Lal, Ansari Road
New Delhi-110 002
Phone : +9111-43580356, 011-23289044, 011-43142548
e-mail: sales@randompublications.com,
info@randompublications.com, randomexports@gmail.com

Reprinted 2024

Type Setting by : Friends Media, Delhi-110089
Digitally Printed at : Replika Press Pvt. Ltd.

Preface

Broadcast journalism is the field of news and journals which are "broadcast", that is, published by electrical methods, instead of the older methods, such as printed newspapers and posters. Broadcast methods include radio (via air, cable, and Internet), television (via air, cable, and Internet), and, especially recently, the World Wide Web. Such media disperse pictures (static and moving), visual text and/or sounds.

Broadcast journalists deliver the news to the public in a variety of formats, including radio, television, and the Internet. They are our trusted sources for the events that shape our lives and our world. A broadcast journalism career can put you in the thick of changing and evolving world events, including politics, the environment, wars, social unrest, or the ups and downs in the nation's, and the world's, economy. A number of television executives and observers say news sharing agreements, driven largely by the wave of station consolidation, offer real benefits for local viewers. For one thing, they say, these agreements make local news available to more viewers by giving them a choice of how it is presented and when to watch it. But critics say that convenience comes at the cost of competition and diversity in news content. In order to properly understand the future of television journalism, one must understand how it grew to where it is today. The past tells us that technology causes journalism to change. In the mid-nineteenth century, the telegraph allowed news publishers to gather and send information across the globe faster than ever before. By the early twentieth century, the camera could create photographic images of people and events that readers had never been able to see. In the past forty years, most afternoon newspapers have disappeared, people's primary news sources have shifted from paper, to television, to the Internet, and our ways of understanding the news has completely changed.

The digital revolution is transforming the news, and this edition explores the new opportunities emerging for journalists and online reporters using the internet. Essential guidance is also given on how you can break into a career in journalism.

– ***Author***

Contents

1

Introduction

Television is a telecommunication system for broadcasting and receiving moving pictures and sound over a distance. The term has come to refer to all the aspects of television from the television set to the programming and transmission. The word is derived from mixed Latin and Greek roots, meaning "far seeing" The origins of what would become today's television system can be traced back as far as the discovery of the photoconductivity of the element selenium by Willoughby Smith in 1873, and the invention of a scanning disk by Paul Nipkow in 1884. All practical television systems use the fundamental idea of scanning an image to produce a time series signal representation. That representation is then transmitted to a device to reverse the scanning process. The final device, the television, relies on the human eye to integrate the result into a coherent image.

HISTORY OF TELEVISION BROADCASTING

Television technology was actually first developed in the 19th century, before commercial radio was conceived of, when, in 1897, Ferdinand Braun invented the cathode ray tube. The first time the cathode ray tube was used to produce images was in 1907. The tube was an essential step in the invention of television, followed by Philo Farnsworth and Vladimir Zworykin's independent developments of the image dissector and iconoscope. By the end of the 1920s, the United States had a total of fifteen experimental stations for mechanical television. In 1929, Herbert Hoover, at the time the Secretary of Commerce, made an appearance on the mechanical television of AT and T. RCA, the pioneer in broadcast development, did broadcasting experiments in the early 1930s.The development of television technology can be partitioned along two lines: those developments that depended upon both mechanical and electronic principles and those which are purely electronic. From the latter descended all modern televisions, but these would not have been possible without discoveries and insights from the mechanical systems.

Electromechanical television: The German student Paul Gottlieb Nipkow proposed and patented the first electromechanical television system in 1885.

Nipkow's spinning disk design is credited with being the first television image rasterizer, however, it wasn't until 1907 that developments in amplification tube technology made the design practical. Meanwhile, Constantin Perskyi had coined the word *television* in a paper read to the International Electricity Congress at the International World Fair in Paris on August 25, 1900. Perskeyi's paper reviewed the existing electromechanical technologies, mentioning the work of Nipkow and others.

From 1907 to 1910, Boris Rosing and his student Vladimir Zworykin demonstrated a television system that used a mechanical mirror-drum scanner in the transmitter and the electronic Braun tube (cathode ray tube) in the receiver. Rosing disappeared during the Bolshevik revolution of 1917, but Zworykin later went to work for RCA to build a purely electronic television, the design of which was eventually found to violate patents by Philo Taylor Farnsworth.

A mechanically-scanned analogue television system was first demonstrated in London in February 1924 by John Logie Baird with an image of Felix the Cat and a moving picture by Baird on October 30, 1925. In 1928 Baird's company (Baird Television Development Company / Cinema Television) broadcast the first transatlantic Television signal, between London and New York, and the first shore to ship transmission. He also demonstrated an electromechanical colour, infrared (dubbed "Noctovision"), and stereoscopic television, using additional lenses, disks and filters. In parallel he developed a video disk recording system dubbed "Phonovision"; a number of the Phonovisionhttp://www.tvdawn.com/tvimage.htm recordings, dating back to 1927, still exist. In 1929 he became involved in the first experimental electromechanical television service in Germany. In 1931 he made the first live transmission, of the Epsom Derby. In 1932 he demonstrated ultra-short wave television. Baird's system was tested by the BBC, who later discontinued its use in 1937 in favour of purely electronic television.

In the U. S. Ernst Alexanderson demonstrated a mechanically-scanned television broadcasting system in 1927.

Electronic television: Although the discoveries of Nipkow, Rosing, Baird and others were extraordinary, little of their technology is used in modern television. By 1934, all electromechanical television systems were outmoded.

A.A. Campbell-Swinton wrote a letter to *Nature* on the 18 June 1908 describing his concept of electronic television using the cathode ray tube, which had been invented in 1897 by the German physicist and Nobel prize winner Karl Ferdinand Braun. He proposed using an electron beam in both the camera and the receiver, which could be steered electronically to produce moving pictures. He lectured on the subject in 1911 and displayed circuit diagrams, but no one, including Swinton, knew how to realize the design. Even though his system was never built, the cathode ray tube is still used in almost all television sets to display images until today. A fully electronic system was first demonstrated by Philo Taylor Farnsworth in the autumn of 1927. Farnsworth, a Mormon farm boy from Rigby, Idaho, first envisioned his system at age 14. He discussed the idea with his high school chemistry teacher, who could think of no reason why it would not work (Farnsworth would later credit this teacher, Justin Tolman, as providing key insights into his invention). He continued to pursue the idea at Brigham Young Academy (now Brigham Young University). At age 21, he demonstrated a working system at his own laboratory in San Francisco. His breakthrough freed television from reliance on spinning discs and other mechanical parts. All modern picture tube televisions descend directly from his design.

Vladimir Zworykin is also sometimes cited as the father of electronic television because of his invention of the iconoscope in 1923 and his invention of the kinescope in 1929. His design was one of the first to demonstrate a television system with all the features of modern picture tubes. His previous work with Rosing on electromechanical television gave him key insights into how to produce such a system, but his (and RCA's) claim to being its original inventor was largely invalidated by three facts: a) Zworykin's 1923 patent presented an incomplete design, incapable of working in its given form (it was not until 1933 that Zworykin achieved a working implementation), b) the 1923 patent application was not granted until 1938, and not until it had been seriously revised, and c) courts eventually found that RCA was in violation of the television design patented by Philo Taylor Farnsworth, whose lab Zworykin had visited while working on his designs for RCA.

The controversy over whether it was first Farnsworth or Zworykin who invented modern television is still hotly debated today. Some of this debate stems from the fact that while Farnsworth appears to have gotten there first, it was RCA that first marketed working television sets, and it was RCA employees who first wrote the history of television. Even though Farnsworth eventually won the legal battle over this issue, he was never able to fully capitalize financially on his invention.

Broadcast television: The first long distance public television broadcast was from Washington, DC to New York City and occurred on April 7, 1927. The image shown was of then Commerce Secretary Herbert Hoover. The first analogue service was WGY, Schenectady, New York inaugurated on May 11 1928. The first British Television Play, "The Man with the Flower in his Mouth", was transmitted in July 1930. CBS's New York City station began broadcasting the first regular seven days a week television schedule in the U. S. on July 21, 1931. The first broadcast included Mayor James J. Walker, Kate Smith, and George Gershwin. The first all-electronic television service was started in Los Angeles, CA by Don Lee Broadcasting. Their start date was December 23, 1931 on W6XAO - later KTSL. Originally, mechanical equipment was used, but in

June of 1936 a 300-line all-electronic service was started. In Germany, regular service started on March 22, 1935, and one year later, the Berlin Summer Olympic Games were televised to places in Berlin and Hamburg.

In 1932 the BBC launched a service using Baird's 30-line system and these transmissions continued until 11 September 1935. On November 2, 1936 the BBC began broadcasting a dual-system service, alternating on a weekly basis between Marconi-EMI's high-resolution (405 lines per picture) service and Baird's improved 240-line standard from Alexandra Palace in London. Six months later, the corporation decided that Marconi-EMI's electronic picture gave the superior picture, and adopted that as their standard. This service is described as "the world's first regular high-definition public television service", since a regular television service had been broadcast earlier on a 180-line standard in Germany. The outbreak of the Second World War caused the service to be suspended.

TV transmissions only resumed from Alexandra Palace in 1946.The first regular television transmissions in Canada began in 1952 when the CBC put two stations on the air, one in Montreal, Quebec on September 6, and another in Toronto, Ontario two days later. The first live transcontinental television broadcast took place in San Francisco, California from the Japanese Peace Treaty Conference on September 4, 1951. In 1958, the CBC completed the longest television network in the world, from Sydney, Nova Scotia to Victoria, British Columbia. Reportedly, the first continuous live broadcast of a breaking news story in the world was conducted by the CBC during the Springhill Mining Disaster which began on October 23 of that year.

Programming is broadcast on television stations (sometimes called channels). At first, terrestrial broadcasting was the only way television could be distributed. Because bandwidth was limited, government regulation was normal. In the US, the Federal Communications Commission allowed stations to broadcast advertisements, but insisted on public service programming commitments as a requirement for a license. By contrast, the United Kingdom chose a different route, imposing a television licence fee on owners of television reception equipment, to fund the BBC, which had public service as part of its Royal Charter. Development of cable and satellite means of distribution in the 1970s pushed businessmen to target channels towards a certain audience, and enabled the rise of subscription-based television channels, such as HBO and Sky. Practically every country in the world now has developed at least one television channel. Television has grown up all over the world, enabling every country to share aspects of their culture and society with others.

By the late 1980s, 98 per cent of all homes in the U.S. had at least one TV set. On average, Americans watch four hours of television per day. An estimated two-thirds of Americans got most of their news about the world from TV, and nearly half got all of their news from TV. These figures are now estimated to be significantly higher. Colour Television: Guillermo González Camarena (1917-1965), invented the first colour TX and first TV XEG. He holds the design and patent to colour television systems from 1940, 1942, 1960 and 1962.In August 31, 1946 he sent his first colour transmission from his lab in the offices of The Mexican League of Radio Experiments in Lucerna St. #1, in Mexico City. The video signal was transmited in 115 MHz. and the audio in a band of 40 meters.RCA claims they did it in 1946 but Camarena's patent has an earlier month. Also, there are previous attempts or designs but none worked properly. Camarena's was the first successful one.

Technology: Broadcasting

There are many means of distributing television broadcasts, including both analogue and digital versions of:

- Terrestrial television
- Stratovision (From aircraft flying in a loop)
- Satellite television
- Cable television
- MMDS (Wireless cable)s

TV sets:

The earliest television sets were radios with the addition of a television device consisting of a neon tube with a mechanically spinning disk (the Nipkow disk, invented by Paul Gottlieb Nipkow) that produced a red postage-stamp size image. The first publicly broadcast electronic service was in Germany in March 1935. It had 180 lines of resolution and was only available in 22 public viewing rooms. One of the first major broadcasts involved the 1936 Berlin Olympics. The Germans had a 441-line system in the autumn of 1937. An example of an early television set is called a rotary dial-tune TV is outdated technology for a television set. This is one of the earliest technologies for TV turners. When the quartz-synthesized turners for TVs came out, rotary dial-tune turner technology was gradually obsolescing.

Rotary dial-tune TVs discontinued production somewhere around the mid and late 90's. Television usage skyrocketed after World War II with war-related technological advances and additional disposable income. Prior to the war, in the 1930s, TV receivers cost the equivalent of US$7000 in 2001, and had little available programming. Rotary dial-tune TVs were the earliest method of channel tuning until it became obsolete in the 90's.

For many years different countries used different technical standards. France initially adopted the German 441-line standard but later upgraded to 819 lines, which gave the highest picture definition of any analogue TV system, approximately four times the resolution of the British 405-line system. Eventually the whole of Europe switched to the 625-line standard, once more following Germany's example. Meanwhile in North America the original 525-line standard was retained. Television in its original and still most popular form involves sending images and sound over radio waves in the VHF and UHF bands, which are received by a receiver (a television set). In this sense, it is an extension of radio. Broadcast television requires an antenna (aerial). This can be an external antenna mounted outside or smaller antennas mounted on or near the television. Typically this is an adjustable dipole antenna called "rabbit ears" for the VHF band and a small loop antenna for the UHF band.

Some early television sets, especially British ones, contained valves and other pre-solid state electronic components which generated a considerable amount of heat even when the set was switched off. As a result, up until at least the mid-1970s, television stations would air announcements reminding viewers to unplug their sets before going to bed for the night, since the heat build-up in the back of the set was a considerable fire hazard.

Colour television became available in the U.S. on December 30 of 1953, backed by the Columbia Broadcasting System (CBS) network. The government approved the colour broadcast system proposed by CBS, but when RCA came up with a subcarrier system that made it possible to view colour broadcasts in black and white on unmodified old black and white TV sets, CBS dropped their own proposal and used the new one.

The first publicly announced experimental TV broadcast of a programme using RCA's "compatible colour" system was an episode of Kukla, Fran and Ollie on August 30, 1953. NBC was the first network to have a regularly scheduled colour programme on the air (*Bonanza*, starting in 1959). The networks slowly reformed into the colour standard, and all three broadcast networks were airing full colour schedules by the 1966-67 broadcast season.

European colour television was developed somewhat later and was hindered by a continuing division on technical standards. Having decided to adopt a higher-definition 625-line system for monochrome transmissions, with a lower frame rate but with a higher overall bandwidth, Europeans could not directly adopt the US colour standard, which was widely perceived as *wanting* anyway, because of its tint control problems. There was no urgency either, since there were still few sets overall and no commercial motivations, European television broadcasters being state-owned at the time.

As a consequence, although work on various colour encoding systems started already in the 1950s, with the first SECAM patent being registered in 1956, many years had passed till the first broadcasts actually started in 1967. Unsatisfied with the performance of NTSC and of initial SECAM implementations, the Germans decided to create PAL (phase alternating line) at the beginning of the 1960s, staying closer to NTSC but borrowing some ideas from SECAM. The French continued with SECAM, notably involving Russians in the development.

The first colour broadcast in Europe was by BBC2 in the UK in the summer of 1967, using PAL. Germans did their first broadcast in September (PAL), while the French in October (SECAM). PAL was eventually adopted by West Germany, the UK, Australia, New Zealand, much of Africa, Asia and South America, and most Western European countries except France.

Apart for France and Luxembourg, SECAM was adopted by Soviet Union, much of Eastern Europe, much of Africa and of the Middle East. Both systems broadcast on UHF frequencies, the VHF being used for legacy black and white, 405 lines in UK or 819 lines in France, till the beginning of the eighties. In the early years of television, losses were common in the industry due to the high costs involved and the relatively low number of sets owned in the U.S.. Profits grew as the market expanded, though, and the size of the network market peaked in 1986. At that time, competition from cable TV, Pay Per View TV and VCRs began to heavily cut into market share. The big three broadcast networks had a 91 per cent share of prime time audiences during the 1978/9 season. This dropped to 75 per cent in the 1986/7 season, and further to 61 per cent in 1993/4. Cable TV was developed very early on and began to be used in the 1950s as a way to expand the reach of network television in areas that had problems receiving broadcast signals, prompted by the desire of businesses to sell televisions in their area. In the 1960s cable stations began to import alternative broadcasts into new markets, fragmenting network reach. The networks demanded FCC regulation of the industry and this regulation slowed growth until the 1970s, when cable TV saw phenomenal growth.

MODERN DISPLAYS

Starting in the 1990s, modern television sets diverged into three different trends:

- standalone TV sets;
- integrated systems with DVD players and/or VHS VCR capabilities built into the TV set itself (mostly for small size TVs with up to 17" screen, the main idea is to have a complete portable system);
- Component systems with separate big-screen video monitor, tuner, audio system which the owner connects the pieces together as a high-end home theater system. This approach appeals to videophiles who prefer components that can be upgraded separately.

There are many kinds of video monitors used in modern TV sets. The most common are direct view CRTs for up to 40 inch or 100 cm (in 4:3) and 46 inch or 115 cm (in 16:9) diagonally; most big screen TVs (up to over 100 inch (254 cm)) use projection technology. Three types of projection systems are used in projection TVs: CRT-based, LCD-based, and DLP(reflective micromirror chip)-based. Modern advances have brought flat screens to TV that use active matrix LCD or plasma display technology. Flat panel LCDs and plasma displays are as little as 4 inch or 10 cm thick and can be hung on a wall like a picture or put over a pedestal. They are multifunctional, because they are used like computer monitors too (VGA and DVI or HDMI connections).

Nowadays some TVs integrate a pair of ports to connect computer cases and peripherals to it or to connect the set to an A/V home network (HAVI) (USB port for cord connection and BlueTooth/WiFi for wireless).

HISTORY OF TELEVISION TIMELINE

Television was not invented by a single inventor, instead many people working together and alone, contributed to the evolution of TV.

1831: Joseph Henry's and Michael Faraday's work with electromagnetism makes possible the era of electronic communication to begin.

1862: Abbe Giovanna Caselli invents his "pantelegraph" and becomes the first person to transmit a still image over wires.

1873: Scientists May and Smith experiment with selenium and light, this opens the door for inventors to transform images into electronic signals.

1876: Boston civil servant George Carey was thinking about complete television systems and in 1877 he put forward drawings for what he called a "selenium camera" that would allow people to "see by electricity." Eugen Goldstein coins the term "cathode rays" to describe the light emitted when an electric current was forced through a vacuum tube.

Late 1870's: Scientists and engineers like Paiva, Figuier, and Senlecq were suggesting alternative designs for "telectroscopes."

1880: Inventors like Bell and Edison theorize about telephone devices that transmit image as well as sound. Bell's photophone used light to transmit sound and he wanted to advance his device for image sending. George Carey builds a rudimentary system with light-sensitive cells.

1881: Sheldon Bidwell experiments with telephotography, another photophone.

1884: Paul Nipkow sends images over wires using a rotating metal disk technology calling it the "electric telescope" with 18 lines of resolution.

1900: At the World's Fair in Paris, the 1st International Congress of Electricity was held, where Russian, Constantin Perskyi made the first known use of the word "television."

Soon after, the momentum shifted from ideas and discussions to physical development of TV systems. Two paths were followed:

1. Mechanical television - based on Nipkow's rotating disks, and
2. Electronic television - based on the cathode ray tube work done independently in 1907 by English inventor A.A. Campbell-Swinton and Russian scientist Boris Rosing.

1906: Lee de Forest invents the "Audion" vacuum tube that proved essential to electronics. The Audion was the first tube with the ablity to amplify signals. Boris Rosing combines Nipkow's disk and a cathode ray tube and builds the first working mechanical TV system.

1907: Campbell Swinton and Boris Rosing suggest using cathode ray tubes to transmit images - independent of each other, they both develop electronic scanning methods of reproducing images.

American Charles Jenkins and Scotsman John Baird followed the mechanical model while Philo Farnsworth, working independently in San Francisco, and Russian émigré Vladimir Zworkin, working for Westinghouse and later RCA, advanced the electronic model.

1923: Vladimir Zworykin patents his iconscope a TV camera tube based on Campbell Swinton's ideas. The iconscope, which he called an "electric eye" becomes the cornerstone for further television development. He later develops the kinescope for picture display.

1924 - 1925: American Charles Jenkins and John Baird from Scotland, each demonstrate the mechanical transmissions of images over wire circuits. Photo Left: Jenkin's Radiovisor Model 100 circa 1931, sold as a kit. Baird becomes the first person to transmit moving silhouette images using a mechanical system based on Nipkow's disk. Vladimir Zworykin patents a colour television system.

1926: John Baird operates a 30 lines of resolution system at 5 frames per second.

1927: Bell Telephone and the U.S. Department of Commerce conduct the first long distance use of TV, between Washington D.C. and New York City on April 9th. Secretary of Commerce Herbert Hoover commented, "Today we have, in a sense, the transmission of sight for the first time in the world's history. Human genius has now destroyed the impediment of distance in a new respect, and in a manner hitherto unknown." Philo Farnsworth files for a patent on the first complete electronic television system, which he called the Image Dissector.

1928: The Federal Radio Commission issues the first television license (W3XK) to Charles Jenkins.

1929: Vladimir Zworykin demonstrates the first practical electronic system for both the transmission and reception of images using his new kinescope tube. John Baird opens the first TV studio; however, the image quality was poor.

1930: Charles Jenkins broadcasts the first TV commercial. The BBC begins regular TV transmissions.

1933: Iowa State University (W9XK) starts broadcasting twice weekly television programmes in cooperation with radio station WSUI.

1936: About 200 hundred television sets are in use world-wide. The introduction of coaxial cable, which is a pure copper or copper-coated wire surrounded by insulation and an aluminum covering. These cables were and are used to transmit television, telephone and data signals. The 1st "experimental" coaxial cable lines were laid by AT and T between New York and Philadelphia in 1936. The first "regular" installation connected Minneapolis and Stevens Point, WI in 1941. The original L1 coaxial-cable system could carry 480 telephone conversations or one television programme. By the 1970's, L5 systems could carry 132,000 calls or more than 200 television programmes.

1937: CBS begins TV development. The BBC begins high definition broadcasts in London. Brothers and Stanford researchers Russell and Sigurd Varian introduced the Klystron in. A Klystron is a high-frequency amplifier for generating microwaves. It is considered the technology that makes UHF-TV possible because it gives the ability to generate the high power required in this spectrum.

1939: Vladimir Zworykin and RCA conduct experimentally broadcasts from the Empire State Building. Television was demonstrated at the New York World's Fair and the San Francisco Golden Gate International Exposition. RCA's David Sarnoff used his company's exhibit at the 1939 World's Fair as a showcase for the 1st Presidential speech (Roosevelt) on television and to introduce RCA's new line of television receivers – some of which had to be coupled with a radio if you wanted to hear sound. The Dumont company starts making tv sets.

1940: Peter Goldmark invents a 343 lines of resolution colour television.

1941: The FCC releases the NTSC standard for black and white TV.

1943: Vladimir Zworykin developed a better camera tube - the Orthicon. The Orthicon (Photo Left) had enough light sensitivity to record outdoor events at night.

1946: Peter Goldmark, working for CBS, demonstrated his colour television system to the FCC. His system produced colour pictures by having a red-blue-green wheel spin in front of a cathode ray tube. This mechanical means of producing a colour picture was used in 1949 to broadcast medical procedures from Pennsylvania and Atlantic City hospitals. In Atlantic City, viewers could come to the convention center to see broadcasts of operations. Reports from the time noted that the realism of seeing surgery in colour caused more than a few viewers to faint. Although Goldmark's mechanical system was eventually replaced by an electronic system he is recognized as the first to introduce a broadcasting colour television system.

1948: Cable television is introduced in Pennsylvania as a means of bringing television to rural areas. A patent was granted to Louis W. Parker for a low-cost television receiver. One million homes in the United States have television sets.

1950: The FCC approves the first colour television standard which is replaced by a second in 1953. Vladimir Zworykin developed a better camera tube - the Vidicon.

1956: Ampex introduces the first practical videotape system of broadcast quality.

1956: Robert Adler invents the first practical remote control called the Zenith Space Commander, proceeded by wired remotes and units that failed in sunlight.

1960: The first split screen broadcast occurs on the Kennedy - Nixon debates.

1962: The All Channel Receiver Act requires that UHF tuners (channels 14 to 83) be included in all sets.

1962: AT and T launches Telstar, the first satellite to carry TV broadcasts - broadcasts are now internationally relayed.

1967: Most TV broadcasts are in colour.

1969: July 20, first TV transmission from the moon and 600 million people watch.

1972: Half the TVs in homes are colour sets.

1973: Giant screen projection TV is first marketed.

1976: Sony introduces betamax, the first home video cassette recorder.

1978: PBS becomes the first station to switch to all satellite delivery of programmes.

1981: NHK demonstrates HDTV with 1,125 lines of resolution.

1982: Dolby surround sound for home sets is introduced.

1983: Direct Broadcast Satellite begins service in Indianapolis, In.

1984: Stereo TV broadcasts approved.

1986: Super VHS introduced.

1993: Closed captioning required on all sets.

1996: The FCC approves ATSC's HDTV standard. Billion TV sets world-wide.

Timeline of the introduction of television in countries

Year	Countries
1928	United States
1929	United Kingdom, Germany
1931	France
1932	USSR
1939	Japan Italy
1949	Cuba
1950	Mexico, Brazil
1951	Argentina, Denmark, Netherlands
1952	Canada, Dominican Republic, Poland, Venezuela
1953	Czechoslovakia, Philippines, Switzerland
1954	Belgium, Colombia, Morocco, Norway, Puerto Rico
1955	Iceland, Luxembourg, Thailand
1956	Algeria, Australia, Austria, Croatia, Cyprus, El Salvador, Guatemala, Iraq, Republic of Korea, Nicaragua, Spain, Sweden, Uruguay
1957	Finland, Hong Kong, Portugal, Romania, Saudi Arabia
1958	Bermuda, Chile, People's Republic of China, Hungary, Iran, Slovenia, Peru
1959	Bulgaria, Haiti, Honduras, India, Lebanon, New Zealand, Nigeria, Panama, Ecuador

1960	Costa Rica, Egypt, Syria, Zimbabwe, Netherlands Antilles
1961	Ireland, Kuwait, Zambia
1962	Côte d'Ivoire, Kenya, Malta, Indonesia, Sierra Leone, Republic of China, Trinidad and Tobago, Cambodia,
1963	Gabon, Malaysia, Singapore, Jamaica
1964	American Samoa, Bangladesh, Ethiopia, Pakistan
1966	Greece, Vietnam, Iran, Tunisia
1967	Turkey, Mongolia
1969	Albania
1970	Qatar
1973	Niger
1974	Palau
1975	Micronesia, South Africa, Angola
1978	Afghanistan, Lesotho
1979	Sri Lanka, Somalia
1984	Tonga
1986	Niue, Papua New Guinea
1989	Cook Islands
1991	Fiji, Nauru, Samoa
1992	Solomon Islands, Vanuatu
1999	Bhutan

TELEVISION BROADCASTING IN AMERICA

Local public radio and television stations have existed alongside commercial broadcasters since the earliest days of broadcasting in the United States. Although no national public broadcast service existed before the late 1960s, in 1952 a grant from the Ford Foundation established the nation's first educational television network, the National Educational Television (NET). In 1957, Senator Warren Magnuson introduced a bill "to expedite the utilization of television facilities in our schools and colleges, and in adult training programmes."

While this bill did not pass at the time, it ultimately resulted in the Education Television Facilities Act of 1962. During the years immediately after, public support grew for transforming the loose association of "educational TV stations" scattered across the country – and supported principally by states, universities and foundation grants – into a strong, inter-connected system for public broadcasting.

This led to the formation in 1965 of the Carnegie Commission on Educational Television, which recommended a blueprint for a broader, national service it called "public broadcasting." The Commission's recommendations quickly found champions in a reform-minded Congress.

On November 7, 1967, within months after the Carnegie Commission issued its report, President Lyndon Johnson signed into law the Public Television Act, which for the first time authorized federal operating aid to public television and radio stations through a new, private agency called the Corporation for Public Broadcasting (CPB). Today, CPB administers close to

15 per cent of public broadcasting's revenue, which it receives through advanced federal appropriations, and distributes these revenues among more than 1,000 public television and radio stations.

On November 3, 1969, CPB and various public television entities incorporated a new non-profit organization, the Public Broadcasting Service (PBS), to connect the nation's public television stations and to serve as a central distributor of national programming produced by its member stations. Today, PBS is owned and operated by 348 member stations that together reach 98 percent of American homes.

In 1970, National Public Radio (NPR) was created as a national production center for news, information and cultural programming, and as a coordinator for national programme distribution. NPR began its national programme service in 1971 with production of All Things Considered, then a daily hour of in-depth, primarily national, news, and is now the primary distributor of content to the nation's public radio stations.

In 1980, local public television stations formed the Association of Public Television Stations (APTS) to support a strong and financially sound non-commercial television service for the American public. APTS works on behalf of local stations to advocate public television interests at the national level.

In 1983, Public Radio International (PRI, originally named the American Public Radio Network) was formed as a producer and distributor of programming for public radio. PRI is now the nation's largest distributor of non-commercial radio content, delivering over 400 hours of news, classical music and contemporary culture programming per week. Several of the signature programmes originally distributed by PRI, such as A Prairie Home Companion and Marketplace, have more recently switched to being distributed by American Public Media (APM), the national production and distribution arm of Minnesota Public Radio.

International Broadcasting Bureau (IBB)

Under the supervision of the Broadcasting Board of Governors (BBG), the International Broadcasting Bureau (IBB) provides the administrative and engineering support for U.S. government-funded non-military international broadcast services. Broadcast elements include the Voice of America (VOA), Radio Sawa, and Radio and TV Martí (Office of Cuba Broadcasting). In addition, the IBB provides engineering and programme support to Radio Free Europe/ Radio Liberty and Radio Free Asia.

The IBB was formed in 1994 by the International Broadcasting Act, which also created a nine-member, bipartisan Broadcasting Board of Governors (BBG). The IBB was initially part of the U.S. Information Agency (USIA). When USIA was disbanded in October 1999, the IBB and BBG were established as independent federal government entities

National Public Radio (NPR)

NPR (National Public Radio) is an internationally acclaimed producer and distributor of non-commercial news, talk, and entertainment programming. A privately supported, not-for-profit membership organization, NPR serves a growing audience of 26 million Americans each week in partnership with more than 800 independently operated, non-commercial public radio stations. Each NPR Member Station serves local listeners with a distinctive combination of national and local programming. With original online content and audio streaming, npr.org offers hourly newscasts, special features and ten years of archived audio and information.

Public Broadcasting Service (PBS)

PBS, headquartered in Arlington, Virginia, is a non–profit media enterprise owned and operated by the nation's 348 public television stations. A trusted community resource, PBS uses the power of non-commercial television, the Internet and other media to enrich the lives of all Americans through quality programmes and education services that inform inspire and delight. Available to 99 percent of American homes with televisions and to an increasing number of digital multimedia households, PBS serves nearly 90 million people each week.

Association of America's Public Television Stations

The Association of Public Television Stations (APTS) is a non-profit membership organization established in 1980 to support the continued growth and development of a strong and financially sound non-commercial television service for the American public. APTS provides advocacy for public television interests at the national level, as well as consistent leadership and information in marshaling support for its members: the nation's public television stations. APTS' affiliated organization, APTS Action, Inc., provides legislative advocacy and seeks grassroots and congressional support

HISTORY OF TELEVISION BROADCASTING IN BRITAIN

The first British television channel was launched by the BBC launched in 1932 and called simply The BBC Television Service. The service used Baird's 30-line system and these transmissions continued until 11 September 1935. On 2 November 1936 the BBC began broadcasting a dual-system service, alternating on a weekly basis between Marconi-EMI's high-resolution (405 lines per picture) service and Baird's improved 240-line standard from Alexandra Palace in London. Six months later, the corporation decided that Marconi-EMI's electronic picture gave the superior picture, and adopted that as their standard. This service is described as "the world's first regular high-definition public television service", since a regular television service had been broadcast earlier on a 180-line standard in Germany. The outbreak of the Second World War caused the service to be suspended. TV transmissions only resumed from Alexandra Palace in 1946.

The BBC Television Service held a complete monopoly on television broadcasting in the UK until ITV was launched in 1955. The station was renamed BBC1 when BBC2 was launched in April 1964.

MAJOR BROADCASTERS: THERE ARE SIX MAJOR BROADCASTERS:

Free-to-air analogue terrestrial networks

Before the advent of digital television in the UK, five main television channels dominated British television. With the increasing popularity of digital television, all are expanding and offering a portfolio of digital-only channels to viewers.

*BBC:*The BBC is the world's oldest and biggest broadcaster, and is the country's first and largest public service broadcaster. The BBC is funded by a television license fee that all households with a television must pay. Its analogue channels are BBC One and BBC Two. The BBC first began a television service, initially serving London only, in 1936. BBC Television was closed during World War II but reopened in 1946. The second station, BBC Two, was launched in 1964. As well as these two analogue services, the British Broadcasting Corporation now also offers digital services BBC Three, BBC Four, BBC News 24, BBC Parliament, CBBC, CBeebies, BBCi and has trialled BBC HD.

ITV: ITV (Independent Television) was the name given to the original commercial British television broadcasters, set up on a regional basis in 1955 to provide competition to the BBC. Almost all of these companies have now merged into a single business. Unlike the BBC, ITV is funds itself by showing television commercials. Despite the proliferation of channels, ITV is still the UK's biggest commercial broadcaster in the country. Its flagship analogue channel is ITV1, though it also now runs digital-only television channels ITV2, ITV3, ITV4, CITV, Men and Motors and ITV Play.

Channel 4 (originally only England, Scotland and Northern Ireland) and S4C (originally only Wales).

They were launched in 1982, and although state owned, Channel 4 is funded by its commercial activities (including advertising). The situation is more complex with S4C~, as the BBC produces some programming, and the channel has Welsh language obligations. Channel 4 has expanded into digital television, now offering E4, More 4 and FilmFour on all digital platforms. S4C~ has also expanded, offering S4C2 in Wales. S4C now also has to compete with Channel 4 in many areas of Wales, even though both channels carry many of the same programmes.

Five: Five (previously known as Channel 5) was the final analogue broadcaster to be launched, in 1997. Its coverage is less than that of the other analogue broadcasters. RTL Group, Europe's largest television broadcaster, took full control of the channel in August 2005, and intends to launch two new digital-only TV channels in autumn 2006 (Five US and Five Life)

All of these channels are also carried on satellite television, cable television and digital terrestrial television services.

Digital Networks

BSkyB

BSkyB (British Sky Broadcasting) operates a satellite television service and numerous television channels *e.g.* Sky One, Sky Two, Sky Three, Sky Movies, Sky Sports etc. It is owned by News Corporation.

Flextech

Owned by the cable provider NTL and operates several channels, *e.g.* Living TV, Bravo, Trouble etc. It also owns 50 per cent of the UKTV company (The other 50 per cent is owned by the BBC). These six broadcasters dominate British television. The terrestrial networks all operate numerous digital channels (except Five, which is set to launch two digital channels later this year) and the bulk of viewing is on channels provided by these broadcasters. The most watched digital channels are owned by these networks also. There are other broadcasters who have secured a notable place on British television including Discovery Channel, Viacom International and EMAP, which all provide multiple channels.

No further analogue broadcasters are expected to be launched, and efforts are being made to popularise the uptake of digital television so that analogue television broadcasts can be discontinued and the bandwidth allocated can be reused. The analogue service is to be switched off over a 5 year plan starting in 2008 and finishing in 2012. 2008 will see ITV Border, ITV Westcountry and ITV Wales analogue service switched off. 2009: ITV Granada, ITV West, stv. 2010: ITV Central, ITV Yorkshire and ITV Anglia, 2011: ITV Meridian, ITV London, ITV Tyne Tees and UTV, and finally 2012: ITV Channel Television.

With the passage of UK's *Communications Act 2003*, there are no longer any foreign-ownership restrictions in the UK's television programming services, cable and Direct-to-Home satellite television sectors. To counterbalance the removal of foreign-ownership restrictions for companies in the broadcasting sector, the UK government has increased the power of the regulatory body, which is called Ofcom.

Digital terrestrial television in the United Kingdom : Digital terrestrial television was originally launched as a subscription-based service by a company called ONdigital, later ITV Digital, which failed commercially. The digital television service was relaunched as Freeview, a free-to-air service which is run and promoted by a consortium which includes the BBC, Channel 4, ITV, BSkyB and National Grid Wireless. The Freeview package includes all of the terrestrial channels mentioned above, some extra BBC channels, and a selection of the specialist channels found on the three subscription services, but not any of the premium ones such as top sport and movie channels. A more limited package of subscription channels has since been added under the name Top Up TV.

Cable and satellite : The major competitors to the old free-to-air analogue broadcasters are the subscription-based services of the regional cable companies NTL and Telewest, and the satellite broadcaster BSkyB, whose Sky Digital system is available nationwide, as well as in Ireland.

In 2005, NTL announced the purchase of its rival Telewest, establishing a single dominant company offering telephone, digital television, and high-speed broadband in the UK. The merger is widely rumoured to be intended to create an effective competitor to BSkyB. Sky have now reacted to this move, with the purchase of Easynet, in a bid to match NTL's "triple-play" offering.

Freesat from Sky: a satellite-based free-to-air service similar to Freeview, is available from BSkyB for an initial installation charge of £150, and includes receiver, dish, viewing card, with access to all FTA and FTV* channels in the UK.

- UK mainland address required.

Alternatively, existing Sky customers can end their ongoing subscriptions, and opt for the Free-To-View viewing card, which is inserted into the Sky Viewing Card slot; effectively giving them the FreeSat from Sky service.Freesat from Sky is not to be confused with the proposed Freesat service from the BBC and ITV, which is yet to be launched.

TELEVISION BROADCASTING IN INDIA

Indian television started off in 1959 in New Delhi with tests for educational telecasts. Indian small screen programming started off in the early 1980s. At that time there was only one national channel Doordarshan, which was government owned. The Ramayana and Mahabharat was the first major television series produced. This serial notched up the world record in viewer ship numbers for a single programme. By the late 1980s more and more people started to own television sets. Though there was a single channel, television programming had reached saturation. Hence the government opened up another channel which had part national programming and part regional. This channel was known as DD 2 later DD Metro. Both channels were broadcasted terrestrially. Interestingly the Government of India required Licenses that TV owners needed to acquire during the initial years of the spread of Television (including the 1970s).A seemingly authoritarian, but obviously poorly thought out scheme that died a silent death and almost surely had no meaningful purpose while it lasted.

Cable Television: In 1992, the government liberated its markets, opening them up to cable television. Five new channels belonging to the Hong Kong based STAR TV gave Indians a fresh breath of life. MTV, Star Plus, BBC, Prime Sports and STAR Chinese Channel were the 5 channels. Zee TV was the first private owned Indian channel to broadcast over cable. A few years later CNN, Discovery Channel, National Geographic Channel made its foray into India. Star expanded its bouquet introducing Star World, Star Sports, ESPN and Star Gold. Regional channels flourished along with a multitude of Hindi channels and a few English channels. By 2001 HBO and History Channel were the other international channels to enter India. By 2001-2003, other international channels such as Nickelodeon, Cartoon Network, VH1, Disney and Toon Disney came into foray. In 2003 news channels started to boom.

INDIAN TELEVISION CHANNELS

Doordarshan: is a Public broadcast Terrestrial television channel run by Prasar Bharati, a board nominated by the Government of India. It is one of the largest broadcasting organisations in the world in terms of the infrastructure of studios and transmitters. Recently it has also started Digital Terrestrial Transmitters. DoorDarshan had a modest beginning with the experimental telecast starting in Delhi in September, 1959 with a small transmitter and a makeshift studio. The regular daily transmission started in 1965 as a part of All India Radio. The television service was extended to a second city – Mumbai only in 1972. Till 1975, only seven cities were covered by DoorDarshan and it remained the only television channel in India. Television services were separated from radio in 1976. Each office of All India Radio and DoorDarshan were placed under the management of two separate Director Generals in New Delhi. Finally DoorDarshan as a National Broadcaster came into existence. National programme was introduced in 1982. In the same year, colour TVs were introduced in the Indian markets with the live telecast of the Independence Day parade on 15th August, 1982, followed by the Asian Games being held in Delhi. The eighties was the era of Doordarshan with soaps like *Hum Log* (1984), *Buniyaad* (1986-87) and mythological dramas like *Ramayana* (1987-88) and *Mahabharat* (1988-89) glued millions to DoorDarshan. Other popular programmes included Hindi film songs based programmes like *Chitrahaar* and *Rangoli* and crime thrillers like *Karamchand' Byomkesh Bakshi* and *Janki Jasoos.* Recent programmes include the serial drama *Lal Kothi Alvida* (2006), based on the novel by Sharat Kumar.

Now more than 90 percent of the Indian population can receive DoorDarshan (DD1) programmes through a network of nearly 1400 terrestrial transmitters. About 46 DoorDarshan Studios are producing TV programmes today. Presently, DoorDarshan operates 19 channels – two All India channels, 11 Regional Languages Satellite Channels (RLSC), four State Networks (SN), an International channel, a Sports Channel and two channels (DD-RS and DD-LS) for live broadcast of parliamentary proceedings.

On DD-1 National programmes, Regional programmes and Local Programmes are carried on time-sharing basis. DD-News channel, launched on 3rd November, 2003, which replaced the DD-Metro Entertainment channel, provides 24-Hour news service. The Regional Languages Satellite channels have two components – The Regional service for the particular state relayed by all terrestrial transmitters in the state and additional programmes in the Regional Language in prime time and non-prime time available only through cable operators. Sports Channel is exclusively devoted to the broadcasting of sporting events of national and international importance. This is the only Sports Channels which telecasts rural sports like Kho-Kho, Kabbadi etc. something which private broadcasters will not attempt to telecast as it will not attract any revenues.

DD Direct Plus: The 'DD Direct Plus' launched on 16th December, 2004, India's first Free DTH service offering 33 TV channels and 12 radio channels, continues to gain in strength. Its all India subscriber base is approximately 4.5 lakhs sets.

Action is underway to increase the number of TV channels in DD Direct Plus from 33 to 50.

List of Channels on DD Direct Plus:

DD Channels

DD National; DD News
DD Sports
DD Bharati
DD India
DD Lok Sabha
DD Rajya Sabha
DD Malayalam
DD Bengali
DD Oriya
DD Gujarati
DD Punjabi
DD North East
DD Podhigai (Tamil)
DD Saptagiri (Telugu)
DD Chandana (Kannada)
DD Sahyadri (Marathi)
DD Kashir (Kashmiri)

Educational Channel

Gyan Darshan

Private Channel

Aaj Tak
Headlines Today
BBC World
Jain TV
STAR Utsav
Zee Music
Smile TV
Kairali TV
Akash Bangla
ETC Punjabi
MH-1
ETV-Marathi

TV-9
SUN TV

Radio Channels

AIR Hindi
AIR Bengali
AIR Telugu
AIR Marathi
AIR Tamil
AIR Punjabi
AIR Gujarati
AIR Kannada
AIR North East Service
Vividh Bharati
FM Gold (Delhi)
FM Rainbow(Delhi)

Cable and Satellite TV

General Entertainment

ETv- Urdu

SAB TV - Sony Entertainment Television's latest Hindi entertainment channel.

Sahara One - Hindi entertainment channel launched in 2006 as Sahara TV.

Sony Entertainment Television - Hindi entertainment channel launched by Sony Pictures Entertainment in 1995.

STAR One - Launched in 2006, promising to deliver the next generation of Hindi entertainment.

STAR Plus - India's No. 1 cable channel for the last six years, owned by the News Corporation.

STAR Utsav - Celebrating the best of STAR's Hindi-language programming.

Zee TV - Launched in 1992, India's pioneering Hindi general entertainment channel.

News and Business in Hindi

Zee News - Hindi news channel from the Zee Network, launched in 1995.

Aaj Tak - Hindi news channel from the TV Today Group.

CNBC Awaaz - Hindi business channel from the TV18 Group.

IBN 7 - Hindi news channel from the TV18 Group, launched in 2005 as Channel 7.

India TV - Hindi news channel from India TV, launched in 2004.

Janmat - Hindi news and views channel from Sri Adhikari Brothers, launched in 2005.

NDTV India - Hindi news channel from NDTV, launched in 1998.

Sahara Samay - Hindi news channel from Sahara India, also available in regional feeds.

STAR News - Hindi news channel from ABP and News Corporation.

TEZ - TV Today Group's Hindi version of Headlines Today, launched in 2005.

Zee Business - Hindi business channel from the Zee Network, launched in 2004.

Bollywood Movies

B4U Movies - B4U's Bollywood movie channel, holding a greater presence in overseas markets.

Filmy - Hindi movie channel from Sahara India launched in 2006.

MAX - Sony Entertainment Television's Hindi movie channel, launched in 1999.

STAR Gold - Launched in 2000 as a channel showcasing the best of classic and modern Bollywood movies.

Zee Cinema - With a strong library, the earliest 24/7 Hindi movie channel to launch in India (1995).

Music

B4U Music - B4U's music channel, holding a greater presence in overseas markets.

Channel [V] India - Popular music network presented by the News Corporation.

ETC - Music channel launched in 1999 by ETC Networks and the Zee Network.

MTV India - India's No. 1 music channel, available on the One Alliance bouquet.

VH1 - English music channel, available on the Zee Turner bouquet.

Zee Muzic - Music channel launched in 2000 by the Zee Network.

Children's

Animax - Popular animation channel in Hindi and English, distributed by The One Alliance.

Boomerang - Classic cartoons channel from Time Warner available on Dish TV.

Cartoon Network - India's No. 1 children's network, available on the Zee Turner bouquet.

Disney Channel - Disney Channel for Indian audiences, distributed by the STAR Group.

Hungama TV - India's only homegrown kids channel, today owned by Disney.

Nick - India's Nickelodeon feed in Hindi and English, distributed by The One Alliance.

Pogo - Cartoon Network's sister channel dedicated to toddlers and younger children.

Lifestyle

Zee Trendz - India's fashion, style, and beauty channel from the Zee Network.

Zoom - Glamour and Lifestyle Television, launched by the Times Group.

FTV - The international 24 hours fashion channel by Michel Adams.

Documentaries

A1 - Asia's only outdoor adventure channel, distributed by the STAR Group.

Animal Planet - Animal Planet for Indian audiences, distributed by The One Alliance.

Discovery Channel - Discovery Channel for Indian audiences, distributed by The One Alliance.

Discovery Travel and Living - Discovery's sister lifestyle network for Indian audiences.

National Geographic Channel - NGC for Indian audiences, distributed by the STAR Group.

The History Channel - NGC's sister network featuring historical programming.

Sports

ESPN - Network with the most comprehensive sports coverage across Asia.

STAR Sports - Offering Indian viewers live Asian and international world-class sports.

TEN Sports - South Asian sports channel featuring cricket, football (soccer), and tennis.

Zee Sports - Sports channel launched by the Zee Network in 2006.

Telugu Channels

Etv (India) - Commonly referred to as ETV.

ETV2

Gemini TV

Teja TV

Teja News

Aditya TV

MAA TV

Zee Telugu

Tamil Channels

Jaya TV

KTV - Sun Network's second Tamil entertainment channel.

Raj Digital Plus

Raj Musix

Raj TV

Sun TV - India's No. 1 Tamil network from the Sun Network.

Sun Music - Tamil music channel from the Sun Network.
Sun News - Tamil and English news channel from the Sun Network.
VIJAY - STAR Network's Tamil entertainment channel.
WIN TV

News and Business in English

BBC World - BBC World news channel, covering South Asia and abroad.
CNBC TV18 - English business channel from the TV18 Group.
CNN - CNN's international English feed for worldwide viewers.
CNN-IBN - English news channel from the TV18 Group and Time Warner.
Headlines Today - TV Today Group's sister news network in English.
NDTV 24x7 - English news channel from NDTV, launched in 2006.
NDTV Profit - NDTV's English business channel, launched in 2006.
Times Now - English news channel from the Times Group and Reuters.
Awaaz TV - www.awaaz.tv.

English Entertainment

Australia Network - Australian Broadcasting Corporation's international television service.
AXN - Action and adventure channel, distributed by the The One Alliance.
STAR World - English entertainment channel from the News Corporation.
Zee Café - English entertainment channel from the Zee Network.
Zone Reality - Zone Vision's reality television channel, available on the Zee Turner bouquet.

English Movies

Hallmark Channel - Providing wholesome family entertainment round the clock.
HBO - English movie channel, available on the Zee Turner bouquet.
MGM Channel - English movie channel, available on Dish TV.
PIX - Sony Entertainment Television's English movie channel.
STAR Movies - English movie channel from the News Corporation.
Turner Classic Movies - Celebrating the golden era of Hollywood cinema.
Zee Studio - English movie channel from the Zee Network.

INTERNET OR ONLINE JOURNALISM

Online journalism is defined as the reporting of facts produced and distributed via the Internet.An early leader was The News and Observer in Raleigh, North Carolina. Steve Yelvington wrote on the Poynter Institute web site about Nando, owned by The N and O, by saying "Nando evolved into the first serious, professional news site on the World Wide Web — long before CNN, MSNBC, and other followers." It originated in the early 1990s as "NandO Land".Many news organizations based in other media also distribute news online, but the amount they use of the new medium varies. Some news organisations use the Web exclusively or as a secondary outlet for their content. The Online News Association is the premier organization representing online journalists, with more than 800 members.The Internet challenges traditional news organisations in several ways. Newspapers may lose classified advertising to web sites, which are often targeted by interest instead of geography. These organisations are concerned about real and perceived loss of viewers and circulation to the Internet.And the revenue gained with advertising on news web sites is sometimes too small to support the site. Even before the Internet, technology and other factors were dividing people's attention, leading to more - but narrower - media outlets.

The Internet has also given rise to more participation by people who aren't normally journalists, such as with Indy Media (Max Perez).Bloggers write on web logs or blogs. Traditional journalists often do not consider bloggers to automatically be journalists. This has more to do with standards and professional practices than the medium. But, as of 2005, blogging has generally gained at least more attention and has led to some effects on mainstream journalism, such as exposing problems related to a television piece about President Bush's National Guard Service. Other significant tools of on-line journalism are Internet forums, discussion boards and chats, especially those representing the Internet version of official media. The widespread use of the Internet all over the world created a unique opportunity to create a meeting place for both sides in many conflicts, such as the Israeli-Palestinian conflict and the Russian-Chechen War. Often this gives a unique chance to find new, alternative solutions to the conflict, but often the Internet is turned into the battlefield by contradicting parties creating endless "online battles."

Most Internet users agree that on-line sources are often less biased and more informative then the official media. This claim is often backed with the belief that on-line journalists are merely volunteers and freelancers who are not paid for their activity, and therefore are free from corporate ethics. But recently many Internet forums began to moderate their boards because of threat of vandalism, which many users see as a form of censorship.

Most important forums based on official or corporate media sources are the BBC message boards and Slate.

Some online journalists have an ambition to replace the mainstream media in the long run. Some independent forums and discussion boards have already achieved a level of popularity comparable to mainstream news agencies such as television stations and newspapers. Particularly interesting are About.com in the United States, Expatica in Western Europe and several others.

LEGAL ISSUES

One emerging problem with online journalism in the United States is that, in many states, individuals who publish only on the Web do not enjoy the same

First Amendment rights as reporters who work for traditional print or broadcast media. As a result, unlike a newspaper, they are much more liable for such things as libel. In California, however, protection of anonymous sources was ruled to be the same for both kinds of journalism.

In Canada there are more ambiguities, as Canadian libel law permits suits to succeed even if no false statements of fact are involved, and even if matters of public controversay are being discussed. In British Columbia, as part of "a spate of lawsuits" against online news sites, according to legal columnist Michael Geist, several cases have put key issues in online journalism up for rulings. Green Party of Canada financier Wayne Crookes filed a suit in which he alleged damages for an online news service that republished resignation letters from that party and let users summarize claims they contained. He had demanded access to all the anonymous sources confirming the insider information, which Geist believed would be extremely prejudicial to online journalism. The lawsuit, "Crookes versus openpolitics", attracted attention from the BBC and major newspapers, perhaps because of its humorous name. Crookes had also objected to satire published on the site, including use of the name gang of Crookes for his allies. Some experts including Mike Godwin believe that libel law is wholly incompatible with online journalism and that right of reply will eventually have to replace it. Otherwise commentary on events in places that give libel plaintiffs too many rights or powers will move to other jurisdictions and most of the comment will be made anonymous. Everyone would then lose rights and remedies, due to a few wealthy people with resources to launch libel suits on weak grounds. Jennifer Jannuska and other legal commentators have, while agreeing with strong protections for publishers who only host journalists, sometimes emphasize that the use of anonymizer technology makes even criminal abuses, not just libel, possible, and so should be avoided even if other rights are lost.

News collections:

The Internet also offers options such as personalized news feeds and aggregators, which compile news from different web sites into one site. One of the most popular news aggregators is Google News. Others include Newsfeedmaker.com and Topisx.net. But, some people see too much personalization as detrimental. For example, some fear that people will have narrower exposure to news.

Internet radio and Podcasts are other growing independent media based on the Internet

Internet radio: Internet radio is a broadcasting service transmitted via the Internet. Not every internet "radio station" has a corresponding traditional radio station. Many internet radio stations are completely independent from traditional ("terrestrial") radio stations and broadcast only on the Internet. Broadcasting on the Internet is usually referred to as streaming. Because the radio signal is relayed over the Internet, it is possible to access the stations from anywhere in the world—for example, to listen to an Australian radio station from Europe or America. This makes it a popular service for expatriates and for people who have interests that may not be adequately catered for by their local radio stations (such as progressive rock, anime themed music, 24/7 stand up comedy, and others). Some of the internet radio services offer news, sports, talkback, and various genres of music—everything that is on the radio station being re-broadcast. One of the most common ways to distribute internet radio is via streaming technology using a lossy audio codec. The MP3 codec is most popular, followed by Ogg Vorbis, Windows Media Audio, and RealAudio; use of HE-AAC (sometimes called aacPlus) is gaining in popularity. The bits are "streamed" over a TCP/IP connection, then reassembled and played within about 2 seconds. Therefore, streaming radio has about a two-second lag time.

There are three major components to an audio stream:

1. Audio stream source
2. Audio stream repeater (server)
3. Audio stream playback

There are many methods for creating the audio stream source. Those more technologically savvy may opt for the SHOUTcast service, which utilizes Winamp and the SHOUTcast DSP plugin to deliver MP3 audio at higher bitrates. Other methods include open source technologies such as Streamcast, stream-db, IceS, and MuSE, and patent-free data formats such as Ogg Vorbis. Using open source stream source tools allows for interesting web interface possibilities like phpStreamcast.

Two of the most popular internet radio networks are Live365 and SHOUTcast. Open source alternatives include Icecast and Xiph.org, which include Ogg Vorbis streamings (that can be played by Winamp and Zinf). Collectively, these internet radio servers list thousands of Internet radio stations covering an ever-expanding variety of genres. The purpose of the server is to repeat the stream source to the audio playback software.

Sites that aggregrate links of Internet radio broadcasts enable listeners to find internet broadcasts by genre, language, or location. Some sort of audio playback software or hardware, that is capable of reading HTTP data streams, is needed to listen to streaming MP3 audio. Some popular software players are Winamp for Windows, iTunes for Macintosh and Microsoft Windows, and XMMS on Unix/Linux. Listening to internet radio through hardware devices has not been very popular in the past, due to the limited number of devices on the market, though the availability of such devices and their consumer popularity is expected to increase significantly during 2006. A list of commercially available devices is available at Internet radio device, but many of these are limited in which audio codecs they can use and consequently the variety of internet radio stations they are compatible with. There is a tradeoff between audio quality and audience size. Stations that encode their streams at a lower bitrate have lower audio quality, but they are more accessible to listeners with a dialup connection, and they can serve more simultaneous users on a given upstream pipe.

There are also a small number of web radio programmes that allow users to rate the songs they are listening to. This allows a user's music listening choices to be correlated against those of others, as with the programmes iRATE radio, Last.fm, and Radio Paradise.

History: The first Internet "radio station", Internet Talk Radio, was developed by Carl Malamud in 1993. Malamud's station used a technology called MBONE (IP Multicast Backbone on the Internet). In February, 1995, the first full-time, Internet-only radio station, Radio HK, began broadcasting the music of independent bands. Radio HK was created by Norman Hajjar and the Hajjar/Kaufman New Media Lab, an advertising agency in Marina del Rey, California. Hajjar's method was to use a CU-SeeMe web conferencing reflector connected to a custom created audio CD in endless loop. Later, Radio HK converted to one of the original RealAudio servers. Today, Internet radio stations such as VoyagerRadio utilize the technologies of web services like Live365 to webcast 24 hours a day.

WXYC (89.3FM Chapel Hill, NC USA) was the first radio station to announce broadcasting on the Internet on November 7, 1994. WXYC used an FM radio connected to a system at SunSite, later known as Ibiblio, running CU-SeeMe. WXYC had begun test broadcasts and bandwidth testing as early as August, 1994. WREK (91.1FM, Atlanta, GA USA) also claims to have started streaming on November 7, using their own custom software called CyberRadio1, although the stream was not advertised until a later date.

KJHK 90.7FM in Lawrence, Kansas, began to stream its live broadcast using CU-SeeMe on December 3, 1994. KJHK was the first radio station to maintain a *continuous*, live signal over the Internet. This has been verified by the National Association of Broadcasters, Sports Illustrated, and CNN.

KPIG also began to transmit a live, 24/7 feed, in August 1995, first using Xing Streamworks and later switching to RealAudio. Bill Goldsmith, who was KPIG's Operations Manager and morning DJ at the time, and the one responsible for starting the webcast, now operates the popular Internet station Radio Paradise. WUEV launched its live simulcast in January 1996, also using the Xing Streamworks technology at first, then adding RealAudio and moving from the Xing platform to Windows Media Technologies as equipment (and budget sizes) changed.

The first radio station to stream 24-hours a day in Europe was the UK's Virgin Radio, who started streaming a live simulcast using Real Networks in March 1996.

Tuning in to a broadcast like a traditional radio is not possible on internet, so finding different broadcasts has to be done with a Search_Engine or a web site that collects on-line radio broadcasts.

In 1996 GBS Radio Networks, founded by radio veteran Guy W. Giuliano, was one of the first to launch an internet radio programming service. The firm syndicated two commercial formats, hip-hop station BombRadio, and hard rock format LoudRadio. In 1998, GBS was purchased by the Emusic.com corporation in a highly publicized cash and stock deal. In 1999, LoudRadio.com became the first online radio station to be syndicated on a commercial broadcast station via KLOD-FM in Flagstaff, AZ.

In 1997, one of the first University/College stations to operate was in Wolfville, Nova Scotia at Acadia University. The popularity of Amedayus Radio grew almost overnight. At one point the station ranked #1 on Shoutcast for 3 straight weeks. With over 5,000 listeners a night the station was forced to close down by the University Administration. The owner of the station Mark Day who went under the alias Tony Bishop was then offered a job by the school to set up and operate a school station sanctioned by the administration. Amedayus has been on again and off again over the last 10 years and still operates under Tony Bishop a canadian comic.

In 1999 a company called BMP released a tool that allowed anyone to Netcast in 10 minutes. The MyCaster tool was cleverly simple. It was basically a software MP3 player, similar to Winamp, that as the user listened to music it simultaneously sent a stream to the MyCaster Web site. MyCaster then amplified the stream and listed it on its site for listeners to access. The free service allowed even people with little technical skill to easily go live with their own Internet radio station. Like many early Internet radio endeavors, MyCaster succumbed to the dot com bust in 2001.

Peercasting uses P2P technology. Its requirement of communicating a URI before transmission and the lack of a centralized repository of such addresses reduced peercasting's widespread adoption.

Podcasts: Podcasting is the method of distributing multimedia files, such as audio or video programmes, over the Internet using syndication feeds, for playback on mobile devices and personal computers. The term, coined in 2004, combines "iPod", a popular portable audio device, and "broadcasting."

The term podcast, like 'radio', can mean both the content and the method of delivery. The host or author of a podcast is often called a podcaster. Though podcasters' web sites may also offer direct download or streaming of their content, a podcast is distinguished from other formats by its ability to be downloaded automatically using software capable of reading feeds like RSS or Atom. Usually a podcast features one type of 'show', with new episodes released either sporadically or at planned intervals such as daily or weekly. In addition, there are podcast networks that feature multiple shows on the same feed.

History: The concept of podcasting was suggested as early as 2000 and its technical components were available by 2001, then implemented in the programme Radio Userland. In 2003 regular podcasts started showing up on well-known Web sites and software support spread. By the end of 2004 thousands of podcasts were available, the term had entered widespread use, and Apple Computer had begun to adopt the technology. For details, see the History of podcasting page.

Even though the name is a misnomer, in that podcasting doesn't require an iPod and no over-the-air broadcasting is required, it has maintained its prominence in the face of numerous alternatives.The use of "podcast" to describe both audio and video feeds seemed natural to some users, while others prefer to reserve the word for audio and coin new terms for video subscriptions. Other "pod-" derived neologisms include "podcasters" for individuals or organizations offering feeds and "podcatchers" for special RSS aggregators with the ability to transfer the files to media player software or hardware..

The "pod" name association came about because Apple Computer's iPod was the digital audio player used by early podcast listeners. The use of "pod" in 2004 probably played a part in Apple's development of podcasting products and services in 2005, further linking the device and the activity in the news media. Ubiquitous usage of the term "Podcasting" may also represent a form of trademark genericisation for Apple. The editors of the New Oxford American Dictionary declared "podcasting" the 2005 word of the year, defining the term as "a digital recording of a radio broadcast or similar programme, made available on the Internet for downloading to a personal audio player".

Various writers suggested other names or alternative interpretations of the letters "P-O-D." Technology writer Doc Searls had proposed "Personal Option Digital" in September, 2004.The "Personal on Demand" interpretation was in international circulation as early as October 2004.In July 2005, Microsoft blogger Robert Scoble mentioned that interpretation while countering reports that his company was pushing the word "blogcasting" to avoid mentioning an Apple product. "Blogcasting" also implied content based on, or similar in format to, blogs, which was not always the case.

Other terms have been suggested, but had shortcomings — "audioblogging", "audio magazines" and "webcasting" could describe other forms of media distribution, and "rsscasting" would be difficult to pronounce. As use of RSS enclosures for video spread in 2005, podcasting of video data was called, among other things, "video blogging", "video podcasting", "vidcasting", "vlogging", "vodcasting", "vicasting", and "videocasting".

WEBLOGS: AN INTRODUCTION

A weblog can be loosely defined as a journal or diary which is published on the World Wide Web. The process of updating and maintaining a weblog is known as blogging and the author is known as a blogger. Weblogs are usually updated at regular intervals using user-friendly software that requires little or no technical background.

The rate of growth of blogging has been astounding. According toTechnorati there are currently (early 2006) there are now over 26 million weblogs in existence. They reckon that:

- The blogosphere (ie: the weblog universe) doubles in size about every 5.5 months.
- A new weblog is created roughly every second and there are over 80,000 weblogs created daily.
- About 55 per cent of all weblogs are active.
- About 13 per cent of all weblogs are updated at least weekly.

It is difficult to come up with a definition that fits all weblogs, or even most weblogs. In essence, weblogs are web pages that have several posts or distinct items of information per page. They are normally in reverse chronological order, with the most recent post at the top of the page and the oldest at the bottom.

Weblogs often contain links to other Web sites or weblogs. Many of the earliest weblogs relied heavily on links, and consisted mainly of short pieces of text, mixed with news items or useful links the author had found that day. Modern weblogs may link to external sites, but they might also have more of an inward focus, acting as a personal journal or diary for the author. Weblogs are often created and maintained by an individual, but they may also be produced by small groups of people, or involve large communities in a single weblog.

Most weblogs are non-commercial in nature, but they are increasingly being added to commercial sites and being used new form of business communication. A weblog can be a small part of a larger site, a small portion of a single page or an entire Web site. Weblogs are usually updated oftener than traditional Web sites, due largely to the smaller changes and lower amount of effort required to add a new weblog post as compared to adding an entire Web page full of content.

Weblogs are based on discrete posts, sometimes known as articles or entries. Each page is usually a collection of posts over a period of time, sometimes several years. Tools are available to automate the creation of new posts, leaving the details of creating archive pages, uploading amended files to a server and applying HTML templates to automated scripts. Bloggers can add new posts using a simplified interface that operates like a word processing application.

Weblogs are a rapidly-developing area, so it is likely that the information given by them will become outdated very quickly.

History of Blogs: It is difficult to specify exactly when the first weblogs appeared, as they weren't defined until much later. No single person was responsible for their invention and they appeared spontaneously on several sites about the same time. The earliest weblogs were simply lists of links and personal filters of billions of pages that were swamping the World Wide Web, but they've since become personal journals or diaries, with much more opinion and editorial content.Pages going back to the earliest days of the Web share many characteristics of weblogs and can be regarded as their predecessors or forerunners. Tim Berners-Lee, the inventor of the Web, used his own web site on the first-ever Web server to keep his colleagues at CERN, the European Nuclear Research Centre, informed about other Web pages and servers within the organisation. The diary and journal formats which appeared soon after the Web's expansion outwith the research community bore some resemblance to the weblog format. They were updated at regular intervals and shared tales from the author's life.

One of the earliest forerunners the weblog was Justin Hall's Links from the Underground web site which the author used to share links to interesting sites and tell stories of his life and travels, beginning in 1994. The site continued to be updated until mid-2005, when the author decided to take a well-earned rest. Another weblog predecessor was Michael Sippey's web site The Filter, a section of a larger site (http://www.theobvious.com), which shared links about technology news. The Filter was updated daily as early as 1996 and was used to publish essays and articles complementing the main part of the site.

The What's New page, seen on thousands of Web sites, has much in common with the weblog format. One of the earliest what's New pages appeared in 1993 at the National Center for Supercomputing (NCSA), producers of the first graphical Web browser, Mosaic. The NCSA/Mosaic what's new page served as a central point for information about new servers, sites and pages coming online.

Around 1997, a few web authors began publishing short bits of text each day without giving this activity a name. For example, Dave Winer of UserLand Software started publishing essays on technology issues on his web site in 1994. In April 1997 he started a new site (http://www.scripting.com) which kept track of Web sites devoted to programming and scripting and gave daily updates about his company's software. The site was still being maintained in late 2005, but now he adds a personal commentary to each day's postings.

Also in 1997, Jorn Barger began compiling a list of links with short descriptions on a regular basis. His site initially consisted of a list of 20 to 30 links, with single sentence descriptions, added at a rate of 5 to 10 a day. He later started writing an online diary to complement the links. Barger coined the term weblog to describe his site, and over the next year or two, the term was adopted by other authors.

Jesse James Garrett, editor of Infosift (http://www.jgg.net/infosift) began compiling a list of similar sites as he encountered them his travels arousnd the

Web. In November 1977, he sent that list to Cameron Barrett, who published it on list on CamWorld (http://www.camworld.com), and others maintaining similar sites began sending him their details for inclusion on the list. Garrett's "page of only weblogs" listed the 23 weblogs known to exist at the start of 1999.

All the earliest weblogs followed a similar format, giving short pieces of text on a single, rapidly changing page which provided links to interesting sites the author had found. The notion of creating a web site purely to direct visitors to other Web sites was a novel idea at the time, as the prevailing wisdom was that commercial Web sites had to be "sticky" in order to keep visitors within the site for as long as possible. In contrast, the early weblogs were eager to provide visitors with links to other sites, rather than confining them to a single site.

It was easy to read all of the weblogs on Garrett's list, and many people did. However, as more and more people began publishing their own weblogs it became difficult to read every weblog every day, or even to keep track of all the new ones that were appearing. In early 1999, Brigitte Eaton compiled a list of every weblog she knew about and created the Eatonweb Portal. She evaluated all submissions by a simple criterion: the site consist of dated entries. This rapidly became part of the definition of weblogs.

1999 also marked the beginning of the "weblog explosion" when tools to enable anyone to create a weblog were initially released. Prior to this, weblog creators had to write their own software and code each day's postings by hand, using HyperText Markup Language (HTML), so people producing weblogs up until 1999 were generally Internet technology professionals or programmers.

July 1999, saw the release of Pitas, the first tool designed for creating, managing and maintaining weblogs. Pitas, which is still in operation today, enables users to sign up for an account and create a weblog, which is hosted for free with an address of the form: http://username.pitas.com. A Pitas weblog has several automated components, including features to let users customise their sites. There is a user-friendly posting page where users can add the title, URL and description of each post.

Pitas weblog authors don't need to know HTML because the software automates the creation of links. However, templates allow knowledgeable users to change the HTML behind the visual design of their site without affecting the automatic elements of each post. Automatic archiving is an important feature of Pitas. As users post regular updates to their sites the software automatically moves older entries to the archive pages.

In August 1999, Pyra Labs released the first version of Blogger, which is also still online at http://www.blogger.com, although it is now owned by Google. Blogger provides similar features to Pitas, but with a number of important differences. Blogger initially required users to have their own Web site. It could take user posts, create static files and transmit the amended files to the users' server when they updated.

The tasks of programming, maintaining and archiving information were handled by Blogger on a central server accessible from anywhere, leaving users to host output on their own sites. Blogger also offered the ability to maintain more than one weblog from a single account and provided additional ways to customise sites, eg: templates could be customised by using a series of special tags, and an archive template allowed users to specify how older posts should appear.

1999 also saw the release of LiveJournal, which actually came out a few months before Pitas and Blogger, but wasn't regarded as a weblog tool until much later. The tools available through Pitas and Blogger led to a massive explosion in the number of people maintaining weblogs. The number of weblog authors grew from dozens to hundreds and then thousands within months of these tools being released. Weblogs were filled with original writing, journals of author's lives and links to interesting sites, including other weblogs.

Additional tools followed, eg: UserLand Software released Manila, a content management system which incorporated weblogs and an integrated discussion system. A public server at http://www.editthispage.com allowed prospective users to try out the software without buying the server. Other tools released that year included Velocinews and Groksoup which also automated weblog posting and offered free hosting for weblogs. All of these services were free and all of them were designed to enable individuals to publish their own weblogs quickly and easily.

The original weblogs were link-driven sites containing a mixture of links, commentary and personal opinions. Their editors presented links to obscure web sites and to current news articles they felt were worthy of note. These links were usually accompanied by an editorial commentary, often with an irreverent or sarcastic tone. The format of the typical weblog, providing only a very short space in which to write an entry, encourages brevity on the part of the writer. Longer commentary is often published elsewhere. These weblogs provided a valuable filtering function for their readers by pre-surfing the web for them.

In 2000, second-generation weblog tools began to appear. Greymatter a weblog management system designed to be installed on your own server, provided dozens of features which were not available in existing weblog tools. Since the software was installed on your own server, there were none of the traffic problems a large, central service such as Blogger sometimes suffered from.

Since 2001, the explosion in weblog growth and popularity has continued. Stories about weblogs have featured in national magazines, and weblogs have supplemented traditional media coverage in some cases. Notable examples include the South Asian Tsunami, the invasion of Iraq and the US Presidential Election.

Weblog tools have continued to develop with the release of packages such as MovableType and Radio, as well as dozens of more specialised tools. Articles about weblogs continue to appear in the mainstream press, and the registered users at popular services, such as Blogger and LiveJournal, are now numbered in millions. Weblogs are appearing on business and media sites, and they are being used increasingly by grassroots organisations as a way of bringing their causes to the attention of the public.

BLOGS AND SOCIAL SOFTWARE

Social software is a broad term used to describe software-based tools that facilitate interaction and collaboration. Social software connects people together intellectually and makes it possible to share and evolve ideas. Social software is not bound just by what features the tool provides, but also by social conventions and etiquette on how to use it appropriately. Such software includes e-mail, Usenet, IRC, instant messaging, blogs, wikis, NNTP, folksonomy, and virtual online communities

E-mail will already be familiar to most people. However it can be regarded as one of the earliest forms of social software, particularly with regard to some of its one-to-many communication features, such as the use of the cc: field and mailing lists, as well as the use of contact lists or address books.

Instant Messaging (IM) allows individuals to communicate privately with one another over a public network. Popular clients include MSN Messenger (http://messenger.msn.com/Xp/Default.aspx) and Yahoo Messenger (http://messenger.yahoo.com/) IM communications were initially text based but they have now been expanded to include audio and video and clients can also exchange files.

Chat is an abbreviated name for Internet Relay Chat (IRC) which lets users join chat rooms and communicate with many people simultaneously. Users can join an existing chat room or create one of their own, on any topic of interest to them. Once in a chat room they can post comments and respond to the comments of others and invite other users to participate in private chats. You can find out anything you want to know about IRC at http://www.irchelp.org/. Popular suppliers include Yahoo. (http://chat.yahoo.com/)

Newsgroups or forums are the Internet version of electronic bulletin boards, popular among computer users long before Internet. A user can post comments on a topic and other users can respond. Messages are visible to all members of the group and some services provide extensions such as file storage and calendaring. The original newsgroup service, Usenet, is now available via Google Groups (http://groups.google.co.uk/). Other services include Smartgroups (http://www.smartgroups.com/) and Yahoo Groups (http://

groups.yahoo.com/). A Wiki is a group of Web pages that allows users to add their own content and permits others to edit the content. It provides a simple method of producing HML content and is an effective medium for collaboration. The term is also used to describe the collaborative software, sometimes known as a wiki engine, used to create such a web site. Examples include: Wikipedia (http://c2.com/cgi/wiki), Wikibooks (http://en.wikibooks.org/wiki/Main_Page), Wikinews (http://en.wikinews.org/wiki/Main_Page) and WikiWikiWeb (http://c2.com/cgi/wiki

Social network services allow people to meet on-line around shared interests or causes. In some cases it is only possible to join a social network by being recommended by an existing member. Examples include Orkut (http://www.orkut.com), MeetUp (http://www.meetup.com), LinkedIn (http://www.linkedin.com) and Tribe Networks (http://www.tribe.net). An offshoot of this area is social network search engines, which allow people to find each other according to their XFN social relationships, eg: XHTML Friends Network (http://gmpg.org/xfn/

Social guides recommend places to visit in the real world such as coffee shops, restaurants and WiFi hotspots, etc. Popular applications include CafeSpot (http://cafespot.net), Tagzania (http://www.tagzania.com/) and WikiTravel (http://wikitravel.org/en/Main_Page).

Social bookmarking sites allow users to post their list of bookmarks or favourite web sites for others to search and view. The object is for people to meet others with whom they share a common interest. Examples include Del.icio.us (http://del.icio.us/), Furl (http://www.furl.net/) and Connectedy (http://www.connectedy.com/

Folksonomy is the name given to the informal classifications (sometimes called tags or keywords) that Internet users invent to categorise the objects with which they interact on-line. Social software makes these classifications available to other Internet users, so folksonomy can be viewed as a distributed classification system. Examples of folksonomy-enabled social software include Furl , Flickr and Del.icio.us.

Evaluating blogs

Blogs are not equal in terms of the quality of information provided and should always be evaluated carefully. The quality of information relates to the following attributes:

Relevance: information is relevant if it relates to the subject under investigation.

Accuracy: information is accurate if it is factually correct – or at least known not to be factually incorrect.

Clarity: information is clear if it is well written in accordance with the rules for clear and simple writing.

Brevity: information is brief if it is succinct and to-the-point

Depth/detail: information is detailed if sufficient information is provided to give the reader a clear understanding of the subject matter.

Timeliness: information is timely if it is up-to-date.

Note that some of these attributes conflict – there is a tension between brevity and depth, and it is difficult to maintain a blog's timeliness and accuracy.

For the purposes of this course you should be able to evaluate blogs according to the following criteria:

Design: see Good Blog Design: Speed, Accessibility, Transparency and Clarity.

Ease of use (usability): generally the same standards are applied as for web site usability. However, there is some discussion as to whether this is appropriate. Both sites provide numerous useful links on usability.

Navigation: a useful article on blog/web site navigation design can be found at: http://www.guuui.com/issues/01_05.php and another one at: http://tapestrydesigns.typepad.com/design_niche/2005/01/navigation_desi.html.

Collaborative features: most blogs support a number of collaborative features, eg:

- Readers can post comments.
- Blogs may be jointly authored.
- There are links to similar blogs (blogrolls).
- Content can be syndicated via automated systems such as RSS.
- Blogs can comment on (or re-circulate) content from other blogs.

A useful summary of blogs as a collaborative tool can be found at: http://cne.sitempower.com/site.cfm/blogs.cfm Links: links are a major component of blogs. They can be made to other blogs or web sites and that links may occur in the main text or in a list of links. Links are discussed extensively elsewhere in these notes (Sections 1.1.5 and 2).

Quality of information: information obtained from blogs must be evaluated critically in the same way as information obtained any other online source. There may be additional difficulties if a blog consists largely of quotations and links. A selection of useful resources can be found at: http://www.library.cornell.edu/olinuris/ref/research/webeval.html

Purpose and target readership

It is important to match the design of your blog to its target readership, for example, blogs aimed at teenagers might be expected to be bright and brash, whilst those aimed at corporate users or researchers would be a bit more businesslike and professional looking. There are a number of steps you can take to help attract the kind of reader you are looking for:

1. Focus on a specific topic and set yourself an editorial calendar to stay on topic, eg: post on a specific aspect of the topic each day of

the week. For example, if your blog is about a local football team, and you post every weekday, you might want to organise your calendar as follows:

- Monday: a review of last weekend's match.
- Tuesday: focus on a particular player.
- Wednesday: a review of a famous historical match.
- Thursday: review of recent activity in the league.
- Friday: information about the team you'll be playing this weekend

2. Visit and comment on other blogs. This allows you to make your voice known. If you make comments that other people find interesting, they're more likely to visit your blog.
3. Contribute to blog carnivals. These are blog articles which contains links to other articles on a specific topic. Blog carnivals are usually hosted by a rotating list of frequent contributors and help generate new posts by contributors and highlight new bloggers posting matter in that subject area.
4. Be passionate about your topic. The more enthusiastic you are about the topic, the more likely you are to generate enthusiasm in others.
5. Try some joint ventures. Ask other bloggers who write on similar topics to write an article for your blog and offer to do the same for them. This will hopefully attract some of their readers to your blog and vice versa.

Keeping your blog up-to-date and relevant

You should always ensure that the contents of your blog are kept up-to-date and relevant to its purpose and target audience. One of the most important features of blogs is currency. A blog which is out of date can rapidly become useless. However, a blog should only be updated when there is something useful to be added; indiscriminate updating, when there is nothing significant to be added, can discourage readers.

One very effective way of keeping you blog up to date is to add newsfeeds from other blogs or web sites which deal with the same topics. We'll be looking at newsfeeds in detail in Section 3 of these notes.

Blogs as an effective information tools

A blog can be regarded as an effective information tool when it succeeds in reaching the target audience, which could be defined by demographics, location, interests or many other variables and communicating the desired information, whether factual or opinion.

Once you've spent hours writing your weblog, you'll want an audience to read it. But how do you attract them? There are millions of weblogs out there, so how is any potential reader going to find yours?

One of the first things you should do is make sure that your weblog is registered with the major portals and search engines. Most search engines and portals allow you to submit your weblog URL to them directly, eg: in Google you can do it from: http://www.google.com/intl/en/submit_content.html. There are also a number of specialized services which will submit your weblog URL too various portals and search engines, free of charge, eg: http://www.addme.com/ and http://www.submitexpress.com/

Unfortunately, it can take a long time before your site shows up in search engines or directories, and there's not much you can do to speed this up without spending money. The sites listed above also offer paid placement services, but these are seldom worth paying for, so just be patient.

An alternative approach is the use of webrings. These are designed to improve links between related sites and they provide a simple way of joining a community of web site owners. The webring will normally have a name which gives some indication of its purpose and each site will provide links to the previous and next sites in the ring, as well as some central location where you can join the ring. If a weblog you enjoy is a member of a webring, take a look at some of the other sites which are members. If you feel that the content of your weblog fits in with the others, it may be a good idea to join. You can find a portal to more than 40,000 webrings at http://www.ringsurf.com/

Another approach is to use update trackers. There are a number off services that provide listings of recently updated weblogs. Some of these generate their directories by checking lists of weblogs at regular intervals while others require weblog owners to notify them. Some blogging tools can be set to notify these services automatically whenever you update your weblog, eg: Blogger can be set to notify weblogs.com automatically. Trackers are a popular way to surf weblogs, and they generate a good response for weblogs that are already known. However, any audience that reaches your site through these services will have already read your site before or heard of it elsewhere. You can submit your site to multiple trackers simultaneously by using http://pingomatic.com/

A simple, but useful technique for generating traffic is to add your weblog URL to your e-mail signature. This will help to remind your correspondents that you are now keeping a weblog. It can also be useful if you participate in any mailing lists (sometimes known as listservs). Although these are often regarded as old-fashioned, they remain an important method of building communities on the internet and of making and maintaining contact with like-minded people. You can find out more about mailing lists at: http://en.wikipedia.org/wiki/Electronic_mailing_list.

Taking part in a mailing list can be a useful way of building your online reputation, through intelligent and relevant contributions. You should ensure that your e-mail signature is included in any contributions you write, but it is not generally a good idea to announce your weblog to the list, unless it is relevant to the list topic. There are a number of etiquette considerations to be taken into account when using mailing lists. You should read the list for a week or two before you begin posting. You want to make yourself known so that people will be more inclined to read your weblog, but to make a good impression you'll need to have a clear understanding of community standards before joining in. If the mailing list has a Frequently Asked Questions (FAQ) document, make sure that you read it before beginning to post. Choose subject lines which are clear and descriptive to ensure that members can decide whether or not to read your message. Remember that almost all mailing list messages are archived, so anything you write is going to be available to any interested Internet user for many years – there are still mailing list messages around from the earliest days of the Internet in the mid 1960s!

Another useful approach is joining weblog community sites like Plastic (http://www.plastic.com) or Meta Filter (http://www.metafilter.com). The etiquette rules for using these sites are similar to those discussed above for mailing lists. Remember that the comments you make on such sites provide the only information other members have about you, so if you want to interest them in your weblog, you will need to interact with others in an interesting and friendly manner. Rebecca Blood (in The Weblog Handbook, Perseus Publishing, 2002) suggests a few rules to be observed when taking part in online communities:

- Do not post when you are angry.
- Always argue the facts, never the personalities.
- Once you have stated your arguments as clearly and cogently as you can, sit back and read what others have to say - you may learn something.
- Respond to personal attacks by ignoring them.
- Do not hijack conversations.
- Do not misrepresent other people's positions.

Once you've joined an online community, there are a number of steps you can take to improve your visibility within it. Can you provide a service to other members of the community? Eg: if you have particular expertise on a specific piece of software, how about providing tips or tutorials to the community. Bloggers occasionally organize community events, which can range in scale from posting on a common theme to face to face meetings of community members. Taking part in events like these can attract visitors to your site. Events which allow you to meet other bloggers face to face can be particularly valuable in building up contacts.

Tracking selected blogs

Over the last few years 'newsfeeds' have become a standard feature of the World Wide Web. Perhaps you've noticed web sites or blogs with a little orange button labeled XML or RSS or simply Newsfeed. These are all examples of newsfeeds. They are links to text files with their content formatted in XML (eXtensible Manipulation Language), containing a set of items in reverse chronological order.

Many major news sources, such as the BBC, CNN and many others now publish newsfeeds and thousands of weblog authors publish feeds to keep themselves connected to their readers. Blogs are the main driving force behind the recent surge of interest in RSS and syndicated content.

One of the commonest feed formats is called RSS 2.0, with RSS meaning Really Simple Syndication. An earlier version called RSS 0.91 or 0.92 is still in use at some sites. Syndication is the name given to the sharing of content among different Web sites. The term is borrowed from the media industry, where it is normally associated with content such as television programmes, which can be syndicated to several different TV stations, and newspaper columns, which can be syndicated to several publishers. Confusingly enough, another major newsfeed format is called RSS 1.0, but in this case RSS stands for RDF Site Summary. (RDF stands for Resource Description framework, a standard way of providing information about web sites, but you needn't bother about that.). There's an updated version called RSS 1.1, but many sites still use RSS 1.0.

The third common format for news feeds is Atom 1.0, released in August 2005 by the Internet Engineering Task Force (IETF). However an earlier release, Atom 0.3 has been around for a long time and some sites are still running this. There are other versions of newsfeeds about, but RSS 2.0, RSS 1.0 and Atom are the commonest ones and the only ones we'll discuss from now on. There are more sophisticated methods of producing and manipulating newsfeeds by using technologies such as ASP (Active Server Pages) or PHP, a scripting language used to create dynamic web pages, but these are outwith the scope of this course. The format and use of newsfeeds is fairly simple. Each feed contains a number of discrete items, usually with a title, content, category, author and date. The overall feed also has information such as source title, last update time, update frequency, site owner and so on. Within these fields, there are various options that can lead to a good deal of variation between feeds, but this level of detail is outwith the scope of this unit.

Though newsfeeds are becoming widespread at many different kinds of web sites, they achieved their current level of popularity today through their use in weblogs. It's difficult to say which was the main driving force behind dated, time-limited, reverse-ordered entries: weblogs or newsfeeds. Most blogging tools provide the ability to generate newsfeeds in one or more formats.

We'll take a look now at several of these tools:

Blogger

As already noted, Blogger was one of the earliest weblogging environments and it still accounts for a significant percentage of weblogs. Blogger provides only Atom as a built-in feed type, though Blogger Pro account holders can also select RSS 2.0. It's also possible to add an RSS newsfeed by using third-party products such a FeedBurner. We'll take a closer look at adding a feed to a Blogger blog shortly.

Six Apart

Six Apart is the supplier of three popular blogging tools, Movable Type, TypePad and LiveJournal. All three support both Atom and RSS 2.0.

WordPress

WordPress supports for all three major syndication feed formats: RSS 1.0, RSS 2.0 and Atom as well as some legacy formats, like RSS 0.9x. As you can see, most tools support RSS 2.0 and Atom, and some support RSS 1.0, along with widely used legacy formats, like RSS 0.92. If you are using a tool which only supports one format and you want to supply another type of feed, you may be able to find plugins or add-ins that can provide support for the relevant format. Another option is to use a service that converts a feed from one format to another, eg: http://2rss.com can generate an RSS 2.0 feed from an Atom feed.

Once you've set up a newsfeed, you'll want let readers subscribe to you. Remember those little buttons labelled Atom, RSS or XML that we talked about earlier? They lead to a newsfeed and clicking on them will open that feed in your browser (or whatever other application you've defined to handle newsfeeds. Your blogging tool may allow you to add a button automatically to your site, or you can create a hypertext link with the appropriate label.

Another way of publicising a feed is to use autodiscovery. This involves putting a line into the Head section of each web document, giving the location of your feed. You must also provide information about the type of feed so that aggregators know how to find it. Your blogging tool may let you to do this automatically. If you add this to a page, and your readers access the page with a feed-sensitive browser, such as Firefox, they will see an indicator that the site has associated feeds that they can subscribe to. If your readers put the URL for your site into whatever newsfeed aggregator they use, it should find the link to the feed, without further effort on your part.

Follow the steps outline above (or the FeedBurner instructions for an RSS feed) to place a newsfeed on your blog.

2

Television and the Public Image

The start of the new millennium brought with it three prime-time television series featuring social workers, the latest of which to debut in the winter of 2001 was Kate Brasher. Was this a sign of greater public awareness of the essential role of social workers? Would this newest series provide a more accurate and flattering portrayal of social workers than other television shows? Unfortunately, the answer was "no" to both questions.

The power of the media to mold public images is well established. The focus here is on one source of image-making—television. Television has high impact and rapid message delivery. A study conducted by the Centre for Media and Public Affairs for the Council for Excellence in Government, for example, found that the vision of elected officials and civil servants as inept (if not corrupt), which had been promulgated and reinforced on prime-time television has undergone a metamorphosis. With new series, particularly The West Wing, government workers are now portrayed—and thus increasingly viewed by the public—as dedicated, sensitive, competent people. If only this were the case for social workers, who could use a boost in public image.

TELEVISION'S RECENT PORTRAYAL OF SOCIAL WORKERS

In the latest, but short-lived, social work entry into prime time, promotions billed the key character, Kate Brasher, as a "single mother, social worker, everyday hero." "She fights hard for the underdog... because she is one". Who was this superwoman of social work? A woman who did not complete high school. Her credentials included experience as a waitress. She landed a job simply by visiting a community centre in search of assistance with a personal problem.

There she confronted a professional staff (including an attorney and a director whose profession remains a mystery) who were rude and overbearing (albeit eventually capable of displaying humanity), and their personal issues and agenda were worn on their sleeves. Open personnel recruitment, selection, and training were simply non-existent in this community centre. To get hired, one apparently had to walk through the door at the right time.

Kate, our social worker, however, was a dedicated mother, conscientious, and possessed other positive virtues, such as the ability to listen well and to mobilize others and advocate on the "case" and "cause" level. These characteristics were in contrast to those of Norm, her colleague on another network. The CMPA (2001) concluded that Norm represented the most negative portrayal of a civil servant to appear on television. His training was as a hockey player. His employment in social services was involuntary; it was either community service or jail for tax fraud. Although social workers walked the picket line to protest the profession's outrage about the portrayal of Norm as a social worker, we should be getting the message: Television is not kind to social workers.

NASW recognized and applauded Tyne Daly's portrayal of a social worker, Maxine Gray, on the series Judging Amy. However, the accolades ate deserved not in an absolute sense, but relative to the consistently negative images that have typified television social work characters. Whereas the character Maxine Gray is certainly a refreshing contrast to that of Norm, she is not the vision of professionalism.

First, we know nothing about her training. Does she hold a BSW or MSW? Is she licensed? Have we ever heard reference to her participation in continuing education? Her behaviour often pushes the boundaries of ethical practice. She engages in insubordination frequently. Although we can applaud the intent of such insubordination—client advocacy—the means are certainly debatable. Even Tyne Daly has acknowledged that the social work situations portrayed may be "overdramatized and some of the outcomes idealized...".

Nevertheless, one would be hard pressed to totally reject the image. Maxine Gray is committed and hard working; she takes her job seriously; she displays realistic burnout and stress; the cases with which she deals often are realistic in their intensity and complexity. However, the accolades bestowed by social workers about this portrayal seem overstated in light of the often questionable practices in which she engages.

Television conveys an anti-professional, disrespectful image of social workers. The message is "no credentials needed; anyone can do it." In reality, Kate and Norm (and perhaps even Maxine Gray, although it is less clear) represent less than 1 per cent of those classified by the U.S. Department of Labour as social workers on the basis of educational attainment at the level of"less than high school diploma." Why, then, would television programme developers focus on characters who are not representative of social workers? Possibly, the answer is that audiences are receptive to this characterization, and such portrayals are consistent with and reinforce public perceptions. There is simply more rating mileage in portraying social work as a job anyone can do.

For social workers, the positive news lies in the cancellation of both Kate Brasher (in April 2001, after only four months) and Norm (in January 2001, after a two-season run). Nevertheless, public perceptions, once formed, are less easily erased.

INFLUENCE OF TELEVISION ON PERCEPTIONS

Television has been referenced as the most powerful of all media, a not surprising revelation in light of the number of hours Americans are reported to spend in front of the screen. Thus, the images portrayed through television, particularly when repeated week after week to millions of people, tend to have a lasting influence on public perceptions. At the same time, television mirrors existing opinions and attitudes.

Ironically, the one groundbreaking network effort to portray a more realistic view of social workers, East Side/West Side, aired for only one season. In this critically acclaimed series, the action was in the issues (child abuse, aging, discrimination, addiction), and the realism portrayed about people and about social work was not popular with viewers. What is marketable is that which is appealing; what is appealing, in turn, is generally consistent with existing sentiments or at least predilections towards certain views. Thus, who is selected by television show developers and, eventually, producers and viewers to represent heroes and villains or intelligentsia versus buffoons often reflects views about people, places, and things about which there is already some general consensus.

Television, in fact, is deluged with series that showcase professionals. ER, for example, portrays the day-to-day work of emergency room personnel, ranging from physicians to clerks. The Practice, Law and Order, Family Law, NYPD, and Third Watch illustrate the work of police, attorneys, judges, tire fighters, and EMS workers, generally in a positive light.

The portrayals of these professionals give appropriate and seemingly accurate recognition of their education and training, the challenges inherent in their work, and their commitment to and compassion about their vocations. The result, in regard to image making, is respect. But the social worker continues to be portrayed as uneducated and bumbling, if not outright laughable. The perpetuation of this view reinforces prevailing attitudes about social work and its labour force.

Substantial consequences accrue to the social work profession from these negative portrayals. How television portrays professions and professionals not only draws attention to these fields, but also affects public attitudes about them. Messages about unqualified and untrained social workers perpetuate the low status afforded the profession by reinforcing stereotypes and substantiating uninformed portrayals of who social workers are and what they do. For youths, the portrayal of social workers exemplified in the three 2001 serials may deter potential recruits into the profession. The consistency of television series—week after week, year in and out—suggests a lasting and powerful forum for image building that denigrates rather than celebrates the work of social workers.

MOVING FORWARD

The use of the media by and on behalf of social workers, the profession, and the clients served by professionals, has conveyed messages that we believe people need to hear. Perhaps it is time to adjust the targeting of our messages and begin by studying and understanding what is important to the audience. Script writers for television shows tap the public pulse, and the success of any show depends on the degree to which research about what will sell to the public is accurate. In other words, the beginning point is the audience, not the message. Messages are then adjusted to the nature of the audience and in language that the audience can comprehend.

The importance of influencing public opinion has certainly been recognized by the profession. NASW, for one, sees public education as among its major roles. For example, Professional Social Work Month activities emanating from one NASW chapter in 2001 included a public awareness campaign "to clarify who professional social workers are and what they do...". However, no matter how many people take note of a public service announcement (PSA) or hear a radio broadcast in which a social worker is interviewed about an issue, the use of media in this manner has far less impact and lasting value than do popular television shows.

The CMPA (2001) found, in its recent study, that the image of teachers in the 1990s was ranked third in terms of positive image, but dropped to 12th place in 2001 after a season's airing of the Fox series Boston Public. Although the impact of the series on public opinion cannot be isolated, the CMPA found some linkage between public views and the television show. In this series, teachers have been portrayed as making racist remarks, pulling out a gun to get students' attention, and having sex with a student. Such negative images neutralize, if not counter, the efforts of teachers' unions to use television PSAs to increase public awareness about the essential and vital role of the teacher—designed both to enhance the image of teachers and to aid in recruitment of the next generation of teachers.

INFLUENCING THE MEDIA

We need to put our networking skills to use in regard to media contacts. We know people who know people in the "industry." Those we want to reach include script writers and executive producers who control the content of popular series. The goal is to gain the ears of those with the power to form images through the medium of television. There are an infinite number and variety of social worker experiences that can forma "script line" that is compelling, dramatic, maybe even amusing, but perhaps most important—an accurate portrayal of professional practice.

The need for social workers to develop skills in working with the media has long been acknowledged. Some schools of social work include knowledge and skill development about the use of media in social welfare courses that incorporate content on advocacy. Perhaps it is time to think about offering discrete learning modules or even courses on public and media relations and to broaden our targeted public to include commercial broadcasting as well as elected and appointed policymakers. Infusing modules about popular media and the means by which to access it will help entering professionals to consider the media as a target of social action.

Continuing education provides a logical target point for specialized content on working with the media. Collaborative continuing education programmes between schools of social work, journalism schools, and public relations programmes might well prove beneficial to each professional group. Social workers can learn to "talk the talk" of journalists and how to cultivate and use media contacts.

Journalists, in turn, might gain knowledge about what social workers do in ways that will augment how they seek and use background information for their story lines, whether print or broadcast. Putting aside admonishments about the deleterious effects of too much time in front of the television, the fact is that a large proportion of our population spends a whole lot of hours "tuned in" to the TV. Popular series that provide misinformation about the profession promote false images based on ignorance and affect the ability of the profession to recruit the labour force of tomorrow. The message is in the medium, and television is surely one medium that cannot be ignored.

Since the label Generation X was first used in Douglas Coupland's 1991 novel to depict the angst of the MTV generation, the label has been used by newspaper and magazine journalists, network and local TV news anchors, print and broadcast advertisers, and TV, cable, and film producers as shorthand to describe the post-baby boomer generation, those born between 1965 and 1977.

While the Generation X label may be convenient for those in the media to use, do those who read, see, or hear it understand that meaning? What are the consequences for the media if the meaning of Generation X, a label that has been used to describe 45 million young adults, is misunderstood by the audience? Would misunderstanding the label Generation X have special consequences for the newspaper industry? This chapter addresses these issues.

BACKGROUND AND USE OF THE LABEL

A 1992 New York Times article on then-presidential candidate Governor Bill Clinton's efforts to court the MTV generation's vote used a variety of labels to refer to this age group: youth vote, youngest voters, young voters, the young, young people, 19 to 30-year olds. But there was no mention of the label Generation X to describe the young adult age group. But over the past six years, the use of the label Generation X, or a variation of it, appears to have become commonplace in describing the generation born between 1965 and 1977.

A headline from a 1994 Washington Post News Service article, for example, said, Marketers tailor pitches towards 'Generation X'. Another headline for a 1996 Austin American-Statesman article, said Groups Give Voice to Generation X. This chapter listed four interest groups that had sprung up to offset the negative portrayals of Generation X in the media, including the National Association of Twentysomethings, Generation X Coalition, The 2030 Centre and Third Millennium.

As early as 1993, academic research began to use the label in conference papers and thesis reports. Books have also used the Generation X label: Generation X Goes to College by Peter Sacks, Managing Generation X by twentysomething author Bruce Tulgan, and Rob Owen's Gen X TV: The Brady Bunch to Melrose Place.

- In creating an advertising campaign for its soft drink, Pepsi Cola used a variation of the Generation X label, Generation Next to appeal to the youth market. Most recently, Time magazine prominently displayed the label in a cover story, Generation X Gets Real.
- From its 1991 debut in Coupland's fictional account of three twentysomethings, the label Generation X has conjured up negative images. Generation X has been portrayed as cynical, apathetic, disrespectful losers and slackers. But a recent Yankelovich study featured as a Time magazine cover story contradicts that negative image. The survey found today's young adult generation should be described as optimistic, savvy, confident, ambitious, determined, independent, and materialistic.
- Author of Managing Generation X Bruce Tulgan adds that the profile of Generation X is "sort of the flipslide of slacker." He described Generation X as "flexible, adaptable, comfortable with technology, independent problem-solvers who constantly monitor the world around them for feedback.
- "But regardless of whether the negative or positive attributes of the label have been emphasized by the media, the relevant question is: How has the label, which has become synonymous with the young adult population, been perceived? Do those who read, see, or hear the label understand its meaning and do they evaluate it positively or negatively?

Just semantics? One might ask whether the use of the term Generation X to refer to young adults is something worth worrying about. As Shakespeare suggested, would not a rose smell just as sweetly, regardless of what name we give it? Is not this just a matter of semantics? The answer is, yes, that's precisely what it is. In fact, the group of scholars who became known as the General

Semanticists offered clear guidance on this matter. Alfred Korzybski, Wendell Johnson and others in this group contributed much to our understanding of how language usage can inhibit communication.

Among the four major misuses of language the general semanticists identified was one they called "undue identification," the failure to observe distinctions among the members of a group. Undue identification has become more popularly known as categorical thinking or overgeneralization, and a particularly pernicious form of it is stereotyping, a term coined by Walter Lippmann in 1922. He said, "In the great blooming, buzzing confusion of the outer world we pick out what our culture has already defined for us, and we tend to perceive that which we have picked out in the form stereotyped for us by our culture."

Those who stereotype others often are not aware that they are doing it. Regardless of intentions, stereotyping occurs. Stereotyping is more likely to occur when communicators are unfamiliar with those about whom they are writing. In 1954, Wilbur Schramm noted that communication becomes more difficult when a communicator's "field of experience" does not overlap much with the fields of experience of those with whom he or she is trying to communicate.

The question is raised whether the term Generation X as applied to young adults operates as a stereotype. What is being communicated when this label is used? Is the audience familiar with the label? How does the age group that this label purports to describe view the label? Are members of this group familiar with the term?

Do they disproportionately consider it to have negative connotations? If answers are yes, these characteristics would suggest that the group to whom the label is being applied may consider it to be a form of stereotyping. What are the implications for those who use the term - newspapers and other mass media - if the label is perceived as a stereotype? A survey was conducted to answer these questions.

METHOD

A random sample of 489 adults 18 years or older in the Austin, Texas metropolitan area was surveyed by telephone. Phone numbers were randomly selected from the Austin area phone book and then 1 was added to the last digit of each number selected and that number was called. This method, called plus-one sampling, gives those in different prefix areas a chance of being selected in proportion to the size of the population holding that prefix and it gives unlisted numbers a chance of being selected. J.M. Lepkowski has noted that this sampling method assumes that unlisted numbers are evenly mixed among listed numbers, which may not be the case. As Paul Lavrakas and Paula Poindexter-Maxwell McCombs observed, however, it is a tradeoff worth making if one does not have the resources to field a true random-digit dialing sample, which results in a large proportion of calls to non-working numbers.

Interviews, which took place between February 20 and March 2, 1997, were conducted by students in an undergraduate class in research methods and graduate students in a seminar in survey research methods. Students in the graduate seminar also helped train interviewers and monitor interviews. The overall completion rate, calculated by dividing all completions by all eligible households, was estimated to be.67.

The survey, which took an average of 20 minutes to complete, focused on knowledge, opinions and behaviours about the mass media. Three questions were used to measure familiarity with and meaning of the label Generation X. Familiarity with the term Generation X was measured by asking: How familiar are you with the term Generation X?

Choices were:

- Very familiar,
- Somewhat familiar,
- Not familiar.

The meaning of the term Generation X was measured by asking an open-ended question with a follow-up probe: When you hear or see the term Generation X, what word or words come to your mind? Any other words?

Evaluation of the term Generation X was measured by asking: In general, would you evaluate the term Generation X as:

- Positive,
- Neutral,
- Negative.

Refusals and don't know also were coded in those cases where it was appropriate.

RESULTS

The survey respondents reflected fairly well the population from which they were sampled but they are somewhat less representative of the state and nation generally. Because Austin is the state capital, the site of the largest university in the country, a major centre of operations for the computer industry and one of the fastest growing cities in the nation, its residents tend to be slightly younger, better educated and wealthier than their counterparts throughout the state and much of the nation.

Almost one in three respondents (30 per cent) were under 30, and almost one in three (32 per cent) had some college or technical school experience. About one-third (32 per cent) had incomes below $30,000 and more than one third (35 per cent) had incomes between $30,000 and $60,000.

More than three out of four (78 per cent) described themselves as white, 11 per cent described themselves as Hispanic or Latino(a), and 6 per cent described themselves as African-American or black. Slightly more than a third (35 per cent) labeled themselves conservatives, slightly more than a third (35 per cent) were moderates and slightly more than a quarter (26 per cent) were liberals. Slightly more than half (53 per cent) were females.

KNOWLEDGE OF THE TERM

Six years after the term Generation X was coined, nearly one out of three respondents (30.5 per cent) said they were unfamiliar with it. Of the rest, 43 per cent said they were somewhat familiar with the phrase and 27 per cent said they were very familiar with it.

Young adults were significantly more familiar with the Generation X label than were older adults. 80 per cent of adults under 30 compared to 65 per cent of adults 30 or older were familiar with the term. Further analysis showed that knowledge of the term Generation X was positively related to education, newspaper reading and TV news viewing. In other words, those who had more education, read newspapers and watched TV news were more likely to be familiar with the term Generation X. Meaning of the term

Of those who said they were familiar with the term, 33 per cent said it represented those who are youthful. Fifteen per cent said the label Generation X had something to do with age, but they didn't specify it as a term related specifically to the young. Another 15 per cent gave the label a variety of miscellaneous definitions.

Almost one in 10 said the label Generation X referred to slackers, apathetic or lazy persons. Six per cent said they considered it a stereotype or an inappropriate, misapplied, misleading label. Five per cent said it referred to a trouble-maker, those who are lawless or irresponsible. Four per cent said the term Generation X described those who are future-oriented or progressive. Other definitions of Generation X included care-free (3 per cent) confused or misdirected (3 per cent), MTV (2 per cent), selfish (2 per cent) and drug-related (1 per cent). Evaluation of the term

Of those who said they had heard of the term Generation X, very few (14 per cent) said it had a positive connotation whereas four in 10 (40 per cent) said it is a negative label. The rest (47 per cent) said they considered it a neutral phrase. When focusing on those who said the term means something decidedly negative - slacker, lawless, dull - those who shared this sentiment had little else in common except the demographic variable, age. The relationship is modest (p=.095) but those in the youngest age groups surveyed (18-24 and 25-29) consider the term as a pejorative in greater numbers proportionally than do their elders. Forty-five per cent of those under 30 said the term Generation X is negative while only 36 per cent of those 30 or older said the label is negative.

In summary, almost one in three adults said they were unfamiliar with the term Generation X, and 40 per cent of those who were familiar with the term said it was negative. That negative evaluation increases to 45 per cent for those under 30. The results of this study suggest that if the newspaper industry is concerned about alienating current and potential readers, it should use the Generation X label with caution when describing the 45 million young adults, born between 1965 and 1977. There are two main reasons to recommend caution. First, almost one-third of the survey participants said they were unfamiliar with the term Generation X, which means that newspapers are not communicating effectively with readers if they are using a term their readers don't understand.

Secondly, the newspaper industry, which has struggled with increasing and retaining its circulation over the past decade, continues to lose readers among young adults. In fact according to a 1997 national survey conducted by the Pew Research Centre for the People and the Press, only 39 per cent of adults under 30 read a newspaper regularly. That per cent increases as age increases. Fifty-five per cent of adults ages 30-49, 65 per cent of those 50-64 years, and 72 per cent of those 65 or older read a newspaper regularly.

These national statistics combined with the findings of this study suggest that the relationship between newspapers and young adults is precarious, indeed. The Generation X label may be convenient for reporters and copyeditors, but it may also have the unintended effect of acting as a repellent to this young cohort.

In trying to increase their young adult readership, newspapers have offered special youth-oriented sections that emphasize movies, music, and technology. In addition to being packaged with dazzling colours and flashy graphics, these special sections have been sprinkled with the terms Generation X, GenXers, and Xers. The data presented here on the Generation X label and its negative connotations, suggest that by using this strategy to appeal to the younger generation, newspapers may be reaching out for young adults with one hand and slapping them in the face, with the other.

PUBLIC RELATIONS IN THE NEW MILLENNIUM

The communication technology revolution and the momentous political changes of the past decade are only two of the many "forces" that will reshape the public relations profession as it evolves from a strictly American concept into a globalized business and management function in the next century.

The purpose of this chapter is to examine the "forces," as explicated by Schranz Distinguished Lecturers during the past 15 years, that are converging to change the way in which public relations will be practiced in the new millennium. From a predicted revolution of "values" to the emergence of a "human climate" that fosters multicultural activism, these "forces" place public relations practitioners in the role of "community" builders responsible for helping link socially, politically, geographically and culturally diverse, and often competing, interests. This chapter looks at the forecasts made by 15 nationally and internationally recognized senior public relations leaders and synthesizes their recommendations as to how the profession, and public relations education, should evolve to accommodate the "global village" of the 21st century. The importance of this may have been underscored by 1987 Distinguished Lecturer David Ferguson:

Public relations are in a state of transition, and in our case, rapid transition. We are forever passing from one order of practice, goals and circumstances into another. The cycles overlap. Change is constant. The implication for educators is more like uranium than gold. What is taught today will have a relatively short life and will have to be altered considerably almost on a yearly basis if education is to continue to keep pace with practice in our profession.

THE SCHRANZ LECTURE SERIES

The Vernon C. Schranz Distinguished Lectureship in Public Relations was established in 1979 by a grant from the Ball Corporation, which has its world headquarters in Muncie, Indiana. The namesake of the lecture series, Vernon C. Schranz, was Ball Corporation's first public relations practitioner. He served Ball Corporation for 25 years in that capacity, and as a corporate officer, until his retirement in 1979. Hosted each year by the Department of Journalism at Ball State University, the lecture series was intended to honour the contributions of Schranz to the field of public relations:

In his 25 years at Ball Corporation, the late Mr. Schranz developed a public relations programme based upon the principles of openness, honesty and community service....The lectureship has enabled Ball State University to recognize leaders in public relations; to provide leaders with a forum for expressing ideas and concepts; and to provide a professional development opportunity for...public relations practitioners, students, and faculty.

Each transcript was reviewed and coded to identify the themes addressed by each of the speakers. These themes were then topically clustered into categories representing each "force" suggested by the speakers. Three principal "forces" or categories emerged from the analysis: changes in the human climate and personal values, the evolving nature of the organization, and changes in the composition of the field of public relations and its practitioners.

THE HUMAN CLIMATE AND A "REVOLUTION OF VALUES"

A principal function of public relations has been, and continues to be, the building of relationships and the management of communication between organizations and individuals. To understand the global forces affecting the enterprise is to first understand how people, in the United States and around the world, are changing and how these changes affect their relationships with businesses, governments, and institutions. In his discussion of attitudinal differences between generations, 1994 Schranz Lecturer John W. Felton, for example, argued that the key to understanding societal change, and why some public relations messages are more effective than others, is to recognize that each generation holds unique values and that those values evolve over time. Felton suggested that practitioners often fail in their efforts because they develop messages that appeal to the wrong generation's attitudes - because a message worked with one group in the past does not mean it will work in the future.

Felton, and several other Schranz lecturers, noted that the current evolution of human values may be more dramatic now than at any time in recent history. Ann H. Barkelew, who presented the 1993 lecture, explained:

There is an explosion, and some would say a celebration, of differences in this country today. We are no longer a culture of sameness. The homogeneous culture of the 1950s is gone, and it's gone forever. In its place is an increasingly diverse culture. We have greater racial and ethnic diversity, certainly, but also diversity in interests, income needs and demands for products, services and information. We are also seeing an explosion in diversity of values. Look at the families we see on television shows today - they reflect the new shape of the American household — where families are defined less by blood relationships, and more by their interests and the amount of time they spend together.

Perhaps, then, no other "force" will have greater impact on business and the public relations profession that what Philip Lesly, the 1982 Schranz lecturer, described as the "emergence of the human climate."

"The human climate," Lesly explained, "is now a determining factor in the future of every organization, institution and nation. It is determining what happens in Poland and Russia; the massive shift towards meeting expectations of Latin America; what shifts in balance will be in the Middle East and what happens in every executive office in the world...(the) emergence of the human climate as the dominant force creates both breathtaking opportunities and serious problems for the field of public relations."

Robert L. Dilenschneider, the 1991 Schranz lecturer, described the emergence of the "human climate" as a "revolution of values." And this revolution, according to Lesly, Dilenschneider and several other lecturers, has manifested itself in several forms: consumerism, global activism, the rise of single-issue groups, and a decline in personal accountability and virtue.

THE ROLE OF INFORMATION TECHNOLOGIES

According to Lesly, a number of factors have contributed to the creation of the current human climate. These include new information technologies which extend the geographical and social spheres of individual experience and influence, and which also create a growing sense of entitlement, particularly to information, and immediate gratification and need fulfillment. He noted that communication technologies can be both "a force for bringing the world closer together and a force for segmenting people into more and more separate groups." A result of this, Lesly explained, is what he termed the "glorification of democracy," the expectation that "every individual can interfere with any process — demand, block, sue, or harass." He explained:

Many follow no leadership and respect no rules. They feel they can interfere with the working of any organization - that they can thwart government, business, education, the armed forces and law enforcement. Refusal to follow any rule is a rejection of all leadership, and without leadership there can only be disorder. The forces I've mentioned create activist pressures to force their type of change. And even when activists attain any of their objectives, they are not likely to fade away but will then seek new and more demanding causes. The pressures for change are now a force in themselves, not to be satiated by the achievement of change.

"SINGLE-ISSUE" PUBLICS

These activist pressures, according to 1980 Schranz Lecturer Douglas G. Hearle, occur as public attitudes become factionalized around highly volatile, self-defining single issues. Hearle explained: The growing national single issue orientation on both sides of the political aisle coupled with the continued disillusionment with political institutions has meant more independence of mind for the Voter - or fickleness of attitude, depending on your point of view. And when you add to that the growing effect of intractable economic problems inflation, unemployment as well as energy - effects which are as much psychological as they are material - we are likely to continue to have a public which is highly volatile in its attitudes as voters and as consumers.

CONFRONTATION AS A TACTIC

As single-issue publics increase and, in particular, as these publics form around sensitive, divisive and volatile topics, Dilenschneider predicted that "confrontation" would increase as a tactic of choice. "Confrontation," he explained, "is definitely back in and not just on the boarders of Croatia or in the alleys of Ulster." More than likely, he said, these confrontations will be played out in the media and in the courtroom. The emergence of "tabloid values" in the media fuels the need for "stories" in which raw emotion becomes more important than simple facts. He explained:

The information revolution is also fueling the trend. The ready availability of vast stores of details about personal lives is helping to etch the character lines of potential victims. And in the courtroom, the opportunity to make public confrontations may be the ultimate goal of single-issue activist groups. Hearle explained:

The courtroom is increasingly where the action is and will continue to be. In that legal arena, special interest groups, like the environmentalists, do not have to "win" by getting a judgement in their favour, by convincing a judge or jury of the correctness of their point of view or by getting a damage award for their cause.

INFORMATION "CLUTTER"

Another bi-product of the information revolution, Dilenschneider explained, is "information clutter." As publics form around all-consuming single issues, their span of attention for, and ability to recall, other information, including corporate messages, becomes seriously eroded. He explained:

I think that we are just now beginning to recognize a clutter problem in recalling messages. There is just too much competition for storage space. If George Bush has trouble leaning on his war laurels within weeks of victory, imagine how hard it is for the average firm to say: Remember the good things we did back in 1989 and 1990.

ACCOUNTABILITY

Perhaps an ironic characteristic of the new "human climate," Dilenschneider argued, is the double standard in how people feel about the "value" of accountability. Americans, he suggested are ambivalent about accountability. While personal accountability is out, corporations, public institutions, and businesses should expect even closer scrutiny in the future than in the past, he said.

The implications for this, according to these Schranz lecturers, is that in the era of the new human climate, organizations will be judged less by their products and services and more by their policies and behaviour related to those values that are "hot" or "politically correct." One "value" is community involvement. Corporations, Ann H. Barkelew argued, will be judged by their involvement in local communities: Strengthening communities has been and is a part of our business strategy - as much a part as operations, distribution or human resources.

THE "NEW" ORGANIZATION

A second "force" frequently identified by the Schranz lecturers dealt with the changing nature of organizations themselves. According to these practitioners, organizations are slowly responding to what has been described as a new "social compact" between employers and their employees. Dilenschneider explained:

There are plenty of disenfranchised white-collar workers out of jobs these days and I expect that you will see more militant efforts towards job entitlement and job protection legislation — closer to what we see in Europe today — arise in the United States.

Companies, he concluded, should expect to face a growing number of accusations that they are not managing work and their employees properly or fairly. Others suggested that the role of the CEO would go through dramatic changes in response to the public's perception that corporate management has become arrogant.

The "new" CEO. "The CEO of the era beginning in the year 2000 will face a legacy unlike anything in our century," explained 1989 lecturer John Budd Jr.

By then, Europe will have faced up to its 1992 challenges; Hong Kong, its reunification with China in 1997; free enterprise will be implanted in the booming nations of East Asia; we'll see deregulation of the economies of eastern Europe and in the bastions of socialism, the Soviet Union and, I'm convinced, in China, under the pressure of its one billion restless population. Perhaps the biggest challenge to be faced, he suggested, would be a crisis of public confidence in corporate management's competence. Dilenschneider called it the "CEO disease" - the overwhelming perception that corporate leaders have become arrogant and have lost touch with employees and customers.

According to Budd, a continuing drop in employee loyalty towards their employers, combined with the crisis of a lack of public trust, is an indication that corporate managements may have to be restructured. He predicted that the nature of the CEO's position will be the first to change. Corporations will create an "Office of the CEO," he said, in which two individuals will serve: one as the CEO for external affairs and the other as a CEO for internal affairs. Reporting to these two individuals, and working to guide their decision making, would be a "cabinet" of executive vice presidents that might include an executive vice president of ideology, an executive vice president of legal affairs, and an executive vice president of human affairs. He explained that what has been traditional public relations would, in this model, fall under the director of "ideology": I think it's time to recognize that public relations as a term has been debased by misuse, overuse, and abuse. More importantly, in a decade's time the enhancement of - and the protection of - the credibility of a company - and its CEOs - will have outdistanced the rote, formula thinking of public relations' accepted wisdom. It will require, as a prerequisite, people skilled in the advancement of ideas, in building broad non-political coalitions and support. It will need people comfortable in dealing with abstracts and converting them to realities. In short, it requires people with minds of originality, endowed with the intellectual resources needed to deal with subjective views, attitudes and behavioural patterns. In short, an ideologist.

Senior management, he concluded, has never been more "in need of truly creative, objective counsel, externally and internally, as now. And, never before has it been in such limited supply."

This may in fact, according to Carole Howard, facilitate the "metamorphosis" of the public relations practitioner to senior management "counselor." This change, she explained, may be so natural that the profession may not even be aware of it until it has occurred. Kerryn King, the 1985 Schranz lecturer, quoted the CEO of a major oil company, who explained:

The modern corporation is no longer perceived solely in economic terms, but as an institution which contributes to society as a whole. These changes in public expectations and in the perception of business are transforming public relations from an ancillary role in the corporation to an essential one.

Globalization. In addition, the opening of new markets in Eastern Europe and Asia have sent many firms looking for overseas opportunities, creating what Carole Howard described as "stateless corporations" with "borderless offices." This, she said, would bring challenges and opportunities:

That's certainly true in my job. With the technological advantages of FAXes, voice mail and satellite hookups at my fingertips, backed by a superb staff at our global headquarters in New York and Reader's Digest Association colleagues in more than 50 offices worldwide, I am as comfortable brainstorming magazine promotions in Sydney as I am giving a speech in Stockholm.

The "human climate," particularly consumerism and environmental movements, may be stronger abroad than in the United States now, and public relations practitioners must be aware of this, she noted.

The Changing "Face" of Public Relations: A third, significant force affecting public relations is the very composition of the field itself and the way in which public relations firms will be owned and operated in the future. Several of the Schranz lecturers intimated that recent studies which have examined the "velvet ghetto" and "glass ceilings" may have been harbingers of what may be the most serious challenge to face the profession in coming decades.

The role of women. As many as 70 per cent of the college students currently preparing for careers in public relations are women, according to Budd. These women, he explained, must be willing to take on leadership roles needed to elevate the profession's status:

If public relations is to achieve the higher destinies its leadership regularly projects for it, women are going to be the catalyst because they will increasingly represent numerically the majority of practitioners. The professional gauntlet is theirs to pick up. Women have to push determinedly upwards by the same measures of personal discipline some men adopt. Men, who currently hold the majority of seniorlevel positions must, for the good of the profession in the long run, must be willing to create opportunities for this to occur. Budd explained: Male executives - and they hold sway in the agency management echelons - for their part have got to be less chauvinistic and give the same encouragement, the same level of mentorship and opportunity they readily provide male interns.

A return to smaller agencies? In the mergerhungry 1980s, small public relations agencies became prey for publicly owned "mega-agencies," whose own gluttony turned themselves into uncreative, non-risk taking, bottom-line-driven shops in which hundreds of clients were served, but none with the close attention that is supposed to be at the heart of what public relations is about.

Budd argued that mega-agencies cannot give personal services to hundreds of different clients at one time. This, he suggests, is a violation of the very tenets of the profession. Because of this, public relations will have to rethink its need to create these mega-agencies. He suggested that future trends will be towards small, specialized agencies looking after the needs of a handful of select clients:

In my opinion, the mega-agencies will not be a material factor then. They will have dematerialized one way or another, most likely cannibalized by new owners to extract maximum profit from the pieces.... These very special needs will become the province of small boutiques - or niches - of senior professionals who bring mature perspectives, independent judgement, front-line experience and a degree of irreverence to conventional wisdom to the assignment.

Generalists and Specialists? "The old notions," Fraser P. Seitel argued, "that people in public relations must be generalists, rather than specialists, simply won't cut it in the years ahead." While it will be important to master the "general" skills of communication, Seitel recommended that future practitioners understand they must become "generalized specialists" who are particularly conversant in and knowledgeable either of a specific aspect of public relations work investor relations or government relations or speech writing, etc. - or of a particular industry - computers or health care or sports or the arts or, as in my own case, banking and finance, or whatever.... Increasingly in the future, specific public relations jobs will be awarded to the practitioner who demonstrates specialized expertise in the particular area at issue.

Douglas Hearle suggested that many of the needed "specializations" will include history, science, law, engineering, education, political science, international affairs, and television production. The Schranz lecturers shared the belief that public relations practitioners must be better trained to understand the dynamics of the business world and, in particular, the international marketplace. At present, public relations has "too many mechanics and too few counselors truly capable of helping management understand the complexities of today's dynamic business environment," David Ferguson explained. As a result, public relations education, he argued, must move away from its exclusive emphasis on "communication mechanics":

Public relations will never reach the status of a profession, as long as people can get into the field and prosper without having completed a fairly rigourous course of study in the field. And, until educations in public relations become sufficiently broad to include study in such subjects as economics, philosophy and law....Any attempt to expand the vision and reach of public relations education must include significant involvement in international affairs and the international business climate. One approach to this, according to Ann H. Barkelew, would be to train future practitioners in "implications thinking." Like issues management or issues tracking, "implications thinking" requires that practitioners be able to critically evaluate the impact of external forces — business ethics, diversity, time-poor customers, health care reform, the economy - on their organizations:

We bring our thoughts to the strategy table, because that is the role of public relations at the table: to identify issues, to respond to concerns, and to position the organization effectively to meet these challenges.

In a sense, this requires practitioners to become what 1981 Schranz Lecturer Dorothy Gregg described as organizational "futurists," forecasting social trends and preparing the organization for their bottom-line impact. "Implications thinking" may be a critical skill in an era of globalization and international business. Douglas G. Hearle explained:

A generalist must have the detailed knowledge and expertise of the specialist when dealing with problems... which have far-reaching legal, social, political and economic implications. Only the specialist can know in full detail what interest groups will be aroused by a particular stand on an issue or by a particular decision. Only a specialist can know how a specific social issue is affecting a country in Europe and might, therefore, affect the United States or a country in the Pacific area. It is this combination of "generalist managers" and "specialist counselors" that "will characterize a successful public relations profession over the next decades," Hearle concluded.

While these three principal "forces" have been identified through the observations and reflections of practitioners who represent the senior leaders of the field, it is likely that the "forces" will continue to change and evolve over time - as communication and information technologies improve, and as social and political revolutions continue to dot the globe.

Because of this, Philip Lesly suggested that public relations professionals and students should be committed to a "lifetime" education, constantly reading "the best thought in this field, on the social patterns, on the psychology of people." David Ferguson, in his lecture, "A Practitioner Looks At Public Relations Education," argued that the only way the discipline will be able to successfully prepare current and future practitioners to respond to these changing global forces is through a partnership between professionals and educators. "It is essential," he explained, "that mutual respect be developed between those who teach and those who practice public relations."

It was recommended by several of the lecturers that public relations professionals be given the opportunity for greater involvement in the education process — through visiting lectureships, presentations, and inclusion in active advisory councils. And it was also suggested that public relations educators increase their involvement with working professionals.

Finally, a consistent theme among the lecturers was the need to move the focus of public relations education away from simply teaching "process" or mechanical skills towards greater efforts at developing critical thinking abilities through the study and application of theory, human psychology, economics, and business philosophies.

Curriculum developers in the field of gifted education raise many critical questions such as:

- What should gifted and talented students learn?,
- For what purpose?

In this chapter, these two questions will be discussed as they relate to and affect the world of gifted and talented students in the first decade of the 21st century. Most of the issues that gifted students will face in the new world landscape, such as ethnic conflict, arms escalation, overpopulation, environmental problems, poverty, and genetic engineering, cannot be solved without integrating knowledge from the natural sciences, the social sciences, and humanities.

This balance is currently not found in the teaching and learning of gifted students, since teaching what is of value, which is called "Philosophy," has less importance than teaching what is, which is called "Science."

I propose that, in order to teach our gifted students elegant problem solving in the arts and sciences (*i.e.*, the parsimonious and e vocative description of patterns to make sense out of a confusion of detail), curriculum developers need to renew their interest in philosophical enquiry in gifted classrooms.

WHY CONSIDER PHILOSOPHICAL ENQUIRY

The value of teaching and learning through philosophical enquiry is not only an intellectual adventure, but also enables learners of all ages to discover and understand elements of the human condition. It is not a new approach, nor is it necessarily unique. Vygotsky valued works of art, philosophical arguments, and anthropological data when building a theory of learning with thought and language early in the 20th century. Bruner believed a curriculum for excelling students ought to be constructed around the great issues, principles, and values that the society deemed worthy of continued concern.

Gardner has said that a culture identifies truths, beauties, and virtues it finds valuable and then gathers resources to ensure their understanding in young learners. These virtues are always being redefined and refined. Educators can not only expect students to learn about virtues such as truthfulness, goodness, and beauty, but can also help students pursue truth, beauty, and goodness in their own lives. It is essential for our gifted and talented youth to become immersed in curricula that inculcate the understanding and application of these virtues. Especially in the new millennium, our brightest students need to discover their deepest ties to the rest of humanity and thereby help ensure that nature and culture survive for future generations. Recently, a colleague of mine, a historian and educator, offered a historian's perspective of the value of teaching gifted students through philosophical enquiry. He said that the way we think—thought at the most reflective levels—determines what will be important in a culture. If the brightest learners have a foundation in philosophical thinking, then the nature of a nation's technology for example, will reflect that thinking. If the brightest learners know only the mechanics or the science of technology, then it is that knowledge alone that will drive its direction. Teaching through philosophy balances the personal worldview with the technical knowledge of a student as he or she becomes a stakeholder in a society.

Philosophy Within the Humanities

One may take the point of view that the legitimate study of mankind is man. The humanities comprise the study of all formal and informal acts of humankind that have resulted in creative products that portray and enhance the human condition in some form. In this light, developers of gifted curricula may view the humanities as providing a link for many disciplines interesting to gifted learners.

Important theoretical models considered for conceptualizing humanities curricula for gifted students include those of Ward and Phenix. Each of these important models incorporates philosophy as a core element in the curriculum experience. Ward's model of teaching philosophy as an integrated learning experience has sought to provide a meaningful structure to gifted curriculum, emphasizing systems of thought and great ideas as organizers. The work of Phenix is a cornerstone of the approach taken by gifted educators as a curriculum-modification procedure designed to provide more in-depth learning experiences for gifted students.

Philosophy as Curriculum

The search for meaning within the domain of philosophy and its subdisciplines is sometimes referred to as ethics, metaphysics, and epistemology. Inviting gifted students to reflect on such philosophical questions as the meaning of knowledge (epistemology), for example, can help them become receptive to all levels and types of experience. It can help prepare them to maximize their knowledge in as many subjects as possible, especially in areas of special interest to them.

Teaching ethics to gifted students expands the teaching of authentic practices in various fields. For example, making explicit to individuals their personal ethical system can help them respond to specific ethical dilemmas. This is an increasingly vital skill to possess when a talented student enters the worlds of microbiology, genetics, fiscal management, journalism, business, or education. Currently, however, teaching gifted students in the philosophical domain of metaphysics seems to be limited, and this may hinder a student from attempting to find meaning personally, as well as in the surrounding world.

The main task of the coming era is...a radical renewal of our sense of responsibility. Our conscience must catch up to our reason; otherwise we are lost. One perplexing problem in the teaching of philosophy to gifted students is that existing curricular models, such as those discussed above, have been too abstract conceptually for easy translation and use by teachers. That can be fixed. As students from one country can easily learn the language of another by extended visits, so teachers of gifted students can allow their students regular extended visits in the realms of truth, beauty, and happiness, all the while doing the business of reading, writing, and arithmetic.

Csikszenrmihalyi has explored the possibility that the next steps in human evolution and human survival will depend on the ability to find flow in activities that nurture human community and protect the environment. In order to do this, schools could promote the activities that bring about flow, including those that could inculcate in students a kind of love for the Cosmos, a cosmic conscientiousness. You don't want to only teach book learning or skills, but also a kind of feeling that the universe is a wonderful place to inhabit and that somehow you love every part of it.

Gifted and talented students, their teachers, and their teachers' teachers should be thinking about, talking about, and doing something about these philosophical ideas as they learn in school. Students need to know that teachers are seekers, too. As educators of the gifted, we must question what to teach our students and to what end. The answers become important as we look beyond the year 2000 and realise the problems facing the next generations of students. Developing curricula for the gifted that incorporate teaching through philosophy is my answer to the first question. Establishing the teaching of philosophy as a cornerstone of the integration of knowledge from the natural sciences, social sciences, and humanities so that gifted students may be able to solve the problems of the new millennium is my answer to the second question.

Once a commitment is made to the teaching of philosophy to gifted students, theoretical models can be developed that are easily understood and used by teachers who then become active partners with students, joining together to build meaningful paths to the future.

3

Newspaper Journalism

There seems to be a shared wisdom among observers of civic (or public) journalism that the most vociferous critics of this emerging movement are the journalists themselves. While public journalism ultimately depends on the "publics" it is attempting to engage, journalists' attitudes are obviously critical to the fate of this movement. Jay Rosen and Davis Merritt, the two principal founders and leading evangelists of civic journalism, have each stated that this new approach to covering communities can succeed only if journalists internalize its values and participate in its evolving definition. Anderson, Dardenne, and Killenberg add that this will require substantial rethinking of traditional journalistic values and the learning of new skills such as listening and mediating.

How can journalists take on such responsibilities if they're opposed to the idea of civic journalism in the first place? Perhaps they're not. This study takes a systematic look at the assumption that most journalists reject the practice of civic journalism. These are the results of a 1996 survey of more than 1,000 newspaper journalists. The study's purpose is to offer a fully explicated definition of the concept of civic journalism, to gauge journalists' support for practices associated with this concept, and to explore possible antecedents of acceptance of these practices.

One reason for the contention over the merits of civic journalism is the absence of a universally accepted definition. In a published debate with Merritt, Paul McMasters rhetorically asked for guidance as to whether civic journalism is "a technique, a theory, a practice, or a philosophy, a new method or a new order, an elaboration on what already exists, or a radical revolution." The most appropriate response would be that civic journalism is some quantity of all of the above. Even Rosen has acknowledged that the term's definition is still in development. Fouhy and Schaffer, fortunately, have offered a simple working definition: It is a set of journalistic "initiatives which make a deliberate attempt to reach out to citizens, to listen to them, and to have citizens listen and talk to each other."

"Initiatives," of course, could refer to intellectual or philosophical innovation or to a pragmatic plan of activity in conjunction with a short-term news project. Merritt and Rosen argue for the former understanding; in fact, Merritt claims that many of those who deride civic journalism are observing only its most superficial manifestations, without attempting to understand its philosophical roots. The two fundamental axioms of civic journalism (in Merritt's conception) are that journalism is inextricably bound up with the public life of a community, whether its practitioners acknowledge it or not, and whether its practitioners like it or not; and that journalists have an obligation to engage citizens with their communities.

Rosen adds that because most American citizens have become disengaged from the public life (which includes political decision making), some institution or institutions must step forward to reconnect people to the public processes that can revitalize democracy. Civic journalists see journalism as an appropriate institution. In this conception, however, the successful public life extends beyond specific political events, such as informing the electorate before an election in order to improve voter turnout. Rosen often cites John Dewey's formulation of democracy not as a form of government but as a way of life.

In order for journalists to serve as the catalyst for such invigoration, Merritt warns, they must set aside a few of the "journalistic reflexes" that traditional journalism has instilled. Such reflexes include placing a premium on conflict; framing issues at their extreme positions (rather than also reporting complex "gray" areas or areas of agreement); adopting "adversary" positions towards those in authority; conceiving of readers and viewers as spectators and not potential participants; and assuming that an attitude of "detached objectivity" will lead to credibility for the journalism. Merritt proposes instead that journalists seek out the concerns of a wide variety of citizens and, through their journalistic practice, motivate them to become involved in solving civic problems.

This notion emerged in the form of experiments at a few different newspapers in the late 1980s, and it attained some national notice when Merritt's own Wichita Eagle and its parent company, Knight-Ridden embraced civic journalism in the early 1990s. But it began to resemble a national movement in journalism in 1993, when the Pew Charitable Trusts hired a staff to develop public-journalism strategies and began funding projects in several cities across the country. Since that time Pew has funded dozens of projects, many of them joint ventures involving newspapers, radio stations, and television stations in the same community.

As Merritt could have predicted, journalists have often framed the controversy over civic journalism in accordance with extreme positions, and those who harbour serious objections to the movement have been given ample voice in the trade press. Consequently, tales of failed attempts at civic journalism have traveled widely. For example, after a project in North Carolina in which several media revised their political campaign coverage in ways that focused on issues of citizen concern, several politicians observed that the new approach had not improved the electoral process.

Editors in the elite media accused their North Carolina colleagues of abdicating their news judgement in order to follow an agenda set by public opinion polls. In California, a paper hosted a town meeting involving an ongoing dispute over building codes, which turned into a brawl. The editors of the paper reportedly recast the originally embarrassing story into a positive account. A Connecticut paper sent reporters out in vans on weekends to give away merchandise and to engage citizens in public conversation on community issues, but the reporters said the citizenry, in a hurry to finish shopping, were not interested in conversing.

Merritt's general response to such stories of misguided efforts, or disingenuous reporting of efforts, is twofold: Many newspaper editors attempt public journalism without understanding its underlying philosophy, and those who understand its philosophy should realise that the results of any one project are unimportant. Civic journalism is not a marketing device or a commitment to report only "positive" news. It is a partnership between journalists and their community, and if it is not undertaken as a long-term commitment it is likely to fail.

The stories of civic-journalism-gone-wrong have also raised deeper concerns, about the movement's philosophy. Some critics worry about its self-conscious rejection of the notion of detachment. McMasters argues that journalists must be dispassionate and detached in their coverage of news in the same way physicians are detached in dealing with patients' medical problems. Too much involvement in community issues compromises their professional competence. Friedland responds that a rejection of detachment does not imply taking sides or reporting with a bias towards a particular group or position. If there is bias, civic journalists assert, it is bias in favour of a smoothly functioning democratic process. Kruh states that the civic journalist's bias should be no more offensive to traditional journalism than the medical writer's bias towards the eradication of disease.

Another concern is a perceived loss of the "watchdog" role of journalism that is strongly implied in the First Amendment. Stepp notes that when journalism commits itself so fully to solutions it inevitably associates itself with the public policymakers who are leading the planning and implementation of a solution. This constricts the journalists' time-honoured (though much debated in academic circles) freedom to criticize governmental officials and policy. Some practitioners respond that they publicly monitor officials' responsiveness to public concerns in a manner resembling traditional "watchdog" journalism.

Some say they have experienced quite the opposite of boosterism. Editors at the Charlotte Observer have reported that during their civic journalism projects they were publicly monitoring local officials' responsiveness to citizens' concerns and that "we told the community hard truths about itself." A third undercurrent of philosophical discomfort involves journalistic pandering. Critics worry that in responding too eagerly to citizens' views, journalism will become little more than market research. Polls and focus groups will replace professional news judgement; that is, news media content will reflect what audience members want to consume, rather than what journalists think their audiences need to know.

Merritt has responded that public journalism is ultimately more concerned with public Life than it is with journalism.23 Journalists who are intent on improving public discourse will not be content to feed their audience inane (but popular) pabulum, regardless of what a focus group may indicate.

As his responses in the foregoing paragraphs indicate, Merritt seems to believe that much of the criticism of civic journalism is rooted in misunderstanding.

He readily acknowledges his critics' "angry dismisiveness." It is entirely possible, however, that if civic journalism were defined in a way that reflected its philosophical tenets (as put forth by Merritt, Rosen, and other early advocates of the movement), journalists might react differently than with dismissive heuristics such as "boosterism," "focus-group pandering," "loss of objectivity" and "same old same old." This study's empirical enquiry, therefore, begins with an explication of civic journalism.

DIMENSIONS OF CIVIC JOURNALISM

The foregoing review of the literature and controversy concerning civic journalism displays recurrent themes that can be aptly transferred into dimensions of the variable concept "approval of civic journalism."

As we have seen, civic journalism involves journalistic initiative rather than reactive coverage; it involves an interest in moving towards solutions to community problems that takes journalism far beyond the detached reporting of the problems; it involves ongoing, long-term commitment to the betterment of the public life; and it involves not only the reporting of important public issues but also non-published efforts to probe citizens' concerns and engage them in the public life.

With the help of Ed Fouhy, former executive director of the Pew Centre for Civic Journalism, the research team for this project developed the following dimensions and indicators of civic journalism.

1. Enterprise. In the view of Merritt, Rosen, and others, civic journalism starts with the initiative of the journalists in reinvigorating the public life. It is rooted in the belief that journalists have a stake in the health of a community's public life, and that journalism stands uniquely poised to engage citizens. This enterprise not only discovers problems of common concern but continues to motivate citizens to seek out

solutions. This is one of the aspects of civic journalism that has prompted the observation that it is no different from traditional enterprise reporting. That is true to some extent, but it is different in two basic ways: It begins with a consideration of what will improve the public life, rather than what will make a good story, and it implies a commitment to solving community problems beyond the publication of one story or series.

2. Information for Decision Making. This dimension speaks to the development of what Charity has termed "public judgement. A principal role for the civic journalist is to enable citizens not only to communicate in a public arena but to be able to work towards solutions without necessarily being led by institutional policymakers. It requires journalists not only to listen to and synthesize public commentary but to present independent research on alternative public views, so that citizens can be informed in their public judgement. This also involves the journalists' close monitoring of official responses to the various alternatives. The effect, Charity states, is that the reporting can "foster a sense of drama and possibility" in the community.

Merritt also sees in this dimension an obligation of the civic journalist to identify shared ideas he calls "core values," to which all participants in the public discussion would adhere. The recognition of core values is often the critical first step in the assessment of alternative solutions.

3. Facilitation of Discourse. Critical to the success of public deliberation is that citizens feel they have an opportunity to discuss issues and concerns themselves in a public forum -not merely to read about them in the news media. The civic journalist does what is necessary to begin and sustain this public deliberation, even if it means taking non-traditional steps to convene participants. The most common practice in this dimension is the news media's hosting a "town meeting," usually to discuss a particular issue. Anderson, Dardenne, and Killenberg and Charity have written extensively about the news media's suitability for such a role, as they comprise one of the few institutions in American communities that regularly address a wide range of issues across economic, racial, and social boundaries. Public agencies and other private organizations have convened innumerable meetings, of course, but civic-journalism proponents cite the failure of current public life generally as an indication of the more traditional institutions' inability to kindle true public discourse.
4. Attention to Citizens' Concerns. This dimension of civic journalism refers to the rejection of agendas set by those in political and economic authority and the substitution of a citizens' agenda. Charity believes

this aspect to be so strange to traditional journalists that retraining is needed, to enable them to elicit, understand, and represent the concerns of ordinary, unaffiliated speakers and to accord those concerns at least as much credulity as they do the concerns of those wielding power.

This dimension is the source of the critique that civic journalism relies mindlessly on focus groups and market research. Merritt and others respond that if such research is truly oriented towards news-consuming preferences, then it is indeed inappropriate as a tool of civic journalism. The value of seeking out public opinion is in setting an agenda for public discourse that reflects popular concerns regardless of political leaders' priorities. This understanding of public opinion resonates with the recent work of political scientist James Fishkin, who urges that public opinion research take place among small, representative groups of citizens who have been carefully informed of the issues under discussion.

The results would represent not an aggregation of individual Americans' uninformed hunches and heuristics but instead the "considered judgements of the public," which would elevate the utility of public opinion. Fishkin observes that this idea "builds on the movement towards public journalism."

As the final stage of the explication, indicators of each dimension were written for inclusion in the survey instrument. Respondents were asked "How do you feel about the following approaches to journalism?" The dimensions were represented by the following sentences:

1. (Enterprise) "A newspaper develops enterprise stories, supported with editorials, to focus public attention on a community problem and tries to help the community move towards a solution."
2. (Information for Decision Making) "A newspaper reports on alternative solutions to community problems, pointing out trade-offs that may be involved."
3. (Facilitation of Discourse) "A newspaper conducts town meetings to discover key issues in the community and follows up with stories focusing on these issues and some possible solutions."
4. (Attention to Citizens' Concerns) A newspaper polls the public to determine the most pressing community issues, then tries to get the candidates to focus on these issues."

While all four dimensions are meant to reflect basic conceptual changes in the way a news organization covers a community, the indicators represent two distinct degrees of departure from current norms. The Enterprise and Information dimensions' indicators represent modest departures from current reporting and editing practices, while the Discourse and Citizens' Concerns indicators represent bolder departures. The indicators were grouped as such in part of the data analysis.

Empirical Research on Civic Journalism

Because civic journalism is a relatively recent phenomenon, what little scholarly work has been done on the movement has been mostly evaluative and prescriptive, rather than empirical. Most of the empirical work has been concerned with the impact of civic journalism projects on political participation and community awareness.

For example, in a comprehensive, Pew— funded study of civic-journalism projects in four cities in 1996, Thorson et al. found that awareness of civic journalism projects was positively associated with citizens' attitudes that are known to bring about political participation.

Their overall conclusion was that civic journalism helps reconnect citizens to public life. In Pew's own report of the same study, 40 per cent of those surveyed in the four cities said the project had made them think more positively about their community.

Less work has been done about the journalists' attitudes and reactions to civic journalism. In a content analysis of the coverage of "The People Project" at Merritt's Wichita Eagle, Riede found that the journalists broke away from only a few traditional routines. He saw a reduction in the political reporting that focuses on personality and political strategy and an increase in substantive reporting of issues. He also noted an increase in stories that encouraged readers to become involved in community organizations and debates. He noted a tone of increased "engagement" and activism, as distinct from detached objectivity.

But he still saw widespread allegiance to experts and politically important people as sources for stories. Voices of "the people" were published more often, but usually superficially and episodically, in ways that could not facilitate discourse. "In fact, the project's doggedly non-adversarial stance, its avoidance of negativism and conflict and its faith in the efficacy of compromise and orderly voluntarism gave it a profoundly conservative tone."

In the Pew Center's own report of the four-city research project in 1996, reporters at the conclusion of the projects were portrayed generally as unimpressed with what they had done. Some thought their stories had been boring and had been read by only a few; others thought their work, focusing in-depth on a single issue, quickly had become repetitive. The Pew evaluators seemed to think that newsroom executives and middle managers were most supportive of the projects, and rank-and-file newsroom employees least supportive.

Webster University researchers surveyed editors and journalism educators to gauge levels of support for various aspects of civic journalism. They found that about half the editors approved the use of polls and focus groups to determine what stories the press should cover.

Majorities of the sample of editors also approved of the notions that journalists should see people not as news consumers but as players in the democratic process; that journalists should devote more attention to what affects ordinary citizens and less on the "major news events of the day;" and that political coverage should include more issue analysis and less "horse race" analysis.

The Webster project does offer a strong indication, however, that civic journalism is not as reviled as the popular, anecdotal accounts would have us believe. But the project surveyed only editors and educators, not rank-and file reporters, photographers, or copy editors-the foot soldiers of this campaign.

The most theoretically provocative finding is found in the most recent study of American journalists by Weaver and Wilhoit. In a replication of earlier analyses, the researchers used factor analysis to identify three "ideal types" of roles for journalism in society. In the analysis of their 1992 survey data, they found renewed evidence of identification with the roles of "disseminator" (whose priority is to deliver information factually and quickly); "interpreter" (whose priority is to provide analysis of complex problems), and "watchdog" (whose priority is to serve as adversary of government and business).

The analysis, however, also revealed a fourth, puzzling factor: journalists who identified with developing the cultural interests of the public, providing entertainment and relaxation, setting the political agenda, and letting ordinary people express their views.

The last item suggested a dimension of civic journalism to the extent that Weaver and Wilhoit labeled this factor "populist mobilizer." Unfortunately, the "ordinary people" item had the weakest loading in the factor, but it obviously intrigued the researchers: "If our analysis is right, the new role ('populist mobilizer') is tantalizing evidence that the spirit of the 'public journalism' movement may have established a foothold among the core values of a tiny minority of journalists."

What sorts of journalists might embrace civic journalism? Another important goal of the current study was to develop a rough profile of the journalist who seems supportive of the indicators of civic journalism, based on a host of independent variables. In this regard the recent research literature provides some guidance. The Pew project's authors found qualitative evidence that younger journalists were less enthusiastic about what they were involved in, which the authors attributed to a sense of professional transience and a lack of commitment to the communities in which they worked.

The size and type of the news organization also may be a factor. In their investigation of the "populist mobilizer factor, Weaver and Wilhoit cautiously suggested that small-market journalists may have more favourable attitudes towards civic journalism than their metro-market counterparts. They found greater resonance for that factor-especially for the item "allowing ordinary people to express their views"-among journalists at radio stations, weekly newspapers, and small-sized dailies.

This is hardly surprising if civic journalism involves a commitment to local issues and community discourse-which are more likely staples in the news diet of small-market media.

From the explication of the term civic journalism and from the suggestions of previous research, a set of hypotheses was developed:

H1: Majorities of the newspaper journalists will approve of each of the four indicators of civic journalism.

One goal of this project was to gauge journalists' approval of civic journalism without explicitly introducing the terms civic journalism or public journalism, thus keeping at bay the generally negative reaction that those terms seems to elicit, and thus keeping the focus of the survey on the concepts and practices of civic journalism rather than on labels. The expectation of approval stems from the findings of the Webster and Pew studies (in which editors, at least, approved of many aspects of civic journalism).

H2a: The smaller the journalist's newspaper, the more accepting he or she will be of these civic-journalism approaches.

This would verify the finding of Weaver and Wilhoit that the "populist mobilizers," few though they were, were more often in small-market media.

H2b: Newsroom managers will be more accepting of civic journalism approaches than will rank-and-file journalists such as reporters, copy editors, and photographers. This would reflect the general sense of the Pew investigators who detailed the complaints of some of the reporters involved in civic journalism projects. It would also reflect Merritt's contention that support of civic journalism results from an understanding of its philosophical underpinnings. Because top editors are the most likely staff members to introduce and assign a civic journalism project, they are the journalists also most likely to have read and thought about civic journalism's purpose.

H2c: The younger the newspaper journalist the less accepting he or she will be of civic journalism approaches.

This last control variable would reflect the Pew authors' impression that younger journalists were less sympathetic to their projects' goals and practices.

H3: The association between identification with the "interpreter role of the media and approval of civic journalism will be stronger than the association between civic journalism and the "disseminator" and "watchdog" roles.

The disseminator and watchdog roles represent two traditional attitudes that Merritt and Rosen find somewhat incompatible with civic journalism.

The disseminator role implies a telling of the news without context or understanding, but rather a detached forwarding of information. The watchdog role implies a state of "adversariness" that delights in conflict and news that splits groups apart in a community. Rosen maintains that civic journalists constantly challenge elected leaders to heed the public discourse, but that bringing down public officials is not a goal of civic journalism.

H4: The stronger the feeling of the importance of neighbourhood and community news, the stronger the approval of civic journalism.

Civic journalism focuses on the concept of community, and because community in journalism is often defined as a geographic community, it seems likely that civic journalism-friendly news people will also be highly interested in issues of local communities. Respondents were asked to rate the importance of "a number of things that newspapers the size of the one you work for do, or try to do, today," which included the item, "Cover community and neighbourhood news." Respondents could choose a response from a fourpart scale ranging from "Extremely Important" to "Not Very Important."

H5a: Journalists who approve of a top editor's involvement in local civic organizations will be more likely to accept civic journalism than will journalists who disapprove of such activity.

H5b: Journalists who approve of rank-and-file staff members' joining civic organizations will be more likely to approve of civic journalism than will journalists who disapprove of such activity.

This set of hypotheses attempts to bring to a personal level the civic journalism tenet of involvement in one's community. One measure of a journalist's rejection of the traditional detachment from the people and issues that one covers would be the attitude towards personal involvement of the journalist in the community-not involvement in a particular faction or political cause, but in a non-political civic organization.

If a journalist feels favourable towards making at least that modest personal connection to the community, he or she will endorse the connection for both the top editors and for rank-and-file staff members.

In the same vein, we might also expect journalists who themselves felt involved in their local communities-actually, not hypothetically-to share that attitude.

H5c: Journalists who describe themselves as involved in their local communities will be more likely to approve of civic journalism than will journalists who describe themselves as uninvolved.

The final set of hypotheses examines attitudes about the current state of journalism at one's newspaper. Proponents and observers alike seem to agree that civic journalism has grown out of a dissatisfaction with the role journalism has played lately, especially with journalism's inability to connect to citizens, and its inability to connect citizens to one another.

H6a: Journalists who feel their own papers do not connect well with readers will be more likely to approve of civic journalism than will those who feel well connected with readers.

H6b: Journalists who feel their own papers are getting worse in quality will be more likely to approve of civic journalism than will those who feel their paper is improving.

THE SURVEY METHOD

The survey was conducted in the fall of 1996 under the auspices of the Human Resources Committee of the American Society of Newspaper Editors. A stratified probability sample of newspaper employees was constructed. From a list of the 1,487 newspapers in the United States, 61 were randomly selected, after measures had been taken to ensure proportionate representation from eight circulation categories. Three of the newspapers in the original group of 61 declined to participate; in these cases the research team randomly chose substitute newspapers from the same circulation groups.

The directing editor of each selected paper was asked to select randomly a sample of journalists from his or her staff. Only full-time employees who fit the categories of reporter, copy editor, photographer, artist, supervisor, or editorial writer were to be included. The number of participating employees depended on the size of the paper, again in order to maintain the validity of the stratified probability sampling procedure.

Each employee participating received a survey packet, which included the questionnaire with instructions and a computer-scannable answer sheet. Participants were assured, both in the written instructions and by the on-site survey coordinator, that responses would be entirely confidential. If an employee declined to participate, a substitute was to be chosen by use of the same "nth name" random process. Editors were asked to give the employees three days in which to complete and return the questionnaire, which in a pre-test in August 1996 had taken respondents about 30 minutes to complete.

Of the 61 newspapers that eventually agreed to participate, only 3 failed to return their questionnaires by the 15 October 1996 deadline. All 3 of these were below 25,000 in circulation. Thus of the 1,191 questionnaires sent, 1,037 were returned, for a response rate of 87.1 per cent.

The four indicators resulting from the explication of civic journalism appeared as closed-ended items in the survey; respondents could choose the degree to which they approved or disapproved of each.

The two "modest" approaches to civic journalism appear first, and more than 90 per cent of the respondents expressed some level of approval. The two "bolder" approaches, involving the polling of readers and the town meeting, appear next, each garnering more than 70 per cent approval. The mean approval for all four measures is 81 per cent, with only 19 per cent on average expressing some degree of disapproval.

It cannot be known what the approval ratings would have been if this section of the instrument had been labeled "civic journalism," but clearly without the labeling these journalists seem to be comfortable with the approaches described in the four items.

It should also be noted that none of the four items cited any of the more controversial or radical examples of civic journalism, such as training editorial employees in mediation and conflict resolution, or having staff members register citizens to vote. This, of course, was in keeping with the explication of the concept, which was based in large measure on the work of the movement's two theoretical founders, Merritt and Rosen.

The "strongly approve" rating for the modest approaches was, predictably, different from the "strongly approve" results for the two bolder measures: a mean of 60 per cent compared to a mean of 28 per cent. The results for "somewhat approve" were 10 percentage points higher for the bolder approaches, however.

The journalists seem to be implying support for town meetings and polling the public for agenda issues, but not as enthusiastically as doing enterprise stories and providing information on alternative solutions.

Survey respondents were asked to attach comments whenever they felt moved to supplement their closed-ended responses, and a few of these were directed to the items on civic journalism.

A staff member at a large East Coast paper wrote, again without using terms like "civic journalism," an eloquent explanation of the movement's rejection of detached objectivity: "Many papers, while remaining objective, led in some way the struggle for civil rights. Now, we do not lead as much as we try simply to report... Unless newspapers make people in their communities feel a part of them, as if they have a stake in them, they will disappear. Papers cannot be observers and reporters of a community. People no longer want to be merely observed. People want to be cared about."

A few others, however, voiced caution about the direction civic journalism may be taking. A journalist at a small paper in New England stated that there is only one place to be a catalyst for community discourse: "A newspaper and the stories it reports should reflect its surrounding communities and should always seek out the input of its readers. It is not a paper's role to 'lead' its readers, but to listen to its readers. There is plenty of room for our own agenda and suggestions of alternative solutions via the editorial and op-ed pages."

To test the remaining hypotheses, an index was created with the four civic journalism measures (Cronbach's alpha =.61) that enabled correlation and regression analysis using "civic journalism approval" as a dependent variable 46.

H2a is supported: the smaller the newspaper, the greater the support for the index of the four civic-journalism approaches. This association was especially pronounced for the two "bolder" forms of civic journalism. The influence of newspaper size remains significant throughout a multiple regression involving the variables with the strongest bivariate associations with the dependent variable.

Newsroom managers did indeed seem more receptive to civic journalism approaches than rank-and-file employees did (H2b), but the strength of this factor pales in the course of the regression. Age appears not to be a predictor of support for civic journalism. While it is likely that older, higher-ranking journalists may be the initiators of a civic journalism project at a paper, a three-way crosstab analysis also revealed that older reporters and copy editors are among the most skeptical about civic journalism.

A few other personal variables were examined for possible correlations with support for civic journalism. Education seemed to make no difference, and while women seemed to approve of civic journalism more often than men do, the difference was never statistically significant.

The third hypothesis sought to learn whether conceptions of journalism's roles have any influence on attitudes towards civic journalism. But the connections seem flimsy.

The "interpreters" were neither less nor more supportive of civic journalism than others; the "watchdogs" and "disseminators" held no significant association with civic journalism either. H3 thus gets no support. It is worth noting, however, that "watchdogs" and "interpreters" both significantly influence approval of the "modest" approaches to civic journalism, but not the "bolder" approaches. Even that influence, however, lost its significance in a regression.

H4 predicted that journalists who accord respect to neighbourhood and community news would applaud civic journalism approaches, and the data support the hypothesis. The influence is particularly strong when the two bolder approaches are considered.

Neighbourhood and community news is one of the few independent variables to hold its influence throughout the regression. In a regression on only the bolder approaches, this variable had a higher beta coefficient than any other variable in the equation.

It was also predicted that journalists who were comfortable with their bosses' and colleagues' involvement with civic organizations would approve of civic journalism techniques, as would journalists who themselves felt "more involved than others" in the community. H5a and HSb, posing the hypothetical questions about staff involvement, both enjoyed strong positive correlations with civic-journalism support. The data suggest that those who approve of these civic-journalism approaches are also likely to approve of journalists at any level becoming personally involved in community organizations.

That approval does not extend to the respondents' personal lives, apparently. H5c enjoyed no support. Whether the respondents were involved in community activities themselves seemed not to make a difference in the attitude on civic journalism. This may suggest that journalists are more open to the personal dynamics of civic journalism in theory, but that there is no connection, at least not yet, between their own actual community involvement and their support for civic journalism. Perhaps they see journalists' personal lives as simply detached from whatever professional values they espouse. The sixth set of hypotheses examined measures of dissatisfaction with the current state of journalism, but the data did not support either H6a or H6b. Whether the journalist felt his or her paper was connecting with readers was irrelevant to his or her feelings about civic journalism. The evaluation of the journalist's own paper, in fact, was significant in the direction opposite that of the hypothesis. It was expected that those who feel their own papers are deteriorating in quality would look to civic journalism as a means of rescue.

However, the data indicate that the higher the journalist's rating of his or her own paper, the more positive the reaction to civic journalism. And this influence held its significance throughout the regression. Apparently those who see their newspapers' quality eroding have no faith that civic journalism is the answer, and those who embrace civic journalism are journalists who think their paper is improving. Perhaps civic journalism will require a sense of collective confidence in the enterprise before it can win newsroom adherents.

Thus only a few independent variables remained, after a four-step regression, as significant influences on a journalist's approval of these four approaches to civic journalism: The smaller the newspaper, the greater the attention to neighbourhood and community news, the greater the approval of journalists' joining community organizations, and the greater the sense that one's own paper is improving, then the more likely the approval of civic journalism.

It must be noted, however, that the regression equation accounted for only 14 per cent of the variance of the dependent variable. Clearly other factors, not explored in this survey, also influence support for civic journalism.

One final piece of analysis was conducted: a factor analysis to follow up on Weaver and Wilhoit's earlier discovery of the "populist mobilizer." The data in the present study were gathered more than four years after the Weaver-Wilhoit survey.

Weaver and Wilhoit had included only one item that could be clearly identified as an indicator of civic journalism ("letting ordinary people express their views"). In a factor analysis of the present data, with a full mix of professional-role items including disseminator, interpreter and watchdog, the four civic-journalism items loaded onto their own separate factor (eigenvalue 1.88).

As the discussion above indicated, approval of civic journalism is correlated with some of the other, older role conceptions, but not robustly so. It could very well be that a new understanding of journalism's role in society has indeed begun to emerge, as Weaver and Wilhoit speculated in 1996, in which a newspaper's commitment to the public life, for at least some journalists in some situations, takes precedence over obligations of disseminating information quickly, analyzing events, or serving as adversary to powerful institutions.

Whether or not newspaper journalists scoff at the term "civic journalism," this much is clear: Many of them seem to approve of four specific manifestations of the movement's guiding principles. It would be inappropriate, however, to draw overarching conclusions about the future of civic journalism on the basis of this study alone. The survey's four approaches to civic journalism were referents of pillars of the movement's philosophical foundation, and while they represented a fundamentally different approach to journalism, not even the two "bolder" approaches seem revolutionary in form.

In fact, it might be argued that the two "modest" items are quite similar to longstanding normative understandings of strong local news coverage. Further research on journalists' conceptions of civic journalism is warranted, and it might begin with a broader selection of approaches and strategies, to see where journalists might finally "draw the line" and begin objecting to certain approaches. Because civic journalism projects increasingly involve broadcast and online media, further studies should include more than newspaper journalists. Rosen has stated that the definition of civic journalism is phenomenological: Ultimately, it will be whatever journalists say it is. For this reason it is important to measure not only what journalists think of a Merritt-Rosen— derived definition of civic journalism, as this study has done, but also to measure how journalists themselves would define the term.

If their definition emerges as similar to the explication of this study, then the future of civic journalism is more promising than even this study suggests. If, however, journalists define it in ways that cause Merritt, Rosen, Charity and others to howl with exasperation, it's more likely that the journalists will also disapprove. Then proponents of civic journalism will truly have their evangelistic work cut out for them.

The most influential independent variables have created a profile of sorts of the pro-civic-journalism practitioner. It suggests that civic journalism may enjoy greater success in smaller communities and in media outlets that are seen by their employees as improving.

But here, too, further enquiry is needed. In carefully steering away from respondents' preconceived notions of civic journalism, the survey instrument did not measure whether the respondent had read or discussed any materials regarding civic journalism, or had participated personally in a civic journalism project. These factors could be expected to influence a journalist's opinion of the movement and its practices.

Even with this early indication that a large proportion of the newspaper workforce seems poised to approve of (at least this conception of) civic journalism, it is still unclear whether this will create any deep changes in journalism, or in the quality of civic life.

Riede's study of Merritt's own paper suggested that journalistic routines are extremely difficult to alter even in one of the pantheons of the movement.

Some scholars question whether civic journalism can survive within a liberal-economic media model like the United States'. Glasser and Craft, for example, suggest that civic journalism, if implemented consistently and seriously, might either risk losing its ratings appeal among advertisers or would challenge power structures in a way that would anger advertisers.

Rosen and Merritt, predictably, have pondered this concern and responded, but with different views. Rosen asserts that civic journalism, properly executed, can draw in a large audience of citizen— participants and thus more advertising revenue.

Merritt acknowledges that civic-journalism content may not compete for audience with the crossword puzzle or "Seinfeld" but that it doesn't have to. As long as it enjoys a permanent place in the mix of programming or editorial features that maximize an audience, it can continue to uplift the public life.

Judgement on the viability and desirability of civic journalism is beyond the scope of this study. Such considerations assume, of course, that civic journalism will indeed catch on among the majority of journalists.

This study suggests that at least one aspect of Weaver and Wilhoit's earlier notion of a "populist mobilizer" attitude towards journalism has taken hold among newspaper journalists.

There may still be only a few journalists actually waving "civic journalism" banners, but in terms of four specific activities that stem directly from the movement's philosophical roots, the movement is quietly finding acceptability. Civic journalism's ultimate reformative power— especially its ability to challenge powerful institutions on behalf of the public and "the public life"-will only be as strong as its support among its practitioners. That support seems to have made important initial strides.

NEWSPAPER COPY EDITORS PERCEPTIONS

Newspaper copy editors have long been known as "the last line of defence" against errors because they do their work near the end of the production cycle. That also means they have the potential to be a last line of defence against violations of ethical standards. In fact, many editing textbooks say copy editors should be prepared to raise questions about potential ethics-related problems, such as a lack of balance or fairness, and to watch for obvious breaches of ethics like plagiarism. There is anecdotal evidence that many copy editors take this role seriously. In recent years, copy editors have been credited with detecting lifted quotations, plagiarized stories and columns and letters to the editor, and fabricated material.

There is also anecdotal evidence, however, that copy editors' ethics-related concerns are not always taken seriously. For example, a copy editor reportedly raised questions "about the level of truth" in Patricia Smith's Boston Globe columns three years before she was forced to resign under fire for fabrication.

Similarly, "growing newsroom unrest" resulted when managers ignored a copy editor's concerns about stereotyping in a Houston Chronicle section on juvenile justice that pictured only minority youths. Articles based on depositions of Atlanta Journal-Constitution copy editors indicate that some tried unsuccessfully to get senior editors to reconsider the fairness of a 1996 column9 likening security guard Richard Jewell-who was never charged with bombing Atlanta's Centennial Olympic Park and was eventually formally cleared10-to Wayne Williams, convicted in 1982 of murdering two people and implicated in the deaths of twenty-two others. The column was published and Jewell filed a 1997 libel suit against the paper that was still pending in late 2005." More recently, John E. McIntyre, managing editor for the copy desk at the Baltimore Sun and former president of the American Copy Editors Society, wrote:

In the endeavor to head off plagiarism and fabrication in news stories, and to ensure the reliability and accuracy of stories . . . the ranking editors and the copy editors are on the same side. The problem is that the ranking editors don't always recognize this. When the American Copy Editors Society presents workshops on structural editing ... a troubling comment keeps surfacing among the participants: "I wouldn't be allowed to raise questions like that at my paper."

Although copy editors' jobs charge them with evaluating stories, their concerns sometimes go unheeded; forces that Shoemaker and Reese identify as stronger "influences on media content" sometimes limit copy editors' authority. Nonetheless, Hank Glamann, former assistant managing editor for editing at the Cleveland Plain Dealer, urged members of the American Society of Newspaper Editors to "create a climate in your newsroom in which any member of the staff can ask any question about any story and expect to be heeded. To restrict who can ask about what is inefficient-and a real waste of talent."

This survey of copy desk workers sought to determine how they perceive their role as "final guardians" of journalistic ethics, and whether there are conflicts between what they think their role should be and what they perceive it actually is. The research is important for two reasons. First, copy editors constitute a significant proportion of the newsroom workforce-nearly 20 per cent in 2005-and are often difficult to hire second, how they see their jobs is important because, as Shoemaker and Reese wrote, journalists' role conceptions affect the content they produce:

"[T]hese roles may determine how they define their jobs, the kinds of things they believe should be covered, and the ways in which they cover them." Copy editors do not cover news, of course, but they produce content as they condense news into headlines, elements that can have a bigger impact on readers' impressions of the news than the words written by reporters. In addition, they may select or help select wire stories for publication and help determine story play as they design pages.

Although there has been an explosion of scholarly interest in journalistic ethics during recent decades and much of the resulting literature describes the ethics, values, responsibilities, or roles of particular types of journalists, almost no work has assessed copy editors' values or how they perceive their role in upholding ethics standards. Other research on copy editing, however, suggests that technological innovations, as well as copy editors' perceptions of how others in the newsroom view them, may have implications for how copy editors think of their ethics roles.

During the past half century, newspaper copy desks have coped with at least four job-altering waves of technological innovation, each forcing copy editors to spend time adapting and some permanently reducing the time available for substantive editing.

First, during the 1950s, newspapers introduced teletypesetting (TTS) equipment, which transmitted wire-service stories via hole-punched paper tape used to automatically activate linecasting machines. This allowed quicker typesetting but forced some copy desks to adopt new style rules, so that local style would match wire-service stories, and was blamed in one study for an increase in errors. second, during the early 1970s, some newsrooms began using optical character recognition (OCR) equipment to produce perforated tape versions of local stories.

This required copy editors to edit stories with a special pen and have their changes input by a corrections typist, changes that one study found led to an increase in published errors. Then, in the late 1970s and early 1980s, newsrooms introduced video-display terminals, which made updating and comparing stories easier but also introduced physical problems, such as eyestrain and headaches, and, some researchers reported, led to newspaper management devaluing editing in favour of production tasks.

Perhaps the most significant technological change was the introduction in the 1980s and 1990s of electronic pagination, which shifted page makeup responsibilities from composing room staffs to copy editors. It gave editors greater control over page appearance, but also cut into the time copy editors had for substantive editing. In 1994, Russial reported that electronic makeup of a page took on average fifteen minutes more than drawing a paper "dummy."

This time drain, which can be exacerbated by malfunctioning pagination equipment, persisted after newsrooms became familiar with the technology. In many cases, pagination turned the desk "from a centre of editing to a centre of production," and it made some copy editors feel they had become computer technicians or proofreaders.

Meanwhile, there are indications that a significant number of copy editors have felt a lack of respect for their work. A1984 report noted that a survey of forty copy editors had "raised disturbing questions about their treatment by senior editors [and] the lack of respect they got in their newsrooms."

Three years later, a survey of 630 copy editors at fifty newspapers found that although 63 per cent said that their work was supported by senior editors, respondents were evenly split on whether the copy desk had "clout within the newsroom." A 2003 survey found that respect remained a problem, with 47 per cent of 337 responding copy editors disagreeing that "most copy editors feel appreciated at my newspaper" and 40 per cent disagreeing that "copy editors at my paper are held in the same esteem as reporters."

It is understandable, then, that copy editor job satisfaction has lagged behind that of other journalists. In 1989, ASNE reported that 43 per cent of 191 responding copy editors said they would be unhappy if they held the same job in five years, compared with about a third of other journalists. Four years later, Cook, Banks, and Thompson found that 39 per cent of fifty-nine copy editors in a study planned to leave journalism within five years, and Cook and Banks reported that copy editors in a sample of newspaper journalists were more likely to be burned out than reporters.

Similarly, in 1997, Voakes reported that 37 per cent of nearly 200 copy editors in an ASNE-sponsored study thought their current job had not met their expectations, compared with 22 per cent of non-copy editors.

Finally, a survey of copy desk workers conducted in 2002 showed that although more than 70 per cent agreed at least somewhat that they were satisfied with their jobs, fewer than a fourth agreed strongly, this during a year when Weaver et al. found that about a third of U.S. journalists in general were "very satisfied" and 81 per cent were at least "fairly satisfied." Intriguingly, the 2002 copy editor job satisfaction study found satisfaction correlated with copy editors' opinions about the ethics standards of their newspapers.

THEORETICAL PERSPECTIVES

Studies of copy editing have not always made good use of theory, but three perspectives from sociology and mass communication appear useful in considering how copy editors perceive their ethics role. First, as Russial and Brill have proposed, some technological innovations may have resulted in the sort of "de-skilling" of copy editing that sociologist Harry Braverman observed when industrial jobs were routinized by automation. Braverman theorized that the introduction of automation or other technology into an occupation could reduce the number of skills used by workers so much that a job became "de-skilled." That resulted, he suggested, in a loss of power by workers, their supervisors, and the occupation itself.

Although pagination initially required copy editors to learn a new skill, one result of having copy editors paginate "may be a limitation in the discretion journalists have in deciding how much time to spend on traditional [editing] tasks." Thus, some copy desks may have lost, if not the skills of editing, then at least some discretion in how much time they can spend on serious editing concerns, such as story fairness and balance. Indeed, 53 per cent of copy editors surveyed in 1987 for ASNE perceived they did not have time to edit well. Such changes could also routinize copy editing so much that the job consists of little more than writing headlines, running spell checkers, and moving copy-very nearly what Bleske found copy editors doing at one 60,000-circulation daily. If routinization results in a loss of copy desk power, as Braverman's theory suggests, then it could rob copy editors of the ability to be ethical "backstops."

Power is also a consideration in Shoemaker and Reese's hierarchy of influences. They suggest that content is affected by "environmental factors" or influences, modeled as a series of concentric circles. The media worker at the center is subject to forces in the outer circles-media routines, organizational influences, extramedia influences, and ideology-which are, in turn, subject to the forces in circles beyond them.

Although ethics does not play a large role in the model, the question of whether copy editors can be final guardians of ethical standards can be viewed in terms of the model. According to Shoemaker and Reese, the judgements of an individual journalist possessing sufficient power can influence content if there is no higher-level factor-such as a strong routine or organizational influence-covering the task at hand. As Shoemaker and Reese note, "institutional position greatly determines the power vested in a role," so copy editors may lack the authority to effectively call into question the actions of writers or assigning editors.

Relevant theory also comes from the sociological study of professional ethics, which generally posits that all professions share certain characteristics: a systematic base of knowledge, community sanction, a code of ethics, a distinctive culture maintained by associations, and a high degree of autonomy and authority conferred by clients. Although some writers have viewed journalism as either a profession or a professionalizing occupation, it has often been seen as lacking several prerequisites of professionalism. For example, Shoemaker and Reese note that journalists are not required to follow specific standards or obtain specific schooling. In addition, their autonomy "is limited by organizational constraints."

Copy editors appear to lack even more of these attributes of professionalism than other journalists. Although copy editors generally possess a broad base of knowledge that is systematic in the sense that it includes detailed information about language, they do not have a great deal of autonomy, they do not have a separate ethics code, and they did not have an association until the American Copy Editors Society was founded in 1996.

Moreover, in many newsrooms, copy editors lack both "community" approval and authority conferred by "clients." The fact that copy editors are hired to be evaluators frequently sets up an adversarial relationship between them and their intra-office "clients," reporters and assigning editors. Copy editors also have external clients, the readers for whom they are pre-publication advocates. However, those reader-clients cannot confer authority upon copy editors, for they generally are not aware that the newsroom's most invisible workers exist. Even if copy desk workers think they should be guardians of ethics standards, they may not feel support in their newsrooms for such a role. As a result:

H1a: Most respondents will report that identifying and seeking to eliminate potential ethics-related problems in stories should be integral parts of copy editors' jobs.

H1b: Respondents will be significantly more likely to say that finding and eliminating errors and identifying and eliminating potential legal problems, such as libel, should be integral parts of copy editors' jobs than they will be to report that identifying and seeking to eliminate potential ethicsrelated problems in stories should be integral parts of copy editors' jobs.

H2: Respondents will be significantly more likely to perceive that eliminating errors and eliminating legal problems actually are integral parts of their jobs than they will be to say that identifying and seeking to eliminate potential ethics-related problems in stories actually are integral parts of their jobs.

H3: There will be no significant differences between respondents' perceptions of what copy editors' roles in eliminating errors and potential legal problems should be and are, but there will be significant differences between perceptions about what copy editors' ethics roles should be and are.

H4a: Respondents will be more likely to agree that copy editors should be encouraged to take questions to managers than they will be to say that copy editors at their newspapers are encouraged to take questions to managers.

H4b: Respondents will perceive more support for taking potential ethics-related concerns to immediate supervisors or assigning editors than they will for taking unanswered concerns to senior managers.

H5: Respondents who perceive that copy editors' actual ethics role differs from what it should be will report lower levels of job satisfaction than respondents whose ideal and real perceptions of their ethics role match.

H6: Respondents whose perceptions of copy editors' ideal and real ethics role do not match will be less likely than others to rate their newspapers' ethical standards favourably.

Data were gathered via a survey63 sent in fall 2002 to journalists at 105 U.S. daily, English-language newspapers listed in the Editor and Publisher International Yearbook64 as having average weekday circulations greater than 25,000. Because copy editors' names generally do not appear in their newspapers, a two-step process was used to identify recipients.

First, a scientifically selected sample of 105 newspapers was stratified66 into the five largest circulation categories used by ASNE. The names of copy editors were obtained from newspaper Web sites, industry contacts, and the newspapers. Then a random sample of 803 copy desk workers was drawn, using a sampling frame designed to match ASNE's estimates of the distribution of copy / layout editors across the five circulation classes.

The study used multiple contacts to improve response rates, and allowed recipients to fill out the questionnaire on paper or online; 470 usable responses were received from 100 newspapers for a 59 per cent response rate. Nearly 81 per cent of respondents identified themselves as copy editors or copy editor/ page designers, though the sample contained copy desk chiefs, page designers, news editors, reporter/copy editors, and others who worked part-time on a copy desk.

H1a, which predicted that most respondents would view seeking to eliminate potential ethics-related problems from stories as an integral part of a copy editor's job, was supported. Nearly 95 per cent of copy desk workers agreed with a statement that made ethics part of copy editors' ideal roles, and more than two-thirds strongly agreed.

Testing other hypotheses involved wading into a long-running methodological debate over how ordinal and quasi-interval data can be analyzed. Ordinal responses to statements about copy editors' roles in eliminating errors, legal problems, and potential ethics-related problems ("strongly agree," "somewhat agree," "undecided," "somewhat disagree," and "strongly disagree") were converted to quasi-interval data by assigning a number to each response so that mean responses could be calculated and compared using f-tests. Although this practice has the support of some scholars, some purists believe that only non-parametric statistics should be used with such ordinal data.

So, while i-test results are reported in the text below, results from the sign test-a conservative, non-parametric test often considered appropriate for non-normal and non-symmetric, paired-measurement data like these-are provided in endnotes.

Both statistical tests offered only partial support for H1b, which held that errors and legal problems in stories would be more likely to be viewed as copy-desk concerns than would ethics-related problems. There was a statistically significant difference between the way respondents viewed copy editors' ideal roles in eliminating errors and potential ethics problems. But there was not a statistically significant difference between support for eliminating potential legal problems and potential ethics-related problems.

H2 predicted greater agreement that eliminating errors and eliminating potential legal problems actually were parts of copy editors' jobs than agreement that seeking to eliminate ethics-related problems was. To test H2, responses to the statements about copy editors' actual roles were compared. H2 was supported. There were statistically significant differences 80 between responses to statements about copy editors' actual roles in eliminating errors and in eliminating ethics-related problems, and between responses to statements about copy editors' actual roles in eliminating potential legal problems and in eliminating potential ethics-related problems.

H3 predicted that respondents would perceive that copy editors' ideal roles matched their actual roles when it came to eliminating errors and potential legal problems but not when it came to identifying and seeking to eliminate potential ethics-related problems. Contrary to expectations, there were statistically significant differences in respondents' perceptions of what copy editors' roles should be and what they are related to all three tasks: identifying and eliminating errors identifying and eliminating legal problems and identifying and seeking to eliminate potential ethics-related problems.

H4a, which predicted that respondents would be more likely to agree that copy editors should be encouraged to take ethics-related concerns to managers than to say that they actually are encouraged, was supported.

First, there was a significant difference between responses to statements, suggesting copy editors should be and are encouraged to bring concerns about ethics-related problems to their supervisors and/or assigning editors. Second, there was a significant difference between responses to statements about whether copy editors dissatisfied with those front-line managers' responses to potential ethics related problems in stories should be encouraged and are encouraged to carry the concerns to senior editors.

H4b, which asserted that respondents would be less likely to support and perceive encouragement for raising questions about ethics-related problems with senior managers than immediate supervisors or assigning editors, was supported.

Respondents were significantly more likely to agree that copy editors should be encouraged to take ethics-related concerns to their immediate supervisors or the assigning editor for the story than they were to support taking subsequently unresolved concerns to senior managers. Respondents were also significantly more likely to say encouragement actually existed in their newsrooms for approaching immediate supervisors or assigning editors than for carrying concerns to senior managers.

H5, that copy desk workers would be less satisfied if they thought their ideal and real ethics roles differed, was supported. Independent samples f-tests showed that among respondents with opinions, those who perceived their ideal and actual ethics roles differed were significantly less likely to agree with five of seven statements about job satisfaction. The editors whose responses revealed a disconnect had significantly lower mean scores on statements about overall satisfaction, the prospect of doing the same work in five years, their prospects for advancement, and satisfaction with supervisors.

In addition, respondents whose responses showed the disconnect had significantly lower scores on intending to remain at their newspapers for the next two years. H6, predicting that respondents whose perceptions of copy editors' ideal and real ethics roles did not match would be less likely than others to rate their newspapers' ethical standards favourably, was supported. Respondents rated the ethics standards of their newspapers lower if their ideas of what copy editors' ethics roles should be did not match their perceptions of reality. The copy editors think they should be the final guardians of journalistic ethics but perceive little newsroom support for that role.

For example, almost three-fourths strongly agreed that addressing ethicsrelated problems in stories should be part of copy editors' jobs, but only about 40 per cent said that was the case in their newsrooms.

Similarly, although all but three respondents agreed copy editors should be encouraged to take concerns about ethics problems to their immediate supervisors and/or the assigning editors, only about 55 per cent said such a simple step was "always" encouraged in their newsrooms.

There was even less perceived support for pursuing ethics-related discussions to a higher level: 90 per cent agreed copy editors should be encouraged to take unresolved concerns to senior managers, but fewer than 15 per cent said such encouragement is "always" given. This suggests that newsrooms are constraining employees willing to serve as ethical backstops from using their niche in the production process to do so.

Constrained Copy Editors. Comments written in the margins of some returned questionnaires or in answer to two open-ended questions90 suggested how these constraints may be working: some come from deadlines, workload, and technological pressures. For example, a news copy editor at a newspaper with 500,000+ average weekday circulation wrote:

If for example there are 35 stories appearing in the paper, more likely than not, 25 of the stories move to the copydesk in the last 45 minutes before the paper is slated to lock upeverything (or much of it) pops near deadline. That puts a strain on the ability to check facts, weigh fairness, check spelling and grammar, rectify inconsistencies, write a good headline and trim the story to fit the hole.

A features/lifestyle copy editor at a major metropolitan newspaper echoed Braverman's de-skilling theory, writing that with the [newspaper's] conversion to CCI [a proprietary electronic editing and pagination system sold by CCI Europe] the "art" of copy editing is being overtaken by the need for copy editors to act as typographers. This is compounded by a recent redesign that is adding a layer of mumbo-jumbo. It's less and less about journalism and more and more about production.

That copy editor's concern may be telling: 58 per cent of respondents designed pages using electronic software; 28 per cent worked for newspapers that changed editing or design software during the previous year; and 52 per cent worked for newspapers or sections that had been redesigned during the previous year. At Issue: Power. Other comments suggested that the issue is power, a central notion in Braverman's de-skilling theory and Shoemaker and Reese's theory of influences on media content. A copy editor at a newspaper in the 25,001-50,000 weekday circulation group wrote: "We're grammarians and headline writers and only rarely deal with the substance of a story except to return it to [the assigning editors] if there's a problem in that area."

A copy editor/page designer at another small newspaper described a similar situation: "The way our system is set up, the city desk determines content and balance on stories, and we merely lay out the pages, write headlines, and edit for AP style. We are not allowed to cut local stories, and not encouraged to question content and balance." Another wrote, "We're not allowed to change local copy."

In those cases-which may be particularly representative of small dailies with beginner copy editors, a powerful city editor, and no highly placed advocate for copy editors (*e.g.*, an assistant managing editor for copy desks)-the ability of copy editors to be ethics advocates may be constrained by their place in the newsroom hierarchy. Shoemaker and Reese suggest that media routines trump the individual's ability to influence media content, except in areas where there is no established routine. At some newspapers, not only is the routine for dealing with potential ethics-related problems in stories well established, but it also ends at the assigning desk. As a result, assigning editors do not grant to copy editors the sanction or approval they need to serve as even backup guardians of ethics standards.

Constraints on copy editors extend beyond ethics-related concerns. Although the largest difference between copy editors' views of their ideal and actual roles involved identifying and eliminating potential ethics-related problems, there were also significant differences between their ideal and real roles in eliminating errors and potential legal problems. Newspapers may also be wasting the talents of key employees by not supporting their efforts to find and eliminate errors and potential legal problems, such as libel. An assistant copy desk chief at a small daily wrote:

The other departments sometimes forget that we are not trained monkeys drawing boxes on the computer. We sift through wire copy and photos to select the most relevant and compelling items for our readers.

When it comes to decisions about local copy and photos, however, comments from the copy desk are often pushed aside. The next afternoon we are the ones questioned about any confusing information, mistakes or questionable remarks. "Why didn't the desk change that?" "How did that get by the desk?" Limits have been placed on our authority as copy editors, yet we are still held responsible for the decisions we cannot make.

One effect of a disconnect between ideal and real roles is a lack of job satisfaction. The nearly one in five respondents reporting that disconnect was more likely to be dissatisfied with aspects of his/her job and to have a lower opinion of the ethics standards of his/her newspaper. However, it is impossible to tell which came first, the disconnect or the discontent.

How should newspapers tackle this situation? If newspapers want to enlist all journalists to help preserve ethical standards and, thus, credibility, managers should encourage copy editors to raise questions when stories with potential ethics-related problems reach them. This encouragement should be delivered in a public way so that newsroom staffers who have traditionally controlled the routine of dealing with substantive questions can see that newsroom policymakers want those routines to include copy editors.

In addition, copy editors who still have concerns after talking with their supervisors and/or assigning editors should be encouraged to approach senior editors. A procedure for doing this should be made public, which could help reduce the perception that copy editors who take concerns to senior editors are acting maliciously, rather than merely doing their jobs.

Meanwhile, both copy editors and senior managers should make increased efforts to get to know each other. As The Poynter Institute's Karen Brown Dunlap has noted, one factor that can make copy editors' position in the newsroom precarious is that "their day begins as many reporters and editors prepare to end the day, keeping copy editors out of the flow of newsroom conversation." Greater connections between copy editors and senior editors would give the former access they need to raise concerns informally and offer the latter a better sense of what is going on in the trenches. It also might introduce senior editors to copy editors with reporting experience (of which there were many in this study) who would be good candidates for assigning editor positions. Considering them would help address two problems reported by this study: a perception that copy editors are not respected and the dissatisfaction of more than half with their prospects for advancement.

Further research might look beyond the copy desk to consider what reporters, midlevel managers, and senior managers consider their ideal ethics roles to be and how those stack up against what newsroom routines allow them to question or take responsibility for. Although media ethics research has often asked journalists "What behaviour do you consider ethical?" it has less often asked "What part of ethical journalism do you consider yourself responsible for?"

A large body of work has tried to determine what influences the behaviour of journalists and other media practitioners. Those studies generally have assumed, though, that media workers will do what they think they should do. This study revealed a disconnect between the "ethics backstop" role some copy editors thought they should have and the roles they perceived they did have. Other journalists may similarly be disconnected from roles they believe they should fulfill.

THE NEWSPAPER'S RESPONSIBILITY

Every reporter or editor who has ever been responsible for the education beat has received "the Call." On the other end of the telephone line is a principal, teacher, or parent. The caller is responsible for public relations at a local school and wants your paper to cover this year's sponsored walk, canned-food drive, or reading marathon. "You write so many negative stories about schools," she begins. "Don't you think it's time you printed something good?"

The Call can take many forms. Sometimes it is from the local superintendent trying to get positive press on a pet project. Sometimes it is from the governor's spokesperson looking for coverage of the latest state education initiative. Teachers, union leaders, college professors, and, of course, professional public relations people make the Call, too. They all deliver the same argument when they phone a newspaper office looking for a story promoting their cause or product: Isn't it time someone wrote something positive about schools?

Exasperated education writers share war stories about the Call whenever they get together at seminars and press events. "Why," they ask one another, "don't people understand that our job is to cover schools, not to make them look good?" They recite all the positive stories they have written about outstanding teachers, curriculum programmes that work, and successful students at the same time as they have probed the more difficult issues of dismal test scores, curriculum battles, school violence, and crowded classrooms. "Is it our fault," they ask, "that people only remember the negative stories?"

Just what is the responsibility of newspapers for shaping public perceptions of education? As a line editor supervising education coverage for a large regional newspaper, I ask myself that question frequently. I have become aware that the public views schools in a harsher light than do either my reporters or I. Parents constantly fret about school violence, even though crime statistics show relatively few serious incidents in most schools. Readers worry that children across the board are no longer learning to read or do arithmetic, even though schools in our region generally score well above state and national averages on achievement tests. Families are considering private schools even in wealthy districts that send most of their public school graduates on to four-year colleges. What is going on here?

Research on the media's impact on public perceptions of the schools is sparse, and what there is mostly dates back to the past decade, before newspapers caught up with the national preoccupation with education. Furthermore, who can separate the influence of newspapers, magazines, television, radio, and even newsgroups on the World Wide Web? To what degree are perceptions also shaped by personal experiences and what people hear from their children, friends, and neighbours? We working journalists are left with little more than our own hypotheses, most of which - naturally - reflect favourably on our efforts and intentions. In any case, there is no question that schools face significant challenges. In such well-documented cases as the school governance reforms in Chicago, inner-city districts appear to be fighting a losing battle against poverty, neglect, and neighbourhood violence, despite the heroic efforts of some dedicated educators. Students in poor neighbourhoods rarely receive as good an education as those in affluent communities. Is that the fault of the media? Only the top students take enough math and science to prepare them for the technological age.

And universities report a steady increase in entering students who need remedial classes in basic subjects before they can tackle college work.

As journalists, my team of reporters and I try to raise public awareness of such problems as a first step towards solving them. Education has become one of the most visible beats at the Mercury News, and the work of those who cover education is often on page 1. Still, in examining the critical issues facing schools, are the media somehow creating the impression that there is nothing worth saving anywhere?

Jim Ritchie, the outspoken superintendent of the respected Moreland elementary school district in suburban San Jose, argued that the Mercury News and newspapers in general play a strong role in forming public perceptions of schools, both good and bad. In his community, he said, "I haven't seen any other entity that has the ability to change public perceptions for the short term. If it appears there and it appears in a strident and dramatic fashion, it will have an immediate effect on public opinion."

The power of specific stories fades over time as parents and readers move on to other issues, in Ritchie's experience, but the impression of critical stories remains strong in the common memory. "I definitely think the image of the public schools reflected in the media is much more negative than it is positive," he said. He pointed to the steady stream of stories about critical reports on education as well as articles about business leaders and politicians who lambaste the schools' inadequacies. In his view, those stories, lumping all schools together in broad, general terms, do little to illuminate the vast differences between schools and even classes within a school. "That constant drumbeat - I really think it's created the impression that public schools do not reflect quality," he said.

Newspapers, indeed, are in the business of news. And ever since 1983, when a blue-ribbon panel warned in A Nation at Risk of a "rising tide of mediocrity" in America's schools, there has been a flood of impressive reports cataloguing education's ills. The country has learned from the National Assessment of Educational Progress how little its children know about history, geography, reading, and math - although their degree of knowledge is probably not significantly different from that of previous generations. Numerous studies, including the Third International Mathematics and Science Study, have found that students in the United States do not stack up as well on academic achievement tests as Americans would like them to do against their counterparts around the world. (U.S. eighth-graders scored below average in math, an area in which their lessons are not as advanced as in the top-scoring countries, and above average in science, an area in which the U.S. curriculum is more focused.) The National Commission on Teaching and America's Future said that many of the nation's teachers are inadequately prepared.

There have been so many reports and studies from this or that commission and think tank that the stories rarely get on the front page anymore. Still, they add fuel to the public debate over the future of schools and cannot be ignored by any responsible reporter or broadcaster.

In The Manufactured Crisis, David Berliner and Bruce Biddle argue that the media have reported the international comparisons, in particular, unfairly and created the impression that America's schools are failing. They contend that journalists have neglected to ask critical questions about the groups tested and the subject matter covered, while ignoring comparative studies in which American students have done well. They insist that schools in the United States, on average, are doing as well as or better than ever, although they concede that there is still much room for improvement.

While the media seem quite willing to report bad news about our schools, they are much less willing to report news about the strengths of American education. One wonders, Why? Is it possible that bad news about education is thought to be more newsworthy? Or have reporters by now been so brainwashed by the critics that they cannot believe good news? Are too many of the reporters' employers friends of powerful people who wish the public schools no good? I find it hard to swallow such hints of a media conspiracy, and I object to inclinations to paint both print and broadcast reporters in the same light.

I suspect, as well, that such criticisms arise from dissatisfaction with the work of the national press rather than with that of the nation's 1,500 daily newspapers, from which most readers get their news.

There may be some truth, though, in the contention that journalists have not done a good job of analyzing the comparative studies. Few reporters are comfortable with statistics - we joke among ourselves that, if we had been good at math, we could have ended up in lucrative jobs instead of in journalism. Also, speed is essential in daily reporting, and we do far too much of our analysis on the fly. We do not come back to a topic for deeper consideration nearly often enough. Compounding the problem, newspapers rarely provide enough space in which to analyse the nuances of a huge study. So, at even the best papers, complex stories on all topics become oversimplified more frequently than reporters would like.

All of this said, education itself has shortcomings that it would be irresponsible for the media to ignore. The national anxiety about education appears justified from many perspectives. As we approach the millennium, parents, business leaders, and politicians alike question whether schools on the whole are producing citizens adequately prepared for the Information Age.

Even educators who are proud of what teachers and students are doing in their classrooms would most probably agree that schools need to reach higher to prepare more students for jobs that require such academic skills as advanced math. Economists maintain that students can no longer expect to graduate from high school with minimal skills and move right into well-paying factory jobs that allow them to join the middle class. It is not enough, others suggest, to prepare only our top students for college. For many jobs, the new standard is becoming at least two years of college.

THE PUBLIC CARES

Education places near the top of the public agenda in most polls, right behind crime and the economy. Even in notoriously tax-stingy California, education is one of the few items on which voters often say they are willing to spend more money. When Policy Analysis for California Education conducted its 1996 poll on public views of education, 38 per cent of the respondents named "improving the quality of public schools" as the most important issue facing the state. In the same poll, 66 per cent said that it was important to increase funding for schools.

Education took on even more significance in a 1996 Mercury News poll, which found that 88 per cent of the people were concerned with the quality of public schools in their community - a notable departure from national polls, in which people have consistently defended their own schools. With that level of public interest, newspapers should not only report the debate but help inform it with stories that explore the issue from all perspectives.

Those who still believe in public education as a social good propose shifting more resources into the schools, setting high academic standards, and helping all students reach them. In his 1997 State of the Union address, President Clinton set forth a 10-point plan "to ensure that all Americans have the best education in the world." In addition to setting national standards and drafting examinations tied to those standards, Clinton called for expanding Head Start, creating 3,000 charter schools, spending $5 billion on school construction, and establishing college scholarships.

On the other hand, some advocates of choice propose subjecting public schools to market forces by giving students vouchers to attend private schools if they wish. They argue that public schools would have to shape up and compete for students or find themselves out of business for want of customers.

In the midst of the debate, David Mathews, president of the Kettering Foundation, warns that the public's connection to its schools is waning. He says that his research has found what other studies have reported: whereas

Americans believe that the country needs public schools, they are torn between a sense of duty to support these schools and a responsibility to do what is best for children. "They are ambivalent and agonize over the dilemma. And, however reluctantly, many are deciding that public schools aren't best for their children or anyone else's." Critics and many educators blame the media for public perceptions that schools are failing because of a combination of growing social problems, declining discipline, and falling standards. Yet, Mathews writes, "The people we talked to based their conclusions on personal experience or the experience of family members and close friends." So discouraged were most of the parents in focus groups conducted for the Kettering Foundation that even those who spoke relatively positively about their public schools said they would send their children to private school if they could receive a "check" to pay for the tuition. It must be noted, though, that voters have consistently rejected voucher proposals that would give parents such checks.

There is no denying that the public has mixed feelings about schools. One of the best indicators is the annual Phi Delta Kappa/Gallup poll.

In 1996, for example, 66 per cent of public school parents gave the school their oldest child attends an A or a B - a figure that gives educators great comfort. At the same time, only 21 per cent of respondents gave the nation's schools an A or a B. Compare that to the 48 per cent who gave top grades to public schools in 1974. Although 54 per cent of the people who responded to the poll in 1996 opposed vouchers that would give families public money to send their children to private schools, most clearly felt that private schools were better: 63 per cent gave private schools an A or a B.

It is hard to tell where the poll respondents obtained the information for that assessment. Most newspapers print very little about private schools, whose business is not conducted in a public forum with taxpayers' dollars.

In most cases, private school students do not take the same tests as public school students, so it is tough to compare them on objective criteria. Perhaps it is their word-of-mouth reputation as bastions of discipline, decorum, and traditional curricula - and not portrayals in the media - that makes private schools so popular with a public committed to discipline and basic skills.

This is not the first era of hand-wringing over American education. Stanford University education professors David Tyack and Larry Cuban have pointed out that the country has been fretting about its schools for more than a century. In Tinkering Towards Utopia, they note that the U.S. has worried most about the effectiveness of schooling at times of crisis, when national leaders obsess about the country's struggle for survival in a competitive world. In the 1890s, the Germans were the source of that anxiety; in the 1950s, the Soviets; in the 1980s, the Japanese. Tyack and Cuban write:

Commentators in the media, muckrakers, leaders in business and unions, government officials, legislators, social reformers, activists in women's associations, foundation officials, leaders of protest movements, and policy makers in education all starkly expose problems and confidently propose educational solutions. Then they pressure legislatures, school boards and public school administrators to adopt their reforms.

What has been different in the latest wave of education debates is the public's current disenchantment with all institutions, from city councils to the Congress. At the same time, college graduation rates are up, and many parents, educated as well as or better than their children's teachers, now appear to be quite comfortable criticizing what goes on in the classroom. For the most part, parents do not buy the education establishment's arguments. They call for a greater emphasis on the basics and turn up their noses at most of the reform proposals from researchers and educators.

The conflicts that arise out of such disagreements are the grist of journalism. It is our job to write about the issues without taking a side. When the media do it right, they help readers and viewers understand what is at stake and explain the arguments. The media must take care, however, not to get caught up in the enthusiasm that educators have for the latest fad or in the ideology of the critics. That role belongs to the editorial writers and the commentators. Although it seems difficult for most readers to distinguish between the editorial pages and the news sections, good newspapers keep them separated by the journalistic equivalent of a fire wall. Editorial writers tell readers what they should think. Reporters give them the information to make up their own minds.

Negativity is in the Eye of the Reader

So what should newspapers be writing about in this time of ferment in education? Robert Frahm, a prize-winning education reporter with the Hartford Courant in Connecticut, says that newspapers have an obligation to help their readers understand what's really going on in schools.

That means going into classrooms to show readers how teachers and students try to cope with difficult issues of learning, often against overwhelming odds. It also means holding the people in charge of the schools responsible for education in the community. "We get some complaints from school officials that we are too negative," says Frahm, former president of the Education Writers Association. "I don't believe that's true. I believe that if you were to count our stories and rate them as positive or negative, there would be more positives." One of the most serious variables, reporters understand, is who is passing judgement on their work. If a story raises critical issues about schools that may lead to the improvement of education for children, most reporters would consider it a positive piece.

In 1996, Frahm and fellow Courant reporter Rick Green did just that when they wrote a revealing study of the Hartford schools' management after its partnership collapsed with the for-profit corporation then known as Education Alternatives, Inc. Their stories, running over four days, chronicled the district's deep problems, ranging from serious financial mismanagement to chronic disputes between the union and the administration that reverberated in the city's classrooms.

As a result of that series, the Connecticut Department of Education announced that it would conduct a comprehensive review of the system. Six months later, the state education commissioner called for sweeping changes in management, curriculum, enrollment policies, and union contracts. At last, it appeared, someone was going to make a concerted effort to fix the problems that had crippled the inner-city school system for years. Many Hartford readers might well view those events as a positive outcome.

Rarely do reporters get to see such a direct link between their work and a shift in public policy. Frahm took great pride in articles in the series that went beyond the facts and figures of the investigation to look at teachers' struggles to make the system work for their students. For instance, the articles cited a kindergarten teacher whose 22 students - all children of unmarried mothers - live in some of the city's poorest neighbourhoods and arrive at school often not even knowing their colours or the alphabet. This was a reality that few Courant readers would recognize. The newspaper's subscribers more often live in the affluent suburbs surrounding Hartford than in the inner city. That is why the story must be told.

Educators, however, frequently appear to misunderstand the reporter's role as the public's eyes and ears. "We are conscious of not ignoring things that are going on in school that are good, but we also believe we can't ignore what is bad," Frahm says. "We feel if we were just to create a rosy picture of the schools, it would be a lie."

Although the Hartford stories were exemplary, such journalism is no longer an anomaly in America's newspapers. The Philadelphia Enquirer catalogued the failings of the city schools in such indisputable detail that in 1994 a new superintendent used the series to launch substantial reform. In Denver in 1995, the Rocky Mountain News so graphically outlined conflicts between research and teaching in Colourado universities that the schools ended up giving more attention to undergraduate instruction. Newspapers from Alaska to Kentucky have explored issues ranging from the inequities of special education to the intricacies of school reform. More and more, ambitious reporters go beyond school board meetings to try to explain why schools are working or not working.

Steve Barkin is familiar with this trend. A journalism professor at the University of Maryland, Barkin has judged the National Awards for Education Reporting since 1985. He has read countless education stories over the years. The newspaper stories Barkin reads for the contest - admittedly some of the best work in the field - increasingly delve into the reality of what goes on in classrooms. There are still the traditional stories about test scores, budget battles, school board politics, and superintendent searches. But there are also many stories that try to explain how schools go about their true work - teaching children. "When I was reading about education 20 years ago, I was reading about test scores," Barkin says, "and I'm still reading about test scores, but the mix is a little richer than it used to be. I think you learn a lot more of what's going on in newspapers."

Even George Kaplan, who has censured newspapers for putting too many inexperienced young reporters on the schools beat and then covering education only superficially via school board meetings, modified his tone in a 1997 interview. Although still fairly critical of the national newspapers for inadequately treating trends in education reform, he cited improvement among all papers. "In general, I think the smaller communities are getting a fairly objective picture. They don't care about national trends," Kaplan said. "For the name papers, the reporting is mixed. But overall I think the reporting is good."

Jay Rosen, a New York University professor and an advocate of public journalism, questions the quality of education reporting. He contends that newspapers are still not giving their readers what they need in order to make informed decisions about education policy and that reporters spend too much time writing about the school board and not enough time writing about schools. "I think the major failing of newspaper coverage of education is the failing of most public institution coverage," Rosen says. "It's institution driven, it's conflict driven and tends only rarely to be concerned with the resolution of issues or problem solving." Rosen wants reporters to get away from their dependence on school trustee meetings for day-to-day education coverage.

As an example of a better approach to education coverage, Rosen points to the 40,000-circulation Sun in Bremerton, Washington. Editor Mike Phillips became frustrated when the Sun education reporter wrote numerous stories about the local school superintendent's salary. Instead, he suggested, the reporter should ask parents what was on their minds and then write about that. The answer that came back was "homework," and the Sun responded by looking into why so many Bremerton students didn't bring home homework. A new approach to schools coverage was born. Phillips says: "What happens in a school board meeting has little to do with the rearing of children, the education of children, most of the time.

A lot of people recognize the problem with that pattern, but they're not very successful in changing it, simply because it's easier." I would argue that many larger papers have all but abandoned school board-related coverage except in the most dramatic cases, such as the very public conflict between Mayor Rudolph Giuliani of New York and former chancellor Ramon Cortines. In an illustration of the new style of education coverage, the Miami Herald in 1996 devoted three months to producing a four-day series that answered Dade County parents' most pressing questions about their public schools.

Mercury News reporters rarely attend board meetings. But in countless other newspapers - particularly smaller publications for which reporters are required to churn out several stories a day - such institutional coverage remains the staple of education reporting. What some critics say about newspapers is true: not all education stories are extensively researched pieces about both the positive and the negative aspects of an issue. By necessity, such thorough articles are only a small portion of what we print over time.

Even if local education reporters fill their articles with context to help readers understand what is really going on, countless stories from other reporters and wire services do not. When Bob Dole attacked teacher unions in the course of his Presidential campaign, it made headlines, but there was very little critical analysis of his charges from the political reporters covering the speech.

When SAT scores go up or down by a single point, it is news, even though the change is insignificant statistically. And papers still run the Associated Press-produced charts ranking the states by SAT scores, even though the College Board notes that only a small proportion of high school students usually those aiming for elite colleges take the test in the highest-scoring states. (Average scores tend to decline when more students take the test.) As a nation, we love benchmarks even if they are flawed. Readers demand them, and newspapers deliver them - usually with caveats that are routinely ignored.

Yet newspapers arguably remain the most complete and objective general source of information on education for the public, producing as true a picture of schools as is possible in limited space and time. Look at the case of the move by the school board in Oakland, California, to recognize as a separate language the dialect of African American students. Within hours of the school board vote, Ebonics - a term taken from ebony and phonics - was topic number one on radio talk shows across the country. Newspapers from Phoenix to London ran stories about the board's action. Within days, Jesse Jackson and Maya Angelou were denouncing the school board's action and Secretary of Education Richard Riley was announcing that there would be no federal funding for bilingual classes in Ebonics.

Through it all, newspapers did a far better job than did broadcast media of reporting just what the board did and what it meant. The school board's resolution referred to "genetically based" African language systems and argued that "recognizing the English language acquisition and improvement skills of African American students is as fundamental as is application of bilingual education principles for others whose primary languages are other than English." It also ordered the superintendent to "immediately devise and implement the best possible academic programme for imparting instruction to

African American students in their primary language" and talked of "maintaining the legitimacy and richness" of Black English. The language of the school board was incendiary, and the intent was obvious: at least some people in the district were hoping to get bilingual funding to help raise the dismal achievement levels of African American students.

Newspapers reported those facts and followed up as the school board subtly revised its position to focus solely on improving achievement by acknowledging and working with the dialect that black children brought into the classroom. Trustees insisted that they had never intended Ebonics to be taught as a separate language in Oakland schools.

Print reporters covered every twist and turn as trustees won Jesse Jackson over to their side and then finally backed off some of the more controversial wording of their resolution. But reporters also took a hard look at the problems that black children face in classrooms across the country when they are expected to speak a language markedly different from their own.

The Mercury News and other California newspapers went into Oakland classrooms to describe just how the district was already using Ebonics to help students master standard English. The Washington Post ran a front-page story on the search for a solution to the national problem of low academic performance by many poor black students. It quoted linguists as saying that the use of Black English as a bridge to standard English might be effective in the classrooms, then explored the views of skeptics.

"I think newspapers handled it a lot more responsibly than the school board acknowledged," says Michael Bazeley, then education reporter for the Oakland Tribune. "Television did a horrible job, in my opinion. On day 6 or 7 they were saying kids were going to be taught Black English in the classroom." Rush Limbaugh had a field day. So did editorial writers and columnists from Los Angeles to New York and beyond. As late as February, a Newsweek columnist expounded on the topic, and Garry Trudeau lampooned Ebonics in a Sunday Doonesbury strip. Yet readers of the news columns got a fairly clear understanding of one of the most controversial education stories of the year.

Explaining the News

That is how it should be. Newspaper articles should help readers understand their world better. The huge, controversial stories are exhilarating. Reporters love it when the world hangs on their words. But they also write smaller, yet still important, stories that they hope will illuminate pressing issues. Often those articles are good news by almost anyone's standards.

Early in 1997, the Mercury News ran a front-page story about a district that consistently performed well against all odds. The report showed how San Jose's Evergreen elementary district, with a large proportion of impoverished students who speak little or no English, had managed to raise test scores and win national recognition for its schools. Evergreen's secret, reporter Maya Suryaraman revealed, was its teachers.

The district emphasized teacher training and curriculum planning and gave teachers a strong role in making decisions that affect their classrooms. As a result, many teachers took a more professional role in diagnosing and solving their students' learning problems. But the story, focused as it was on solutions, received only slight notice from readers. The public seems to have a better memory for the negative story.

As a case in point, Jodi Berls, education reporter for the Austin American-Statesman in Texas, likes to tell the tale of two big projects that her paper produced in 1996. One was on the local district's efforts to get parent volunteers into the schools. The other was on lunchtime violence in schools. "Both packages got front-page play, with extensive space inside; both had lots of photos and some graphics; both involved numerous campus visits and myriad phone calls; both took about a month to put together," she says. "The cafeteria violence story got a lot of response - parents, teachers, and students called afterwards to tell us they liked it, offer us tips and ideas related to it, et cetera. The volunteering story... went down a black hole except for one guy who referred to it in a board meeting in a snide comment suggesting that I'm in the school district's pocket." Even as they are berated for their work, most reporters realise that public opinion often seems to have a life of its own, with little relation to journalistic enterprise. Conventional wisdom quite frequently rules, in spite of evidence to the contrary.

To see how newspapers can fail to sway public opinion, consider the series that the Mercury News produced in 1996 looking at the otherwise unquestioned push for more computers in the schools. The newspaper performed its own computer analysis in concert with a University of California researcher, working with data from a national technology data collection firm. When they were finished, the reporters concluded that there was no hard evidence that California schools with large investments in technology performed any better academically than comparable schools without similar equipment - except in low-income neighbourhoods.

Evidently, few readers bought the idea. Letters ran heavily in favour of a bigger investment in school technology in all schools. Local superintendents called for a meeting with the publisher and executive editor to complain that the Mercury News was anti-education. And the paper, located in the heart of Silicon Valley, continued to run story after story about high-tech executives trashing the schools for not doing enough with computers, as well as articles on politicians urging greater expenditures on technology. Even though the newspaper included a paragraph in most of those stories about our reporters' findings, it was clear that most people still believed that computers are the answer to schools' academic shortcomings.

Such experiences are frustrating, but journalists are accustomed to them. So most journalists decide that they just have to do their best to keep their minds open, their eyes peeled for good stories, and their judgement unclouded by ideology. Journalists try to keep up with research and the broad range of emerging thought in the field. They look for issues and trends that may make a difference in their readers' lives as well as interesting features that illuminate what's going on in schools. In the end, journalists cannot allow themselves to be swayed by consideration of whether a story will be good for the public image of schools. Their job is to tell the truth and help readers understand the challenges that society is facing. And the truth is often unpleasant.

4

The Evolution of Journalism

Looking into the future, we can forecast with total certainty that the nature of journalism and the stories that it tells will change. Journalism always has been changing. Today's norms about what is news are far from absolutes. Contemporary discussions about blurring the line between news and entertainment usually are interpreted as meaning that this behaviour is a violation of the standards of journalism.

A viable alternative interpretation is that this behaviour is simply a major contemporary feature in the ongoing, albeit not always salubrious and straight-line, evolution of journalism. It is possible to identify many of the prominent characteristics of this evolution over recent decades and even over past centuries. However, we cannot with any certainty predict the course of this evolution and identify precisely which characteristics of journalism will be paramount in future decades.

We can with certainty predict two things: The change will be neither orderly nor even, and some changes will be thoughtful and deliberate, whereas others will be reactions to immediate drastic circumstances. At least for the short term, Sept. 11 swept mainstream journalism's years of preoccupation with the scandalous, salacious and sensational off the agenda and turned its attention to more significant topics at home and abroad.

Was this a temporary aberration, or a significant, long-term shift in the focus of journalism? Even if the effects of Sept. 11 were temporary, no one can predict with any certainty what other events or trends might reshape journalism in the future.

From one perspective, this indeterminacy is fortunate because a major goal of this book is to foster discussion and debate—perhaps even have some influence—on the course of this evolution in the new media setting.

Although no one knows exactly what will emerge in the next decade or two, individuals can have some influence on what does emerge because the creative and entrepreneurial spirit of journalists, singly and in various combinations, has been a potent force in the evolution of American journalism during the past two centuries.

An important point to keep in mind is that the shifting nature of journalism over the 19th and 20th centuries and now in the opening decade of the 21st century basically has been evolutionary rather than characterized by abrupt shifts at specific historical junctures.

This is the case because the changes in journalism—and, more broadly, the changes in mass communication—over these centuries result from the confluence of three major factors:

- New developments in technology.
- Changes in the undergirding social conditions.
- And creative and entrepreneurial impulses.

In the 1830s, when mass communication began with the penny press, the convergence of influences producing this phenomenon was the new technology of steam-driven printing presses capable of producing large numbers of copies of newspapers; widespread literacy as the supporting social condition; and a key entrepreneur, Benjamin Day, who launched the *New York Sun.* But Day alone did not create the style and the norms for this new journalism.

Those were the product of numerous editors and working journalists, a few well known to us, such as James Gordon Bennett and Horace Greeley, but most anonymous.

THIRTY-YEAR VANTAGE POINTS

Any activity such as journalism that results from the creative and intellectual efforts of hundreds of different organizations geographically scattered across many cities will be characterized largely by evolution. It is difficult, if not impossible, to perceive distinct changes from day to day or even from month to month.

But as these shifts and changes accumulate over time, they do become apparent. An optimum strategy for observing the evolution of American journalism from the days of the penny press to the present is to dip into this historical stream at intervals of 30 years.

Not only is three decades a sufficiently broad interval of time to make changes in the nature of journalism readily apparent, an interval of three decades also means that a new generation has come onto the scene and made its mark. Those persons who would have been novices at one point in time will have become, 30 years later, the cadre of experienced journalists and editors occupying most of the key positions in news organizations.

Today's 22-year-old graduating with a bachelor's degree in journalism may well be, by age 52, the managing editor or even editor of a daily newspaper—or occupying a similar high level position in other news media. No generation is a perfect clone of its predecessor. Each generation brings change and by the time that 30 years have passed, each new generation is likely to have made its mark on the practice of journalism.

This situation is not unique to journalism. Arthur M. Schlesinger Jr. noted the utility that the concept of generation has generally for historical analysis and explanations of change: In traditional societies, where change was imperceptible and each generation lives as its parents and grandparents had lived before it, the passage of generations made little difference. But, with the acceleration in the velocity of history, new generations began to undergo novel experiences and thereby to achieve distinctive outlooks.

He also noted the influence of Auguste Comte—in Schlesinger's view, the first person to recognize the historical significance of generations—on John Stuart Mill who asserted that historical change should be measured by "intervals of one generation, during which a new set of human beings have been educated, have grown up from childhood, and taken possession of society."

Although both Jose Ortega y Gasset and Karl Mannheim identified a generation's lifetime as 30 years—an interval also used by Schlesinger to analyse the 20th century political history of the United States as alternating cycles in the dominance of public purpose and private interest—Ortega y Gasset urged caution: There is no arithmetical inevitability in the generational sequence. A generation is a rough, not an exact, unit; almost a metaphor.

This idea of generations, in particular generational replacement, also has been used to explain fundamental changes in public opinion over time. Few people radically shift their opinions about the issues of the times, but over time, one generation of opinion holders is replaced by a new generation with new perspectives and opinions on the issues of the day.

Journalist Samuel Lubell attributed the long-running success of the Democratic Party in the 1930s and 1940s to the generations of voters that came of age during the Great Depression. Later generations shifted the tide to the Republican Party.

As an international example, the strongest support for social welfare policies in both the United States and western Europe is found among the generations that attained adulthood after these programmes were already in place in the societies in which they grew up. There are many other examples of differences between generations and their differing approach to the times.

Without delving too deeply into the historical details, think about a historical timeline of American journalism from the 1830s to the present. Thirty years after the appearance of the penny press is the time of the Civil War with news stories frequently constructed in inverted pyramids and modeled on the principle of objectivity.

Thirty years later is the end of the 19th century and a time when the yellow journalism of William Randolph Hearst and Joseph Pulitzer epitomized much of mainstream journalism.

Next are the 1920s and the perceived need in the complex aftermath of World War I to offer news analysis as well as spot news about the events of the day. By the mid-20th century, television news was a major part of mass communication and a continuing influence on the style of journalism.

The final decades of the 20th century are the ones that define for many journalists, including us as the authors of this book, significant portions of their professional careers. Contemporary journalism is delivered through far more channels than it was when we were college undergraduates in journalism.

Daily newspapers and both network and local television still command significant, though shrinking, audiences. Now these media share the public arena with a multitude of cable news channels, online newspapers and a variety of other news sources.

CHANGING STYLES OF NEWS

Much more has changed than the variety of media that deliver the news. The style of that news also has changed significantly. A succinct portrait of this evolutionary pattern in contemporary journalism during the final decades of the 20th century is found in Thomas Patterson's *"Out of Order"* an analysis of how the news media covered our presidential elections from 1960 to 1992. Again, an interval of approximately 30 years proves a useful vantage point for sketching these changes.

In 1960, an interpretative framework—rather than the more traditional descriptive framework used to report the presidential election—was found in only a small fraction of the news stories on the front page of the *New York Times.*

By 1972, there was parity between the two styles of election reporting; in the 1988 and 1992 elections, interpretative stories dominated the front page of the *New York Times* by a ratio of 4-to-l. Over a period of approximately 30 years, the preferred style for reporting the presidential election had turned upside down.

By 1960 there already was an emphasis on politics as a game in which reporting a candidate's strategy for winning and conjuring with such things as "who won the day" and "who is ahead by how much" were key elements.

That is, the thrust of the reportage was on the campaign as a contest between parties and politicians rather than on the election as a method for the public to make a decision about its future.

In that 1960 election, the split between reporting on the game and reporting on the issues was close to 50-50. This already was very different from elections in earlier periods, but that 50-50 split was just the baseline for major changes appearing in the 1972 and 1976 elections.

By 1972, reporting on the game prevailed by about 2-to-l. By 1976, the ratio of game coverage to issue coverage had reached a new plateau of about 4-to-l. Among the most powerful influences driving the startling shift to a 4-1 ratio of strategic, insider reporting over issues reporting was Theodoure H.

White. Starting in 1960, White, a veteran reporter, produced a best-selling series of quadrennial books, *"The Making of the President.* " Remarkable in their detailed reporting from inside the presidential campaigns, the books set a new standard for depth and insight into the strategic and human calculations that elected presidents.

White was writing history, but the seemingly authenticating details that his books contained proved irresistible to the political press; never mind that they were reported months after the votes were cast.

The Associated Press, for instance, messaged its political reporters, "When Teddy White's book comes out, there shouldn't be a single story in that book that we haven't reported ourselves.

" And A. M. Rosenthal, managing editor of the *New York Times*, instructed his staff, "We aren't going to wait until a year after the election to read in Teddy White's book what we should have reported ourselves. "

The impact of such commands was to drive political reporting further and further inside the campaigns and away from issue coverage. The narrative illusion was if you can report what's in the candidate's stomach, that is, if you know what he had for breakfast, then you surely must also know what's in his head and heart.

What journalists failed to recognize was that White's books were not helpful to the public in terms of picking a leader, for the rich details they contained were published months after the votes were cast. They were conceived and executed as history, not contemporary journalism. Nevertheless, the hunger for glimpses into the inner circles and thoughts of the campaigns moved political reporting ever further from anything that could be useful, or even very interesting, to average voters.

Even White himself came to regret his reportorial invention. "It's appalling what we've done, " White said during the 1972 campaign, the fourth of the five he chronicled. "All of us are observing him (the candidate), taking notes like mad, getting all the little details. Which I think I invented as a method of reporting and which I now sincerely regret. If you write about this, say that I sincerely regret it. Who gives a ... if the guy had milk and Total for breakfast?"

Not surprisingly, as shifts occurred among the aspects of the campaign that were emphasized in news reports, the journalist's voice also became more prominent in setting the tone of election reports. Back in 1960, the candidates themselves and partisan participants in the election set the tone in two-thirds of the stories. Praise for a candidate came from his supporters, attacks and criticism from his opponent and the opponent's supporters. By the 1972 presidential election, journalists were setting the tone of most articles.

Looking more closely at the nature of that tone reveals another pattern that turned upside down across those nine elections from 1960 to 1992; good news versus bad news. Back in 1960, the ratio of good news to bad news was about 3-to-1. This ratio seesawed up and down over the next four elections but in 1980 moved to a new plateau where the ratio of good news to bad news was 2-to-3, another 30-year reversal in the prevailing style of political reporting.

This 30-year trend is graphically illustrated by the titles on *Time* magazine's cover stories. In 1960, they were simply "Candidate Kennedy" and "Candidate Nixon.

" In 1992, they included "Nobody's Perfect: The Doubts About Ross Perot" and "Waiting for Perot: He's Leading in the Polls, But Can He Lead the Nation?. " Bush's cover story was "The Fight of His Life" and Clinton's cover stories included "Why Voters Don't Trust Clinton" and "Is Bill Clinton for Real?. "

In sum, the pattern of presidential election coverage that evolved bit by bit from 1960 to 1992 resulted in a fundamentally different election journalism. In 1960, journalists described the campaign, issue coverage was priority, partisans set the tone of the coverage, and good news prevailed over bad news. Thirty years later, journalists interpreted the campaign, game coverage was the priority, the tone of the coverage was set by journalists, and bad news prevailed over good news.

The sequence of these steps in the evolution of a new style of political reporting is where the Xs mark elections with significant increases over past journalistic practice. This stair-step pattern is a succinct portrait of shifting professional perspectives, the evolution of a new set of "cookie cutters" that shape contemporary political journalism.

Beyond political journalism and presidential elections, there are numerous other cookie cutters used to shape the daily news, many with long histories of use. Noting the repetition of master narratives—even rather specific stories—over and over through the years, even centuries, Robert Darnton metaphorically summarized his time as a journalist:

We simply drew on the traditional repertory of genres. It was like making cookies from an antique cookie cutter.

Among the most ancient sets of journalistic cookie cutters are political, financial and sexual scandals, cookie cutters extensively employed in the final decade of the 20th century whose historical origins are in the broadside ballads, news books and French canards of the 16th and 17th century.

In reporting the news of the moment, journalists depend for the most part on a set of standard conventions about how a news story should be written. Some of these are very ancient, some very recent.

The mix of cookie cutters in common use is constantly evolving, and an interval of 30 years is a useful vantage point for observing what has changed and what has remained constant in reporting the news.

Journalism changed in the closing decades of the 20th century, in particular adding a strong interpretive element to the reporting of public affairs in general, not just political campaigns.

Undoubtedly, journalism will change again during the opening decades of this century. Part of the change will result from the tremendous changes in communication technology and its diffusion among the public.

In *"Mediamorphosis: Understanding New Media"* Roger Fidler cited Paul Saffo, a director at the Institute for the Future in Menlo Park, Calif., who "posits that the amount of time required for new ideas to fully seep into a culture has consistently averaged about three decades for at least the past five centuries. He calls this the 30-year rule. "

EVOLUTION OF JOURNALISM

Our purpose here is not to present a history of journalism using intervals of 30 years or any other vantage point. That is a massive undertaking for another book. Rather, our purpose is to make the point that the nature of journalism constantly evolves in response to the social, technological and creative environment in which people work.

Furthermore, the defining characteristics of this evolution need to be made explicit and the subject of intense scrutiny and debate, especially in this time when a rapidly changing technological environment arguably offers more options than at any time in the past.

Not all of these options—or even the current emphases of news, however long they last—are beneficial ones for society or for journalism. It is especially important to note "wrong turns" along the way or the failure to shed some bad habits.

And there is the need to more explicitly guide this evolutionary pattern of the new journalism, not a new style of newspaper journalism or broadcast journalism, but rather a journalism resulting from the convergence of many media on the contemporary stage.

JOURNALISM CULMINATES IN PERSUASION

The need for persuasive writing is based on the recognition that even when people are well informed about what is happening, when they understand what is happening and are able to determine whether it is good or bad or best or worst, even then they may not be able to decide what should be done about what is happening. It is the task of persuasive writing to provide knowledge about what should be done and even, on occasion, to motivate people to do what should be done.

On April 1, 1988, for example, the Labour Department reported that, although the national unemployment rate had dipped to 5.6 per cent, the lowest level since May 1979, the jobless rate for blacks had increased from 12.6 to 12.8 per cent. Most readers probably had no difficulty determining that the increase in black unemployment is a bad thing, not only for blacks but also for the entire country. But what should be done about it?

Should minimum wages be lowered, with the hope that increased hiring would result? Should embargoes be slapped on imports, with the expectation that domestic production and employment would increase? Should public works programmes be initiated? Should job training programmes be expanded? The possibilities are numerous, but what specifically should be done? Decisions have to be made. Even the decision not to do anything is a decision.

Although, in this case, the general public can do little directly, they can rally behind one or more courses of governmental action. That mysterious force called public opinion, can have a powerful effect, but only if it is aroused and directed. To achieve such an intellectual movement is one of the tasks of the journalistic persuasive writer. On some public matters—especially the election of persons to fill executive, legislative, and judicial positions—the decisions of the people do have direct effects. Media endorsements, at least when they are well argued, help the public make these choices. When Sig Gissler was editor of the *Milwaukee Journal*, he said:

We simply recommend, or state a preference, for two main reasons. One is to stimulate thought and discussion. The other is to provide some guidance, not in the know-it-all sense but rather as a sharing of judgements based on research. Most readers don't make public affairs a full-time job. Our editorial conference does, investing much time and effort in sorting out issues. Consequently, our election suggestions can play a useful role.

What Gissler said about the members of his editorial conference applies also to most full-time journalists who are persuaders: columnists, broadcast commentators, editorial cartoonists, and the others. All earn their living by thinking and communicating about public affairs. When they do their jobs well, those persuaders perform an important public service by helping the people make both personal and public decisions. If we recognize that persuasive communication primarily attempts to determine what should be done about some person, event, or situation, we can see that the answer sometimes involves decisions on a great number of possibilities. For example, faced with large and increasing deficits, Congress, in 1985, passed Public Law 99-177, better known as the Gramm-Rudman-Hollings Act.

Two years later, partly to avoid constitutional challenges, the law was revised; the Balanced Budget Reaffirmation Act of 1987 established new targets and extended the date for achieving a balanced budget until 1993. But what should be done to reduce the deficit, which the Congressional Budget Office (CBO) projected would be $183 billion for fiscal year 1988? The CBO, required by the Congressional Budget Act of 1974 to submit an annual report on budgetary options, listed some alternatives.

In fact, without making any recommendations—it is prohibited by statute from doing so—it set forth in some detail 26 possible cuts in national defence spending, 26 in entitlements, 7 in agricultural programmes, 38 in non-defence discretionary spending, and 8 in federal workforce costs. In addition, it described 25 means of revenue enhancement. Thus, on this one issue of deficit reduction, this one source alone presented 130 options for the consideration and decision of Congress and, supposedly, public opinion. In 1988, numerous persuasive journalists were attempting to provide additional guidance on decisions about budget surpluses.

journalists were described as the persons who have at least some control over the content of the journalistic product. But who is the journalist when a reporter quotes another person, especially a news source who offers explanations, utters criticisms, or proposes courses of action?

This happens with great frequency. For example, when Los Angeles County Assessor John J. Lynch sent a letter warning that he might strip churches of their tax-exempt status if they provide shelter to undocumented refugees, reporters Glenn Bunting and Paul Feldman turned to the Reverend Philip Zwerling of the First Unitarian Church and obtained this evaluation: "Mr. Lynch is acting in a very un-American manner and his strategy is better suited to the state in Poland than to that in California."

When *Christian Science Monitor* reporter Barbara Bradley asked Georgetown University law professor Paul Rothenstein to comment on the news that President Reagan's former political director Lyn Nofziger was guilty of illegal lobbying, she obtained this reply: "Because of Mr. Nofziger's high political profile, this will have a great preventive effect."

A *Chicago Tribune* reporter obtained this evaluation of the U. S. Supreme Court decision denying damages to evangelist Jerry Falwell for a parody in *Hustler* magazine: "Richard Schmidt, legal counsel for the American Society of Newspaper Editors, hailed the ruling as 'a great victory for free speech'".

Are the reporters or are the persons quoted by the reporters the real journalists? Both are; both have important control over the useful knowledge that is communicated to a public. The former are full-time journalists; the latter are occasional journalists. But all are journalists.

Journalists are not only those who own or are employed by the media of mass communications. All those who provide journalistic knowledge—including some free lance writers, public relations practitioners, advertisers, participants in call-in shows, writers of letters to the editor—belong in that category. To ignore this is to misunderstand the true nature of journalism.

ONE OF THE DANGERS OF JOURNALISM

But the fact that interpretation, criticism, and advocacy can be incorporated into news reports does give the media owners and operators a great and potentially dangerous power. If those in control of a journalistic medium wished to do so, they could influence the people's attitude towards public affairs by including only material that agreed with the view of the medium's managers.

Paradoxically, the policy of many American media—again, newspapers in particular-to maintain an evident distinction between news and "opinion" material may increase the power and the danger.

People tend to read news stories less carefully and critically than they read obvious critiques and editorials. Thus when a news story quotes judgements—especially those representing only one side, from reputable sources, and not too contrary to accepted values—the readers do not erect the same defences that they build when they read explicit opinion articles.

Most journalists try to abstain from exploiting this power by insisting that a judgement in one direction must confront one or more judgements in other directions. Even then, however, a problem may occur, not because of the full-time journalists but because of media manipulators who know how to twist the conventions of the press to their advantage.

As many scholars have pointed out, one of the persons most adept at using the media to his own advantage was Senator Joseph R. McCarthy of Wisconsin. About persons and institutions—especially the State Department—he would make judgements that the press thought it dared not ignore.

And he warded off the desire of journalists to compose balanced stories by releasing his statements so close to deadlines that the reporters, driven by the fear of competition or the unavailability of other sources, thought they could not delay their stories long enough to obtain additional viewpoints. Jack Anderson and Ronald W. May (1952, 266) dramatize the situation that existed in the 1950s:

Say you're an editor of a big afternoon paper. It's fifteen minutes before the deadline for the final home edition—the edition that goes into people's homes and makes up 95 per cent of your circulation. And you've got no hot stories. Sure, there's an automobile wreck, and a mayor's announcement, and maybe a riot in faraway Iran—but these aren't exactly banner headlines in a big city. So what do you use for an eight-column black "line" in the Night Final?

By this time you're scratching around, desperate. And then the wire editor pushes across a piece of yellow paper, marked WASHINGTON (AP). And you read: "Sen. Joseph R. McCarthy (R. Wis.) charged today that Ambassador-at-Large Philip Jessup had an unusual affinity for Communist causes. In a speech on the Senate floor, the Wisconsin senator said he has the proof for his sensational charge."

Quickly you scribble a headline across the copy and mark it "P. 1." Then you stuff it in the capsule and send it up the airtube to the composing room. And you've got your Night Final banner headline! There, in a nutshell, you have 99 per cent of the reason for Joe McCarthy's success.

The introduction of computers has made present-day newsroom procedures much different from those of the McCarthy period, but most of the pressures and many of the conventional beliefs still exist. In particular, the existence of deadlines is still used as a reason, and sometimes an excuse, for publishing incomplete stories, even in situations in which a delay would not place a publication at any conceivable disadvantage. Thus, when the *Milwaukee Journal* published a front-page article containing adverse criticisms of the local Roman Catholic archbishop by the leader of a small conservative group, reader-contact editor Thomas Heinen agreed with those who objected that the story was deficient, but then added: "That doesn't mean the story, which was written on deadline with limited time for additional telephone calls, was incorrect as published." Most widely discussed, however, as the reason for journalists being trapped into reporting one-sided criticisms is their desire to be objective. Even when they personally believe that the judgements being expressed are grievously wrong, and even when they cannot obtain any counterbalancing statements, reporters believe the goal of objectivity requires that those "wrong" judgements be set forth without any indication of the reporter's own evaluations of them. This difficulty will be discussed in the chapter on objectivity.

Although the various types of journalistic communication sometimes raise difficulties, the solution to those difficulties does not lie in attempting to do away with them. Publishers, editors, and station managers could prohibit their reporters, commentators, editorial writers, critics, reviewers, and documentary producers from presenting disputable material. The result, if such discipline could be maintained, would not only be a devitalized, but also an unrealized, journalism. A great part of the ultimate achievement—providing the knowledge people need to make good, timely decisions—would be cut off at the knees. On many subjects, members of the public, in order to make up their own minds, need access to and consideration of the judgement of others.

For many of the journalistic media, especially those that direct their messages to the masses of readers, listeners, and viewers, the persuasive genre is often employed reactively rather than actively, especially when public affairs issues are at stake. Instead of initiating their own proposals for solving current problems, too many editorial writers simply react to proposals made by others. If a community is suffering from poor student achievement or if a state faces a budgetary shortfall, the writers will usually wait for the governor or appropriate legislators to set forth possible solutions, and then will oppose or support those suggestions. If the State Department announces that a foreign country is not living up to international agreements, most editorial writers will wait until the President or other government officials describe a possible solution and only then will step in, launching their praise or condemnation.

Of course, the more complicated and distant the issue, the more reasonable it is for editorial writers to hesitate to leap into murky waters. Unfortunately, though, the tendency to be reactive rather than proactive often extends to local affairs. Locally, editorial writers can often be as knowledgeable about the issues facing the city or the town as the elected officials of a community. Journalistic media pride themselves on being known as "the fourth branch of government." They can deserve that title if they contribute new proposals to the public forum and if they encourage the people themselves to join in the debate about public affairs.

PERSONAL AFFAIRS PERSUASION

In matters of personal affairs, on the other hand, the journalistic media extensively advocate courses of action. Much of this is done by columnists, both syndicated and staff, by hosts on radio call-in programmes, and by the writers of newsletters. The topics range over the gamut of personal concerns: finances, sex, child care, home repairs, etiquette, health, automobile maintenance, interpersonal relations, and the like.

Unfortunately, viewed strictly from a journalistic perspective, a good portion of this material involves an inefficient use of the mass medium. For example, Andrew Leckey, who writes on personal finance for the *Chicago Tribune*, led off one of his columns with this query from a reader: "I'm a newlywed and trying to get ahead financially. My husband and I own 400 shares of Burndy Corp. and wonder what its future looks like long- and short-term."

Leckey replied that the stock was good, gave reasons for his thinking so, and advocated "holding or buying for short- or long-term goals". Other pieces in the personal-writing category can be almost voyeuristic.

Ann Landers began one of her columns with a long letter from a woman who, nine years ago, had married a man she had known for four years. This was the man's third marriage, and she said he had supplied good reasons for his previous divorces. But the woman discovered that the man had lied to her, and she began to distrust him.

He was making so many sexual demands that she became physically and emotionally ill. His high-school-age daughter was having sex in an open car in front of school, his son had stolen money and was thought to have burned a car to collect the insurance, and another son was living with a prostitute.

Three years ago, she continued, the man had divorced her and moved in with a woman 20 years younger. The writer said she now doubted her ability to evaluate men and wondered what she should do.

Ann Landers suggested that, from now on, the writer learn a great deal more about boyfriends before considering marriage. Two major problems are suggested by these and similar examples of personal affairs advice. First are the risks involved when a journalist gives personal advice to persons the journalist doesn't know and, except in live broadcasting, to persons the journalist can't question or engage in dialogue.

The more personal the problem, the greater the danger the adviser might give counsel that is actually harmful, like the doctor who prescribes medicine over the telephone to a patient the doctor has never seen. One way to avoid this is by giving advice that is general and innocuous, but in thus doing something harmless, the writer also provides responses that are close to useless. Both generality and uselessness work against the goals of journalism.

The second problem grows out of a paradox. For the persuasive writer to give good personal advice, the writer needs to know the specific characteristics, situations, background, and objectives of the person seeking the advice.

Thus it undoubtedly helped Leckey to know that the person he was advising was a newlywed concerned about her financial future, and the joint owner of 400 shares of Burndy Corp. And it probably helped Ann Landers to know the many details of the marriage of the woman who had asked her for help. But the more these columnists know those individuals and the unique details of their situations, the more the writers' advice about what should be done, if it is to be appropriate, applies only to those distinct individuals.

Although a large number of persons may find it interesting to peek in on discussions of the personal concerns of others, catering to such interests is not the function of journalism. Strictly as journalism, therefore, much personal affairs persuasive writing involves, at best, an inefficient use of the mass media.

Media that reach many thousands of persons are providing practical help, in some instances, only to very few persons. Among the thousands of readers of the *Chicago Tribune* there are not likely to be many other newlywed brides who are joint owners with their husbands of 400 shares of Burndy Corp, nor, among the much more numerous readers of Landers' syndicated column are there likely to be, many, even any, other readers who had experiences identical to those of the woman who wrote to Landers. There are some exceptions, of course—some questions on such topics as home repairs or gardening that might have a degree of commonality—but, generally speaking, personal affairs persuasion does not contribute to the journalistic roles of the mass media. Such persuasion is best and most efficiently done on a one-to-one basis. People with sexual problems should go to sex therapists or doctors, those with financial problems to accountants or lawyers, those with family problems to ministers or social workers. It is important to recognize, however, that the claim that the mass media are usually not the best place for personal affairs persuasion does not mean that all personal affairs journalism should be excluded from mass communications.

The reportorial and, to a lesser extent, the interpretive genres of journalistic writing serve both public and personal affairs. But, since the ultimate question in personal affairs is "What is good for me?" (in contrast to the ultimate publicaffairs question, "What is good for the community, for the commonweal?"), the standards for determining whether something is good or bad and for analyzing what should be done have a great personal and individual component.

Taste, feelings, private inclinations play a great part, and these are not well suited to public debate. The person does need to know and understand what is going on in his or her life and in the surrounding world, and, having this knowledge, the individual may wish to consult experts of his or her choice, but this is best done within the boundaries of interpersonal communication and with respect for privacy. An exception should be noted for the situations in which the personal welfare of a large number of individuals is so common and linked together that personal affairs persuasion is appropriate.

Efforts to persuade young people to never start or to stop smoking, to promote exercise, healthful diets, and appropriate medical care could have far-reaching, beneficent effects.

THE HIERARCHY OF JOURNALISTIC GENRES

Perhaps it would be helpful to consider the point just made from another perspective. The four journalistic genres of reporting, explaining, evaluating, and advocating possess a logical, cumulative order. They provide the knowledge that we the people need, first, to know what is going on, then to understand what is going on, then to evaluate what is going on, finally to determine what should be done about what is going on.

Often journalists need to provide only the first type of knowledge; once we, the people, know what is going on we can often supply the rest of the knowledge ourselves. Once we have been informed that our favourite route from home to work will be under repair for the next three months, we don't need any journalist to explain to us what this means, to tell us whether, at least temporarily, it is good or bad, or to urge us to find a detour.

Less often we need both information and the interpretation that helps us understand that information, but, having that, we then can judge the event and decide what to do about it. If we read that a Thai restaurant that has opened in town serves food that is hotter than Szechuan cuisine, those who like spicy food now have information of which they can take advantage.

Still less often is there a need for persuasion after the public has received adequate reports, interpretations, and evaluations. This is most obvious in the area of the arts. If a drama critic, for instance, gives us information about a new play, explains portions that might confuse us, and gives a strong, reasoned evaluation of the play, the critic does not also need to try to persuade us to go see it if it is good or stay away if it is poorly done.

On personal issues, we are usually quite capable of making those decisions for ourselves. In fact, in the journalistic situation, one in which (by definition) the critic is addressing a mass of readers, viewers, or listeners, the critic is frequently incapable of adding any useful persuasion on personal issues. Each member of the public is an individual with private good involving unique factors.

Let's say, for example, the critic gives the play a rave review. In spite of that, many people might decide, often for reasons the critic cannot penetrate, that the play is not a good one for them to see. One man may like only musicals, and this play is not a musical. One woman, who likes plays of this type, may have an ill parent whom she does not want to leave. One man may think the decor of the theater is so revolting that he cannot tolerate being there.

One woman may think the leading man looks like an old boyfriend she now dislikes; another is planning to marry in six months and wants to save every dime for the wedding and honeymoon. The journalistic critic, the mass-communication persuader, cannot be aware of all these contingencies, and, even if he or she could become aware of them, there would be no efficient way in which the persuader could deal with all of them in one of the mass media.

Of course, it is possible that all these people could be individually persuaded by friends or relatives to overcome their reluctance to see the play, but the means would not be journalistic persuasion but interpersonal persuasion.

JOURNALISTIC PERSUASION

In some instances, on the other hand, idiosyncratic differences are ignored, and the journalist attempts to persuade masses of people on personal issues. In many such cases the good to be achieved seems so important that it transcends all individual objections. This occurs most often in a situation in which the public already agrees on what should be done; they are not yet, however, moved to action. We probably have all experienced the circumstance in which we know we should do something, yet we do not do it: stop smoking, show parents our love, exercise, wear our seat belt while driving, install a smoke detector in our home, aid starving children. One of the more famous examples of mass media, personal-issue persuasion was just such a piece. In an effort to dissuade automobile drivers from speeding, J. C. Furnas wrote, "—And Sudden Death." It was published in the *Reader's Digest* in August 1935, and millions of reprints have been distributed since then.

PUBLIC AFFAIRS MOST NEED JOURNALISTIC PERSUASION

Yet the differences between public-affairs persuasion and personal-affairs persuasion are essential for an understanding of the broad field of journalism. The most important of those differences stems from this: public affairs issues are and ought to be publicly debatable. They are and ought to be subject to multiperson, public persuasion.

They are issues that affect entire groups, entire communities, *even those members of the groups or communities who are not interested in the issues*. Many persons in the United States may not be interested in revisions in the Federal Tax Code, yet those revisions affect them whether they are interested or not.

Even if a person's income is so low that he or she does not have to pay any tax, that person is affected by the provision in the tax code that exempts low-income people from having to pay income taxes. Even if the revision under consideration pertains explicitly only to those involved in offshore drilling for oil, all of us are benefited or disadvantaged, at least to a small extent, by any exemption or penalty applied to that small portion of the population.

Good citizens will make their decisions on the basis of whether a proposed course of action is good, not solely for them individually but also for the group or community, for what is sometimes called the common good.

Whether or not that is the goal in mind, however, the decisions on public issues, since they affect the welfare of the group or community, do, in fact, affect all who are members of that group or community. And thus it is good that any persuasion concerning those public issues comes at least from all who represent distinct positions on the issues.

This is not true when private affairs issues are involved. Should I learn to roller skate? My family, well aware of my physical capacities and temporal limitations, might try to persuade me that I should or should not. But this is no subject for public debate. Those who do not know me would waste their time trying to persuade me, and I would waste my time paying any attention to what they have to say. A company that rents roller skates might run ads aimed at convincing the public that skating provides ideal exercise and a way to share fun with friends and family. But if I feel compelled to resist those suasions, I do not also feel compelled to debate the issue in public with the advertiser. Private issues are often the basis for interpersonal discussions rather than general public persuasions.

ADVERTISING AND THE JOURNALISTIC GENRES

Much advertising is primarily news. That is, many ads simply tell the public that some items or services are available for sale at a location that is open at specified days and hours or that can be ordered from a specific business. Most supermarket, catalogue, department store, automobile, and entertainment ads are of this type. Usually, of course, the item or services are described or pictured as attractively as possible. In general, in fact, advertisements are similar to many editorials or opinion columns in that the writers select and present the factual knowledge in ways that support the views of the writers or of the organizations that employ them.

By the very fact that advertisements, editorials, and opinion columns are labeled as such, the readers are alerted to the possibility that the news content is selected to advance the cause of the writers. The reporting, in other words, is not what is often referred to as "objective."

Nevertheless, advertisements predominantly present knowledge in the form of information that helps large numbers of people make good decisions about issues that are facing them. To help compensate for the lack of objectivity in the reporting content of ads (and of editorials and columns), the reader or listener usually will be able to compare and evaluate other available ads or opinion pieces.

Many ads also include the journalistic genres of explanation and evaluation that are no different from what we find in other areas of journalism. But if they also employ explicit persuasion, that persuasion relies heavily on either the other journalistic genres or the later communications of sales people. The latter, being interpersonal, is not journalism as we have been using that term.

Thus, the more advertising aims strictly at *personal* affairs persuasion, the further it moves away from journalism. The more decisions need to be based on individual criteria the less the media of *mass* communication become the efficient means by which the grounds for making those decisions can be conveyed to readers, listeners, or viewers.

Let us take, for example, the merchants who are attempting to sell lamb chops, ten-speed bicycles, Picasso prints, or tickets to a rock concert. News, explanation, and evaluations may be of value, but persuasion, which aims at urging individuals to action, cannot take into consideration all the factors that may affect the decisions that those individuals will have to make.

Interestingly, advertising is often claimed to be enormously influential in the decisions that people make. And, to some extent, it is. But the influence in personal decisions, at least as far as journalism and thus the mass media are involved, comes rarely from the advertisers' efforts at persuasion.

This surprises the many who recognize that advertising is a powerful and effective category of journalism. But its strength comes more from the attractiveness and selectivity with which the facts are presented and from the selective use of the other genres of journalism, such as explanation and evaluation, than it does from any explicit use of persuasion.

When we turn to public affairs decisions, the situation is significantly different. Prior to that, however, we need to bring to the surface two points that have so far been swimming under water.

DISTINCTION MAY NOT REQUIRE SEPARATION

First, although the journalistic genres are distinguishable, they are not always presented in separate articles or programmes. In fact, critical and persuasive pieces almost always include some news and often include some explanatory material. This is most evident in newspaper and magazine editorials, in persuasive columns such as those by William Safire or Cal Thomas, in film documentaries such as Leni Riefenstahl *1937 Triumph of the Will*, in television documentaries such as the 1960 CBS Report "Harvest of Shame," and in books such as Allan Bloom *The Closing of the American Mind*.

Efforts are often made to keep evaluation and persuasion (often simply called "opinion") out of news and interpretive reports, and some media, newspapers in particular, are criticized if they fail to do so. No efforts, on the other hand, are made to keep news and interpretation out of critical and persuasive articles.

The 1987 revision of the Society of Professional Journalists' Sigma Delta Chi "Code of Ethics" states, "Sound practice makes clear distinction between news reports and expressions of opinion," but this usually works, if it is achieved at all, only in one direction: explicit statements of opinion may be excluded from news reports, but news reports are rarely excluded from opinion articles. The mere fact that two things can be and ought to be distinguished from one another does not necessarily mean that those two things must be separated from one another.

DETERMINING WHAT IS "FIT TO PRINT"

Second, the same criteria used for evaluating what news is "fit to print" can be employed in determining what material in the form of the other journalistic genres ought to be printed, screened, or broadcast.

For example, a piece of persuasion would be most fit to appear in a specific journalistic medium if it advocated a decision on an issue that was vital, that affected a large proportion of the audience of that medium, that had to be decided urgently involving something close at hand that could be effected directly, and that could reach the audience only or most probably through this specific medium. The only major qualification is this: these criteria apply primarily to personal-affairs journalism. Clear, thorough reporting often provides all the knowledge that readers, listeners, or viewers need to interpret the event or situation, evaluate it, and decide what needs to be done. Likewise, reporting plus interpretation sometimes make criticism and persuasion unnecessary, and reporting, interpretation, and criticism sometimes make persuasion unnecessary. If we turn this around, we then see another set of criteria for determining what is fit to print: the less reporting alone is adequate for enabling the public to make good decisions, the greater is the need for the subsequent journalistic genres; the less reporting plus interpretation are adequate, the greater the need for criticism and persuasion; the less reporting, interpretation, and criticism are adequate, the greater the need for persuasion.

These genres of journalism are most completely realized and most highly respected in public affairs journalism. Why is this so? And is the presentation of effective public affairs journalism an unattainable ideal for the mass media or is it a realistic and achievable goal? It is now time to try to answer these questions.

5

News Writing Style

Body subsidiary points in order of importance The inverted pyramid model of newswriting starts with an *introduction* (*intro* or *lead*) which will usually be no more than 25 words and contain the key elements of the story. The *body* of the story will cover remaining details in descending order of importance. The model of writing works for print and online news. It does not work for radio and television, where stories need a strong ending.

Putting the most important details first didn't just ensure that they weren't lost if the transmission by wire was interrupted. It also allowed sub-editors to trim stories from the bottom without losing any valuable details.

This form of news writing is called the "inverted pyramid" and, as its name suggests, it turns the traditional form of story telling on its head. Instead of being left until the end, the conclusion goes at the top as the "intro". The second sentence, or "par", expands on the intro and the remaining story details are then set out in descending order of importance.

WRITING TO SPACE

Starting a story with the punch line is the opposite of the narrative way of telling a tale. But these days, long after we stopped sending stories by telegraph wire, and despite the fact that editing from the bottom is no longer so common, it remains a useful technique. For one thing it allows readers to take in the most important points of a story without reading the rest, and that's all some readers want.

In recent years, some analysts have predicted the demise of inverted pyramid writing. It was seen as outdated at a time when many newspapers were turning to a more personalised or magazine style of writing.

In addition, the compilation of newspaper pages on computer screens means reporters these days usually know the number of centimetres allocated to their story when they write it.

The day after bushranger Ned Kelly was hanged in Melbourne in November 1880, *The Sydney Morning Herald* ran the following report on the bottom of page five.

Much has changed in news delivery since then but in this report we can see the development of the style of news writing we work with today.

For one thing, though some of the language used may seem unfamiliar, the report is a factual account of Kelly's death. And while much of the report follows the events of the day in the order in which they occurred, there is a clear hierarchy of information, with the main news elements—Kelly's death, after the failure of his hopes for clemency—placed at the top of the story.

Newspapers were not always written this way. Earlier in that century, a commitment to reporting factually was of far less importance than presenting a point of view, and the information in stories was presented chronologically or thematically rather than in the order of its significance.

In his *A History of News,* American writer Mitchell Stephens points to the role of the communications revolution of its time, the telegraph, in establishing a more factual and hierarchical style of news writing.

During the American Civil War in particular, journalists rushing to transmit their most newsworthy information over often unreliable telegraph lines had begun to develop the habit of compressing the most crucial facts into short, paragraph-long dispatches, often destined for the top of a column of news ... From here it was not a long distance to reserving the first paragraph of their stories, the "lead", for the most newsworthy facts and then organizing supporting material in descending order of newsworthiness.

That means they can write to fit the space and the story needn't trail off at the end because it's unlikely to be trimmed by the sub-editors. Certainly, if you read some news stories these days, particularly in the metropolitan newspapers, they do not follow the inverted pyramid style. But the basics of the style are far from out of date. They're still a staple of tabloid news writing and of news delivered online or to portable hand-held terminals.

As we'll see shortly, different media apply the hard news model in different ways. But the basics of the style remain much the same and it's with these basics that reporters begin learning to write in news style.

STRUCTURING THE NEWS STORY—FIVE Ws AND H

In news writing, brevity is a virtue, but not at the expense of the facts. Making sure they've covered all the main elements of a story is one of the first things reporters have to learn. Lucky for them there's a mantra for checking the main points. It's the five Ws and H and it stands for:

Who What When Where Why How

These are the questions that the readers/audience will expect to have answered in the story:

- Who (or what or how many) did (or will do) something? –What did (or will) they do? –When did they (or will they) do it? –Where?How? And Why?

THE INTRO

In most cases, the intro will contain the *What* and the *Who:* either someone doing something or someone saying something. The *Who* can involve a person's name, an explanation of who a person is, or both. If the subject, or one of the subjects of the story is very well known, their name will form part of the intro. But if the *Who* is not a household name, that can. This intro contains the What and When, but the detail of the Who (the name) would just slow down the intro and can be left to the next par.

In this case, the Who belongs in the intro, because it involves a household name.

An aged pensioner from Sunshine is the winner of last night's $20 million lottery draw.

Olive Yang said...

Premier Fay Dushki said last night she would not be quitting politics, despite her $20 million lottery win.

be left until lower down the story and a tag is used in the intro instead, as in the example below.

The *Why* often involves the greatest amount of explanation so that, too, will usually be part of the body of the story, not the intro.

Example: The angle

Before you can write the intro to the story, you have to settle on the approach or *angle* you are going to take. You can see from just the simple example above that there's usually more than one possible angle, and the choice you make will be dictated by the nature of the story itself and the audience for which you are reporting.

In choosing an angle, the reporter is shaping the raw information and turning it into *news.*

WARNING

It's not news, for example, to report the lottery draw as a linear sequence of events, as in:"State lottery officials presided over draw 203 last night. They drew the winning ticket followed by those that would receive the five secondary prizes. The owner of the winning ticket has been revealed to be the state premier, Ms Fay Dushki ..."

Choosing a news angle means finding the most newsworthy element of the story and putting that at the top. The angle a reporter takes to a story will also influence the way they conduct the interviews and the quotes they choose to use.

To develop your skills in choosing angles and writing news intros, compare the ways in which at least two different news outlets approach the same story each day.

Different Media Outlets—Different styles

While "inverted pyramid" writing sets out information in a hierarchy, from most to least important, the way in which it's applied varies considerably according to the news style of the paper or programme. The style of writing at a tabloid is different from that of a broadsheet. The metro, suburban and regional papers will all have different approaches. Radio, television and online will be different again.

There's a metropolitan broadsheet style, which can be found not just in those papers directed at the educated, white-collar readership but also in those like-minded broadcast services including the ABC and SBS. Tabloid style is a little racier, more populist. The smaller, more commuter-friendly format of tabloid papers encourages the use of shorter stories. "Short, concise and sharp" is how the Victorian Leader Newspaper group's Jane Cafarella describes the style of her suburban tabloids. She says their stories don't include a lot of detail, just "the bare facts" told in a manner that is "as interesting and snappy as it can be".

Radio and online news are news in a hurry. They offer rapid turnaround services for people who want to find out what's going on, be brought up to date with events and feel that they're in touch. Paradoxically, while online news services generally exploit the medium's potential for the use of images and graphics, the audience seems more focused on the text.

Research conducted by Stanford University and the Poynter Institute tracked the eye movements of a group of Web news users and found that they were drawn first to text and only later to photos and graphics. The style of television news is driven by the need to integrate pictures and narration.

News agencies, such as Australian Associated Press, provide stories to subscribers who can either use the stories as provided or rewrite the copy, often including material of their own. That means news agencies have to keep their product fairly unvarnished, so that it appeals to the broad base of users. AAP's Melbourne bureau chief, Joanne Williamson, describes its style as "fair, accurate and tightly-written".

We try to be factual, take no sides, straight down the middle basically. But not so it's dull and uninteresting. We also try to ensure that there's some flair in the writing. Because we have such a wide and diversified subscription base, there's no point in doing it in *The Age* style when it's also going to other clients.

To illustrate some of these differences between various news styles, we've chosen to write the fairytale "Little Red Riding Hood" as a hard news story. It's not an entirely original idea but it is a timeless and effective way of illustrating news style.

Readers familiar with the tale, published by the Grimm brothers in the 19th century, will recall that it begins with Little Red Riding Hood being dispatched by her mother to take cake and wine to her sick grandmother who lives in a house in the woods. As the narrative unfolds, Little Red Riding Hood encounters a wolf, which then speeds over to granny's, devours the old lady before donning her clothes and getting into her bed to wait for the girl.

In the Grimms" version, the story ends happily (except for the wolf) after a huntsman rescues both the girl and her grandmother by using a pair of scissors to open up the wolf's stomach.

This form of story telling, which has been successfully used to send generations of small children off to sleep with wild nightmares, is far too slow and boring for hard news. Instead, we need to start with the conclusion. But, as we've seen already, the conclusion we choose will vary depending on when the paper, site or programme is published or broadcast, and also the nature of the media outlet and its audience.

The examples below represent a typical hard-news lead in the main news formats. We've taken a few liberties with the story (which you would *never* do in real life) to allow us to give it a location, use quotes, and to project the original tale into "follow-up" news items for non-daily papers. To avoid repetition, we've written just the intro to some versions of the story.

TABLOID DAILY

A girl and her grandmother had a miraculous escape after being eaten by a wolf in Oakville forest yesterday.

Both the 10-year-old and her frail grandmother were ripped alive from inside the savage beast's stomach.

Covered in entrails, the girl was carried from the scene of the terrifying attack by local hero, ranger Brad Gore. The little girl's grandmother,

Mrs Betty Hood, 82, also survived the horrifying ordeal.

Brad Gore said he had been on the trail of the carnivorous canine for some weeks and had been alerted by loud snoring from inside the house. Gore said he used scissors to cut the little girl and the old woman out of the wolf.

"The old lady was more dead than alive when I got her out," Brad said.

"When I went into the bedroom, I found the wolf in her bed. I was going to take a shot at him but then I thought it might not be too late to save Mrs Hood and the kid."

Covered in bandages and heavily sedated in her hospital bed, Mrs Hood was too traumatised to comment on the attack.

STYLE TIPS

- Emphasise the drama/human interest elements of the story.
- Emphasise the pictorial elements.
- Keep the story brisk and to the point. The lead should be short and punchy; a maximum of 25 words, preferably fewer.
- Use words that everyone can understand. Write your copy so that it has a "readability" age of 12 to 14 years.

- Newspapers generally use the past tense and terms such as "yesterday" or "last night" because they are reporting events that have concluded. But there is an increasing trend, in newspapers, towards the use of the present tense, because it can make events seem more current. Your choice of tenses will be guided by the story itself and by house style.
- Use the active voice, wherever possible, and strong verbs (*i.e.* "ripped" rather than "lifted" in this example) and nouns.
- Use quotes to liven up the story.

Note: The first of the shaded items also applies to other print news media listed below. The remaining shaded items apply to most news media— print, broadcast and online. Note also "Taking the story further" at the end of this section.

BROADSHEET DAILY

Metro police yesterday warned residents of Oakville to be vigilant against roaming wolves from the nearby forest after a near-fatal attack on two residents. Their warning followed an incident in which an elderly woman and her young granddaughter were initially eaten by a wolf and then cut free by a passing ranger. The woman, 82-year-old forest resident, Mrs Betty Hood, is recovering in St Oakville hospital.

Last night, officials described her condition as serious but stable. Her granddaughter, 10-year-old Red Hood, did not require hospital treatment and was reunited with her parents after being rescued. The ranger, Mr Brad Gore, said "The old lady was more dead than alive when I got her out, but the little girl was in pretty good shape."

He said he had been hunting the rogue animal for some months and it was just a matter of luck that he had found him when he did. Mr Gore revealed he had thought of shooting the wolf but realised there might still be time to save the victims. It is expected Mr Gore will be nominated for a state bravery award.

Style Tips

- Consider the market for which you are writing.
- Remember that readers are likely to have already heard the details of a story such as this on other media (*e.g.* radio and television) so you need to look for a slightly different angle.
- Consider including wider issues as part of your report.

Suburban or Regional Daily

Oakville identity Mrs Betty Hood, aged 82, is recovering in hospital after being attacked by a roaming wolf. The beast also attacked her 10-yearold granddaughter, Red Hood. The pair was eaten by the animal, but rescued shortly afterwards by a passing forest ranger.

Style Tips

- Focus on the local angle or the local identity.
- Personalise the story for local readers using terms like "us" or "our" where appropriate.
- Use the standard features of tabloid writing style, including short, punchy sentences.

Suburban or Regional Weekly

Local forest ranger, Brad Gore, has been hailed a hero after saving a grandmother and her granddaughter from a wolf this week. Mr Gore went to the aid of Mrs Betty Hood and Red Hood after he heard unusually loud snoring coming from her house in a remote part of Oakville forest. Inside, he found a wolf dressed in the elderly woman's clothes and sleeping in her bed ...

Style Tips

- Find a different angle from the one(s) that will have been used by the daily press. Usually this will mean looking for an angle in the aftermath of the initial event.
- The same need to make the story relevant to the local community, and personalise it for the audience, noted above, applies here too. So does the use of tabloid writing style.

RADIO—VOICER, PRERECORDED (NEWS RADIO FORMAT)

Newsreader: An elderly Oakville grandmother is recovering in hospital after she was cut free from the stomach of a wolf.

Sonia Clack reports the animal also ate a young girl, but she was rescued relatively unharmed.

Reporter: Police can't remember the last time a wolf-attack was this vicious. They say the beast stalked 10-year-old Red Hood as she was walking through Oakville forest taking some cake and wine to her sick grandmother.

He then broke into the elderly woman's house and ate her before disguising himself in her clothes and waiting for the girl. The pair was saved by local ranger, Brad Gore, who cut them free with scissors. The Old Lady Was More Dead Than Alive When I Got Her Out. Mr Gore says the girl seemed okay, despite her ordeal. Sonia Clack, Oakville.

Style Tips

- Radio and television stories start with an intro, which usually includes the main news point(s) and sets up the rest of the report.
- Wherever possible, radio news likes to include the voices of newsmakers themselves—in this case the ranger. These small

interview segments are called *soundbites* or *grabs.* In fact, some commercial FM radio news services rarely run reporters" voicers, like the example above. Their stories mostly consist of an intro followed by a soundbite.

- Write short, punchy sentences, or sentences that have easy places to pause for breath. Remember, you have to be able to read your script aloud.
- Use the active voice and the present tense, wherever possible.
- Radio and television stories can't be allowed to trail off at the end in the way some newspaper or online reports can. Instead they need a conclusion, to alert the listeners/viewers to the fact that the story has ended and another one is about to begin.
- Radio uses conversational language and contractions such as "can't" and "he's", etc. FM radio news takes this even further. An FM service, with a young audience, might personalise the story and use very colloquial terms such as "cops", "guys", "granny" and so on.

ONLINE—METRO MEDIA OUTLET

News prepared for online delivery is structured so that readers can scan the headline and then drill down to more detailed versions of the story if they are interested. In this form of writing, it is important that the headline tells the gist of the story. It can't be enigmatic or cute because readers won't get the point straightaway. In a newspaper, a reader can take in the story at the same time as reading the headline.

The precis will often serve as the first paragraph of a longer story, so it needs to stand alone and set up the rest of the piece.

HEADLINE

Police have warned residents of Oakville to be vigilant against attacks by wolves from the nearby forest. Their warning follows an incident in which an elderly woman and her young granddaughter were initially eaten by a wolf and then freed by a passing ranger.

FULL STORY

The woman, 82-year-old forest resident, Mrs Betty Hood, is recovering in St Oakville Hospital where her condition is described as serious but stable. Her granddaughter, 10-year-old Red Hood, did not require hospital treatment and was reunited with her parents after being rescued.

Ranger Brad Gore said he was alerted by strange noises from the house. He used scissors to cut the victims out of the wolf's stomach. "The old lady was more dead than alive when I got her out, but the little girl was in pretty good shape, " he said. He said he had been hunting the rogue animal for some months and it was just a matter of luck that he had found him when he did. Mr

Gore revealed he had thought of shooting the wolf but realised there might still be time to save the victims.

Style Tips

- The style used for an online news story will be influenced by the nature of the originating medium (*i.e.* whether it's a metro, suburban or regional newspaper or broadcast site). Many newspapers post the newspaper versions of stories online with few changes. Broadcasters have to ensure scripted stories work as text, which includes turning soundbites into quotes or indirect speech. Some newspapers and broadcasters may sub-edit the copy to ensure that references to locations and people make sense to an audience that can range from local to global.
- The headline should be a clear pointer to the story.
- The first par may need to both stand alone and serve as the story intro.
- Some sites also require a separate story precis of a single par.
- Different online outlets have different ways of handling time references. Both the present or past tenses may be used, depending on the site and the story.
- Online sites tend to use newspaper-style quotations and attribution.
- Try to include at least one still photograph. Stills play a greater role in identifying stories online than they do in print. Some outlets would compile a photo gallery to accompany the story.
- The issue of whether to include links to external sites is a matter of house style. But note that if you do link out it is usually better to link to an external site's *home page* rather than using a *deep link* to within the site. This is for legal reasons. Deep linking can create ambiguities over who created the copy being linked to and can bypass advertising that site owners use to generate revenue. Deep links should be restricted to appropriate information sites and used only with thought and care. Any external links should have a purpose within the full story and should be editorially responsible. Think about where you are taking your audience.
- Consider "value adding" to the story by including additional background information and interview transcripts as separate pages linked from the main story.
- Consider opening a readers" forum on the story and inviting e-mail responses.
- Not all information is best presented as text. The online environment lends itself to using bullet points and displaying information in graph or table form, where appropriate. You might also attach a map of the area.

- Our example is free of potential defamation or contempt of court. But reporters working in an online environment need to remember that while their site may originate in one state, it may draw a substantial audience in other states and this has legal implications.

In particular, journalists handling court reports need to respect any restrictions that might apply in any particular part of the market regarding the identification of the accused. The same issue arises in television and in print, where journalists working on national bulletins or publications have to remember the restrictions that apply in individual states within the viewing or circulation footprint.

SPECIAL-INTEREST MEDIA

A financial newspaper or news agency would, naturally, look for an angle of interest to the business community. For example, when the financial media report natural disasters, it is usually in terms of the insurance implications.

In the case of this story, they might take one of the following approaches. Landowners in the outer suburban area of Oakville are concerned that their property values may fall after a savage attack by a wild animal on two local residents. An elderly woman is recovering in hospital after being eaten by wolf which also devoured her 10-year-old grandchild. The pair was rescued by a local ranger. However, the incident highlights the danger to surrounding properties posed by rogue animals. President of the Oakville Realtors Association, Ms Shelley Novella, said repeated pleas to council to eliminate the problem have had no effect. "We are concerned that this attack and the widespread attention it has received will drive away potential new residents," she said. The Utility Scissor company received the sort of publicity you just cannot buy when its product was used in yesterday's headline-grabbing rescue of an elderly woman and her granddaughter in Oakville ...

The financial press, programmes and sites are the largest specialist news outlets, but they are not the only ones. You might like to imagine how, for example, the agricultural press or a medical magazine might handle the above story, or how it might be reported in a paper aimed at older people.

Style Tips

- Look for an angle that fits the objectives of the specialist media outlet.
- Seek out interviewees who can present a different perspective from that offered in mass-audience news outlets.

TELEVISION NEWS

Television news is a picture medium and so the way in which this story would be written would be driven, to a large extent, by the type of pictures available. In this case, we can assume the news crews would have rolled up at about the same time as the ambulance came to take the injured to hospital.

That means they would have shots of the grandmother being taken out on a stretcher, and the girl being escorted to the ambulance. They'd probably have the body of the wolf being removed. They would almost certainly have scored an interview with the ranger and one of the emergency service officials. They might have a comment from the girl or her family. They would probably try to get shots of the two victims being taken *into* hospital and they might also have some helicopter shots of the forest. Finally they'd check the station library for shots of roaming wolves, preferably in the same environment as the one in which the attack occurred. For the purposes of this exercise, we are going to assume that the two victims were so traumatised by their experience that they were unable to talk to reporters at the scene and also that police kept reporters away from the girl. We can assume that a number of media organisations would be chasing the family, chequebooks in hand. But that's another story.

- Mrs Hood being taken into ambulance outside cottage
- Wolf's body being removed Photo of girl
- orest track
- Exterior of house
- Brad Gore showing scissors
- Gore interview file shots of wolves
- More shots of crime scene
- Gore interview
- Reporter's piece to camera

Most television stories begin with a presenter's intro, followed by a reporter's package. There are other story formats, though the variations are too detailed for inclusion here. Television scripts are set out in two columns, to cover the words (the narration, captions and so on), which go on the right-hand side of the page and the pictures, which go on the left. Our example is written in the television equivalent of broadsheet style. *Newsreader* An elderly Oakville grandmother is recovering in hospital after she was cut free from the stomach of a wolf. Sonia Clack reports the animal also ate a young girl but she was rescued relatively unharmed. Police say they can't remember a wolf-attack as vicious as this one. They say the beast stalked 10-year-old Red Hood as she was walking through Oakville forest taking some cake and wine to her sick grandmother. He then broke into the elderly woman's house and swallowed her before disguising himself in her clothes and waiting for the girl.

The pair was saved by local ranger, Brad Gore, who cut them free with scissors.

THE OLD LADY WAS MORE DEAD THAN ALIVE WHEN I GOT HER OUT

Mr Gore says the girl seemed okay, despite her ordeal.

The ranger says he'd been hunting the rogue animal for months and he was lucky to find him when he did.

I was just passing the house when i heard an animal snoring. that's what alerted me. With news of today's attack still filtering through the community, police are warning oakville residents to be on the look-out for more wolves from the forest.

- Interview with police spokesperson
- Grandmother being wheeled into hospital
- Police taking granddaughter home

THE BEST PROTECTION AGAINST THESE ANIMALS IS PUBLIC VIGILANCE

- Tonight, Mrs Hood is in a serious but stable condition in St Oakville Hospital.
- Her granddaughter is recovering at home with her parents.
- Sonia Clack, Oakville.

Style Tips

- Television news shares the conversational writing style of radio (and some online services). But it's not enough to add pictures to a radiostyle script. Television stories need to be written to their pictures, not least to maintain continuity in the visual part of the narrative.
- Don't make the viewers wait too long before they hear and see an interview segment (soundbite). These help to break up the narration and add pace to the story.
- Television stories need a conclusion and this usually includes a reporter's sign-off (or "tag").

BREAKING OUT OF THE "PYRAMID" NEWS STYLE

Of course, not all news stories these days are written in "pyramid" style. The computer software programmes now used in newspaper production mean that reporters often know the amount of space allocated to their story as they write it. That means there's less need to crop stories from the bottom, which gives reporters more freedom in constructing the story, and it has encouraged some reporters to adopt a more expansive style of writing.

THE NON-PYRAMID PRINT STORY

This type of format has slipped into journalism under the influence of literary traditions.

New journalism, as expounded by writers like Tom Wolfe, has also encouraged some journalists to deliberately "toy" with readers by delaying the news angle or by starting their stories with background information or description. Australian writer and journalist, Bob Jervis, also argued that deliberately creating information gaps or delays in supplying information could itself act as an enticement to readers. Told in non-pyramid style, our wolf-attack story might go something like this:

Forest ranger, Brad Gore, had no idea what he might find when he went to the rescue of Oakville grandmother, Olive Hood, yesterday.

Certainly the loud, guttural snoring from inside the 82-year-old's bedroom had been sufficient to shock his adrenalin system into full alert.

But it wasn't until he pulled back the delicate, pink lace which enveloped the grandmother's bed that the full horror was revealed ...

A final word of caution: This style is probably best left to more experienced writers who are confident in their own approach to news.

ISSUES OF BALANCE AND FAIRNESS

By now you might have realised that most stories lend themselves to a wide variety of different angles, and the ones reporters choose are determined in part by their own approach to the story and also by the nature of their audience.

In framing angles, and in writing their reports, journalists also need to bear in mind the need for balance and fairness, enshrined in the codes of ethics and practice that inform the work of Australian reporters.

Warning

One of the lessons journalists learn early in their training is the need to set aside their own opinions and report fairly, paying due attention to the different opinions in society on the issue at hand. Of course, journalists" own opinions do creep into reports, most commonly in the choice of interviewees. But outside of the opinion pages of the newspapers or similar clearly flagged segments of broadcast programmes, journalists are expected to keep their own opinions in check.

That means that, among all the acceptable angles for our wolf-attack story, there are a few that would warrant an immediate rewrite.

For instance:

- Roaming wolves should be immediately cleared out of Oakville forest after an attack on an elderly woman and her granddaughter.
- This style of writing is called "editorialising". The writer is standing on a metaphorical soapbox shouting their own opinion. It's tedious and almost always unacceptable.

TAKING THE STORY FURTHER

We've spoken earlier about the ways in which news stories generate other stories—including breakouts, follow-up news items and features.

Our example of the wolf-attack on Little Red Riding Hood and her grandmother is no exception.

Breakouts

Newspapers often supplement some of their news stories with breakout reports. These can be separate news items on different aspects of the main subject including background reports. Alternatively they can be brief "value adding" pieces, such as fact boxes or a sequence of "vox pop" comments from ordinary people asked to give their opinion on the issue.

An item such as our example could easily warrant any of the these.

- A Fact box could include short bullet points on
  - Information on earlier wolf-attacks
  - The number of wolves estimated to live in the forest
  - The size of the forest and other wild animals living there
  - The number of state forests that are home to wolves, and so on.
- A Backgrounder could cover similar material but in story form rather than as bullet points. Or it might profile forest residents and their views on the risk from wild animals.
- Vox pops would be several short comments from local people giving their opinion on the attacks.
- A box beside the main story could detail the number of serious wild animal attacks in the state or country over the past 12 months. Or the breakout box might cover the regulations that protect wildlife living in close proximity to people.

THE FOLLOW-UP

This story definitely lends itself to a follow-up and the perfect time would be when either victim speaks to the media for the first time. This would be a particularly good story for the tabloid press and commercial television. You've heard this type of story many times before.

A tabloid newspaper version would go something along the lines of:

- An 82-year-old grandmother yesterday told how she thought she would die when a wolf attacked her while she was lying sick in bed.
- Mrs Olive Hood had been suffering from anemia and was too weak to resist when the animal burst into her home and devoured her ...

On television, the story would begin:

- *Newsreader:* An elderly woman has spoken for the first time about a terrifying attack by a wolf, which nearly claimed her own life and that of her granddaughter ...

FEATURES

Of course, a news story of between 200 and 600 words can do only so much justice to a riveting human-interest story such as this one.

This is the type of item that cries out to be given the feature treatment.

In this case, it might begin along the lines of: As she prepares to celebrate her 83rd birthday, Oakville grandmother Betty Hood knows she has more to celebrate than most people her age.

Her physical injuries are fading but 82-year-old Oakville grandmother Betty Hood is still reliving the terror that swept over her when a wolf gripped her in his powerful jaws. As the jaws of a wolf snapped shut on her, Oakville grandmother Betty Hood's biggest fear was that her 10-year-old granddaughter would be the beast's next victim.

REMEMBER

The angle you take to a story will depend not just on the story itself but also on the nature of the publication or programme and its audience. The intro needs to be punchy and make the audience want to know more.

BASIC GUIDELINES

It's important to recognise that there is no single formula for news writing. Different outlets require different approaches. But no matter what the outlet, the main characteristics of news writing remain much the same. Here are some of the guidelines for writing hard-news stories.

- News writing is concise. People turn to the news pages or news programmes or sites to get the facts, fast. So reporters need to tell the gist of the story in the first couple of sentences and then elaborate in the body of the item. That way, people who have neither the time nor inclination to read beyond the lead will still have been given the main elements of the story.

  Keeping copy concise, while still presenting all the essential facts, means sticking to these rules:

  – Don't use many words when one will do.

Examples

Avoid at this point in time *Instead use* now got under waybegan, was an employee of worked for crisis situation crisis at an early date soon in excess of more:

- Delete unnecessary adjectives and adverbs. Sometimes adjectives and adverbs just weigh down your writing, clogging it with unnecessary words. An over-reliance on these qualifying words can be a sign of poor writing style. That noted, your relationship with adjectives and adverbs will depend greatly on the kind of news outlet you work for. Tabloid news style makes more use of adjectives and adverbs than broadsheet news style. Indeed, tabloid news favours descriptions such as "*violent* sequel", "*brutal* arrest". It also likes alliteration (*i.e.* the repetition of a letter at the head of consecutive words) *e.g.* "terrorist tragedy" and "flood fury as wild waters keep rising".

Examples

Avoid ran *quickly Preferred* ran or sped *Avoid* the *noisy* protesters *Preferred* the protesters shouted abuse shouted abuse:

- Eliminate other unnecessary words.

For example, the words "that" and "which" can often be cut out with no loss of meaning.

Example

Delete the word that from this sentence. Infrastructure Minister Freya Yang said that the new road works were essential.

- Use short, easily understood words instead of longer alternatives.

Examples

Instead of exacerbate *Use* worsen *Instead of* commencement *Use* start *Instead of* employees *Use* workers *Instead of* employment *Use* jobs

- *Avoid repetition*: Don't use the same word twice in a single sentence if you can avoid it.
- News writing requires language with a bit of edge. Use strong verbs and nouns.

Examples

Tip

Most of the rules listed here can be set aside if there is a compelling reason to break them. But sidestepping the rules only works when it's done thoughtfully, rather than out of ignorance.

Avoid: The company *attributed* the job cuts to the poor economic environment.

Avoid: The team captain *said* officials *paid insufficient attention* to the poor condition of the ground when they scheduled the game.

- *Stronger wording*: The company *blamed* the job cuts on the
- *Stronger wording*: The team captain *accused* officials of *ignoring* the poor condition of the ground

More Rules

- Avoid using clichés. We say this advisedly because, in reality, clichés do creep into news writing. One reason is that news writing favours brevity and some clichés are the shortest way of conveying an idea. But others are simply silly or overworked.
- For instance, at the time of writing, the word "raft" had become the term of choice for journalists needing to describe a group of non-physical things such as a "raft of proposals", "raft of measures" and so on. When this happens to a word, someone should put it out of its

misery. At the very least, individual reporters should think before automatically reaching for the trendy but meaningless term of the moment.

Examples

Avoid gunned down in a hail of bullets bit the dust *Avoid Avoid* dawn of time ground to a halt...etc. *Avoid* lost in time Of course, if an interviewee uses a cliché, you can include it in the quote. But you should avoid writing them yourself.

- Avoid clichéd intros. Just as certain terms have become over-used, so too have certain formulas for leads. British writer Philip Norman identified several "clunky" styles of intro that he reckoned usually stopped him from wanting to read any further.
  These included:
  - "Such and such is alive and well and ..."
  - "I have seen the future and it ..."
  - "Just when you thought it was safe to ..." (*The Weekend Australian,*

January 22–3, 2000: Features p. 8).

Another over-worked intro is the kind that begins "You don't often see ...".

- Avoid tautologies: A tautology is saying the same thing twice. Sports presenters, who do a lot of live commentary, sometimes reach for tautologies in the heat of the moment, as in, "There goes Freddy, the tall, lofty, Argentinian ..." But anyone who has time to think about what they're saying or writing has little excuse.

Examples

Don't use razed to the ground *Alternative* razed (it means the complete destruction of something)

- *Don't use* past history *Alternative* history
- *Don't use* true facts *Alternative* facts OR truth
- *Don't use* completely empty *Alternative* empty
- *Don't use* 2am in the morning/*Alternative* 2am OR two O'clock in the

5pm in the evening morning/5pm OR 5 O'clock in the afternoon (am and pm convey morning or afternoon/evening)

- *Avoid mixed metaphors*: A metaphor is a term or phrase used to describe something to which it's not literally related. Familiar metaphors include "the iron curtain", "a horse of a different colour", "the hand that rocks the cradle", "one foot in the grave". A mixed metaphor occurs when two of these descriptions are jumbled together.

Example

Mixed metaphor the hand that rocks the grave:

- Avoid the "bleedin" obvious". Some statements are so self-evident that they are not worth writing.

Example

Avoid constructions which labour the obvious:

- *Don't use*: If the Australians don't make enough runs, they'll end up losing this match.
- *Don't use*: One thing is certain, only time will tell (*or simply* time will tell).
- *When artist*: Joe Bloggs was alive, he was an outspoken environmentalist.
- *Alternative*: *(The version on the left states the obvious "When Joe Bloggs was alive". A small amount of rephrasing will fix this.)* Throughout his life Joe Bloggs was an outspoken environmentalist.
- *Alternative*: The Australians need... runs for victory.
- *Alternative*: There isn't really an alternative. If you reach for an expression such as this, it means you've run out of sensible things to say and you need to think again.

Example

- *Don't use* helping police with their enquiries
- *Don't use*: At this moment in time an enquiry is ongoing with officers conducting residential interviews on a face-to-face basis.
- *Alternative* being questioned/interviewed by police
- *Alternative:* Police are asking local people if they saw anything.
- *Don't use will facilitate*: *Alternative* will help to assist

• Avoid euphemisms. Journalists sometimes have to temper the way they write to avoid causing unnecessary distress or offence. But there is no point in taking this to extremes.

Example

Avoid Passed on, gone to meet *Alternative* Died (and, on rare his (her) maker, etc occasions, passed away)

- Attribute thoughtfully. Quotes are an important part of any story. They help improve its audience appeal by introducing the voices of newsmakers themselves. In broadcast and online journalism, listeners and viewers have the chance to hear the actual voices of those making the news and the inclusion of soundbites in stories also punctuates the reporter's narration.

When quoting someone either directly or indirectly, you often need to attribute the remark, for example: "The economy is in good shape, " the prime minister said. In most cases, the verb "said" (or "says" if you're using the present tense) is the most appropriate one to use when attributing information.

It's the shortest word for the occasion. But the verb you use when attributing remarks needs to be chosen carefully because it can convey a loaded meaning, depending on the circumstances. There are occasions on which the alternatives, including "claimed", "agreed" and so on, are acceptable or preferable. But the choice needs to be made with some care.

In print journalism, the news comes first, then the attribution. Anything controversial needs to be attributed to an authoritative source so it does not give the impression that the journalist is writing their own opinion or that of their news organisation.

Examples: Direct quotes (also applies to indirect quotes)

- The economy is in good shape," the prime minister *insisted.*
- My opponent will double parking fees in the inner city," Councillor Caselli *claimed.*
- My opponent will double parking fees in the inner city," Councillor Caselli *revealed.*
- The economy is in great shape," the treasurer *averred.*

Indirect Quotes

The prosecutor *alleged,* cricket star Laura Tiger, had been driving with a blood alcohol level of.09. *Insisted* is fine if the person being quoted is being insistent for some reason, such as countering criticism, but it's a stronger word than "said", not a simple substitute.

In cases such as this, *claimed* is preferable to *said* because *said* would imply the statement was correct rather than an allegation.

The term *revealed* implies a statement is true and that the information was previously secret. Use it with caution. In this case, *claimed* is more accurate.

Occasionally the word *averred* can be used to make a point, particularly in a slightly humorous situation. But in most circumstances the word is not one you would use in daily conversation and "said" is preferable.

In court reports, the word *alleged* is important to convey the fact that something is an accusation and not a fact until proven in court.

The term *alleged* can be used in some other, similar, circumstances ("Police arrested 10 protesters *alleged* to have crossed their lines").

But it should not be used to try to reduce the defamatory implications of a statement ("the *allegedly* corrupt politician") because it doesn't work. The treasurer *denied* the economy was in poor shape. Take great care with the word *denied* because it gives credence to whatever it is that's being denied. The example opposite would be the correct wording if the treasurer were responding to claims that the economy was in poor shape.

But, in other circumstances, it would likely lead readers to assume that there *was* something wrong with the economy. Other verbs that need similar care include "commented", "stated", "laughed", "sighed" and so on. Terms such as "declared" and "chuckled" should be reserved for the novel in your bottom drawer.

News writing shouldn't be colourless. But don't use words in an effort to be clever without thinking about what they really mean or the implications they might convey. One thing all the above examples make clear is that language is not neutral.

Even quite simple words can require political choices. Journalists need to think about the words they use and what they imply to ensure that they are not unwittingly putting emphasis on a particular position, backing a cause, or slighting a person or group of people.

Certainly, there's no shortage of lobby groups prepared to monitor news outlets" use of language and push for changes.

The types of language use that require special attention include the following:

- Disabled persons" lobby groups have fought to have news organisations adopt certain terms and reject others. As a result, the word "handicapped" is rarely used now. "Disabled people" is used.
- AIDS lobby groups have fought a largely successful campaign to have the media avoid terms such as "AIDS sufferer", "AIDS victim" and "AIDS carrier" in favour of "person with AIDS" and so on.
- Mental health is another area in which the media have been urged to take special care with their reporting standards and use of language. Lobbyists in this area have urged that terms such as "insane", "lunatic" and "mental patient" be avoided.
- Many media outlets now follow the requests of Aboriginal communities in respecting cultural sensitivities, particularly with regard to the naming or showing images of people who have died.

Inclusive Language

Using language with care means using language which is inclusive rather than exclusive. It means avoiding terms which are gender specific—such as airline hostess or fireman—in favour of gender neutral terms, in this case flight attendant and firefighter. Apart from anything else, gender specific terms usually sound rather old-fashioned these days.

Equally unacceptable is language which assumes that one particular race, nationality, religion, sexual orientation and so on, is normal, at the expense of everyone else.

Most of the codes of ethics and practice applying to the Australian media make reference to the need to avoid stereotyping particular members or sections of the community.

For example, clause 2 of the Journalists" Code of Ethics says: Do not place unnecessary emphasis on personal characteristics, including race, ethnicity, nationality, gender, age, sexual orientation, family relationships, religious belief, or physical or intellectual disability.

But careful writing requires more than just avoiding the most obviously prejudicial terms. It means writing in a way that gives credence to more than one idea or position.

To take one example, it is common to read or hear that police were "forced to use" tear gas, capsicum spray or some other deterrent to pacify an individual or group of people. The word "forced" sounds dramatic, which is why it's used. But it also paints a picture of the person or group in question, which is usually open to dispute.

It's just as easy, and more honest, to write "police used capsicum spray to ..." and leave the justification to a quote, if explanation is required.

Another circumstance in which loaded language is common is in the reporting of industrial disputes. Stories that suggest that workers are "holding (employers) to ransom" or "bringing (employers, the country, etc) to their/its knees" reflect a one-sided view of a dispute.

Reporters need to think about the meaning— both intended and implied— of what they write. They also need to consider the inferences audiences might draw from their reports and try to write in a way that eliminates any unwanted confusion or conclusions.

6

Newsroom Cultural Change in Journalism

Less than a decade ago, there was a growing concern among corporate executives, scholars, and even many editors about the future of the newspaper industry. Newspapers faced stiff challenges on every horizon: circulation was stagnant, and a smaller percentage of the public was reading newspapers than at any time in the past half-century; the Internet was competing for the populace's time and advertisers' money; the costs of doing business were rising and unpredictable; and, for public companies, profit pressures were increasing as corporate managers sought to maintain control over their companies amidst waves of hostile buy-outs and takeovers. The message to those leading the industry was clear: change or fall victim to the forces redefining your environment.

There were also rumblings within the industry for change. Some influential editors and journalists became outspoken critics of how newspapers had lost sight of their public service mission and lost touch with their communities. These critiques often focused on the insular nature of journalism, emphasizing that journalists are "insider-oriented" elitists.

This inner directedness could be understood in at least two ways: first, journalists tended to assess the value of their work in relation to how it is viewed by other journalists, not the public; second, working close to politicians and other powerful sources resulted in reporting more focused on power struggles and personal political battles than the issues that affect the daily lives of average citizens. Some editors - buoyed by support from scholars, a small body of research, and philanthropic organizations - became convinced that if journalists were able to get closer to readers, reconnect with their democratic mission, and begin framing stories from the centre of their communities, then newspapers would reclaim their relevance.

It is within this framework that newspaper executives - addressing both internal and external issues - re-evaluated the goals and practices of the industry and set out to put it back on course. In 1994, the American Society of Newspaper Editors created a Change Committee, a group of editors given a 5-year period to develop and experiment with initiatives that would ensure the long-term viability of the industry. Founded on the heels of a recession that had lingered since the late 1980s and resulted in smaller newsroom staffs and budgets, the committee focused its attention on exploring ways to: (1) reorganize newsrooms for better efficiency and (2) realign journalists' values more closely with those of readers and citizens.

Change initiatives emerged that attempted to transform the culture of the newsroom, making it more externally focused on markets and readers, while internally changing the nature of work by abandoning the century-old beat system of news coverage and replacing it with collaborative teams. "Change" became the mantra of many leading editors and executives, and the new, restructured approach to producing newspapers was labeled "strategic," "reader-driven," or "market-driven" journalism.

Newsroom managers, recognizing that they lacked the organizational background to plan, execute, and monitor fundamental change, increasingly looked to outside consultants to guide their efforts and alleviate employee resistance. The process of change, seldom easy in any organization, became a target of skepticism for journalists, who worried that initiatives jeopardized core journalism values and credibility.

Organizational development (OD) is the study of how organizations evolve, learn, and adapt. This line of enquiry is well suited, although it lies been rarely used, to explore and understand the process of change in the newspaper industry. The research reported in this monograph uses OD theory as a framework for assessing the perceptions and attitudes that top newsroom managers and rank-and-file journalists have about initiatives aimed at changing the newsroom culture.

This study also explores the impact of two newer, largely unstudied variables that have been a part of change initiatives - newsroom restructuring and the reader-oriented redefinition of news values - to better understand how journalists perceive change and its impact. Organizational development scholarship is rooted in social psychology and management. OD scholars concede that because organizations vary in size and resources and have different goals, OD research has generally focused on one organization at a time. Argyris acknowledges that this situation-by-situation approach, which relies on on-site observations, in-depth interviews, and situation-specific variables, makes the task of generalizing results and theory building more difficult.

This study takes a different approach than most OD research and attempts to advance OD theory building and the practical understanding of ongoing newspaper change by surveying a relatively large probability sample of rank-and-file journalists and a census of top newsroom managers from 17 newspapers most experienced in ASNE-sanctioned change initiatives.

The logic of the approach is that journalists working at newspapers that have experimented with similar change initiatives create a population of cohorts who have clear perceptions regarding change based on their common experiences. This commonality should permit valid research that extends beyond single organizations and site-specific variables, producing results that can benefit newsrooms embarking on change initiatives. Accordingly, this study extends newspaper change research by addressing the problem differently, both in terms of its theoretical framework and methodological design.

The extent to which change initiatives can be tied to economics is uncertain. By 2001, a recessionary national economy led the nation's largest public newspaper companies to downsize their workforces between 5 and 10 per cent to maintain profit levels attractive to investors.

However, the late 1990s, a period of a strong economy and fast and furious change, saw the same high profits that had characterized the industry a decade earlier. Publicly owned companies, which account for nearly half the nation's daily circulation, returned an average profit of 20.7 per cent in 1998 and 22.2 per cent in 1999.

Advertising revenue was also at record levels, reaching $46.3 billion in 1999, the eighth consecutive year of record highs, casting doubt on prognosticators who only a half-decade earlier had predicted the Internet would spell doom for newspapers.

CHANGING NEWS VALUES

Aware that their readership is stagnant and influence declining, newspaper managers and journalists have been reexamining their news values. This introspection has manifested itself in several ways: an increased marketing consciousness, a desire for more credibility, the involvement of readers in deciding news and how it should be reported, and a sense the media are failing to live up to their historic democratic role of informing people of issues important to successful governance.

American Journalism Review, in a 2000 cover story titled "Reader Friendly," reported that the emerging culture of restructured newsrooms around the country is characterized by:

- Enthroning readers as the "invisible giants," elevating them to near equal partners in decision making;
- Erring on the side of caution rather than aggressiveness, rejecting stories that might offend readers as lacking compassion or sensitivity;
- Promoting cooperation with everyone, from City Hall to the paper's advertising departments.

The long-time taboo of "pandering" to readers has been swept away by an attempt to reverse what some editors have called a "disconnection" between newspapers and the public. Following a series of meetings called the Journalism Values Institute in which 30 editors from around the country debated the problems of the industry, Peck (1996) wrote, "The essence of these evaluations comes down to this: American journalists continue to say they practice good journalism in the public's interest - but the public doesn't believe we deliver".

Editors left the meetings agreeing that newspaper content includes too much gossip, not enough substance, bias but no balance, and a preoccupation with conflict and few solutions. The Oregonian's Bhatia summed up the problems: "Our comfort zones are painting the world in black and white. And our comfort zones are seeing the traditional good side and evil side of whatever issue it might be. We've got to blow that up".

Many of the editors most active in the ASNE Change Committee borrowed ideas from and adopted the language of civic (or public) journalism. Civic journalism broadens the concept of journalistic social responsibility into a more active role, with the goal of journalism becoming a catalyst for the revival of civic life by promoting citizen engagement and dialogue.

Merritt insists the practice of civic journalism requires journalists to abandon several common and traditional practices, including: valuing conflict as the primary narrative device, framing issues at extremes, maintaining an adversarial role with institutions, treating the readers as audiences rather than participants, and insisting that journalism credibility arises from detachment.

Stopp wrote that a cross-country tour of newsrooms left him impressed by how many newsrooms were using the language and techniques of civic journalism. he notes that when he raised this issue many editors and journalists dismissed it, suggesting civic journalism is a project-driven formula that they don't understand.

Stepp, however, concluded: "Perhaps the resistance to the civic journalism label simply underlines how much some of the techniques have seeped into the newsroom groundwater".

CHANGING THE NEWSROOM CULTURE

Nearly all editors who have involved their newsrooms in change initiatives have suggested the key to making change work is to create a new culture. Weaver said changing the newsroom culture requires "getting the staff to think of the whole paper, as opposed to their own story or small piece they contributed." She said that reporters need to be trained to work in a new system, as many lack the editing, headline writing, and design skills required in the team structure.

Managers, too, have more pressure, as the staff is often competing for the attention of fewer bosses. And, because of the changing nature of journalism work, job performance evaluations need revision to reflect the standards and goals of a new system. She admits that "newsroom stars" under the old system often fool stifled by the team structure. Teams require a "new breed" of journalist with different personality traits and skills than the "lone wolf" who worked well alone and often produced breakthrough stories.

Sue Deans, editor of The Sun News, said for change initiatives to work staff members need to understand that change is a constant; it will not go away after a short time or a few experiments.

The two "core issues" of change are continuous product improvement, and keeping aware of what readers want and the market demands. She said changing the newsroom culture requires emphasizing "passion" for the newspaper business and:

- Impressing on people who do not want change that they must change or leave;
- Eliminating "silo" thinking by creating cross-departmental approaches to work and evaluating work quality;
- Staying focused on strategy and on the market.

Campbell, who resigned in April 2000 as Si. Louis Post-Dispatch editor after a stormy 3 1/2 years, had embarked on an ambitious attempt at "cultural transformation" at the paper. He claims the existing newsroom "judgemental culture" is part of the problem with American journalism, and he attempted to change the Post-Dispatch's culture from one based on "judgementalism" to one based on "collaboration."

By the millennium, the ideas for change that began in a couple dozen newsrooms in the mid-1990s were becoming the industry norm. Stepp (2000) wrote: "From civic journalism to New Directions for News, from credibility reforms to the Committee of Concerned Journalists, a host of foundations, trade groups and other forces have been pouring millions of dollars into attempts to remodel how journalists think and act".

IMPACT OF CHANGE ON MORALE

Change initiatives have required journalists to rethink some fundamental principles of their work: their sense of news, audience, organization, and even the purpose of journalism. Signs of eroding morale were present before change began in the mid-1990s, and morale problems in relation to change initiatives have been reported in trade journals.

Gassaway used observation and survey to study the social construction of a journalist's reality. he found news judgement decisions were most often the result of "preordained news," determined by coverage beats and how editors decide to use their resources. Editors and reporters struggle for control of information because they often disagree on what should be communicated to the public. Editors' authority is derived from organizational hierarchies, but reporters can deny editors' authority by controlling information obtained in iiewsgathoriiig. Gassaway concluded editors and reporters negotiate for control to prevent confrontations and reduce resorting to power.

Jeffers and Lewis studied organizational communication at a midsized newspaper and found rank-and-file journalists perceived their communication with their immediate supervisor and publisher as poor. They suggested the organizational climate could be improved by increasing the amount and frequency of communication at all levels. The authors concluded their study supported the findings of Pincuss, Knipp, and Rayfield, who found rank-and-file employees' communication relationship with their immediate supervisor is a predictor of job satisfaction; however, employees' sense of having meaningful communication with top-level managers was as strong a predictor of satisfaction as immediate-supervisor communication.

In the mid-1990s, several scholars began to assess organizational structure and goals, often considering profit motive and its impact on normative journalism values. Deniers integrated organizational and economic theory in his book, The Menace of the Corporate Newspaper: Fact or Fiction?, to define the corporate newspaper, its characteristics, and organizational dynamics. Demers asserted that corporate newspapers are complex bureaucracies controlled by trained managers, not owners.

These managers are best understood as innovative professionals or "technocrats" who are morn interested in professional, organizational, and technical goals than profit goals. Demers juxtaposed the roles of managers to those of owners, defining the latter as "capitalists" most interested in returns on their investments. In the 20th century, managers replaced owners as the driving force; in corporations because the organizations had become complex bureaucracies that required professional management.

Further aiding the transition was the death of the original owners, whose influence was dispersed over time and divided among heirs. Deniers wrote the result is that corporate newspapers are efficiently managed and structured to maximize profits, but they place less emphasis on profit than non-corporate newspapers, which tend to be family-owned, less bureaucratic organizations. In two studies, his results indicate that newspapers become more rigourous editorially as they become larger, more complex organizations.

In studies that both support and refute Deniers' work, Beam studied the conditions that influence newspapers' market orientation and whether market orientation affects content. To define and measure market orientation, Beam explored the extent that newspapers: (1) have one or more departments active in understanding customer needs and the factors affecting the needs, (2) share this information across departments, and (3) have various departments engaged in meeting select customer needs. He found that ownership by a large group is the most important predictor of a newspaper's market orientation, suggesting the corporate parent may not be involved in specific content decisions but is more likely to require certain general processes be followed in making content decisions.

He concluded that traditional journalistic values are important at market-oriented papers, and while more market-oriented newsrooms are more committed to special interest and visual content, they are not less committed to traditional content, including public affairs. Beam (2000) has also found that newspapers that are part of privately owned companies are more market oriented than those of public companies. Using his survey data, Beam (2001) then chose 10 newspapers for a content analysis - 5 papers with strong market orientation and 5 papers with weak market orientation.

He found the majority of items on page one of both orientations was "public sphere" content, which includes government affairs; however, the percentage of public sphere items on page one for weak market orientation newspapers was significantly higher (65.6 per cent) than for strong market orientation papers (54.9 per cent). Overall, Beam analysed the display pages (section front or topic lead page) and found papers with strong market orientation have proportionately more items devoted to private life, coping, and sports, while proportionately fewer items about government and public life.

Martin compared profits earned by 15 public newspaper companies to profits of publishing companies and yields from corporate and government bonds over an 11-year period. For the entire period, newspaper profits averaged 90 per cent higher than publishing companies, 78 per cent higher than government bond yields, and 54 per cent higher than interest payments from corporate bonds. Using a scale created by an economist that labels profits 50 per cent above those of comparable measures as "excessive," Martin found that in 23 of 33 annual comparative indices (70 per cent) the newspaper companies in the sample earned excessive profits. In some cases, these excessive comparative profits occurred in the early 1990s during what an analyst called "the biggest advertising recession since World War II".

After newspapers embarked on broad, and in some cases bold, change initiatives in the 1990s, a few researchers began to study these initiatives through the lens of organizational development.

Gentry observed while a small California daily embarked on several change initiatives aimed at better aligning its content with community interests. The year-long efforts, orchestrated by New Directions for News, led Gentry to conclude the following elements were essential for successful newspaper organizational change: (1) strong leadership; (2) management communication about: why change is needed, management's vision, and new performance standards; (3) staff involvement in the change process; (4) management rewarding correct behaviour and extinguishing improper behaviour; and (5) anticipating problems of acceptance and implementation.

Working a few years later with the American Press Institute, Gentry developed a model he calls "A Roadmap for Change" that added several variables, including: (1) prechange analysis of the current culture to determine the extent and types of changes needed; (2) use of mission statements to clarify core values for employees; (3) flexible management strategies and putting people in the proper roles to execute them; (4) enabling structures, such as job training; and (5) creating visible symbols of the new culture.

Testing the model, Gentry (1997) surveyed management and rank-and-file at six newspapers and found management thought it was doing a better job than the staff thought it was doing on all 10 elements of change the study addressed. In a longitudinal case study, Gade and Perry measured newsroom employees' perceptions of change initiatives led by editor Cole Campbell from 1996-2000 at the Si. LOUJS Post-Dispatch. Over 4 years, Campbell, known as an industry innovator, had some success making news values more reader driven, but the 1999 reorganization of newsroom coverage from beats to teams left much of the staff confused about their roles and job responsibilities.

Campbell's embrace of public journalism did not resonate with a majority of the staff. Morale declined and was lowest among respondents with management duties. Respondents consistently indicated they wern open minded towards change until after reorganization, which apparently was the last straw in a series of changes that underscored Campbell's tenure as editor (he resigned under pressure in April 2000). Over the course of the study, respondents consistently indicated that they failed to see how change initiatives contributed to better journalism.

At a time when cross-departmental teams were still new to the industry, Sylvie studied how department heads of news, advertising, and circulation perceived their identity and ability to cooperate with each other. News managers named advertising as the most difficult department, while the advertising directors named the news editors as least cooperative. Newsroom managers were the only department heads of rank their respective department's concerns as most important, ranking circulation success the most important. News editors showed a significantly greater tendency to say more cooperation between departments is needed. Sylvie concluded the news managers exhibit a "surprising sensitivity" to market-oriented concepts, which gives credibility to journalists' anecdotal claims that the newspaper industry is moving towards a greater market orientation.

A meagre amount of research exists on newspaper team performance. Russial studied changes in health and science content at The Oregonian after that paper created a Health and Science team. He found that the team produced more coverage that received better play (Al or Metro section front) than before the team was created. Russial suggested that although his study did not measure coverage quality, the creation of a team-based system represents a realignment in the use of newsroom resources that may have important consequences on news content.

Neuzil, Hansen, and Ward surveyed Minneapolis Star Tribune and St. Paul Pioneer Press journalists working in teams and found most thought they had less authority and less success getting story ideas in the paper than before teams were created. Those who thought they had less authority also said they were unsure of the chain of command, worked on larger teams, and wore reporters more than editors. The researchers concluded if a goal of team work was to "empower" journalists by granting them more autonomy to be innovative, this goal was not being met. In sum, trade journals and a developing body of research provide evidence that newspapers are changing in some fundamental ways: flattening organizational structures, replacing traditional beats with teams, revising job descriptions and required skills, rethinking organizational values, and redefining news judgement.

USING ORGANIZATIONAL THEORY TO MAKE SENSE OF CHANGE

The study of "organizations" is a relatively new discipline. Drucker wrote that "no one in the United States - or anyplace else - talked of Organizations' until after World War ?" Drucker said that the modern idea of an organization - as a purposely designed and specialized entity that is defined by its task and is distinct from society's other institutions - emerged in the second half of the 20th century with what he calls the "management revolution." Initial theoretical assumptions of this revolution were largely shaped by turn-of-the-century scholars: Taylor's views on "scientific management" and Weber's ideas on the rational and specialized bureaucracy.

This organizational model is characterized by a hierarchical division of labour where managers are the "thinkers" and laborers are the "doers". Employees develop highly specialized skills that increase performance and productivity, while management's job is to ensure the conditions exist for the organizational "machine" to run smoothly. Recognizing that organizations must evolve and adapt to survive in changing environments, Lewin suggested a "natural" (as opposed to mechanical) metaphor to explain organizational dynamics; change, he wrote, can be best understood and managed through a process of "unfreeze, change, refreeze."

These early attempts to understand organizations and their dynamics prepared the intellectual soil for the growth of organizational development, which attracted the interest of U.S. scholars and corporate managers in the last quarter of the 20th century as the changing global marketplace threatened U.S. dominance.

Although Taylor's and Weber's (and to a lesser extent Lewin's) ideas are considered outdated, they have proven resilient and modest adaptations of them are still very much alive in both theory and practice. Bergquist wrote that most organizational theorists have conceived organizations as pendulum-like mechanisms, which value "simplicity in motion" and homeostasis. When organizations experience turbulent times, they tend to seek equilibrium by returning to their previous form and function. However, the structured and predictable environment in which U.S. companies once thrived no longer exists, and Bergquist contends a more accurate metaphor in the postmodern world is that of the organization as a liquid, "poised on the edge of order and chaos". The liquid system, he wrote, contains at the same time both elements of stability and change, especially along the edges, or shifting boundaries.

In an organizational sense, it is the shifting boundaries that offer potential for understanding the change process. It is these places on the "edge" where innovation occurs and where organizational traits such as mission, communication, and leadership become integral to success.

In perhaps the seminal book on organizational change and development, Kanter wrote American companies that value "innovation" are better placed to use their employees' creative capacities and stay ahead in changing environments. Interviews with 65 corporate executives led Kanter to conclude the innovative companies are integrated (my italics); they grant power to individuals to encourage fresh thinking and create opportunities for new ideas to cross organizational boundaries.

She juxtaposed integrated companies with "segmented" companies, which are characterized by an "ovorspecification" of resources and consider themselves successful when every segment works well independently, without much need for communication. Segmented companies, Kanter wrote, seek stasis, because they are constantly looking to the past to define the future; accordingly, habits and routines that maintain the course are valued.

Kanter identified five major building blocks in change initiatives that increase the company's capacity to meet new challenges:

- Departures from tradition: activities or ideas that require the organization to think and behave in new ways.
- Crisis or galvanizing event: a critical event that cannot be solved by traditional means. This allows a non-traditional idea to be pushed forward.
- Strategic decisions: the opportunity for management to create a vision by articulating a deliberate and conscious direction.
- Individual "prime movers": people who push the innovative strategy through the organization by communicating strategic decisions and manipulating the symbols of the organizational culture towards the direction of change.
- Action vehicles: mechanisms that allow new action. These include training programmes, successful results for people using new practices, new organizational rewards that support new practices, and ongoing messages of the benefits experienced by individuals using the now practices.

Kanter wrote that managers need three new sets of skills to operate effectively in integrated, innovative environments: "power skills" used to persuade others to invest in new initiatives; ability to manage problems associated with teams and greater employee participation; and understanding of how organizational change is designed and constructed. She concluded that "the art and architecture of change" requires managers to abandon their reliance on traditional analytical tools, which measure what already exists or has occurred. "Change efforts have to mobilize people around what is not yet known, not yet experienced ... they require a leap of faith that cannot be eliminated by presentation of all the forecasts, figures, and advance guarantees that can be accumulated". Accordingly, the paradox of managing changes, she wrote, is "there needs to be a plan, and the plan has to acknowledge that it will be departed from". Most attempts at organizational development involve efforts to transform an organization's culture. Schneider, Brief, and Guzzo wrote that the values and beliefs that are the foundation of an organization's culture can be changed by focusing on the tangible things - such as practices, policies, and procedures - that define daily life in the organization.

It is these tangible phenomena that comprise an organization's climate, and for real cultural change to occur, management must change the climate in which the employees exist. The authors contend that many efforts at cultural change are focused on "macro" issues such as values and beliefs, while overlooking the more tangible issues that create the organizational climate in which employees experience everyday life.

They wrote: "Sustainable organizational change is most assured when both the climate - what the organization's members experience - and the culture - what the members believe the organization values - change".

Successful companies have increasingly educated workforces, and they are creating cultures that are more innovative and flexible. The new, desired culture is one in which power and accountability are shared between managers and employees in a manner that allows companies to respond quickly to challenges and opportunities. The goal of these efforts is to unleash and channel the power of employees' knowledge in an organizational "culture of contribution."

Fisher acknowledges that this is a major cultural shift for most U.S. companies because - unlike the Japanese, whose collective society adapted easily to a team-building, egalitarian corporate model - "America's professional workers value their individualism and often express it in counterproductive ways". Corporate America also clings to some values that work against creating a culture of contribution; most prominent among these, Fisher wrote, is the corporate view on job attachment. Workers are expected to accept such surprises as downsizing, job reclassification, or relocation with quiet stoicism, which contradicts companies' claims they are striving to empower employees as co-partners with management.

Fisher contends that U.S. managers need to be aware that there is no single ideal corporate culture; rather, corporate culture is better understood as a combination of macro and micro cultures. Many senior managers claim to embrace a culture of contribution, but Fisher contends that few have ideas about how to put a programme or process in place to let the transformation occur.

On the other hand, the changing nature of professional work, driven by new technology, has organizations acting as though they are horizontally constructed even though most corporate organizational charts still reflect a vertical hierarchy.

If management is to be successful creating the culture of contribution, it must cede some of its "span of control" and forge a "span of relationships," with workers and managers acting more as "learners than knowers, listeners than tellers, partners than adversaries". Fisher cautions that management should not be too optimistic that a reorganization into teams will solve the ills of the company; rather, a culture of contribution is more likely to develop in a climate where workers are trusted and have the freedom to think and act like owners. At the core of many organizational development efforts over the past two decades has been the restructuring of organizations from vertical hierarchies into more horizontal, "flattened" designs where most of the work is done by self-directed teams.

In theory, teams "empower" employees by giving team members more decision-making authority and eliminating vertical chains of command. However, empowerment efforts not only require management to share power, they also demand that individual team members think differently about the nature of work. Labianca, Gray, and Brass (2000) found that empowerment efforts require a change in "schemas" - cognitive frameworks that give meaning to experience - for both management and lower level employees.

The authors analysed a 2-year organizational development project involving team building and increased participation of lower level employees in decision making. Before the project, the "schema-in-use" for organizational decision making was that management should maintain control of events and decision making, and this schema was understood by both management and employees. The expected new schema for management included: making the organization more team oriented and collaborative, empowering lower level employees, aligning organizational structure effectively, and keeping current workers.

For the ruiik-aiid-filu, the expected new schema was characterized by working on team building, creating more avenues of communication, and encouraging employees to air their "beefs."

The authors found: a great amount of employee skepticism at the outset about the likelihood of real change; despite a series of organization-wide meetings, interviews revealed both managers and non-managers were unclear about the project's goals; resistance was heightened when managerial behaviour failed to conform with its stated expectations; and management incorrectly assumed that employees would postpone judgement of the reorganization plan until after it was implemented. Randolph (2000) wrote that few managers or employees fully understand how empowerment affects traditional patterns of corporate hierarchy and behaviour. Management confuses empowerment as "giving people the power to make decisions," and this perception misses the essential notion of empowerment, that a great amount of power already exists in employees' knowledge, experience, and motivation.

Rank-and-file perceive empowerment to mean they will be given the freedom to make all major decisions about their jobs. Randolph wrote that empowerment efforts do require a cultural shift; however, the shift is from one person making decisions to team-based shared decision making.

He asserts that empowerment makes employees more accountable than the older, hierarchical culture, and it is best understood as a strange combination of opportunity and risk. An organization moves towards team-based empowered culture through three stages: (1) starting and orienting the process of change, (2) making changes and dealing with discouragement, and (3) adopting and refining empowerment to fit the organization.

Each stage utilizes three "interlocking tools" - sharing information, creating autonomy through boundaries, and replacing the hierarchy with self-directed teams. Hirschhorn, a management scholar whose work focuses on team-based organizations, wrote that the entire philosophy of management is changing as corporations flatten hierarchies and adopt new team environments. Successful managers develop roles for team members and "manage the boundary," communicating the company's needs to the team and the team's needs to the company. Managers lead by creating a structure in which the team can be successful and by positioning themselves to defend the team's efforts.

Managers must realise they are both cause of and solution to many team problems. To be successful, managers must show their vulnerability (a traditional management faux pas) and willingness to learn from team members. Exhibiting these traits shows that managers are open to new ways to solve problems and encourages team members to respond to challenges that can enhance team performance. Although development efforts are characterized by dispersing power throughout an organization, management's ability to provide leadership remains a key to organizational success. Kets de Vries, a psychologist who focuses on the "psychodynamics of organizations," wrote that organizational culture depends on the psychological contract that exists between its leaders and followers.

Effective leaders need to: articulate a vision of the future; create symbolic impressions to communicate the vision; build networks; empower followers; make choices (often painful ones); and keep perspectives of the followers based in reality. he wrote that the leader/follower relationship a process of social comparison that involves power, authority, hero worship, flattery, ambition, and attention seeking - provides tremendous opportunities for distorted management reasoning. The key is for managers to "preserve their hold on reality." Trust is essential for a healthy organization, and trust is dependent upon communication, support, respect, fairness, competence, and consistency on the part of the leaders. he concluded, "In order for the leader to understand the meaning of these words, it is important that he or she realise what it means to be a follower, how it feels to be in that position".

The importance of communication in organizations, especially during times of change, has spawned its own discipline of study. Lewis wrote that a growing body of empirical research indicates that the communication process and organizational change efforts are "inextricably linked processes".

Communication plays an important role in several aspects of the change process, including: creating and articulating a vision; soliciting input and channeling feedback to and from all levels of the organizational hierarchy; and propelling and altering the paths of change.

The organizational communication literature reveals that communication has been shown to reduce uncertainty associated with change efforts, increase accuracy in perceptions about the reasons and goals of change, and increase willingness to participate in planned change.

Studying the methods and channels organizations use to communicate change, Lewis found change agents consider themselves to be the primary sources of change-related information, and they solicit input much less frequently than they disseminate information.

She suggests that management's lack of use of channels of communication, especially upward channels, limits feedback from lower level employees who do the work of the organization.

This approach can affect the success of change efforts, as "changes in status, reward structures, job descriptions, roles, work methods, work relationships, and procedures bring significant organizational issues to the surface" that increase rank-and-file employees' need to communicate with their supervisors.

There is a small body of literature; on organizational attempts to initiate market-oriented cultural change. Narver and Slater described a market-oriented culture as one that most effectively and efficiently creates superior customer value. Harris defined a market-oriented culture as "the dominant, dynamic segment of an organization whoso orientation, attitudes and actions are geared towards the market".

Harris contends that most reseachers err when they assume an organization has a single, unitary culture. This approach ignores the dynamic interaction of many aspects of an organization's culture and denies the possibility of the existence of multiple cultures. Generally, developing a market-oriented culture can be understood as a means to improve organizational efficiency and effectiveness. However, Piercy maintains the success of developing such a culture is largely dependent on internal power relationships and organizational politics, which - at least in the short term - do not necessarily lead to high levels of organization-wide motivation, commitment, or satisfaction.

When understood in this context, developing a market-oriented culture can be seen as one of many ways that an organization can impose cultural control over the attitudes, actions, and behaviours of its members. Overall, Harris and Ogbonna wrote that the literature on the effects of developing market-oriented cultures is inconsistent, with some studies suggesting that the new culture improves employee satisfaction and commitment and others indicating this is not the case. However, researchers tend to agree that the success of any attempt at creating a market-oriented culture is contingent on employees who have to implement it. In nearly all cases, this is the front-line employees who are the primary link between an organization and its customers. The authors also contend that developing a market-oriented culture should be concerned with the long-term generation of values, attitudes, and behaviours, but the underlying assumption of the market culture is continuing responsiveness to customer needs.

The dilemma for organizations is how they can craft short-term responses to "increasingly fickle" customer needs in a manner that does not conflict with long-term organizational objectives. Harris and Ogbonna concluded that this condition is "a contradiction yet to be resolved or fully understood". Change, because it requires giving up what is known and routine for something new that may not be understood, is often met with resistance. De Jager (2001) wrote that many managers perceive employees who resist change as a problem. he contends this a short-sighted view that fundamentally misunderstands the causes of resistance and the potential benefits resistance can exert on an organization. De Jager wrote that businesses today acknowledge the need to change, but there is so much change that employees become confused and see themselves pushed in conflicting directions. Management is wise to understand that resistance to change is a tool that can be used to guide an organization. "Another way of looking at resistance is as a gateway or filter. Resistance to change helps us select from all possible changes the one that is most appropriate to the current situation". Because change involves replacing old organizational routines and values with new ones, managers must be able to provide answers for employees to some fundamental questions:

- Why is the old status quo no longer sufficient?
- What will it cost to make the transition from the old to new ways of doing things? De Jager identified several likely costs: disruption of routines, training, temporary low morale, new hires, people leaving, and the emotional cost of destroying what was.
- Is the cost of change justified by the incremental benefits of the change proposed?
- Does the proposed change support and reinforce existing core values?

As the millennium approached, the newspaper industry faced imposing, concurrent challenges on several fronts: stagnant circulation and a slowly dwindling base of readers; a fragmenting mass modin market; new electronic media that are changing the way people access and use information; threats to traditional sources of advertising; and unpredictable but rising costs of production. In the wake of a mid-1990s recession that saw significant cutbacks, layoffs, and downsizings, newsrooms were restructured and reorganized. Hierarchical newsroom designs were flattened, and the beat system of coverage centered on social institutions was replaced by a team system that defined coverage areas by topics believed of greater interest to readers and consumers. What becomes apparent from the industry trade journals is that "change" became the guiding light of the industry in the late 1990s.

Feeling out of step with the social patterns and interests of the public, the industry questioned its news values and management has focused on changing the culture of the newsroom to include greater marketing awareness and knowledge. Editors are increasingly taking on marketing duties, working in cross-departmental teams with advertising, circulation, and marketing directors to create strategies to attract readers, often in specific demographic groups that advertisers are willing to pay to reach. Rank-and-file journalists are expected to accept restructuring, redefined news values, and a greater sensitivity to marketing as part of a larger cultural change process that is redefining their jobs and norms as journalists. Organizational theory suggests that integrated organizations are more innovative and flexible and respond more quickly to opportunities and challenges. The basis of power and decision making in integrated organizations shifts from being solely in the hands of management to a shared arrangement that empowers employees to use their knowledge and skills in team-based systems.

Teams, and their individual members, respond to more decision-making power and autonomy by taking more responsibility for the quality of their work and becoming more productive. Organizational change and development is understood as a process with several stages, including planning, executing, and monitoring the progress and results.

Because organizations have different values and goals, the study of OD has usually focused on one organization at a time, identifying the impact of site-specific variables on organizational development. This approach, while making theory building more difficult, has, however, led to researchers identifying several variables that impact the success of OD efforts.

These variables include an organization having a clear mission, employees who understand the mission and organization's core values, effective organizational communication, employee participation in Grafting and implementing change initiatives, strong leadership, trust, flexibility, and mechanisms that monitor the progress of change initiatives and reward desired behaviour. The effect of successful OD efforts should be empowered employees who, in self-directed work teams, are more motivated, productive, and responsible for their work. In theory, at least, successful OD efforts should in the long term improve employee morale.

However, change is also understood as a difficult and risky process. It requires employees (both management and rank-and-file) to embrace new values, to alter routines, and to think differently about their organizational roles and the nature of their work. It requires greater accountability from empowered rank-and-file and a new, less autocratic style from management. Accordingly, resistance to change should be expected, and in some cases is rational. For management, successful OD includes understanding the reasons for resistance and having the flexibility to find ways of working through resistance.

In short, the challenge of conceiving and leading change falls on management, while rank-and-file are expected to enact and embrace change initiatives that affect many of their conventions and values.

Management perceives it is initiating change in the best interests of the organization and industry, while rank-and-file ponder the reasons for change and are sensitive to how it is implemented.

Organizational theory and change models provide conceptual guidelines that should help predict effective organizational development (OD) initiatives. Given the vast amount of change in the newspaper industry and the relative dearth of research studying these OD initiatives, this study of top newsroom managers and rank-and-file journalists at newspapers leading industry change explores the following research questions and tests three hypotheses.

RQl: What are the attitudes and opinions of management and rank-and-file journalists towards organizational change?

RQ2: How do management and rank-and-file perceive the change process in relation to organizational development theory?

RQ3: How do management and rank-and-file perceive organizational change in relation to the normative values of journalism and marketing?

RQ4: Have change efforts affected rank-and-file perceptions of news values and organizational structure?

RQ5: Have change efforts affected rank-and-file morale?

RQ6: Does organization size (measured by circulation) affect how rank-and-file perceive change?

H1: Management will perceive it has done significantly better at organizational development than rank-and-file.

H2: Morale among rank-and-file will be low.

H3: Rank-and-file perceptions of organizational development will predict morale.

This study used two survey instruments: a 62-statement survey sent to a sample of rank-and-file at 17 newspapers that have been engaged in change initiatives and a 20-statement survey sent to a census of top newsroom managers at the same papers. The rank-and-file survey was designed to explore respondents' attitudes towards concepts important to all newspapers experimenting with change: news values, organizational structure, and morale. The survey included statements that allowed measuring the degree to which the newsroom change process has adhered to organizational development theory.There were also statements asking rank-and-file to assess the relationship of change with journalistic and marketing goals. The 20-statement management survey focused primarily on issues of organizational development, asking managers to assess the change process and their leadership of it.

These 20 statements also appeared on the rank-and-file survey, allowing for a comparison between managers and rank-and-file on issues important to successful organization development. On both surveys, respondents were asked to record their level of agreement or disagreement to stimulus statements along a 5-point Likert-like intensity scale.

VARIABLE MEASURES

Most of the 62 rank-and-file survey statements were written to probe change initiatives in relation to news values, organizational structure, organizational development, and morale. The statements exploring news values incorporate ideas from trade journals about the changing nature of news, but also reflect norms articulated in the Libertarian and Social Responsibility theories of the press.

The statements that construct the organizational structure variable were taken from trade journal and organizational development literature. The statements in the organizational development construct were all derived from the OD literature.

Morale statements were written to explore both individual respondents' attitudes about their own morale and their perceptions of morale in the newsroom. Factor analysis of the rank-and-file data assisted construction of the four concepts: 14 statements measure news values; 12 statements measure organizational structure; 14 statements measure organizational development; 6 statements measure morale.

Statement responses - on a 5-point scale with 1 strongly agree, 5 strongly disagree, and 3 neutral - were coded so that a positive response indicated support for the concept (*i.e.*, positive response indicated high morale). Conceptual quotients were created by calculating the mean response to the set of statements measuring the concepts. Accordingly, a quotient significantly below 3.0 (the assumed population mean on the 5-point scale) indicates positive agreement with the concept, and a quotient significantly above 3.0 indicates that respondents disagree with the concept (*i.e.*, disagree with statements suggesting high morale).

Comparisons between Management and Rank-and-File

Organizational Development. The literature indicates that cultural change is difficult, requiring management and rank-and-file to adapt to new values, structures, routines, and goals. However, management and rank-and-file have different roles in the change process. Management is responsible for conceiving, guiding, and monitoring change, while rank-and-file must execute management's vision and live with the new roles and values associated with change.

Management is expected to perceive OD initiatives more broadly, in concert with strategic organizational goals, and guide and assess the change process from a position of leadership and accountability. It is expected that management will perceive that its OD initiatives are rooted in sound strategies and practices, while rank-and-file will question the reasons for change and be sensitive to how it is implemented. This logic is the basis of the following hypothesis:

Hl: Management will perceive it has done significantly better at OD than rank-and-file.

At test of independent samples was used to compare the OD quotients (mean value of the 14 statements in the construct) of management and rank-and-file. This hypothesis is supported.

The data indicate that management believes OD initiatives have generally followed theoretical guidelines, as the OD quotient for management shows modest overall agreement with the statements (quotient is less than 3.0). Conversely, the rank-and-file OD quotient shows general disagreement that change initiatives are in accordance with the parameters defined by OD theory. Thus, there is not only a significant difference between the OD quotients, there is also a clear difference of attitudes: management perceives it has generally implemented change in accordance with OD, while rank-and-file think the process of change has not adhered to ideas and practices consistent with successful OD. This finding is further reinforced by looking at the pattern of responses to the variable statements. Of the 14 OD statements, management agrees with 9 and rank-and-file agree with only 3.

T tests wore also used to compare individual statement means, and there are significant differences on 11 of the 14 statements. Because the OD variable is a broad measure of change, with survey statements addressing planning, training, commitment, leadership, communication, participation, and a system of rewards, the significant differences on so many OD aspects reflect both the intensity and broad-based nature of the differences between the groups.

Six of the statistically significant OD statements show a clear difference of attitudes, with management agreeing with the statement and rank-and-file disagreeing. The two groups have differing opinions on some of the most basic aspects of change (means noted parenthetically). Management believes the newspaper's mission and core values are understood by newsroom employees, while rank-and-file are apparently unsure about their paper's mission and values. Management believes the staff has participated in drafting change, while rank-and-file disagree; and management says that it has asked for staff feedback about change, while rank-and-file apparently think management is not interested in feedback, or at least not interested enough to ask.

The importance of communication in the change process is also shown, as management agrees that change initiatives and the reasons for change have been continually communicated, while rank-and-file disagree.

Most telling about communication is the large difference of opinion concerning honesty. Management shows quite strong agreement that it has been open and honest with staff about the reasons for change, but rank-and-file exhibit equally strong disagreement. This .8 mean difference on honesty (on a 5-point scale) is the largest gap between the groups' responses to any of the 14 statements in the OD variable.

Even on the eight statements where the groups tend to agree, there are significant differences in their intensity of agreement on five statements. Although rank-and-file credit management for its strong leadership role and unified commitment to change, management assesses its leadership role and commitment in significantly more optimistic terms. In those areas where management is relatively self-critical, rank-and-file tend to be more critical.

Management's response is a candid assessment of an unpleasant reality and a subtle admission of a failure of change; yet, rank-and-file are significantly harsher in their assessment, with their strongest level of disagreement to any of the 14 statements. These differences underscore that even when management and rank-and-file find areas of common ground, they still tend to disagree. Of the 14 OD statements, management has a stronger level of disagreement to only 2, and these 2 statements are among the 3 statements that do not have significant mean differences. Management disagrees that it has overestimated resistance to change, while rank-and-file are neutral; and managers disagree that the staff is open-minded towards change marginally more than rank-and-file. Although not significant, taken together, the ideas that management perceives more resistance and less open-mindedness suggest that management believes their staffs are generally resistant to change initiatives. This perception is likely to influence how managers approach leading change. Managers would be likely to view with more optimism the task of managing a staff that is open to new ideas and practices. Conversely, managers who perceive a resistant and inflexible staff are more likely to judge the task of leading change as more difficult.

COMPARISONS OF STATEMENTS NOT IN THE OD VARIABLE

There were six statements appearing on both surveys that were not part of the OD variable. T tests were performed on the responses, and significant differences were found on four of the statements. Two of the significant statements show a clear difference of attitudes. Management, consistent with other responses that show more optimism about change than rank-and-file, agrees that there has been a noticeable change in the newsroom culture that has improved the organization, while rank-and-file disagree quite strongly. This large difference of opinion (.82 on a 5-point scale) underscores the different experiences and perceptions the two groups have about the impact of change on the newsroom culture. But the pattern of management optimism is reversed when the groups are asked about an indicator of journalism quality. In this case, rank-and-file agree that newspapers arc doing a boiler job portraying a representative picture of society than in the past, while management is significantly more pessimistic, disagreeing with the statement. This finding could help explain why management sees a need to get closer to readers and redefine news to be more aligned with the lives of people in a changing and diverse marketplace.

This trend might be best shown with management's relatively strong disagreement to the statement that change initiatives have helped build stronger trust between management and rank-and-file.

Management's response is a candid assessment of an unpleasant reality and a subtle admission of a failure of change; yet, rank-and-file are significantly harsher in their assessment, with their strongest level of disagreement to any of the 14 statements. These differences underscore that even when management and rank-and-file find areas of common ground, they still tend to disagree.

Of the 14 OD statements, management has a stronger level of disagreement to only 2, and these 2 statements are among the 3 statements that do not have significant mean differences. Management disagrees that it has overestimated resistance to change, while rank-and-file are neutral; and managers disagree that the staff is open-minded towards change marginally more than rank-and-file. Although not significant, taken together, the ideas that management perceives more resistance and less open-mindedness suggest that management believes their staffs are generally resistant to change initiatives.

This perception is likely to influence how managers approach leading change. A one-sample t test indicates the quotient mean is significantly higher than the assumed population mean. Accordingly, rank-and-file have a negative attitude about changes in news values. In general, respondents think they are doing what they can to preserve some traditional journalism values in an era when newspapers are more market driven.

Responses to the individual statements shed some light on specific news value issues that shape respondents' attitudes (statement means noted parenthetically). Journalists agree that newspapers are doing a better job portraying a representative picture of society than in the past, but they are neutral about whether papers are doing better at providing a truthful account of the day's events in a meaningful context than in the past.

The rank-and-file journalists do not believe that content decisions are based solely on journalism criteria, as they agree strongly that more gossip, trivia, and non-news features are used to fill the paper and recent changes in design stress style over substance to the point that look and feel of the paper are more important to editors than the depth of the news.

They have slight agreement that their newspaper has less breaking news than before change initiatives, and significant disagreement that changes in the industry have made papers more thoughtful and provocative. Journalists feel the impact of new methods and structures on their news values.

They agree focus groups, surveys, and community meetings are good methods to generate ideas for news coverage, but they acknowledge an impact of organizational integration, showing strong agreement that journalists working at papers that have eliminated divisions between news and business are more likely to engage in self-censorship when writing about issues important to advertisers.

And they disagree that change has increased resources for practicing journalism and led to more investigative reporting. This point is underscored by journalists' agreement that an important issue is less likely to become news if it takes a great deal of time to uncover and report. The respondents see journalism independence, a traditional benchmark of news values and credibility, as on the road to obsolescence. Journalists agree that the opportunity for independent-minded publishers or editors to run their own newsrooms is coming to an end and are neutral when asked whether the role models for today's managers are those editors and publishers who in the past told the truth when it was not popular or profitable to do so.

ORGANIZATIONAL STRUCTURE

The quotient for the 12 statements that construct this variable is 3.55, which a one-sample t test shows is significant to the assumed population mean. This finding suggests that journalists generally responded negatively to the impact of changing newsroom structures. When viewed individually, the statement means indicate that journalists recognize that changes in structure (the most common being from beats to teams) have impacted their work, but seldom in ways theory would predict nor management would desire.

Journalists indicate modest (but significant) agreement that they work more closely with their colleagues than in the past, but they agree much more strongly that newsroom changes have too often meant attending meetings that cut into time spent on journalism. Contrary to theory, rank-and-file don't see that restructuring the newsroom has flattened the hierarchy, disagreeing strongly that the number of layers of management has decreased. This finding is reinforced by nearly equally strong agreement that newsroom restructuring seems to require more editors who send out memos about the new goals of restructuring. The journalists in this sample are still wary of the impact of cross-departmental teams, indicating strong disagreement that directors of advertising, circulation, and marketing should participate in news planning.

Also, they do not see a connection between the team structure and better journalism, disagreeing that reorganization has helped the staff better understand readers and that work teams have improved product quality. Moreover, the rank-and-file see media executives as having different values than they do, with executives more focused on market and strategy than on the experiences of their employees; respondents also disagree strongly that structural changes place more emphasis on nonprofit goals (organizational efficiency, the latest technology, product quality, and worker autonomy and creativity) than profit goals.

VARIABLES AFFECTING MORALE

Considering the vast amount of change being implemented at newspapers in the sample and the difficulties associated with OD in general, a particular interest of this research project was to measure the impact of change initiatives on morale. Towards this end, the variables constructed to measure the three concepts common to change efforts at newspapers - OD, news values, and organizational structure - were used as independent variables in a regression model to assess their relative impact on morale.

Because OD is a broad measure of change and OD initiatives impact an organization's structure and values, it was expected that the 4 variables (OD, news values, structure, and morale) would be highly correlated. This was indeed what occurred, as the correlations were all significant at the $p < .001$ level. A colinearity test for tolerance showed these correlations did not violate the assumptions of multiple regression. A multiple regression model was then built to test:

H3: Rank-and-file perceptions of organizational development will predict morale.

To control for the demographic variables of age, ethnicity, gender, experience, and duties, these variables were entered as a block into the regression model before the three independent variables. Experience, duties ("some managerial duties" or "no managerial duties"), and age were significant predictors in the block. Together, the demographic variables accounted for 5.77 per cent of the variance.

H3 is supported. Organizational development, entered as the second block in the model, explained 45.8 per cent of the variance after controlling for demographies. OD is clearly the strongest predictor of morale among all the independent variables. Accordingly, the data indicate that as rank-and-file's attitudes towards OD become more positive their morale increases; or, as rank-and-file's attitudes towards OD become more negative their morale decreases.

After all the independent variables were entered in the regression model, OD, structure, and news values are significant predictors of morale. However, after controlling for demographics, the explained variance each variable adds differs notably. OD explains 45.8 per cent of the variance, organizational structure accounts for 7.8 per cent of the variance and news values accounts for 2.0 per cent. What is interesting is that news values, so basic to journalists' jobs and how they perceive their roles, explains a relatively small amount of the variance. Perhaps this is because in the midst of organizational changes that affect the most basic elements of work - schedules and routines - journalists continue to see the basic elements of news as information gathering, interviewing, writing, and editing.

It is logical that news values impact morale, but change initiatives that require training and re-ordering of work priorities, as well as newsroom restructuring, are tangible symbols of a new culture. Because they are the most easily identified signs of change, they are the most likely targets for acceptance or resistance. Thus, it appears that changes most affecting morale are those OD and restructuring initiatives that management believes will eventually reconstitute news. News values are changing, but the results suggest that among the types of change, rank-and-file see changing news values as having a smaller impact on their morale.

After all the variables were entered in the model, duties were also shown to be a significant predictor of morale. A dichotomous variable (0 = no managerial duties, 1 = some managerial duties), the negative beta weight indicates an inverse relationship.

In other words, journalists who have some managerial duties have significantly lower morale than those who have no managerial duties; or, those with no managerial duties have higher morale than those with some managerial duties. This result supports anecdotal evidence that change has been most difficult for low- and mid-level managers. These managers tend to get "squeezed" by change, expected to execute the change initiatives of top management while working most closely with non-managers.

Statements Not Part of Variables. The statements not part of variables also provide some useful insights. One of the research questions in this study was whether newsroom employees think the direction of change better fits the goals of journalism or marketing. As noted in the comparative results, of the 62 statements in the survey, rank-and-file's strongest agreement was with the statement: "There is more emphasis on maintaining or increasing the paper's profits than there used to be".

There was also strong agreement that newsroom managers have become increasingly aware of the concerns of stockholders and capital investors.

Respondents think this increased awareness or pressure created by financial performance does not need to be expanded, as there is significant disagreement to the statement that the newspaper industry needs a culture that requires greater marketing intelligence in the newsroom.

Taken together, these statements indicate rank-and-file journalists believe newspapers are becoming more sensitive to marketing and this movement has gone far enough.

There is also a concern about the ethical issues and threats to journalism independence that removing the wall between the news and business may initiate. There is strong agreement that ethical committees are needed to draft guidelines for editorial staff participation in promotional events and significant agreement that journalistic independence has helped establish newspapers as credible. The journalists in this sample still use journalism excellence as the standard for quality, and they like competition. Even in the era of increased profit pressures, there is significant disagreement that most newspaper companies would trade Pulitzer Prizes for consistently high profits, and, in an apparent longing for days past, respondents show strong agreement that journalism has suffered in the era of one-newspaper towns.

There is additional evidence that rank-and-file do not perceive OD as progressing in accordance with theory. Rank-and-file disagree that management has done a good job preparing employees for change, and they disagree that management has done a good job measuring the results of change. Respondents have even stronger beliefs that management is ego driven and inflexible. Rank-and-file agree that some managers have embraced formulas of change because they have invested so much money, time, and ego in them that they can't admit their lack of success. And there is a similar strong agreement to the idea that managers who have found resistance to change have responded by saying in effect, "The train is leaving the station, you can get on or get off".

Furthermore, journalists don't see change meeting its stated objectives, as they show strong agreement there is little evidence that common changes (*i.e.*, redefining of news, newsroom restructuring, and use of emerging technologies) are attracting more readers and advertisers.

The data also lend support to the idea that news managers and the growing number of consultants employed in newsrooms misunderstand journalists' resistance to change.

The journalists in this study do not see themselves as opposed to change; in fact, they show significant disagreement to the statement that they look forward to when change is no longer such a large part of work. But journalists tend to like to be left alone to do their jobs which runs counter to theory that predicts workers are happier when they collaborate and more productive in teams. The more than 450 rank-and-file in this sample significantly agree with the statement: "I am happier when I can work alone".

ANALYSIS BY CIRCULATION

Because organizational resources are determined in part by an organization's size and group dynamics can be impacted by group size, this study explored whether newspaper size (measured by circulation) impacted respondents' attitudes towards change. To test for differences by circulation, means for each variable were calculated by circulation size.

The data show that small newspapers are having more difficulty with change as it relates to two variables: OD and morale. A one-way analysis-of-variance test indicates that morale is significantly lower at small papers; also, small paper respondents indicate significantly higher disagreement that OD initiatives have been in accordance with theory. It is worth noting that the means for all four variables are higher for small papers.

These results also reveal no significant differences between mid-size and large papers. But perhaps more telling about this analysis is that there is not a positive attitude towards any of the variables at any size paper. In other words, even though some aspects of change are more difficult at small papers, these strata show that respondents do not believe change has gone well (or in accordance with theory) on any of the measures, regardless of newspaper size.

The challenge of change from the standpoint of management is getting rank-and-file to accept the core values that embody management's vision for a transformed newsroom culture. The data provide strong evidence that management's OD initiatives are failing to win rank-and-file support - regardless of whether the initiatives are in concert with theory. What is surprising in these findings is the extent to which management and rank-and-file disagree and how often. Of the 20 statements that appeared on both surveys, there are significant differences on 15 of them. Of these 15, the responses to 9 statements indicate clear differences of attitudes, with one group agreeing and the other disagreeing. Of the 14 statements that construct the OD variable, there are significant differences on responses to 11 statements. Taken as a whole, the responses show that many important divisions exist between management and rank-and-file, and even when the groups can agree, they often disagree on their level of agreement. In many instances the gap between responses is so large that it is hard to understand the two groups are sharing the same experiences, and perhaps they are not. The groups' roles in the change process differ.

The sample of newsroom managers in this study is comprised of many of the nation's leading editors. Their involvement in the ASNE Change Committee reflects their interests beyond the walls of their newsrooms, and suggests they positioned themselves as leaders in an industry-wide effort to respond to the forces mandating change.

The rank-and-file in this sample must adapt to management's vision by executing their jobs in accordance with the new procedures and goals of change. Despite these different roles, however, as part of the same organizations, management and rank-and-file should share similar values. Both groups are journalists. Management's self-assessment may be a bit optimistic, but it is grounded in reality and is at times unflatteringly candid. Managers have a great deal invested in change initiatives, both in terms of organizational resources and their individual careers.

A role of management is to "see the big picture," which suggests that management should be able to assess the process and progress of change within its overall strategic goals better than rank-and-file.

Thus, management's general optimism regarding change may be a reflection that the broader process is proceeding in the right direction, even if certain aspects tend to get off course. The data support this. Management gives itself high marks for leadership and generally following the prescriptions for change articulated in OD models and theory. Management views itself as trying to do what should be done to enable change to succeed.

Yet, as Kanter suggests, change requires a "leap of faith" to get people to embrace an organizational reality that is not yet known. And on this issue, the data show management to be quite honest, admitting the entire change formula has not been worked out. Even more candid, however, is management's admission that certain parts of the process that it can control have not been well-managed. Management concedes that it has not adequately thought through the long-term implications of change, and it acknowledges there is not a system of rewards for work that meets the goals of change initiatives.

Accordingly, it is not surprising that management recognizes that its short-comings have contributed to a breakdown of trust with rank-and-file, while at the same time perceiving a cultural change that has improved the organization. This apparent contradiction must be perplexing and difficult for newsroom managers. There is some evidence in the data that managers are a bit frustrated, placing the "blame" for a lack of success on rank-and-file, who are perceived as close minded and resistant to change.

However, the results from the rank-and-file survey suggest it is not accurate to simply dismiss journalists as resistant to change. Rank-and-file indicate they accept change as a part of work and are personally committed to their paper's change efforts. They credit their managers for taking leadership roles and being committed to change. However, they question the factors motivating change and are able to distinguish between intentions and results. In brief, while management says it has articulated a vision, included employees in creating changes, been flexible, and sought feedback about the change process, rank-and-file respond that they are confused about the vision, fool loft out of the process, and perceive their managers as inflexible.

Rank-and-file also sense management's vulnerability and frustration in leading change, showing strong agreement that change is ego driven by inflexible managers who, refusing to recognize its lack of success, resort to authoritarian measures to counter pockets of resistance. Rank-and-file's perception that management has failed at nearly every step of the process, combined with their sense that profit is increasingly important to newsroom managers, further explains the low level of trust rank-and-file express towards their managers. Numerous scholars cite trust as a prerequisite condition for successful OD initiatives. Thus, despite management's general optimism about an improving newsroom culture, the breakdown of trust that both management and rank-and-file acknowledge does not bode well for continuing efforts at change, as theory suggests and common sense reveals that people do not readily accept the ideas of those whom they do not trust.

Beyond the organizational development issues associated with change, rank-and-file's skepticism about change can be understood by an apparent lack of producing successful results. Change initiatives are not only failing to create more efficient, productive, and happier newsrooms, they are also falling short on their stated goals. Journalists don't perceive changes as attracting more readers and advertisers, or helping to produce better newspapers. Instead, rank-and-file connect change initiatives with fewer resources for journalism in a more market-driven culture and industry.

Kanter, Drucker, Bergquist, and many organizational scholars would suggest that "breaking down the wall" between the newsroom and other departments in the news organization is an important step towards creating the "integrated" and "innovative" organizational culture required to meet challenges swiftly and capitalize on opportunities in the postmodern business world. The data in this study suggest that rank-and-file perceive the new, integrated culture as a threat to their values, most of which are rooted in journalism.

Much of rank-and-file's resistance to change is related to a sense that the "journalism-based" culture of their newsrooms is being replaced with a culture that places less value on journalism norms. In this way, there is a cultural "battle" unfolding in news organizations as they become more integrated.

Harris, writing about the clash that occurs when an organization attempts to create a market-oriented culture, asserts that the market-oriented values that define the culture must come to dominate the existing cultures for the transformation to succeed.

This study indicates that this type of cultural struggle is being waged in newsrooms experimenting with change. When viewed in this regard, resistance to change can be understood as both rational and part of a cultural conflict. However, if cultural change is achieved through a combination of macro (values and beliefs) and micro forces (the tangible things such as practices, policies, and procedures that define daily life in the organization), then management's attempt to change the newsroom culture by changing the organization's structure and work routines appears to be well-advised and well under way.

This study also opens for re-examination several theoretical assumptions. The idea that modern newspaper organizations are characterized by complex, hierarchical bureaucracies and specialized labour appears to be less accurate today than it was before "change" became an industry buzzword and organizational goal. Media corporations, no doubt large bureaucracies, can however be understood to be "disassembling the assembly line." The goals of OD and change most often focus on creating flatter corporate flowcharts with the expectation that employees need to be more versatile and multiskilled.

Clearly, this is the opposite of labour specialization. Furthermore, the empowerment assumptions of restructuring hierarchical organizations into flatter, team-based units have not materialized for the rank-and-file journalists in this sample. Rank-and-file understand restructuring as a mechanism that affords them fewer resources to practice journalism, and, contrary to theory, rank-and-file perceive restructuring has created more layers of managers and a more "managed" newsroom. The journalists in this sample say that the team-based structure has not brought them more autonomy, nor has it provided more decision-making authority.

It is possible that the empowerment expected to result from restructured newsrooms is misconceived. A primary rationale for less hierarchical organizations is the team-based structure unleashes the knowledge and creativity of lower level employees. This view presupposes that management, under the hierarchical structure, has not previously afforded employees the power to effectively utilize these assets. However, this assumption seems to neglect the nature of newspaper work, which has traditionally afforded rank-and-file a great deal of latitude, encouraging journalists to apply their knowledge and be creative. Long before empowerment became a management cliche, Gassaway's 1984 social construction work found that rank-and-file journalists and newspaper managers negotiate for power, with rank-and-file having considerable leverage, because as newsgatherers they control the initial flow of information. Furthermore, journalism is one of the few occupations where employees at the bottom of the corporate ladder consider themselves professionals. Valuable newsroom employees have long been those who could work well on their own, digging for stories and building relationships with sources. Interviewing is a craft, writing and design are forms of self-expression, and editing is a skill built on an individual's grasp of language and professional values. To require journalists to give up the individual nature of their work asks them to sacrifice some of the skills that have become a part of their professional identities. There is strong evidence in this study that journalists have not accepted the idea that team-based newsrooms empower them or better utilize their skills.

This finding supports previous research and reinforces the idea that the organizational theory that managers are using to empower their employees and restructure their newsrooms could be misapplied, as it misunderstands the nature of newspaper journalism work. The assumptions about the organizational role of management are changing, too. This study finds little support that newsroom managers are "technocrats" who value organizational and technical development more than the profit goals of their "capitalist" owners. The data indicate it is more accurate, as Kanter and others suggest, to understand change as a process of integration, where the marketing goals of the traditional "business side" of the news organization have become more apparent to journalists and more valued by management throughout the organization. Galbraith's "approved contradiction" concept - that innovative managers will focus on professional and organizational goals while returning just enough profit to keep their capitalist owners satisfied - is a core assumption of Demers'research on the corporate newspaper. This study found little support for the existence of an approved contradiction; rather, managers and rank-and-file perceive change as both market and profit driven at the expense of organizational issues thought to be of prime concern to professional managers (product quality, technology, and employee development).

These findings suggest that modern news executives are no longer "technocrats" in the sense Galbraith defined them, but are closer to the "capitalists" who sought maximum financial return on their investments. The practice of offering newsroom managers incentives (salary bonuses or stock options) tied to the financial performance of the company is one way corporations subtly "disapprove" of the approved contradiction.

LIMITATIONS OF THE STUDY

An obvious shortcoming of this survey method is that it can only provide a "snapshot" of attitudes at the time of the study. Change is an ongoing process, and the instruments used can only provide a one-time glimpso of the process. As the change process unfolds in newsrooms across the country, it would be wise to continue to monitor change initiatives and journalists' attitudes towards them. Also, this study did not attempt to measure the amount of change orthe phases of the change process. Thus, while all the respondents have a commonality of change experiences, it is not clear if attitudes towards change differ based on the amount of change or stages in the change process.

There is also a chance to refine the instruments and measures of change used in this study. Organizational development research has generally focused on one organization at a time, using site-specific variables. By taking a different approach, there were very few established measures. Accordingly, the attempt here was to create "tools" from which scholars can begin to empirically assess change. Suggestions for future research. The findings in this study point to several theoretical areas that should prove fertile ground for exploration. This study adds to the small amount ol research thai suggests restructuring newsrooms into team-based systems does not "empower" journalists in the manner theory predicts. If team-based newsrooms are the future of the industry, then changing organizational relationships spawned by restructuring offer interesting opportunities for study. Among some of the questions these changes suggest: Do team-based structures impact the ways journalists work with one another? Do teams impact the ways journalists develop relationships and interact with their sources?

Do teams require and reward different personality traits? How does the resourceful journalist, the "gumshoe" who worked well alone, often producing front page stories in the beat system, perform in the team structure?

Do team-based newsrooms produce different content than the beat system does? And possibly most important to understanding the values that will drive the industry in the future are the questions of management influence and power. Do newsroom managers and editors see themselves as the innovative "technocrats" that theory presupposes?

How much influence do newsroom managers have when it comes to setting the vision for change? To what extent do newsroom managers embrace the changes they are expected to lead? These questions, along with the need to develop better change-related measures over time (throughout the process of change], provide an abundance of directions for research.

This study surveyed a purposive sample of the nation's newspaper managers most experienced in industry-wide change initiatives; it also surveyed a much larger sample of rank-and-file from those same papers. The managers in this study have, in effect, used their newsrooms as laboratories to experiment with new and far-reaching change initiatives. These changes have become - depending on whom you ask - new standards of excellence or points of controversy and resistance. Although the results from this purposive sample cannot be generalized to the entire industry, the relatively large sample gives a good indication of what change has meant to journalists at newspapers on the cutting edge of industry-wide change. These findings should prove useful for the many news managers and editors who find their newsrooms embarking on or considering similar change initiatives. This study has also tested the key concepts of organizational development, making it one of only a few attempts to understand the complexities of newspaper industry change through the lens of organizational theory.

Given the size of the sample and the scope of the newspapers (circulations ranging from 5,000 to more than 1,000,000, including public, private, and family-owned papers that are located in every major geographic region of the country), this study represents one of the largest scale attempts to date to assess journalists' perceptions about change initiatives that are sweeping through newsrooms nationwide. Management, despite some res- ervations about the market-driven nature of change, thinks it is doing reasonably well following the guidelines of organizational development in a manner consistent with creating a more outer-directed and reader-driven newsroom culture. In short, management believes it has "managed" the change process in general accordance with theory.

Rank-and-file, on the other hand, feel more victims of change than participants in it. The gulf between management and rank-and-file experiences with change has facilitated a breakdown in trust that could seriously hamper ongoing change initiatives. Morale among rank-and-file is low, and data suggest it is getting worse. The newspaper industry finds itself in the throes of a cultural revolution precipitated by internal and external forces. Yet, the industry remains highly profitable and has shown resiliency in the information age, remaining a respected and widely utilized source of news and information. The predictions of doom are far from materializing, but many of the challenges that served as catalysts for cultural change remain. The findings of this study suggest there is a struggle unfolding between the core values of two cultures - marketing and journalism - and rank-and-file perceive organizational development efforts are focused on creating a more dominant marketing culture, often at the expense of journalistic norms.

This study has extended previous change research by approaching the problem differently. Organizational research has seldom been conducted on more than one organization at a time, and its methods are usually qualitative. The constructs in this study held up quite well to tests of reliability and statistical analysis, showing the depth of common experiences of journalists at newspapers implementing change. An important methodological finding of this study is that change can be studied at more than one newspaper at a time. Studies that go beyond site-specific variables are possible, which should encourage more research using larger, representative samples with the goal of testing and building theory.

7

Television News Texts in Journalism

While researchers have paid increasing attention to the study of global news in recent years, relatively little attention has been paid to two aspects of this process. First, studies of television news have focused on issues of news flows or news agendas but have not explored the "meanings" television news reproduces on a global level. Second, the sense that global audiences make of television news (*i.e.* the commonalities of news reception across countries) has not been studied.

In studies of global news agendas or flows the emphasis has been on quantifying news coverage and balance. In contrast, the aims of this project are on qualitative issues of how news events become narratives and how audiences relate to these narrative frames.

The analysis presented here is drawn from a study of television news texts and audience reception in four countries (Britain, Germany, France, and the United States). Two cases of political conflict—rioting by South Korean students and a politically motivated massacre of train passengers in South Africa—were covered by individual stations in each of those countries (The German stories aired on ZDF, the French on A2N, the British on ITN and BBC and the American stories on ABC).

These broadcasts were shown to six focus groups in each of those countries. Each country's audience was shown the version of the story broadcast in their country. "Political conflict" stories were chosen, because they are staples of foreign television news coverage. At the level of texts, our reading was informed by narrative theory which sees news as "purposive storytelling", functioning to present a "particular symbolic universe, a relatively stable and recognizable 'world of television news,' that is self contained and coherent" with recurrent patterns and themes of coverage or what Gurevitch, Levy and Roeh term, the "stability of narrative forms".

Specific to the representation of political conflict, we drew on the work of Dahlgren and Chakrapani who suggest that television news coverage is usually critical of violence against the state and has a proclivity for using violence-in-itself as sufficient explanation for events.

Their argument overall is that western foreign news is dominated by discourses such as social and political violence, governmental corruption, natural disasters and cultural traits such as primitivism and barbarism. Such a focus, they argue, provides for an implied bi-polar opposite, such as order and stability, ethical government, modernism and high civilization as attributes of the self.

At the level of audience analysis, we drew on the qualitative reception analysis tradition, working with its central assumption that watching television is a persistent social practice through which audiences carry out considerable rhetorical, political and cultural work. The specific work that foreign news performs is the perpetuation of certain "ways of seeing" and the imaging of cultural others.

Two research questions informed the study. These were:

How does television news portray foreign events (What is its narrative construction of the outside world)? Specific to stories on "political conflict", what vision of cultural "others" becomes narrative? How do audiences make sense of foreign news on television? What patterns of mediation of the narratives on political conflict emerge as constructed by television news?

Method News broadcasts in the four countries were taped during September and October 1990 and in February and June 1987. Narrative analysis of the news broadcasts focused on a range of features. These included verbal features such as lexicon, syntax, metaphors and mythic phrases. Visual features included type of shot (closeup, wide), content, sequencing, graphics, etc.

From close analysis of the features identified, summary statements or themes were abstracted. For details of thematic and narrative analysis as a method. The comparative analysis followed the initial thematic analysis for each country. The next step was to identify the commonalities of these themes across stations to develop a comparative chart of themes. In fall of 1990, six focus groups were conducted in each country (9-12 people per group).

The six focus groups were made up of individuals from different occupations (school teachers, bank clerks, sales people, factory people). The aim was to have representatives from different income levels. Groups were recruited by academic institutions in each country. The method of recruitment in France, Germany and Britain was through the snowball sampling method. People known to the investigator(s) in each occupation were contacted; they, in turn, contacted other members (and so on).

Participants were recruited from the town or city in which the academic institution was located. The audience was not segmented by age, race, gender or other demographic features. In the United States, respondents were recruited through random telephone calls in the Prince Georges and Montgomery Counties of Maryland. Participants in the United States were paid twenty five dollars to participate in the study. No incentive payment was made in the other countries.

The study was not designed to produce any social scientific measures and to echo Leibes, "one cannot make claims of formal randomness or representativeness, but, on the other hand there is no reason to suspect any systematic bias." Given the complexity and difficulty of comparative work, focus groups can represent a useful sample, but cannot represent the diversity of a "nation."

Focus group transcripts were analyzed for issues of variation across countries and power (the extent to which the audience reiterated the discursive features of the text).

Each question by the moderator was followed by discussion. A transcript was divided into discussion segments. Summary statements were written for each discussion segment. These statements were used as the basis for identifying modes of interpretation comprising audience mediation.

Each focus group began with viewing of the news story aired in that country. The audience was asked to retell the story in their own words. This was followed by questions about media coverage and content, including the dominant themes identified by the researchers.

Korean Unrest: Thematic Analysis. Across the four news stations, three dominant themes were identified: "A violent world," "The fight for democracy," and "endangered Olympics."

All four stations used footage provided by Eurovision of rioting students who attacked/chased policemen and of policemen who attacked/chased students while tear gas bombs burst amidst scenes of general pandemonium. This compelling (and commonplace) footage provided part of the basis for the thematic frame of "a violent world." To give details from one story (ZDF) the following visuals were shown: students throwing stones and running; pushing against a police picket line; police pushing against the students with their shields; students running pell-mell, covering their faces from the tear gas; students protesting, pumping fists and marching in a demonstration. In addition to these visuals, the A2N story showed a confrontation between an armored car spewing tear gas and students who had attacked it.

The students were shown running around the vehicle hitting it with rods but eventually retreating. Supplanting these images of an violent out of control world was the reporters copy which used words such as "a sea of tears" and "a strip of gas fumes." The ABC and BBC story developed the theme of a violent world, but framed it within the context of the students' democratic struggle. In other words, the violence was particularized within a specific narrative and thematic frame ("the fight for democracy"). Overall, both stories presented a liberal/democratic perspective on events, and through their rhetoric legitimized the students (and others) as agents of a democratic revolution.

The ABC story began with rioting students being tear gassed and chased by policemen wearing gas masks and brandishing batons. This was followed by an account of the day's events, in which students who had been holed up in a cathedral were allowed to go without harm by authorities. Their departure in buses waving flags and fists, was followed by a night-time candle light procession.

Ted Koppel's lead-in said that the government's attempts at controlling student "protests for democratic reform" was not having much of an impact, and that the movement had begun "spreading." The story thus began with the theme of democratic revolution, which then became its governing principle.

Reporter Jim Laurie reinforced the positive nature of the students protest with the assertion that "even the state controlled Korean news agency admitted that 80,000 students took part in anti-government rallies nationwide." The implication was clear: the political strife was of such a magnitude that even the official state controlled news agency—presumably given to lying—had to concede to the sheer magnitude of the protests. While the students were one of the revolution's primary protagonists, the text focused on other protagonists in the on-going performance: the "wide cross section of the Korean population... clergy, middle class office workers, the old and the young."

A performance needs a setting, and in the ABC story the establishment of protagonists was intertwined with two scene setting events—the student hold-out at the church and then a candle light demonstration.

The "impressive candle light rally attracting some 10,000 people," Laurie said, constituted a "growing movement for greater democracy in Korea."

While all the ingredients were there for a revolution, it was evident that this was an early moment. Much depended on how the other protagonist in this performance—the government—acted its role. The government, Laurie said, had not only allowed the rioting students to go (from the Catholic church) but now was realizing the "extent of these protests and the depth of support that has developed in six days."

Still, the government was not expected to quietly accept the inevitable, and much depended on its next move—a choice between "drastic emergency measures or a new plan of political reform." Either way it was clear that the audience was in for a sequel that could follow one of two options—continued struggle, or a victory for the students. The story told us the revolution would continue. The BBC story, in similar fashion, began with the frame of "a violent world" and then contextualized it with the notion of "the fight for democracy." The reporter said the "students, whose support is growing, are demanding democratic election."

The justification for those elections was then set in terms of conflict with a focus on the third theme (endangered Olympics): "President Chun says that they will have to wait until after South Korea stages next year's Olympic games. But the protestors say democracy first and Olympics later." Overall, the story framed the students as the "conscience of the nation" and the fate of their democratic revolution as a "struggle (which) cannot stop until the present government is swept away."

South Africa train violence story: thematic analysis. Only two themes were present—"A barbaric world" and "a political struggle."

However, the dominant theme across all countries was "a barbaric world." It was a visually driven story and reiterated images of a violent world "out there," in even more emphatic terms than the KU story. If violence in the KU story was contextualized through issues of democracy and the Olympics, the SATV story presented the train killings with little context.

In the ABC story, all but one of the frames displayed pictures of the dead and dying. Scattered in stark poses of death, the victims—all Black men and women—lay in pools of blood. Harsh police lights and the hard gray floor emphasized the grotesque. A close up of a woman huddled in death was followed by shots of her shoes and handbag.

The rush and noise of ambulances and the revolving lights of police cars punctuated the darkness of the night beyond the railstation. The camera focused and lingered on each body, zooming in to show details of bloody faces, shot up bodies and agonizing survivors. The natural soundman eerie silence punctuated with the whine of police sirens—was interrupted only by the comments of one bystander and one relief official.

The platform scene framed both as they spoke. Visually, the narrative did not move outside the violence of the platform and the pictures of the dead, except for an insert of Nelson Mandela speaking to reporters. Little context or background material was offered, only one line by the reporter ("the violence has been blamed on a power struggle") and by a Mandela sound-bite("The government could have stopped this if they wanted to").

The reporter's closing emphasized the story's dominant theme: "After tonight's slaughter of helpless commuters, the cycle of violence seems to have been raised to an even more vicious level."

In the British story, the violence was framed as a "rampage." The station was described as a "battlefield" where the commuters had been "butchered indiscriminantly." Following sound-bites from onlookers describing the killings, the reporter developed the secondary theme (*i.e.* political struggle) and said that "the carnage represented a frightening escalation in a month long war between the African National Congress and the Inkatha."

As with the American story, the reporter ended with promises of more to come:The conflict is now threatening to engulf the disenfranchised black community and undermine attempts to negotiate a new democratic society. The most ominous aspect of this indiscriminate slaughter is that after several weeks of bloodshed, South Africa's township war seems to be spilling over into the cities. The German and French stories showed similar dependence on the theme of "a barbaric world" with little contextualization provided for the violence. The German story used terms such as "a bloody attack" and "bloodiest massacres." The station "seemed like a morgue as fear spread around South Africa." The event was described in a tense dramatic style: unidentified men attacked travelers with rifles, knives and axes, the attackers butchered whoever came near them without saying a word, without regard for women and children. A senseless blood bath.

The second theme was developed with excerpts from a press conference given by Mandela. The reporter summarized Mandela's views about government interference and his comparison of the violence to the Renamo movement in Mozambique (a South African supported insurgency aimed at toppling the Marxist government). The French story began with Mandela's response to the attack. In other words, the theme of "a political struggle" was in foreground, but the story focus remained on "a barbaric world" with extensive use of visuals of the platform with the dead and injured. Audience Mediations.

How did audiences respond to these stories? The major finding is the sweeping similarities of the critical or "reflexive" treatment of the news stories. Audiences across these countries showed similar trends of media criticism.

Their criticisms were

- Criticism of the discursive content
- Criticism of textual strategy
- Criticism of institutional principles (of journalism).

Criticism of discursive content. The two dominant themes in the Korean unrest story ("A violent world" and "the fight for democracy") and the dominant theme in the SATV train violence ("A barbaric world") were critically reviewed by respondents. For purposes of brevity, groups are identified by initials (for example, the British Focus Group number 1 is referred to as BFG1).

Stories with such themes are unclear, repetitive and largely negative of the "other world.' Respondents discussed the theme of "a violent world" in the KU story and focused on how such stories are stereotypical of reporting on international issues.

One respondent said "they were a type that we've all seen over and over again" (BFG3). Another respondent pointed out that such coverage "always (looks) the same, only that the policemen are wearing different uniforms in different countries" (GFG2). A third respondent elaborated:

What I don't like about reports from abroad, in general, is that you always see some bloody faces, some policemen hitting somebody and vice versa. This could really be skipped. It's enough to mention that there are violent conflicts and then to report some background information, facts, numbers (GFG1).

In discussing the theme of "the fight for democracy," respondents said that such coverage is unclear and repetitive. One respondent said "you never hear why they were rioting and only they want democracy" (AFG3) while another participant, referring to repetitiveness said

In any political demonstration, average or big, they are the same images. These same scenes are filmed, no matter what event, whether it's the Middle East, in Seoul or in Africa, because they are the same demonstrations (FGF3).

In discussions of "a barbaric world" in the SATV train violence story, one respondent pointed out how such stories are "so confusing that you hardly know who is doing what. The reasons given are very confusing" (BFG1). Making a similar point, another respondent said, "It didn't quite become clear to me who was actually fighting against whom.

It also didn't become clear why they're fighting each other and what their demands are" (GFG5). Another respondent asserted that such an event would have been covered differently if it had been local: "They show us that everything is barbaric and wild. If this was in France, they wouldn't have treated the information like that" (FFG4).

Stories with these themes provide little context to events. Respondents also focused on the differences between local and international coverage when discussing the low level of context in foreign news. In discussing the theme of "a violent world," one respondent pointed out that if:

A fight is happening in Bordeaux or Marseilles, you will know that there is a political party on one side and the policeman on the other-that people are fighting for such a reason. Here they are beating up on each other and no one knows who is having a go at who. We don't know why it happened. One has a right to know the reason why (FFG1).

In discussing the theme of "the fight for democracy" another respondent said, "1 think two big distinctions between that and the China news report (reports on the Tiananmen Square massacre) was that they actually went to the students and interviewed them. They asked them, 'Why are you actually doing this?' Not just masses of kids, running around throwing bombs at the army or whatever. You got the overall picture given by the reporter. You got government reaction" (BFG1). In focusing on the SATV story theme of "a barbaric world" respondents emphasized the effects of using violence without a context to understand it. One example:

It's about violence. I can't exactly say why there are such problems. I only understand that this violence is for nothing. This reporting is unbearable. They are sensationalistic and do it in order to make people watch. It's a kind of absolute violence (FFG4).

The impact of such stories is problematic. In addition to criticizing the themes in terms of context and repetitiveness, respondents discussed how such stories may have an impact on viewers in some specific ways. The discussion focused on what was termed the "emotional" impact (where audiences felt the stories played on emotions rather than providing information); the "voyeuristic" impact (where audiences viewed violence as entertainment rather than as shocking); the "affirmation" impact (where audiences said such stories allow for a continuation of the negative image of the "other" and a positive image of the "self") and the "political" impact (where audiences said the news item favoured one side of the conflict).

Emotional: One respondent criticized the theme of "a violent world" in the KU story and said that "it played on emotions. It started off with anger and guys kicking at the police and that sort of thing and then you went to a more sympathetic side and seeing them calmly walking around with a candle. It played on show biz by getting your emotions involved". Another respondent said that, by emphasizing the emotional elements, the story remained "very blurred...we see people who fight and scuffle, but what remains? What have we retained? We retained that there was a crowd who fought against the army, against the police, and we retain the gas masks and the emotional side of the issue, but the emotion passes, and things remains distorted".

Voyeuristic: Respondents repeatedly emphasized that excessive violence on television news numbed them to the reality of violence and made it entertaining. One respondent in discussing the KU story said, "By watching these pictures we feel voyeuristic. We are pleased with the violent images, with all these problems which are someone else's, no like natural disorder".

Another respondent, discussing the SATV story, said that having little context for such violence allows for not taking it seriously:

It's shocking because it's violent...but one can switch from violent pictures to the exhibition room or to a fashion parade or something frivolous, and we could unscrupulously switch from one to another, from something serious to something very light. It makes you angry to see things like this, and you understand nothing. You're shocked and then two minutes after, you forget it.

Affirmation: Respondents discussed how such a story would have been covered in their own country (as evident in some of the other examples). Beyond issues of coverage, respondents criticized how such stories were aimed at a sense of self affirmation. As one respondent put it, "we feel good when we see all these events" (FFG2). Another respondent said that:

those German citizens sitting in front of the TV with a bottle of beer in their hands. They don't get upset about these things, they don't mind them at all. And you know why—because they are in a better situation (GFG3).

Political: Respondents said the political impact of such stories was that it framed the actors within each story positively or negatively. In the KU story context, the discussion focused on how democracy was foregrounded. In the SATV story, the issue was how the story constructed Black South Africans and their struggle against apartheid. Two examples:

Well, to me, it tells us that the ANC and the Inkatha are fighting between each other, and, since it doesn't specify the White South Africans part in it, it makes us think, goodness, if these people are going to get independence and they're going to get to vote, it's going to be an absolute bloodbath. It's going to be really horrendous in South Africa. It totally makes no sense. There are more than twenty dead people. The reasons—we don't know—it's totally crazy. The message that is probably being transmitted is that in South Africa when the Blacks recover all their rights, and when the whites will no longer have the upper hand, there will still be problems as there always will be this inter-ethnic conflict. Instead of fighting between Blacks and Whites, the Blacks will fight between themselves.

CRITICISM OF TEXTUAL STRATEGY

In addition to the general critique of news story content, respondents across the four countries focused on specific textual features in the news stories. Criticism of the news stories' structures focused on issues of framing (discussion of a story's key verbal and visual elements) and perspective (discussion of how television news itself is a construction of events rather than an objective report). Framing.

Respondent discussion of verbal elements focused on lexical and syntactic features within different stories. Words/sentences such as "Fear is haunting South Africa" (German SATV story), "Olympics" and "Berlin as a substitute site" (German KU story), "river of tears" (French KU story), "growing movement for greater democracy" (American KU story), "Black on Black violence" (American SATV story)," "democracy," "violence" (across both stories and all countries) were critically reviewed. The discussion of these choices was interlaced with criticism of the discursive features outlined above.

Respondents in all of the countries discussed the closeups of the killings in the SATV story and the police/student violence in the KU story. One example from the KU story:

I mean, basically what we saw was that there were some lovely pictures—of tear gas monsters, guys dressed in the paramilitary outfits with helmets and shields and clubs. You know, it looked like an ominous confrontational type situation...which makes for great pictures (AFG3).

PERSPECTIVE

In discussing how television news is a construction of events rather than a report of these, respondents focused on specific issues of coverage (as identified in issues of framing and discursive content) but also raised more general issues about representability and accuracy. Three examples:

Television news is like an iceberg, they only show us a little part, and I always ask myself what they haven't shown us. Behind these images, we could only imagine what they did not show us (FFG1). I mean what I find is that, as I keep seeing this, [it] makes me think more about what I see on television. I mean, how close to any truth, is this bulletin? You don't know about what other footage there was or what other people could have been interviewed or how many people refused to be interviewed (AFG5). I really don't know if the events follow each other or not. I don't know right now. I hesitate, you know. News is not reliable. You don't know what to believe, because you see it once one way and another time another way. You face a dilemma (GFG3).

CRITICISM OF INSTITUTIONAL PRINCIPLES

In addition to the discursive and text based criticisms above, respondents used the stories to raise questions about the rules governing journalism as a profession. The main criticism was the news value accorded to violence. Respondents said repeatedly that television has too much violence and too little concern for the victims of violence. Some examples:... blood, blood. If there is blood, then it is good.

This is a characteristic sample of broadcasts from abroad. A lot of disasters, a lot of wars (GFG4). The news shown on TV. It's all gloom and doom. Very rarely do they show real news which is not gloom and doom. Some things are interesting which not necessarily violent (AFG3) are.

They have no inhibitions about filming directly into their open wounds or to interview the woman mourning for her shot husband five minutes ago with the camera ten millimeters from her face, asking if she is still sad (BFG2). When someone is gunned down, murdered, victimized give them a little bit of dignity. Don't flash them on the screen (AFG4).

Television News narrativization of foreign events: Different stations use similar themes that represent the "other" world as a violent, unstable world. The violence the stories suggested threatens democracy and peace in South Korea and tears at the social fabric (and implicitly the political process) of South Africa. While some differences emerge in how each event was narrativized by the different stations, the sweeping similarities stood out.

In the KU story, the "violent world" theme presented the "other" world as an essentially unstable world, one that was unknowable outside from the violence that seemed to be inherent in it. Violence here was not political; politics was violence. Once riots, tear gas, destructive demonstrations, fights between protestors and policemen become staples of foreign news coverage, they do not require any special reflection on the viewers, only the retrieval of standard images and frames. The second theme—a democratic revolution—raised a different set of issues. Dahlgren and Chakrapani have argued that there is an unspoken but organic value in Western democratic societies that violence is defensible only when employed by the state. However, one can argue that there is an exception to this rule.

Violence deployed as part of a process of political change towards a Western style democratic system is often regarded as legitimate. The violence within this frame, as seen in the actions of Korean students, is portrayed as part of a process towards democracy.

In the SATV story, not only was the violence not contextualized in political or historical terms, it seemed to suggest that it needed no explanation. Violence as a frame for the violent act became a tautology—a violent act occurred, because there was violence.

Foreground explained background, which in turn explained foreground. The perpetrators of such an act can be explained in terms of their acts: as violent, brutal beings living in a violent, brutal world.

The effects of television news discourse we suggest is discursive, *i.e.* the news the narrative constructs in each country draws on frameworks common in each country. But the news also display cross-cultural, global trends. These cross-cultural trends provide a narrow and negative construction of the "other."

This observation takes on additional significance when we realise that television news is the primary provider of international news and hence the most frequent and recurrent provider of cultural material from which audiences shape their perception of the "other." Television news can be seen to function inter-culturally, presenting and re-presenting every night the other and the self. Audience Mediation of foreign news: In the stories examined here, three major trends of news criticism were evident—of discursive content, textual strategy, and institutional rules. In each case, what stood out was the detailed critical attention audiences gave to issues of encoding and of purposiveness. Part of the political and cultural work that television news audiences perform is reflexive, re-articulating the terms of the news texts through a specific set of analytical practices.

If television news does function discursively at a global level, it is clear that audiences have become sensitive mediators of such texts. The second global trend in television news is the emergence of a global culture of critical media consumption. This critical mode is born of a familiarity with the narrative conventions of the genre; an awareness of the institutional imperatives of the media industries and, more generally, the cultural, political and ideological contexts of media coverage.

A final issue is related to the normative sense of "a global village" (sustaining the popular vision of globalization). The globalization of television news agendas has not created "global villagers" but has built cultural identities in ways that perpetuate historical and contemporary power relationships. The "other" remains an underprivileged area—where violence and death remain the norm even it strives for the values of the West.

It is equally clear that audiences living in an age of mass information watch news critically, filtering and rationalizing modes of representation even as they make judgements about the news' discursive content.

The most prominent and notorious West German underground left wing terrorist organization from the 1970s, the Red Army Faction (RAF) continues to be a source of entertainment, in pop culture, documentary films, docudramas, (auto)biographies, and fiction. The fashion and film industries, as well as the book market, profit from the particular aura that surrounds the radical activism of the 1970s. While popular accounts often narrate the events of the "German Autumn" as a polit-thriller or crime novel, the fact that they are told from different perspectives, by ex-activists, ex-terrorists, or conservative politicians, results in ambiguous fictions of the drama of "state versus the terrorists."

Instead of simply discounting these pop obsessions as part of a capitalist marketing strategy or criticizing them as depoliticizing and popularizing what once was a deeply political and historically specific project, this chapter understands these fictionalizations as part of an attempt to create meaning out of events that continue to be unsettling and disturbing.

To examine aspects of this ongoing interest in "the story of the RAF" the following media analyses trace the frantic reaction of the 1970s into the next decade: How did media discourses transform; how did fears shift; and how were the actors in the drama recast? Which aspects of "the drama" continue to be unsettling? Histories of German left wing terrorism often begin with the year 1968 and end abruptly with the end of the year 1977. Cultural histories describe the following decade of the 1980s as characterized by a political "backlash" and a new stage in global capitalism—a decade that is simultaneously conservative and postmodern; exciting and boring.

By searching for the connections between the events of the fall of 1977 and the cultural and political developments of the 1980s, the reactions to and the obsessions with left wing terrorism become visible as part of the complex process of re-imaginations and reinterpretations of space and identification in the aftermath of global social change.

These perceptions enticed Chancellor Helmut Schmidt to proclaim in January 1980: "the whole world is in uproar." This sense of instability and change, extending well beyond the borders of the nation state, contributes to the continued fascination with the story of the RAF today.

After introducing the theoretical framework for the media analyses and presenting a brief summary of the events leading up to the German Autumn, this chapter offers a close analysis of media responses in major German newspapers and political magazines in the months following these violent and confusing political developments.

The second portion compares these responses to reports in the same media sources in January 1980 that look back at the 1970s and make prognoses for the next decade. This analysis will not offer another version of what happened, but rather an attempt to theorize the effects of the German Autumn on concepts of security, stability, and order at the beginning of the 1980s.

The anxieties that crystallized around the issue of left wing terrorism and the state's response to terrorism served as a catalyst for fears of global change that threatened the stability and identity of the West German nation state in the late 1970s and into the 1980s. At the beginning of the 1980s, media articulate these fears in increasingly vague and generalized terms—the global situation is "out of control." The following analysis shows further, however, that in mainstream West German media this discourse of fear, loss of national control, and global instability remains highly ambivalent.

CHANGING POLITICAL LANDSCAPES

Historian Wolfgang Kraushaar has pointed to some of the most significant gaps in RAF research that surfaced in the discussions about the planned RAF exhibition in 2005 at the Kunst-Werke in Berlin.

The controversies about the exhibition showed "the lacking emotional distance on the parts of politics and society to be able to engage with a now three decades-old challenge to the democratic society.

The Federal Republic is far from having coped with the conflicts of the 1970s; an exceedingly neurotic reaction apparently remains dominant." Likewise, the writer Friedrich Christian Delius suggests that with the increasing historical distance to the events, Germans are starting to re-evaluate this "dynamic of fear" and draw attention to "a pathological addiction to or search for the enemy and the origin of the violence" that was indicative of the time.

These "pathological addictions" and "neurotic reactions" relate directly to questions of law. Post-Lacanian theorist Renata Salecl understands the neurotic as someone who "has doubts about the consistency of the law," while at the same time feeling guilty before the law. In the context of the panicked reactions to left wing terrorism in West Germany in the late 1970s and in the attempts to write its history, the neurotic is connected to questions of "law" on various levels.

The 1972 Radikalenerlass, the decree against radicals, implemented new policies permitting stricter controls for state officials and teachers and allowed for more invasive surveillance techniques.

Specific laws that were passed during the trials and the imprisonment of RAF terrorists in the mid 1970s, the so-called Baader-Meinhof Gesetze, allowed the trials to be held in the absence of the defendant and to restrict even further communication between lawyers and their clients.

Moreover, it is no coincidence that the Notstandsgesetze (Emergency Laws), which fueled protests in the mid 1960s were passed in 1968. These laws permitted the government to make quick decisions without consulting the parliament in case of a national disaster. The West German Basic Law, heavily influenced by the Western Allies after World War II, had not granted the West German state that particular right.

The Allied forces had taken this measure to prevent another "Hitler" from rising to power, since it was well known that Hitler, as soon as he had been elected, declared "exceptional circumstances" to justify the consolidation and concentration of his power. Nonetheless, twenty years after the foundation of the Federal Republic, at the height of the student protests in major cities, the West German government decided to pass the proposed emergency laws.

As Jeremy Varon in his comparative study on left wing terrorism in the United States and West Germany points out, the student movement and radical left wing protest movements in the West seemed more threatening to global stability because they explicitly referred to global liberation and guerilla movements, such as Castro's revolution in Cuba or the war in Vietnam.

A particularly alarming aspect of left wing terrorism was that the activists seemed to escape the law by moving across borders, into the socialist East, the Middle East, and the global South—into cultures that seemed distant and foreign. Salecl sees a shift away from the Cold War perspective that clearly located the enemy as someone coming from the outside.

By contrast, "in the age of globalized capitalism the enemy takes the form of a wandering terrorist (an image which, in its elusive character, strangely resembles the antisemitic one of the dangerous wandering Jew), while at the same time the inner antagonisms that mark Western capitalist societies are perceived in the form of viral dangers." Over the course of the 1970s, communication channels, violence, and surveillance, within and across the border of the nation state, conveyed a feeling of an elusive and ever-present threat. The Federal Republic is far from having coped with the conflicts of the 1970s; an exceedingly neurotic reaction apparently remains dominant." Likewise, the writer Friedrich Christian Delius suggests that s" can be more accurately described as an "oil price shock," West Germans' realization of continued dependency on the United States and other international forces, as well as a general sense that the seemingly unlimited progress of the West had come to an end, help to explain this lasting, panicked reaction.

In respect to the perceived "oil crisis," historian Jens Hohensee describes the beginning of an oil-psychosis, and the continuing propagation of the antagonism between Orient and Occident. Furthermore, during and in the aftermath of the Vietnam War, international security seemed once again in jeopardy and the German public perceived the political association with the West as unstable and shifting.

THE STUDENT MOVEMENT AND RADICAL POLITICS

In the face of such global changes and confronted with increasing police brutality during the 1967 visit of the Iranian Shah, the student movement of the 1960s split into a collection of dissenting subgroups. Some argued that only by becoming organized in structured groups, the so-called K-Gruppen, could this kind of state violence be countered and a truly "international" revolutionary movement emerges.Others continued a more spontaneous kind of activism and advocated forms of creative protest.

A small number of underground groups, which believed in armed resistance, emerged from this perceived need to change strategies. The motivation for early terrorist activities, *i.e.*, to protest the War in Vietnam and the West German government's support of that war, are certainly in line with the goals of parts of the student movement.

Gundrun Ensslin's and Andreas Baader's activities during the late 1960s—the bombing of two Frankfurt department stores in 1968 for instance—were not meant to put civilians into danger, but to force the state and the public to realise that West German wealth and consumption were based on imperialist and deadly wars elsewhere.

"Consumption terror" was the target of these attacks, as much as the idea of "bringing the war home." Global capitalism and global warfare, both issues that caused intense anxiety at this particular point in time, inspired these early terrorist activities.

In 1969, the activists were released on parole under an amnesty for political prisoners after having served three years in prison. When, by the end of the year the court ordered them back into prison, Ensslin and Baader went underground and fled to Paris.

In 1970, they re-entered the Federal Republic whereupon Baader was arrested and put back into prison to serve his remaining years.

Ensslin, Ulrike Meinhof, and others freed Baader from prison in the spring of 1970. Following this, the RAF published its first official communique, demanding that the red army be built up. Due to the heated political climate after Baader's escape, the terrorists decided to leave the country, allegedly via the German Democratic Republic, and join a Fatah training camp.

Images of the time portray Ensslin and Baader as glamorous revolutionary outlaws. After burning department stores in their war against the terror of consumption and bombing U.S. army bases in their fight against imperialism, in 1970 the most prominent RAF terrorists, Baader and Ensslin are pictured sunbathing with their cohort in Jordan. Baader and Ensslin, it seems, were able to move around freely "underground," cross borders, exit and enter courtrooms, prisons, and the country. After a few months of dissension within their own ranks and with the Fatah leaders, Baader, Meinhof, and Ensslin returned to West Germany, most likely via the East. Bank raids and fire bombings were the most common activities of the RAF in the early 1970s, but the bombings in the year 1972 targeted mostly U.S.military installations, killing General Paul A. Bloomquist and injuring thirteen others.

In a letter following this attack, the terrorists stated that this was a response to the landmines that the U.S.military had put into the harbours in North Vietnam. The hostage crisis during the summer Olympics in 1972 shows similarly complex transnational connections. International media broadcasts, Cold War politics, as well as relations between Israel and West Germany influenced the outcome and the reaction to the hostage crisis during the 1972 hostage crisis.

While West Germany deliberately wanted to appear peaceful in the eyes of the international community—to counteract the image of the 1936 Nazi Olympics—security guards and the police were utterly unprepared to respond to terrorist violence. As a response to this embarrassing display of "weakness" in front of the international media, the West German state started to remilitarize its police and security systems.

Technological progress further allowed for increasingly sophisticated surveillance techniques. By the fall of 1971, Horst Herold was appointed chief commissioner of the Federal Criminal Investigation Agency (BKA) and he started work on an elaborate database, storing names of organizations and individuals, as well as addresses, fingerprints, and hand writing samples.

Yet, these new global networks, infrastructures and communication systems posed both a chance and a particular threat to the state and the terrorists. Technologies that allowed the Left, and later the radical and militant Left to make their causes known, also allowed the state to watch, record, and catch terrorists and activists. Left wing terrorism in West Germany relied on the media and only worked under the assumption of a functioning media society—advances in surveillance and information technology helped the state to capture and arrest terrorists.

The arrests of Baader, Ensslin, Meinhof, Jan-Carl Raspe, and Holger Meins in 1972, followed by their first hunger strike, sparked support from large numbers of young political activists, who were visiting the political prisoners and publishing reports about the oppressive prison conditions. The death of Meins as a result of the hunger strike combined with a lack of medical care increased the popularity of the RAF.

At this point in time, the image from the beginning of the 1970s of terrorists as wild and romanticized Bonny-and-Clyde style freedom fighters had been complemented with the image of the self-starving political prisoner tortured and mistreated in German prisons.

Two images of the left wing terrorists co-existed in the mind of their supporters: one of the young rebel moving freely across borders with a false passport and a made-up identity, and the other of the victim of a repressive state apparatus. At the same time, the nation state appeared to be on the defensive, both fragile and violent. While, on the one hand, sympathy for the incarcerated RAF members had reached its peak, a discursive shift in reaction to the state's response also can be detected. When the June 2nd Movement kidnapped conservative candidate for mayor of West Berlin Peter Lorenz, the state agreed to exchange the prisoners to save the politician's life.

Media and conservative politicians, however, voiced concerns that the state's response seemed to indicate that the terrorists could get whatever they demanded. In response to the hostage taking at the German Embassy in Stockholm in 1975, where the terrorists demanded that Baader, Ensslin, Meinhof, among a long list of other terrorists, should be released, the newsmagazine Der Spiegel published an issue with the title "Attack in Stockholm—the State Stays Tough."

Following these events, Der Spiegel published statistics showing that more and more Germans were indeed leaning towards demanding a stronger state in order to deal with this threat. The 1976 death of Ulrike Meinhof in her prison cell spurred further controversy, discussion, and confusion.

Did the state kill Meinhof and make it look like a suicide to end the permanent threat of further kidnappings? Or did Meinhof kill herself out of despair? In both scenarios, should the state have been held responsible for this death? Could this be understood as a new strategy on both sides, leading to further deaths and killings?

The prison cell, the ultimate black box, became a metaphor for the black box of the state: the more confined and confining it appeared to be, the more deadly and—in the eyes of the left wing terrorists and activists—fascist it was becoming. The relationship between the terrorist threat and the measures taken by the state had become highly ambivalent.

AMBIVALENCE AND MORAL PANIC

In the first half of the year 1977, once again a different picture of the relationship between the state and the terrorists emerges. In the spring of 1977, the "Ulrike Meinhof Commando" executed Federal Persecutor Siegfried Bubak, the judge responsible for the RAY trials, on his way to work. The shock of this murder was twofold: for the first time it appeared that the goal was not a kidnapping, but simply assassination; secondly, this murder took place on a public street in broad daylight.

Despite roadblocks, police raids, and a large-scale search effort, the murderers were nowhere to be found. In response to the Bubak murder, Der Spiegel wrote: "The first terrorist killing of a leading representative of the federal law enforcement harshly reveals the boundaries of security in a democracy." On the front page of Die Zeit from 15 April 1977, Hans Schueler asked: "Is the murder of Siegfried Bubak a reason to renounce liberal politics?"

In his answer, he registers a shift in terrorist tactics: "But now: The planned bloody murder of a specifically targeted person. This can be called, in its specific significance and the means of execution, a completely new, and the most horrific form of terrorist crime."

Only three months after Bubak was killed, RAF terrorists shot Jurgen Ponto, head of the Dresdner Bank, in his own house during what was most likely an attempted kidnapping. Christian Klar, Brigitte Mohnhaupt, and Susanne Albrecht entered his house in the afternoon, Klar pulled his gun, and Ponto was shot during the struggle. The press reactions to these two murders show the growing sense that new tactics needed to be employed to counter such increasingly violent and brutal acts. In the liberal West German media, however, this call for stricter measures in the fight against terrorism was always complicated by voices that warned against the erosion of democracy and democratic rights. Fear of the state becoming too authoritarian and a sense that it needs to reassert itself go hand in hand.

Likewise, fear of the terrorists and sympathy for the situation of political prisoners exist side by side. This particularly anxious political atmosphere precedes the events of the German Autumn in 1977 when, in two separate attempts, terrorists aimed to free prominent members of the West German Red Army Faction (RAF) from the high security prison in Stuttgart-Stammheim; a group of RAF members kidnapped the West German manager Hanns Martin Schleyer and took him to France; and under the leadership of a Palestinian terrorist, another group hijacked a Lufthansa passenger plane.

In the night of the 17 October 1977 the West German special police force GSG 9 stormed the plane, and freed all the passengers.

That same night, three terrorists were found dead in their prison cells and a few days later, the corpse of Hanns Martin Schleyer was found in the trunk of a car. Despite differing reports of the exact chronology and various versions of who was responsible for the deaths, almost all historical accounts agree that this series of events in October 1977 significantly changed West German democracy. The same night as the West German special police force GSG 9 successfully stormed the hijacked Lufthansa plane in Mogadishu, Somalia, Baader and Ensslin were found dead in their prison cells. Raspe died on the way to the hospital—all presumed to be suicides. Only a few days later, Hanns Martin Schleyer, who had been held hostage for over a month at this point, was found dead in the trunk of a car.

The exact chronology of the events was never determined. The question of how guns ended up within the confines of the "Fortress Stammheim" remained unclear. For both sides—the terrorists and the state—these events could be interpreted as a moment of success as well a moment of complete despair.

These ambivalent images of the state and the terrorists set a "moral panic cycle" into motion. Stuart Hall uses the term "moral panic," to describe a social reaction to forms of political "crisis," where fears "converge and overlap... the enemy becomes both many-faceted and 'one.'" The law and order society of the 1980s is, in Hall's analysis, a result of this cycle:

This is where the cycle of moral panics issues directly into the law-and-order society.... Meanwhile, the state has won the right, and indeed the inherent duty, to move swiftly, to stamp fast and hard, to listen in, discreetly survey... charge or hold without charges, act on suspicion, hustle and shoulder, to keep society on the straight and narrow.... The times are exceptional. In the aftermath of the events of the year 1977 in West Germany such a movement towards this particular law and order state went swiftly. It was, however, contested and contradictory from its onset. The concept of the moral panic cycle captures the two poles between which media reactions shift back and forth in what Kraushaar describes as a "neurotic reaction."

The events of the autumn of 1977 come to signify both a newly found confidence that "we" West Germans could win the fight against terror, and a deep skepticism concerning democracy and civil rights in the Federal Republic. Nevertheless, it always remained unclear who this "one" and "multi-facetted enemy" actually was. After the West German GSG 9 stormed the hijacked plane, the news magazine Der Spiegel published a cover story leading with a quote from the Wall Street Journal: "Germans can be strong and human: The successful German action-commando in Mogadishu fostered an unexpected wave of solidarity for the Germans—among their friends in the West as in the Third World, where until recently, the "ugly German" still haunted the imaginaries." On top of the page is an image of the West German chancellor Helmut Schmidt smiling proudly and a group of people holding up signs congratulating him as well as the GSG 9.

The chapter is written in the typical ironic voice of Der Spiegel that makes it hard to tell who is being made fun of: is it the Germans for being so proud of this single successful event in the year of the German Autumn? Or is it the foreign press for only now, after this spectacular media event, proclaiming that Germany has finally redeemed itself?

Is it the German public for being fooled into believing that they are indeed protected by their antiterrorist task force? Or is it the "black Somalia ambassador" or the various "New York Jews" the article quotes—or the German press and public in general for being naive, as the end of the article suggests?

The tone of this chapter once again conveys both, a sense that the state is strong, and will protect its "good" citizens, as well as the feeling that somehow this event was just an embarrassing display of a state that is otherwise weak. In the fall of 1977, critical and complicated discussions about what to do in response to terrorism increased. Other articles in Der Spiegel reflected the worried discussions of the state in crisis, highlighting the fear that the Federal Republic of Germany was moving towards becoming a fascist police state. Again, this situation was ambivalent: could the terrorists be blamed? Should the state be held responsible?

A similar ambivalence can be seen in other major newspapers of the time. The liberal daily paper Suddeutsche Zeitung celebrated the success of the GSG 9 in a similarly ironic tone.

It reported in detail on other nations congratulating the Germans for their successful rescue mission, next to articles on the continuing, or even greater threat of international terrorism. With headlines like "Threats of More Violence" and reports on radical groups demonstrating against Germany in other European countries like France and Italy, the success of the German GSG 9 and the state in general turned into a reason to be even more afraid, insinuating that this publicity might lead to further terror activities against Germany and Germany might become a fascist police state.

The fact that either the Stammheim terrorists managed to smuggle weapons into the cells of a high tech, high security prison or were murdered by the state, in combination with the knowledge that the terrorists had international allies, provided more reasons for West Germans to remain worried, as various articles and commentaries in the following months attested.

On 21 October 1977 the Suddeutsche Zeitung introduced a lead article with the following paragraph: "Parliament worried about further attacks. United in the fight against terror: The chancellor and the government refrain from any partisan decisions/Schmidt: The people in the Federal Republic have come closer to each other/are closely united." Even the less conservative weekly paper Die Zeit admitted that there was some pride in the relief that people felt after the successful end of the hijacking drama. In the same article, however, Theo Sommer pointed out the tension in this newly found pride:

The fight against terrorism is not over yet. The drama of Hanns Martin Schleyer continues. The RAF is alive, even though Andreas Baader, Gudrun Ensslin, and Jan-Carl Raspe killed themselves—an other sign, by the way, for the outrageous incapability of the Stuttgart law enforcement agencies, that something like that could happen in this particular manner.

In the following month, Die Zeit published various articles—first a series entitled "Kidnapping Drama 77" and then a collection of articles under the title "State, Society, Terror" that tried to explain and make sense out of the events of the past year. Where Der Spiegel and the Suddeutsche Zeitung followed the ambivalent strategy of conveying both pride and fear, Die Zeit offered yet another version of the permanent state of emergency. Aside from looking for psychohistorical and sociopolitical explanations for the events, Dieter Buhl acknowledged that the idea of international terrorism, clearly a reality as the Mogadishu hijacking revealed, added another dimension to this crisis: nothing less than a threat to the Western, capitalist, democratic, world order.

It exemplified the "fear of a cartel of international and centrally organized terror-gangs, who can take the world order out of its hinges." This quote suggests that the worries went far beyond the borders of the nation-state-the real concern was the collapse of a world order, and more specifically the potential redistribution of order, power, and wealth.

Nevertheless, as Dieter Zimmer in a separate article in the same issue of Die Zeit suggests, this is not only located in the international sphere but also within the each individual: "Maybe the reason [for the path into terrorism] is so easily made plausible because the deadly consequences lie just underneath normality, and maybe that is precisely the unsettling puzzle, that terrorism asks us to solve." The unsettling puzzle that the weekly paper Die Zeit offers relied on the tension between an individualized and psychological notion of the "the terrorist within" and the vision—however vague—of a transnational threat to the stability of "the West." Prognoses for the Future: The Beginning of a New Decade?

These ambivalences and tensions in the emergency discourse transformed in the beginning of the 1980s and entered current debates on security of the nation state and the European Union in the form of a hardly disguised debate over "the West and the rest." Media responses to the German Autumn show that in connection to terrorism the tension between the territory of the nation state and transnational terrorist networks led to increasingly neurotic and anxious reactions. Anxieties over the transnational connections of left-wing terrorism—linked to issues like the Oil Crises, the Cold War, and the relationship to the United States—survived the decade and dominated the visions of anxiety in the 1980s.

While the crises of the 1970s were still very much on people's minds, the Iranian hostage crisis in 1979, and the Soviet invasion of Afghanistan in December 1979 opened the door for another collection of vague, but intense anxieties over the stability of the "world order" and the effects on West Germany. On 4 January 1980, Rolf Zundel in Die Zeit saw peace and energy supply as the main concerns: "Is the [energy] supply still sufficiently secure? Can we ensure enough peace so that this society can still pursue its business? Where Zundel simply supplied his readers with a set of anxiety-provoking questions, other articles provided a laundry list of elusive threats. Reports on the chaos in the stock markets, the brutal Khomeini regime in Iran, the second oil price shock of 1979, and a revival of the Cold War due to the Afghanistan crisis dominated the daily papers in the first weeks of January 1980.

On 2 January 1980 the Frankfurter Allgemeine Zeitung reported on a survey on fears and hopes for the future, entitled "Optimistic Angsthasen:" "Didn't we use to believe that everything would be possible: wealth, better relations between East and West, yes even talent and happiness?

Germans are therefore optimistic chickens; their demands are growing, but every risk frightens them." The article went on to suggest that even if the relationship between East and West Germany might not be scarred forever by the Afghanistan crisis of 1979, international relations—referring to crises in the Middle East and in Southeast Asia, as well as the expansion of "Soviet Imperialism"—posed an immanent threat to world politics. The most frightening aspect of this development was, according to the author, that it showed that "the West" was dependent on "the Rest." We do not live in a "space void of air", a metaphor that implied that "our" existence depended on "others." The same week the more left-leaning Frankfurter Rundschau reported on Franz Josef Strauss, Bavaria's Minister President and candidate for chancellor at the time. In an article in the Bavarian Christian Social Union party paper, the Bayernkurier, Strauss found Germany to be threatened in an apocalyptic way at the beginning of the new decade.

He provided a list of countries and regions that belong to "the Rest:" the Middle East, Southeast Asia, Africa, Latin America. Oil producing counties in general are potential sites of crises. He demanded that the West show leadership and responsibility—and be proactive.

The Germans, he insisted, had to stop their cowardly assimilation. He did not further explain this process of "emancipation," but justified this display of power by calling it "our historical responsibility." In Strauss' opinion, Germans had to engage in world politics—they owed it to world. Strauss' contender for office, Schmidt, offered a slightly different perspective in his new-year speech: Ladies and gentlemen, the next decade might be difficult, not only because of the insecurities concerning energy supply. The whole world is in uproar. Let us think about Africa, the Near- and Middle East, the American hostages in Teheran, with whom we declare our solidarity, let us think about South-East Asia. He demanded a strong partnership with "our friends in the West," as well as collaboration with "our neighbours in the East." Die Zeit reviewed Richard Lowenthal's book, Societal Change and Cultural Crisis: Future Problems of Western Societies at length on January 4th of the same year.

The thesis of the book is that this cultural crisis, which originated in global capitalism, is enhanced in Germany since German society has traditionally been founded on values like community, self-reflexivity, and contemplation (Innerlichkeit). This crisis, in Lowenthal's opinion, is a result of rapid changes and a "wrong development (Fehlentwicklung) in capitalist society."

The sense at the beginning of the 1980s was not that the crises of the 1970s were solved. Quite to the contrary, they had become increasingly unmanageable. One argument was that "the West" should finally begin with serious, and if necessary forceful, crisis management. Others suggested cautious global negotiations. The issue of terrorism is strikingly absent in the media in January 1980. Discussions of an uncertain future focused on increasingly elusive and global threats to the stability and security of the western world in general.

Robert Young in White Mythologies summarizes this crisis of "the West" as a "sense of the loss of European history and culture as History and Culture [with capital letters], the loss of their unquestioned place at the centre of the world." "The West," the nation state, and West Germany, were experienced as penetrable, and fragile from the inside out and from the outside in. The events of the late 1970s in West Germany highlighted this instability and functioned as a catalyst for fears of slippage in the rule of law (Rechtstaat) that this series of events triggered. Media accounts clearly show that the resulting "moral panic cycle" continued to influence national political discourse in the following months and years. An ambivalent discussion of the power and influence of the nation state continued to foster anxieties about alliances, stability, reliability, and law. These anxieties fuelled the "conservative" politics of the 1980s—threatened territory needs to constantly be policed, secured, protected, and defended.

The discussions in this chapter suggest, however, that these anxieties and neuroses reveal tensions, interruptions, and gaps in this "conservative" fantasy of security and protection. Today, films, novels, memoirs, and television shows still tell and retell the story of the RAF.

While their depictions neither strive for historical accuracy, nor try to do justice to the political agenda of the activists of the time, their popularity is based on the continuing appeal of the drama of "moral panic" and anxiety of "the West" in the face of global change—perhaps even more pronounced in today's post-9/11 world.

8

Radio Journalism

The pre- and early history of radio is the history of technology that produced instruments that use radio waves. Later in the timeline of radio, the history is dominated by programming and contents, which is closer to general history. Radio owes its development to two other inventions, the telegraph and the telephone; all three technologies are closely related. Radio technology began as "wireless telegraphy". Radio can refer to either the electronic appliance that we listen with or the content listened to. However, it all started with the discovery of "radio waves" - electromagnetic waves that have the capacity to transmit music, speech, pictures and other data invisibly through the air. Many devices work by using electromagnetic waves including: radio, microwaves, cordless phones, remote controlled toys, television broadcasts, and more.

RADIO BROADCASTING

Various scientists proposed that electricity and magnetism while both capable of causing attraction and repulsion of objects, were linked. In 1820, Hans Christian Ørsted performed a widely known experiment on man-made electric current and magnetism. He demonstrated that a wire carrying a current was able to deflect a magnetized compass needle. Ørsted experiments discovered the relationship between electricity and magnetism in a very simple experiment. Ørsted's work influenced André-Marie Ampère to produce a theory of electromagnetism.In 1831, Michael Faraday began a series of experiments in which he discovered electromagnetic induction. The relation was mathematically modelled by Faraday's law, which subsequently became one of the four Maxwell equations. Faraday proposed that electromagnetic forces extended into the empty space around the conductor, but did not complete his work involving that proposal. Between 1861 and 1865, James Clerk Maxwell made experiments with electromagnetic waves.

On July 30, 1872, Mahlon Loomis was issued U.S. Patent 129971. In 1873, as a result of experiments, Maxwell first described the theoretical basis of the propagation of electromagnetic waves in his paper to the Royal Society *A Dynamical Theory of the Electromagnetic Field*. Towards end of 1875, while experimenting with the telegraph, Thomas Edison noted a phenomenon that he termed "etheric force", announcing it the press on November 28. He abandoned this research when Elihu Thomson, among others, ridiculed the idea. Between 1893 and 1894, Roberto Landell de Moura, a Brazilian priest and scientist, conducted experiments. He did not publicize his achievement until 1900. In 1878, David E. Hughes was the first to transmit and receive radio waves when he noticed that his induction balance caused noise in the receiver of his homemade telephone. He demonstrated his discovery to the Royal Society in 1880 but was told it was merely induction.

In 1884, Temistocle Calzecchi-Onesti at Fermo in Italy invented a tube filled with iron filings, called a "coherer". Between 1884 and 1886, Edouard Branly of France produced an improved versions of the coherer. In 1885, Edison took out U.S. Patent 465971 on a system of radio communication between ships (which later he sold to Marconi).

Between 1886 and 1888, Heinrich Rudolf Hertz validated Maxwell's theory through experiment. He demonstrated that radio radiation had all the properties of waves (now called Hertzian waves), and discovered that the electromagnetic equations could be reformulated into a partial differential equation called the wave equation. Between 1885 and 1892, Claims have been made that Murray, Kentucky farmer Nathan Stubblefield invented radio, but his devices seem to have worked by induction transmission rather than radio transmission. Claims have been made that Nathan Stubblefield invented radio before either Tesla or Marconi, but his device seems to have worked by induction transmission rather than radio transmission.

WIRELESS RADIO BEGINNINGS

In the history of radio and development of "wireless telegraphy", there are multiple claims to the invention of radio. The identity of the original inventor of radio, at the time called wireless telegraphy, is contentious. The key invention for the beginning of "wireless transmission of data using the entire frequency spectrum", known as the spark-gap transmitter, has been attributed to various individuals. Marconi equipped ships with life saving wireless communications and established the first transatlantic radio service.

Tesla developed means to reliably produce radio frequencies, publicly demonstrated the principles of radio, and transmitted long distant signals. Nikola Tesla developed means to reliably produce radio frequencies, publicly demonstrated the principles of radio, and transmitted long distant signals. He holds the US patent for the invention of the radio, as defined as "wireless transmission of data". In 1893, at St. Louis, Missouri, Tesla gave a public demonstration of "wireless" radio communication. Addressing the *Franklin Institute* in Philadelphia and the *National Electric Light Association*, he described in detail the principles of radio communication. The apparatus that he used contained all the elements that were incorporated into radio systems before the development of the "oscillation valve", the early vacuum tube. Tesla was the first to apply the mechanism of electrical conduction to *wireless practices*. Also, he initially used sensitive electromagnetic receivers , that were unlike the less responsive coherers later used by Marconi and other early experimenters. Afterwards, the principle of radio communication (sending signals through space to receivers) was publicized widely. Various scientists, inventors, and experimenters begin to investigate wireless methods.

On August 19 of 1894, British physicist Sir Oliver Lodge demonstrated the reception of Morse code signalling using radio waves using a "coherer". In November of 1894, the Indian physicist, Jagdish Chandra Bose, demonstrated publicly the use of radio waves in Calcutta, but he was not interested in patenting his work. Bose ignited gunpowder and rang a bell at a distance using electromagnetic waves, proving that communication signals can be sent without using wires. in 1894, the Russian physicist Alexander Popov built a coherer. On May 7, 1895, Popov performed a public demonstration of transmission and reception of radio waves used for communication at the Russian Physical and Chemical Society, using his coherer: this day has since been celebrated in the Russian Federation as "Radio Day". Popov was the first to develop a practical communication system based on the coherer, and is usually considered by the Russians to have been the inventor of radio.

In the beginning of 1895, Tesla detected signals from his New York lab's transmissions at West Point (a distance of 50 miles). In 1895, Marconi received a telegraph message without wires, but he did not send his voice over the airwaves. In March of 1895, Popov transmitted radio waves between different campus buildings in Saint Petersburg, but did not apply for a patent. In 1895, the New Zealander Ernest Rutherford, 1st Baron Rutherford of Nelson was awarded an Exhibition of 1851 Science Research Scholarship to Cambridge. He was instrumental in the development of radio.

He arrived in England with a reputation as an innovator and inventor, and distinguished himself in several fields, initially by working out the electrical properties of solids and then using wireless waves as a method of signalling. Rutherford was encouraged in his work by Sir Robert Ball, who had been scientific adviser to the body maintaining lighthouses on the Irish coast; he wished to solve the difficult problem of a ship's inability to detect a lighthouse in fog. Sensing fame and fortune, Rutherford increased the sensitivity of his apparatus until he could detect electromagnetic waves over a distance of several hundred metres. Thomson quickly realised that Rutherford was a researcher of exceptional ability and invited him to join in a study of the electrical conduction of gases.

Guglielmo Marconi was an electrical engineer and Nobel laureate known for the development of a practical wireless telegraphy system. In 1896,

Guglielmo Marconi was awarded a patent for radio with British Patent 12039, *Improvements in Transmitting Electrical Impulses and Signals and in Apparatus There-for*. This was the initial patent for the radio, though it used various earlier techniques of various other experimenters (primarily Tesla) and resembled the instrument demonstrated by others (including Popov). During this time spark-gap wireless telegraphy is widely researched. In 1896, Bose went to London on a lecture tour and met Marconi, who was conducting wireless experiments for the British post office. in 1897, Marconi established the radio station on the Isle of Wight, England. In the U.S. during 1897, Tesla applied for two key radio patents. Those two patents were issued in early 1900.

In 1898, Marconi opened a radio factory in Hall Street, Chelmsford, England, employing around 50 people. In 1899, Bose announced his invention of the "iron-mercury-iron coherer with telephone detector" in a paper presented at Royal Society, London. In 1900, Reginald Fessenden made a weak transmission of voice over the airwaves. Around 1900, Tesla opened the Wardenclyffe Tower facility and advertised services. In 1903, Wardenclyffe Tower neared completion.

Various theories exist on how Tesla intended to achieve the goals of this wireless system (reportedly, a 200 kW system). Tesla claimed that Wardenclyffe, as part of a World System of transmitters, would have allowed secure multichannel transceiving of information, universal navigation, time synchronization, and a global location system. In 1904, The U.S. Patent Office reversed its decision, awarding Marconi a patent for the invention of radio, possibly influenced by Marconi's financial backers in the States, who included Thomas Edison and Andrew Carnegie. This also allowed the U.S. government (among others) to avoid having to pay the royalties that were being claimed by Tesla for use of his patents.

Early radio telegraphy and telephony

Donald Manson working as an employee of the Marconi Company (England, 1906) Using various patents, the company called "*British Marconi*" was established and began communication between coast radio stations and ships at sea. This company along with its subsidiary American Marconi had a stranglehold on ship to shore communication. It operated much the way American Telephone and Telegraph operated until 1983, owning all of its own equipment and refusing to communicate with non-Marconi equipped ships. Many inventions improved the quality of radio, and amateurs experimented with uses of radio, thus the first seeds of broadcasting were planted. Around the turn of the century, the Slaby-Arco wireless system was developed by Adolphus Slaby and Georg von Arco (later incorporated into Telefunken). On Christmas Eve of 1906, Reginald Fessenden used an Alexanderson alternator and rotary spark-gap transmitter to make the first radio audio broadcast, from Brant Rock,

Massachusetts. Ships at sea heard a broadcast that included Fessenden playing *O Holy Night* on the violin and reading a passage from the Bible. In 1909, Marconi and Karl Ferdinand Braun were awarded the Nobel Prize in Physics for "contributions to the development of wireless telegraphy".

In April of 1909, Charles David Herrold, an electronics instructor in San Jose, California constructed a broadcasting station. It used spark gap technology, but modulated the carrier frequency with the human voice, and later music. The station "San Jose Calling" (there were no call letters), continued to eventually become today's KCBS in San Francisco. Herrold, the son of a Santa Clara Valley farmer, coined the terms "narrowcasting" and "broadcasting", respectively to identify transmissions destined for a single receiver such as that on board a ship, and those transmissions destined for a general audience. (The term "broadcasting" had been used in farming to define the tossing of seed in all directions.) Charles Herrold did not claim to be the first to transmit the human voice, but he claimed to be the first to conduct "broadcasting". To help the radio signal to spread in all directions, he designed some omnidirectional antennas, which he mounted on the rooftops of various buildings in San Jose. Herrold also claims to be the first broadcaster to accept advertising (he exchanged publicity for a local record store for records to play on his station), though this dubious honour usually is foisted on WEAF (1922).

In 1912, the RMS *Titanic* sank. After this, wireless telegraphy using spark-gap transmitters quickly became universal on large ships. In 1913, the International Convention for the Safety of Life at Sea was convened and produced a treaty requiring shipboard radio stations to be manned 24 hours a day. A typical high-power spark gap was a rotating commutator with six to twelve contacts per wheel, nine inches to a foot wide, driven by about 2000 volts DC. As the gaps made and broke contact, the radio wave was audible as a tone in a crystal set. The telegraph key often directly made and broke the 2000 volt supply. One side of the spark gap was directly connected to the antenna. Receivers with thermionic valves became commonplace before spark-gap transmitters were replaced by continuous wave transmitters.

Audio broadcasting (1915 to 1950s)

In the 1920s, the government publication, "*Construction and Operation of a Simple Homemade Radio Receiving Outfit*", showed how almost any family having a family member handy with simple tools could a build a crystal radio. This is a modern reproduction of an early receiver. The most common type of receiver before vacuum tubes was the crystal set, although some early radios used some type of amplification through electric current or battery. Inventions of the triode amplifier, generator, and detector enabled audio radio. The invention of amplitude-modulated (AM radio), so that more than one station can send signals (as opposed to spark-gap radio, where one transmitter covers the entire bandwidth of spectra) was pioneered by Fessenden and Lee de Forest.In the 1920s, the Westinghouse company bought Lee De Forest's and Edwin Armstrong's patent. During the mid 1920s, Amplifying vacuum tubes revolutionized radio receivers and transmitters. Westinghouse engineers developed a more modern vacuum tube. In 1920, Regular wireless broadcasts for entertainment began in Argentina, pioneered by the group around Enrique Telémaco Susini.

Also in 1920, Spark-gap telegraphy stops. On August 31 of 1920, the first known radio news programme was broadcast by station 8MK, the unlicensed predecessor of WWJ (AM) in Detroit, Michigan. In 1922, regular wireless broadcasts for entertainment began in the UK from the Marconi Research Centre at Writtle near Chelmsford, England. Early radios ran the entire power of the transmitter through a carbon microphone.The question of the 'first' publicly-targeted, licensed radio station in the U.S. has more than one answer and depends on semantics. It's commonly attributed to KDKA in Pittsburgh, Pennsylvania, which in October of 1920 received its license and went on the air as the first US licensed commercial broadcasting station. (Their engineer Frank Conrad had been broadcasting from his own station since 1916.). But on February 17 1919, station 9XM at the University of Wisconsin in Madison had already broadcast the first human speech to the public at large (9XM sent music over the air two years earlier, was originally licensed in 1914 and sent its first transmission in 1916). That station is still on the air today as WHA. On August 20 of 1920, at least two months before KDKA, E.W. Scripps's WBL (now WWJ) in Detroit started broadcasting. It has carried a regular schedule of programming to the present. Then there's the history noted above of Charles David Herrold's radio services (eventually KCBS) going back to 1909. Settlement of this 'first' question may hang largely upon what constitutes 'regular' programming. Technically, KDKA was the first of several already-extant stations to receive a 'limited commercial' license.

Broadcasting was not yet supported by advertising. The stations owned by manufacturers and department stores were established to sell radios and those owned by newspapers to sell papers and express the opinions of the owners. In the 1920s, Radio was first used to transmit pictures visible as television. During the early 1930s, single sideband (SSB) and frequency modulation (FM) were invented by amateur radio operators. By 1940, they were established commercial modes.

In 1933, FM radio was patented; Edwin H. Armstrong invented it. FM uses frequency modulation of the radio wave to minimize static and interference from electrical equipment and the atmosphere, in the audio programme. In 1937, W1XOJ, the first experimental FM radio station, was granted a construction permit by the FCC. In the 1940s, standard analog television transmissions started in North America and Europe. In 1943, Tesla's patent (number *645576*) was reinstated by the U.S. Supreme Court shortly after Tesla's death. This decision was based on the fact that prior art existed before the establishment of Marconi's patent. Ignoring Tesla's prior art, the decision may have enabled the U.S. government to avoid having to pay damages that were being claimed by the Marconi Company for use of its patents during World War I (as, it is speculated, the government's initial reversal to grant Marconi the patent right in order to nullify any claims Tesla had for compensation).

After World War II, the FM radio broadcast was introduced in Germany. In 1948, a new wavelength plan was set up for Europe at a meeting in Copenhagen. Because of the recent war, Germany (which was not even invited) was only given a few medium-wave frequencies, which are not very good for broadcasting. For this reason Germany began broadcasting on USW, "ultra short wave" (nowadays called VHF). After some amplitude modulation experience with VHF, it was realized that FM radio was a much better alternative for VHF radio than AM.

Later 20th century developments

In the early 1960s, VOR systems finally became widespread; before that, aircraft used commercial AM radio stations for navigation. (AM stations are still marked on U.S. aviation charts). in 1954, Regency introduced a pocket transistor radio, the TR-1, powered by a "standard 22.5V Battery". In 1960, Sony introduced their first transistorized radio, small enough to fit in a vest pocket, and able to be powered by a small battery.

It was durable, because there were no tubes to burn out. Over the next twenty years, transistors displaced tubes almost completely except for very high power, or very high frequency, uses. In 1963, Colour television was commercially transmitted, and the first (radio) communication satellite, TELSTAR, was launched. In lLate 1960s, the U.S. long-distance telephone network began to convert to a digital network, employing digital radios for many of its links. in the 1970s, LORAN became the premier radio navigation system. Soon, the U.S. Navy experimented with satellite navigation. In 1987, the GPS constellation of satelliotes was launched in 1987. During the late 1990s, the digital transmissions began to be applied to broadcasting. In the early 1990s, amateur radio experimenters began to use personal computers with audio cards to process radio signals. In 1994, the U.S. Army and DARPA launched an aggressive successful project to construct a software radio that could become a different radio on the fly by changing software.

Telex on Radio

Telegraphy did not go away on radio. Instead, the degree of automation increased. On land-lines in the 1930s, Teletypewriters automated encoding, and were adapted to pulse-code dialing to automate routing, a service called telex. For thirty years, telex was the absolute cheapest form of long-distance communication, because up to 25 telex channels could occupy the same bandwidth as one voice channel. For business and government, it was an advantage that telex directly produced written documents.

Telex systems were adapted to short-wave radio by sending tones over single sideband. CCITT R.44 (the most advanced pure-telex standard) incorporated character-level error detection and retransmission as well as automated encoding and routing. For many years, telex-on-radio (TOR) was the only reliable way to reach some third-world countries. TOR remains reliable, though less-expensive forms of e-mail are displacing it. Many national telecom companies historically ran nearly pure telex networks for their governments, and they ran many of these links over short wave radio.

21st century development

Internet radio consists of sending radio-style audio programming over streaming Internet connections: no radio transmitters need be involved at any point in the process.

- *Early technology wars*: Push or pull, streaming media or multicast
- Run your own station with live365 or almost like Geocities or Hotmail

Digital audio broadcasting (DAB)

Appears to be set to grow in importance relative to FM radio for airborne broadcasts in several countries.

IMPORTANT HISTORICAL FACTS OF RADIO BROADCASTING

A. Scientists

- Heinrich Hertz - first to detect radio waves in 1887 by causing a spark to leap across a gap that generated electromagnetic waves - built oscillator and resonator by 1893
- Oliver Lodge in Britain, Alexander Popov in Russia, Edward Brauley in France - filled a glass tube with metal filings that would cohere under electromagnetic waves and when the tube was tapped, the filings would collapse to break the circuit - built coherer to detect radio waves by 1894

B. Inventors

- Guglielmo Marconi invented his spark transmitter with antenna at his home in Bologna, Italy, in December 1894. He took his "Black Box" to Britain in Feb. 1896 and although it was broken by custom officials, he filed for British Patent number 12039 on June 2, 1896. He formed his first Wireless Telegraph and Signal Company in Britain in 1897 at age 23 and the world's first radio factory on Hall Street in Dec. 1898. The American Marconi Co. was formed in 1899. Marconi controlled patents for the Lodge tuner of 1900 with dial, and Fleming valve of 1904 that acted as a diode tube to amplify electrical current in one direction. His company sold spark transmitters to the U.S. Navy for point-to-point transmission.

- Reginald Fessenden of Canada invented a continuous-wave voice transmitter 1905 using a high-frequency alternator developed by Charles Steinmetz at GE 1903, made voice broadcast over North Atlantic Christmas Eve 1906; this broadcast was heard by wireless operators on banana boats of the United Fruit Company that developed crystal receivers for its ships; Fessenden sold to Westinghouse in 1910 the patent for a heterodyne receiver that used the joint operation of two AC currents for a third frequency.
- Lee de Forest patented his audion tube 1906, had visited the Fessenden lab in 1903 and stole the design for a "spade detector," promoted idea of multi-point broadcasting, sold patents to AT and T.
- Harold D. Arnold at AT and T developed the amplifying vacuum tube in 1913 that made possible the first coast-to-coast telephony and the first transatlantic radio transmission in 1915.
- Edwin Armstrong patented the regenerative circuit in 1913 that fed a radio signal through an audion tube 20,000 times per second to caused stronger oscillations in the tube that generated radio waves. He made long-distance voice transmissions 1914, developed superheterodyne circuit during World War I that combined high and low frequency waves, was promoted to Major in the Signal Corps, sold patents to RCA 1920, discovered FM transmission 1933 but rejected by Sarnoff at RCA who was trying to develop television.
- De Forest began the longest lawsuit in radio history in 1915 when he sued Armstrong over the basic regenerative patent, but lost in 1921 and 1923 when it was demonstrated in court that de Forest could not explain how or why his audion tube oscillated; Armstrong did understand and made a clear explanation of regeneration. De Forest would win the final court battle in his 13th lawsuit in 1930, on a technical interpretation of the words used to describe oscillation, and was awarded the basic radio patent, causing him to become known as the "father of radio." The Ken Burns 1991 documentary *Empire of the Air* focused on the 3 men who "made radio" - de Forest, Armstrong, Sarnoff - but unfortunately ignored the contribution of many other important engineers and amateurs and pioneers.

C. Amateurs

- Charles Herrold began regular broadcasting in San Jose 1912
- Prof. Earle Terry in Madison, Wisconsin - 9XM

- Fred Christian in Hollywood with 5-watt transmitter in his bedroom - 6ADZ
- William Scripps in Detroit broadcast music from office of his newspaper, the Detroit News, on station 8MK that became WWJ
- Hiram Maxim of American Radio Relay League testified at Congressional hearings in 1918 - 8500 amateurs transmitting to 200,000 receivers - many had returned from World War I with experience using Signal Corps SCR-70 vaccum-tube radios - most popular were simple inexpensive crystal radio receivers rather than tube sets
- Frank Conrad was engineer for Westinghouse, built SCR-70 receivers during war for Signal Corps and began broadcasting music from his garage in Pittsburgh - 8XK
- RadioShack Corporation formed in 1921 in Boston to sell equipment to "ham" operators, taking its name from the small wooden building for radio equipment on ships.
- The American Radio Relay League in Dec. 1921 made the first successful transatlantic shortwave broadcasts with small superheterodyne receivers, and Frank Conrad would develop regular commercial shortwave broadcasting.

D. Government

- Law of 1912 - due to *Titanic* disaster April 14, all ships required to have radios with 2 operators and auxiliary power and all transmitters must be licensed.

E. Corporations

- RCA incorporated Oct. 17, 1919, to control patents of GE, AT and T, Westinghouse, United Fruit, according to the plan of GE lawyer Owen D. Young to buy out American Marconi and create American monopoly. The Navy approved of plan to keep radio out of the control of British Marconi, German Telefunken, French interests. David Sarnoff became General Manager of RCA in 1919, sought mass production of "radio music boxes" using Armstrong's superheterodyne circuit.
- Westinghouse VP Harry Davis joined Conrad Sept. 30, 1920, to create 100-watt transmitter in Pittsburgh - given call letters KDKA by Commerce Dept. Oct. 27 - transmitted election returns Nov. 2 - began regular scheduled broadcasts every evening 8:30-9:30 pm - power of transmitter increased to 500 watts 1921 - Midcontinent chain of 6 stations by 1925.
- AT and T toll broadcasting began 1922; the first radio commercial was broadcast on Aug. 28 by the Queensboro Corp. that paid $100

for 10-minute message promoting the sale of apartments in Long Island; the AT and T stations were anchored by WEAF in New York with a "clear channel" and featured a broadcast of the opening of Congress 1923, and the Democratic National Convention 1924.

- RCA anchored by WJZ (classical) and WNY (popular) - RCA licensed other companies to make receivers, *e.g.*, Philco, Zenith, Emerson, Sylvania.
- New York radio station WJZ made broadcasting history when it used a live studio audience for the first time for a show called *The Perfect Fool* on February 19, 1922.
- Hazeltine Electronic Corp. developed automatic volume control 1924.
- Herbert Hoover and Commerce Department favoured large corporations; the 1923 allocation of frequencies from 187.3-100 MHz created high power "clear" channels, medium and low power channels.
- NBC was formed July 7, 1926, owned by RCA (50 per cent), GE (30 per cent), Westinghouse (20 per cent), leased telephone lines from AT and T, bought WEAF from AT and T for its "red" network of popular music to complement "blue" network from WJZ and the Pacific network, for a total of 48 affiliate stations; sold "sustaining" programmes to affiliates and broadcast "sponsored" programmes produced by advertisers such as American Tobacco Co.
- Arthur Judson in 1927 created United Independent Broadcasters with 16 stations, helped by William Paley of La Palina Cigar Co. and the Columbia Phonograph Co., and is reorganized in 1928 as the Columbia Broadcasting System (CBS) with 47 affiliate stations including WABC that would later become WCBS in New York.
- Paley gave CBS affiliates free "sustaining" programmes in exchange for ad time sold to national advertisers.

  In January 1928 NBC produced a 47-station coast-to-coast programme The Dodge Victory Hour with Al Jolson in New Orleans, Fred Stone in Chicago and Paul Whiteman in New York and Will Rogers from his home in Beverly Hills (he did a Coolidge imitation, the first time a presidential imitation was done on radio), to the largest national audience since Lindberg's return in 1927, estimated at 35 million, sponsored by Dodge new Victory Six auto, the front page of the *New York Times* next day declared "All America Used As a Radio Studio"; a second show of the "Dodge Victory Hour" was broadcast in March 1928, again with Hollywood stars and Whiteman's band; United Artists installed extra speakers in theaters so a greater audience could hear the show.
- The Mutual Broadcasting System (MBS) was created in 1934 as a cooperative shared by WOR in New York, WGN in Chicago, WLW in

Cincinnati, and WXYZ in Detroit. Unlike the two larger networks, it had no production studio or centralized corporate owners and owned no stations. The network carried popular programmes such as the *Lone Ranger* and *The Green Hornet,* and attracted a larger number of affiliate stations than the other networks, but mostly in rural and small markets.

F. Programmes

- Radio programming would shift from music and local talk programmes to drama and news by 1940
- Interwoven singing commercial by the Happiness Boys, Billie Jones and Ernie Hare 1921-1939
- Major Bowes and His Original Amateur Hour, (variety, 1935) with "the wheel of fortune" catchphrase and a gong sound if contestant lost
- Jack Benny Programme (comedy, 1932) featured character interacting with his "gang" of Mary (Mary Livingstone), Dennis (Dennis Day), Phil (Phil Harris), Don (Don Wilson), and Rochester (Eddie Anderson), one of the first regular black radio performers, at 7 pm Sundays on NBC for Jell-O
- Fred Allen Show (comedy-variety, 1932) had a "feud" with Jack Benny and a face-to-face meeting March 14, 1937, for one of the largest radio audiences of the 1930s.
- Jack Armstrong, the All-American Boy (adventure, 1933) on CBS sponsored by Wheaties
- Let's Pretend, (children, 1934) in the "public interest" without commercials by CBS until the 1940s
- Amos and Andy, (comedy, 1928) originated as "Sam 'n Henry" in 1926, then syndicated nationally using transcription records of shows mailed to radio stations; early example of the sitcom genre with Freeman Gosden as Amos and Charles Correll as Andy, at 7-7:15 pm 5 nights per week on NBC, dramatically boosted the sales of Pepsodent in 1929, appealed to families and was the most popular show during the depression 1930-32, with 40 million listeners, emphasizing optimism and traditional values
- Easy Aces, (comedy, 1930) from Kansas City written and acted by Goodman Ace, a witty, urbane domestic comedy
- Fibber, McGee and Molly, (comedy, 1935) created for Johnson Wax with commercials integrated into the show's narrative, at 9:30 pm Tuesday ("comedy night" on NBC), with opening closet by Fibber at home on Wistful Vista, running for 15 years, one of radio's longest shows

- NBC allowed its local stations to make and use recordings May 1, 1932, but not for network use. In 1935, NBC created a division to make disc recordings of radio programmes.

Old Time Radio Moments of the Century

The Flight of Alan Shepard 5/5/61

America's entry into the Manned Space Age comes as the OTR Era enters its final year, but millions of Americans follow the flight by means of portable radios, car radios, and other receivers — as if to confirm that there'll always be a place for the audio medium.

Truth or Consequences: The "Mr. Hush" Contest. Winter 1945-46

A harbinger of things to come, this guess-who-it-is contest ushered in a new era of listener-participation quiz shows that would help change the face of radio in the postwar era.

Sherlock Holmes on the Air. 10/20/30

Famed actor William Gillette is the first Holmes to take the network air — the first of many to follow. The Holmes story format is ideally-suited for radio, and the programme proves to be one of the most successful dramas of the Depression era.

Cruise of the Seth Parker. 1934-35

Radio listeners follow the adventuring Phillips Lord around the world by shortwave — an adventure that takes on a harrowing real-life flavor when Lord's schooner is wrecked by a tropical storm. The program's reputation is wrecked as well, when it's revealed that Lord wasn't exactly living up to Seth Parker's Yankee-parson image during his adventure: accompanied by wine, women, and the sort of songs that weren't found in the hymnals back in Jonesport

The Rise of Dorothy and Dick. 1945

Charming chit-chat in the morning with Richard Kollmar and Dorothy Kilgallen — foreshadowing the modern man/woman TV talk show teams. Think of them as the Regis and Kathie Lee of the forties.

The Rise Of Wendell Hall. 1923-24

He was a bombastic Southern-fried ukulele-playing balladeer — and radio's first national superstar, thanks to his long series of appearances on the pioneering "EverReady Hour." Everyone who owned a two-tube regenerative in the twenties knew all the choruses to "It Ain't Gonna Rain No' Mo'," and thousands flocked to his personal appearances, helping to prove the power of the new medium.

Walter Winchell Hits His Peak. 1941

Loud, brassy, and abrasive, Winchell was the most influential newspaperman in the country at the dawn of the forties — and his Sunday night news-and-comment programme was by far the most-listened-to news-related programme on the air in the last months before US involvement in WW2.

Arthur Bagley, Network Radio's First Morning Man. 1926

He's forgotten today, but he paved the way for all the network early-bird shows. His "Tower Health Exercises" programme for Metropolitan Life got NBC listeners up and doing from the formation of the network well into the mid-thirties, even as his zany antics with his mascot, the Goofus Bird, set the tone for a legion of morning-men who would follow.

One Man's Family goes National. 5/17/33

Already a hit on the West Coast, Carlton Morse's sensitively-written and deeply-textured study of an upper-middle-class San Francisco family gained a national reputation over the full NBC network, and ran for nearly three decades. There was never another a show quite like it: too serious to be a soap opera, too thoughtful to be a melodrama — and sometimes, even too adult for the kiddies. Morse's mystery shows may have a stronger modern-day following: but for me, "One Man's Family" stands as his greatest accomplishment.

The Talent Raids 1948-49

CBS skims away the cream of NBC's comedy crop by means of some complicated tax maneuverings, and the revenues from these programmes gives the junior network a needed boost at the dawn of the television era.

Elsie Hitz and Nick Dawson and the rise of Romantic Adventure: 1932

Sexual tension in serial drama is nothing new. The smoldering relationships of Elsie and Nick brought a vicarious thrill to Depression-weary women thruout the mid-thirties. The couple starred in three different series of "exotic, romantic adventure" during these years — "Dangerous Paradise," "Follow The Moon," and "The Magic Voice." Different titles, different settings — but the sublimated passion never changed. The concept of the "Super-Couple" is key to soap opera technique to this day, and it can be argued that Elsie Hitz and Nick Dawson were the pioneers. Granted, "Mary and Bob" of the Macfadden True Story Hour came first — but Elsie and Nick had the mystique.

Who's Yehudi?? Spring 1940

Bob Hope was just another fresh-guy comedian thru the late thirties, and while he was a rising star on the Pepsodent Show at the dawn of the new decade, it took a chance exchange with stooge Jerry Colonna over possible names for announcer Bill Goodwin's infant son to capture the national imagination. Was "Yehudi" a figment of Colonna's imagination? A reference to violinist Yehudi Menuhin? Or a mysterious personification of prewar jitters? No one knows — but that didn't stop all America from asking. And as Americans became Yehudi-conscious, they soon made Bob Hope the top-ranked radio comedian in the land.

National Defence Test Day 9/12/24

Broadcasters and the military join forces for an impressive demonstration of how radio can link the country together in the event of an emergency. The substance of the evening — a series of rather tedious speeches, livened only by one general's seemingly-tipsy rendition of an old barracks song — is less important than the technical skills necessary to make it all happen, as engineers flawlessly shift from point to point along a coast-to-coast network: demonstrating techniques that would become essential in the years to come.

A Christmas Carol: 12/25/34

A holiday tradition begins as Lionel Barrymore appears for the first time as Dickens' covetous, grasping old sinner, in a segment of a three-hour Christmas Day broadcast over CBS, under the sponsorship of the Nash-Kelvinator Company. The tradition would endure in various formats for the next twenty years — and, in recorded form, to this day.

The Death of Will Rogers 1935

The "Cowboy Philosopher" was a fixture on radio thruout the Depression years, and while he had a successful career in movies and as a syndicated newspaper columnist — to say nothing of his many years on the stage —by the early thirties, most Americans knew him as the man with the alarm clock, giving out wry and sometimes even caustic commentary on the passing scene. His sudden death in the summer of 1935 sent a nation into mourning.

Don Becker's Weak-End Satires 1928

Before he became a soap-opera writer/producer ("Life Can Be Beautiful"), Don Becker was a ukulele playing utility man at WLW Cincinnati. And he was also the medium's first notable satirist, parodying the conventions of radio at a time when they had barely been established. While recording artists like Jones and Hare had kidded the emerging medium on phonograph records, Becker took the idea even further: creating an entire fictitious network and making the day-in day-out effluvia of broadcasting into one big running gag. His weekly presentation of the programmes of the "Lavender Network" and his depiction of the behind-the-scenes chaos have been echoed by innumerable comedians. Stoopnagle and Budd, Brad Browne, Raymond Knight, Fred Allen, Stan Freberg, Bob and Ray, even Saturday Night Live and Second City have all done it since — but the forgotten Don Becker blazed the trail.

Shakespeare Summer 1937

Imagine a season in which the two major networks battled for listeners not with comedians or swing bands - but with the Bard himself. NBC's "Streamlined Shakespeare" offered condensed plays starring John Barrymore, while the CBS presentation of "Hollywood Salutes Shakespeare" gave movieland favourites a crack at the Classics.

The Fall Of William L. Shirer 1947

Was he fired for being too liberal? Or was he fired for being lazy? Was Shirer, later to be blacklisted, the victim and Ed Murrow the villain? Or was it all just a massive misunderstanding? To this day, arguments rage over the departure from CBS of the legendary newsman. The real, full story will probably never be known, but that didn't make the issues raised any less significant, as radio moved into a dark new era.

The Rise of Joe Penner Fall/Winter 1933

Tens of millions of otherwise reasonable radio listeners are captivated by a bizarre, manic child-man, whose piercing catchphrases echo across playgrounds and schoolyards, offices and street corners for nearly two years before the craze fades away.

Academics have tried to dissect the Penner phenomenon — but in fact there is no rational explanation for it. It just *is*.

Fall Of The City 4/11/37

Earle McGill's spectacular production of Archibald McLeish's chilling vision of a not-so-future war brings the Columbia Workshop to maturity. Hardly anyone was listening — but many of those who did were themselves creative radio people, who were profoundly influenced by the program's power.

Bob and Ray Present The CBS Radio Network 1959-60

The best-loved satirists of their era, Bob Elliot and Ray Goulding rose out of local Boston radio in the late forties to epitomize the postwar approach to radio comedy. Inspired by the works of Stoopnagle and Budd and Raymond Knight twenty years before, Bob and Ray kidded radio with a unique, stream-of-consciousness sensibility, and their 1959-60 series for CBS presented them at the peak of their creative powers.

The Rise of Jessica Dragonette 1930-31

No one who listened to the "Cities Service Concerts" series in the early 1930s will ever forget her fragile soprano voice — but the woman behind that voice was a tough, no-nonsense professional who firmly stood her ground in battles with sponsors and the network over programme formats and choice of material. Her appeal crossed the boundaries of popular and classical music, and though her career was compromised by conflicts, her legend remained.

"The Great Gildersleeve" Spins Off 1941

The term "spin-off" really didn't come into wide use until the early 1970s — but the seeds for the concept go back to Fibber McGee's puffed-up neighbour. While "Gildersleeve" wasn't strictly the first programme to "spin off" from another if you think in terms of variety-hour derivatives like "The Aldrich Family" and "We The People," it was the first important series to be based on a supporting character from another programme — and it was also the most enduring. Harold Peary's textured performance in the title role (until 1950), a solid supporting cast, and brilliant writing — especially by the team of John Whedon and Sam Moore — helped give "Gildersleeve" the longest first-run life of any "spin off" series, radio or TV.

The Rise and Fall of the Liberty Broadcasting System 1948-1952

It all started with the mercurial Gordon McLendon, and his need to fill time on his Dallas radio station, KLIF. Looking for cheap, appealing programming, he decided to feature recreated Major League baseball games. But he didn't figure on the results — in an era in which the westernmost Major League clubs were located in St. Louis, the entire western half of the United States was hungry for big league action. McLendon began to line up regional affiliates, and by 1951, his operation had gone national. McLendon was an innovator, no question about it — but he was also, to put it bluntly, a pirate. He had no legal right to air the games he was airing — and Major League Baseball went after him in court. Liberty was driven into bankruptcy, but McLendon was a survivor — who would go on to be one of the innovators of the "Top Forty" Format.

Hollywood Speaks on the Dodge Victory Hour 3/29/28

As the "talkie revolution" terrorizes the film capital, a phalanx of Hollywood's biggest names faces the microphone: Mary Pickford and Douglas Fairbanks, Charlie Chaplin, D. W. Griffith, John Barrymore, Dolores Del Rio, Norma Talmadge, and Gloria Swanson. Fairbanks was MC, Chaplin told Jewish and Cockney dialect jokes, Barrymore offered a scene from Hamlet, Del Rio performed a song, and the others delivered short talks —as millions of Americans heard the voices of these film favourites for the first time. And judging from the reviews, many of those listeners weren't at all impressed. Nonetheless, the show marks the start of a long liaison between Big Time Radio and Hollywood.

Gunsmoke and the rise of the Adult Western 1952

The heroes don't wear white hats or shoot silver bullets. The villains don't snarl and twirl their mustaches. And the endings are rarely happy. Norman

MacDonnell and John Meston gave radio a searingly-realistic drama: a western for people who hate westerns, and perhaps the most relentlessly *adult* programme of the entire OTR era — and its success contributes to a final "golden age" flurry of quality radio drama.

A Fireside Mystery Chat 10/17/36

A paid political broadcast over CBS by the Republican National Committee takes the art of "negative campaigning" to new heights, as Senator Arthur Vandenburg conducts a mock debate — pitting himself against out-of-context recordings of President Roosevelt. The programme itself is controversial and is made even more so by the fact that CBS cuts it off the air — not on political grounds as charged by the GOP, but on the grounds that the use of recordings violates the network prohibition on transcriptions! Nevertheless, the programme pioneers the use — and abuse — of political "sound bites."

The Rise and Fall of "Pot O' Gold" Fall-Winter 1939/40

A venal twist on the old carnival wheel-of-fortune gimmick, this big-money quiz is the first network programme to offer large sums of money to listeners waiting by their phones at home. The series becomes a national craze before NBC decides it's too close to a lottery for comfort. The basic concept would resurface on ABC after the war as the infamous "Stop The Music."

Unemployment Relief Programme 10/18/31

Stars join forces for a spectacular dual network programme urging the "haves" to help the "have-nots" as the Depression nears rock bottom. President Hoover delivers a speech stressing his belief that relief is the responsibility of the states and local charities and not the federal government — and Will Rogers doesn't sound like he's smiling as he delivers an uncharacteristically bitter critique of the American Way Of Doing Business.

Hugo Black Defends Himself 10/1/37

For the first time, an embattled national political figure uses radio to directly answer charges against him. A decade before, this Supreme Court nominee had belonged to the Ku Klux Klan — and over an all-network hookup, he came before the American people to explain himself and to repudiate the organization. Black went on to a career as one of the court's most distinguished liberals — and his speech set a take-it-to-the-people precedent that would be followed in years to come by such figures as Richard Nixon and Bill Clinton

The London Naval Conference 1/21/30

World leaders gather in the British capital to discuss Naval arms limitations — and radio allows the world to listen in. NBC listeners follow the conference by BBC shortwave relay in a day-long special broadcast — the first international news story to be covered in such a manner. It's also the first time American audiences hear a broadcast by a British monarch, as King George V opens the ceremonies.

Dragnet - a new era in police drama 1949

Just a cop doing his job, for thirty minutes a week. No wisecracks, no gum-chewing gun molls, no threadbare private eye cliches. Jack Webb created a whole new genre of radio crime drama — a world of hard-working, down-to-earth law enforcement professionals who always finished their paperwork. His influence is with us yet.

Superman Battles Intolerance 1946-47

Juvenile adventure characters had always fought well-defined, simplistic villains: robbers, smugglers, pirates, Nazis. But in the first postwar spring, the mightiest hero of them all tackles a terrifying new enemy— terrifying because he lives in every child's hometown. Terrifying because he might live right next door. Terrifying because he or she might be your own father or mother. Or, maybe, might even be you yourself. "Superman's" crusade against hate and bigotry is by far the most complex subject matter ever taken on by a children's programme — and over the next year, is a recurring theme in the series: breaking new ground for a genre which is usually concerned with issues no more complicated than selling cereal — and, hopefully, helping to open the eyes of a generation of kids.

Mae West meets Charlie McCarthy 12/12/37

"Why Don't You Come Play In My — Woodpile," purrs the sultry movie star to a flustered wooden puppet, to the nervous laughter of the studio audience. Earlier in the evening, Mae West had traded mild ribaldries with Don Ameche in the famous "Garden of Eden" sketch as a guest on the Chase and Sanborn Hour — and it's that sketch that generates all the uproar, thanks to complaints from Catholic religious authorities in New York. But the truly explicit material comes later in the evening in Miss West's innuendo-filled exchange with Charlie McCarthy: possibly the bluest ten minutes the Red Network ever aired.

Kate Smith's War Bond Marathons 1944

Radio stars are wholehearted in their support for the war effort, but none more so than Kate Smith. Twice, she mounts round-the-clock marathon appeals for War Loan Drives — appearing every hour on the hour on CBS to urge listeners to support the campaigns. By wars' end, Kate Smith is by far the show-business bond-selling champion: personally responsible for raising more than $600,000,000 for the war effort.

Lux Presents Hollywood 6/1/36

He doesn't produce the show. He doesn't direct it. He has nothing to do with casting it or choosing the scripts. He sometimes doesn't even show up for rehearsals. All he does is read lines someone else has written for him. But to listeners, none of that matters. Cecil B. DeMille *is* Hollywood. And when a two-year-old dramatic anthology moves to the film capital in mid-1936, the J. Walter Thompson Agency makes a brilliant move in tapping him to host. In interviews, he often takes public credit for work he didn't do — a nod here to the unsung agency men who were the real masterminds of the programme: Danny Danker, Tony Stanford, and Frank Woodruff — but nevertheless DeMille wraps the programme in his own mystique: and makes the Lux Radio Theatre a national institution.

Flood Tide for Demagogues 1935

Senator Huey P. Long, Father Charles E. Coughlin, The Reverend Gerald L. K. Smith, Dr. Francis Townsend. Names that may not mean much today, but to radio listeners in the spring of 1935, they represent the thundering voice of political extremism. Promoting a weird blend of free-silver populism, anti-Semitism, and what can only be described as an Americanized "national socialism," Long, Coughlin, Smith and Townsend are all over the airwaves — both the mainstream networks, and in Coughlin's case over a coast-to-coast private hookup — and millions of Depression-weary listeners are paying close attention to what they have to say.

The assassination of Long removes the movement's most popular speaker from the scene — but his colleagues carry on, sponsoring a third-party presidential candidate in 1936. Pressure from this radio-driven movement has a lasting effect, as the Roosevelt administration defuses one of its most potent weapons — the Townsend Revolving Old Age Pension Plan — by promoting an alternative: the Social Security Act. One is left to ponder — with a shudder — what might have happened had Long been alive to head the "Union Party" ticket in 1936.

Amos' Wedding 12/25/35

Seven years to the night after they became engaged, Amos Jones and Ruby Taylor are wed in a simple, dignified Christmas Night ceremony that caps the golden era of "Amos 'n' Andy," and marks the culmination of one of radio's most memorable love stories — the tale of an unschooled but earnest young man from the country in love with a well-bred, college-educated young city woman. It was a tender, gentle romance which endured economic hardship, family tragedies, misunderstandings, and a near-fatal illness, all the while helping to establish precedents which would be followed in soap opera and "family drama" for decades to come.

Arthur Godfrey Goes National 1945

It isn't the first time he's heard on a network, but when Arthur Godfrey greets his coast-to-coast listeners on the morning of April 30, 1945, he stakes out a claim that would keep him there for twenty-seven years. Along the way, he becomes CBS's greatest moneymaker, and an influence on an entire generation of broadcasting personalities. One can make a convincing case that Godfrey was the greatest simple *communicator* ever to face the mike.

WLS National Barn Dance moves to the "Hayloft" 1928

Chicago was the capital of country music during the twenties and early thirties — and WLS was its headquarters, reaching a vast audience all over the midwest. The primary showcase for the station's impressive roster of musical talent is the Saturday night "National Barn Dance" programme —on the air since 1924 — and when this series moves to Chicago's Eighth Street Theatre, soon to be known as "The Hayloft," it enters its golden era. In 1933, the show goes national: and Lulu Belle and Scotty, the Hoosier Hot Shots, the Vass Family, the Maple City Four, Uncle Ezra, and all the rest find a whole new audience.

We Hold These Truths 12/15/41

An eloquent paean to the Bill Of Rights by Norman Corwin, featuring a cast of big-name stars and heard over all networks becomes one of the most-heard single broadcasts of the entire radio era, with an estimated audience in excess of sixty million. Coming just a week after the US entered the Second World War, the programme sets the tone for Corwin's wartime output — programmes stressing a uniquely populist brand of patriotism.

Sorry Wrong Number 5/25/43

It's lost a lot of its impact from constant repetition — is there anyone out there who *doesn't* know how it ends? But Agnes Moorehead's handwringing tour-de-force performance in Lucille Fletcher's tight little murder story is, in many ways, the essence of the radio suspense drama. Its notoriety helps land CBS's sustaining "Suspense" series a big-budget sponsor, and helps lay the foundation for a twenty-year run.

Light's Golden Jubilee 10/21/29

Radio joins the nation together in tribute to the fiftieth anniversary of the invention of the electric light bulb. Thomas Edison himself is the guest of honour in an elaborate ceremony broadcast from Dearborn, Michigan under the auspices of Henry Ford, and President Hoover heads a long list of dignitaries on hand for the festivities. Even Albert Einstein joins in by shortwave from Germany. Graham McNamee, at mikeside for NBC, and Ted Husing for CBS, give a stirring descriptions of the highlight of the evening — the reenactment of the lighting of the first electric bulb. The entire event is one huge publicity gimmick, orchestrated for General Electric by PR mastermind Edward Bernays — and points the way for a long succession of self-congratulatory Corporate Media Events to follow.

The Rise of Information Please Summer/Fall 1938

Bright people sitting at a table talking. No scripts at all — just questions sent in by listeners, the sort of things we'd call "trivia" today. It doesn't sound like a particularly promising idea — but "Information Please" proves to be the surprise radio hit of 1938. It's a highbrow show that even a lowbrow can love, with questions ranging from Shakespeare to baseball, and panelists able to cover all that ground with energy left over for sparkling repartee. The series spawns a number of forgotten imitators — "So You Think You Know Music?" "Fun in Print" — as well as a sort of precocious little niece known as "The Quiz Kids", but none of the imitations ever rise to the level of the original. And one could argue that in the unscripted, spontaneous "Information Please" format one finds the true ancestor of the modern talk show.

Mrs. Wicker and Miss Mack. 1930-31

Radio for children splits into two directions at the dawn of the 1930s — the heavily commercialized and hyperactive adventure serials, and the quieter, more contemplative sort of entertainment best represented in the works of Ireene Wicker and Nila Mack. Both come to prominence as the 1930s are getting underway: Wicker as NBC's "Singing Story Lady" and Mack as the director of CBS's "Adventures of Helen and Mary," a precursor to the better known "Let's Pretend." There are formatic differences between the two — Wicker is essentially a solo performer, while Mack works behind the scenes of a fully-dramatized production — but they share a similar outlook on the sort of entertainment they offer to youngsters. And together, they blaze a trail to be followed in later years by such thoughtful creators as Paul Tripp, Bob Keeshan, Shari Lewis, and Fred Rogers: a trail that leads to a world of gentle imagination.

And Now Get Ready To Smile Again... 1932

Husband-and-wife situation comedies first show up in the late twenties, with shows like "The Jenkins Family" and "Graybar's Mr. and Mrs." They're all pretty much the same sort of thing: harassed white-collar husband dealing with a more-or-less ditzy wife. Even bright spots like the urbane "Easy Aces" are simply variations on this standard format. But in 1932, an NBC-Chicago staff writer named Paul Rhymer takes this cliche and turns it sideways. "Vic and Sade" isn't a sitcom, isn't a drama, isn't really a serial. It's easier to say what it isn't than to figure out what it is — a fun-house-mirror held up to a quiet midwestern family that manages to be both profoundly ordinary and awesomely bizarre. And it echoes down thru the years in the works of such performers as Jean Shepherd and Bob Newhart.

Little Orphan Annie and the rise of Juvenile Adventure. 1931

With a new decade comes a new approach to childrens' programming — rollicking, rousing, blood-and-thunder serialized adventure: epitomized by a blank-eyed frizzy-haired funny-paper heroine. On radio, Annie loses the harsh ultra-right-wing political overtones of Harold Gray's comic strip — and becomes the personification of an aggressive childhood: solving mysteries, exploring the world, and horrifying Concerned Parents for more than a decade. From the drooling hard-sell of the Ovaltine commercials to the endless send-away-premium offers, "Annie" sets the tone for an entire genre: Jack Armstrong, Tom Mix, Captain Midnight, Hop Harrigan — they're all her children.

The Lone Ranger Hits The Big Time: January 1934

The Mutual Network wasn't founded by the Lone Ranger, no matter what they claim at WXYZ. But when the Masked Rider Of The Plains rides onto stations in Cincinnati, Chicago and New York — by arrangement of the Gordon Baking Company — he strengthens the links that already exist between WOR and WGN, stations that are already on the way to becoming the nucleus of that new chain. And more important, The Ranger goes on to become radio's most enduring contribution to American popular culture — and one of the best-known fictional characters of all time.

Dr. Brinkley almost wins the Kansas Governorship Fall 1932

Today, we see him as a quaint sort of quack — a bearded face right off a patent medicine bottle, a twanging Kansas voice offering up spicy barnyard metaphors. To the AMA, he was a dangerous fraud — parlaying a phony medical degree and an eccentric idea for revitalizing impotent men into a national reputation over his radio station KFKB. But to his heartland followers in the 1920s and early 1930s, John Romulus Brinkley is a champion — fighting for their interests against them slickers from the Big City, and their support makes KFKB, for a time, the most popular station in the United States. Following investigations by the AMA and the Kansas City Star, Brinkley's fraudulent background is made public — but that doesn't stop the Doctor. Eventually, from an ultra-high-power radio station just over the Mexican border, Brinkley blankets the entire nation with his graphic condemnations of Internationalism, the Medical Establishment, and prostate massage. On the strength of his down-home line of patter — and his unstoppable signal — he comes within 30,000 votes of winning Kansas' highest office. Brinkley's station is finally muzzled by Mexican authorities in 1941, and he dies bankrupt in 1943 — but his tradition of medical/political charlatanism is alive and well today on dozens of shortwave and small-time AM stations.

Orson Welles becomes The Shadow 9/26/37

It isn't great art. It's never a ratings blockbuster. But this Sunday-afternoon superhero saga has captivated generations of listeners. And many of those listeners will tell you that the 22-year-old Welles was the greatest Lamont Cranston of them all. Others (including me) may find him a just bit too callow compared to the more mature Bill Johnstone. But no one will dispute that Welles makes an impression in the role — and even more important, the part helps pave the way for even more impressive roles to come.

The 1936 Olympics 8/36

Thru the crackle of shortwave static, American listeners sit spellbound by the descriptions of Jesse Owens' track and field triumphs in Berlin— victories that carry significance far beyond the stadium. The announcers are rather circumspect in their descriptions of the events — reluctant, perhaps, to offend broadcasting authorities in the host country — but Owens' triumphs speak for themselves.

Let's Dance, and the Rise Of Swing Winter 1934-35

Suggesting that swing music began with Benny Goodman will earn you a derisive, deserved sneer from fans of Duke Ellington, Fletcher Henderson, Don Redman and other great Harlem bands of the twenties. But that distinctive span of time we think of as the "Swing Era" did begin with Goodman, and his tenure on the Nabisco "Let's Dance" programme. For many listeners, it's their first real exposure to "hot" music — and the programme starts Goodman on the way to being crowned King of Swing. Maybe some people tuned in "Let's Dance" for the mellow melodies of former Clicquot Club Eskimo Kel Murray, or to rhumba with Xavier Cugat — but it's Goodman's contribution to this three-hours-a-week series that's earned it a place in history.

The Metropolitan Opera Begins Its Run 12/24/31

The Met made its radio debut back in the prehistoric DeForest days of 1910 — but it takes another two decades before a regular series of Metropolitan Opera broadcasts begins, even though individual Met stars were network radio celebrities as early as 1925.

But the Met organization makes up for lost time, rapidly building its Saturday afternoon broadcasts into a radio tradition. Part of the tradition is in the packaging — with the gently-unctuous Milton J. Cross occupying a permanent seat in Box 44, inspiring three generations of listeners with his endearing, wide-eyed love for the music and its performers.

The Rise of Experimental Drama 1934-38

Radio goes thru a quantum change between 1931-1933 — the days of freewheeling experimentation with programme formats are replaced, so far as sponsored programmes are concerned, by tight advertising agency control. But there is still unsold time to fill — and the experimenters find a haven in sustaining dramatic programmes like the NBC Radio Guild and the Columbia Workshop, as well as the more outre offerings like "Lights Out." During the mid-thirties, people like Vernon Radcliffe, Irving Reis, William N. Robson, Earle McGill, Wyllis Cooper, Arch Oboler and Orson Welles push the envelope of what can be done in radio drama. Though their audiences are small-to-negligible, much of their work retains its power even today.

Coronation of King George VI 5/12/37

All the world is listening as a slender, stammering man known to his friends and family as "Bertie" mounts the throne of the British Empire in the wake of his brother's abdication. Millions of Americans get up early in the morning to follow all the pageantry via shortwave relay, described in meticulous detail by BBC commentators. The response to the broadcast suggests that even a hundred and sixty years after the Revolution, Americans are really still just Colonists at heart.

The Lindbergh Baby Tragedy 1932-1936

Radio listeners are glued to their sets in horror on the night of March 1, 1932 as NBC and CBS broadcast a steady stream of bulletins detailing the story: the toddler son of aviator Charles A. Lindbergh has been kidnapped from his New Jersey home. Perhaps the most poignant radio moment in the entire case comes the day after the kidnaping, as NBC staff announcer Ben Grauer reads an urgent message to the kidnappers from Anne Morrow Lindbergh — giving the recipe for the baby's special formula. The first chapter of the story comes to a tragic conclusion on May 12th, when the child is found dead — leading to a two-year search for the killer. On September 19, 1934, a German-immigrant carpenter from the Bronx is arrested and charged — and radio is once again in the thick of coverage, as Bruno Richard Hauptmann is placed on trial for his life — a trial which, with radio's help, quickly degenerates into a media circus the likes of which wouldn't be seen for another sixty years. Two important radio careers get a boost from this case: disc jockey Martin Block rises to fame over WNEW in Newark as he spins records during breaks in that station's trial coverage; and WOR commentator Gabriel Heatter grabs attention for his nightly summations of action in what truly is the Trial of The Century. The final chapter is written on April 3, 1936, when Heatter reports from outside the New Jersey State Prison at Trenton as, to the chants of an angry mob, Hauptmann goes to the electric chair — proclaiming his innocence to the very last.

Irna Phillips joins NBC 1933

If Correll and Gosden are the Fathers Of the Broadcast Serial, then Irna Phillips is its mother. Joining NBC with "Today's Children," a thinly disguised version of her WGN serial "Painted Dreams," Phillips begins an enduring career as one of the leading creators of network soap opera — her shows always a cut above the treacly productions of her major competitors, Frank and Anne Hummert. And the Phillips influence is still pervasive in modern-day soaps, with her longest-lived creation, "(The) Guiding Light," still very much alive after sixty-two years.

Hollywood Hotel brings movieland to the mike fall 10/4/34

Hollywood and radio were a natural match, and as far back as the late twenties, there had been efforts to bring the two together. Programmes like the "Sunkist Musical Cocktail" and "Hollywood On The Air" had featured movieland gossip and celebrity interviews - but these shows were expensive to produce, thanks to the exorbitant AT and T line charges for programmes originating on the West Coast. In 1934, columnist Louella Parsons (who had been featured a few years earlier on the Sunkist programme) hits upon a solution: she would use her considerable influence to coerce stars into appearing for free on a big-time weekly variety hour. Campbell Soup underwrites the project, and "Hollywood Hotel" is on the air. Unionization eventually brings an end to Parsons' use of free talent, by which time AT and T has changed its rate policy, allowing radio to thunder westward with a vengeance.

WSM Barn Dance begins 11/28/25

It all goes back to George D. Hay, one of the great announcers of the mid-twenties. Styling himself "The Solemn Ole Judge," Hay had been one of the movers behind the "WLS Barn Dance" in Chicago, and when he moves on to Nashville in 1925, he brings the idea along with him. By the end of the year, WSM is featuring a block of home-grown melodies every Saturday night, with Hay as announcer and rustic fiddler "Uncle Jimmy" Thompson the best-known attraction. Within two years, the "WSM Barn Dance" takes on a new name — and the "Grand Ole Opry" is well on its way to becoming one of the true landmarks of twentieth century popular culture.

H. V. Kaltenborn covers the Spanish Civil War 9/3-4/36

He doesn't fit the dashing, romantic image of a war correspondent — a lanky, balding middle-aged man with thick glasses and a scribbly moustache. But Hans von Kaltenborn makes journalism history when he becomes the first American reporter ever to broadcast live from an actual war zone. Crouching between a haystack and a cornfield on a farm in the Spanish town of Irun, his microphone lines clipped onto a farmhouse telephone, Kaltenborn brings CBS listeners the actual sounds of battle — the whizzing bullets, the chatter of machine guns, the thunder of artillery, all broadcast live — just three hundred yards from the front lines. Thru it all, this Harvard-trained newspaperman keeps up an extemporaneous commentary which offers a vivid description of the scene and a detailed explanation of what is happening and why. The next day, Kaltenborn's listeners hear the outcome of the battle: the entire town lies in flaming ruins, sacked by Franco's forces. Kaltenborn's gone down in history as a rather self-absorbed, pontifical man — but there is no questioning his front-line courage.

Mary Margaret McBride Hits Her Prime 1941

Women's programming in the OTR era is, for the most part, a hopeless wasteland — banal, condescending, and trivial. But there are bright spots — none brighter than Mary Margaret McBride. A veteran journalist, critic, and author with a deceptively folksy style, McBride moves beyond the ossified formats of "womens' radio" to present thought-provoking, substantial programmes. Her best series by far is her 1940s local show over WEAF — a forty-five minute midday feature in which she brings to the microphone important authors, journalists, politicians, celebrities — the only requirement being that they have something worthwhile to say.

Murrow reports on Buchenwald 4/15/45

There are really no words adequate to describe what Edward R. Murrow saw as he toured one of the most notorious of the Nazi concentration camps - but he finds words non-etheless. Other Murrow broadcasts are more famous — but none are more eloquent.

First Transatlantic Relay Broadcast 3/14/25

You can barely make it out thru the overwhelming roar of static — there! there it is! Dimly, you sense the rhythm of a familiar tune — a dance band squawking out "Alabamy Bound." And there — that voice, that halting British voice, saying something about 5XX, Daventry — the High Power Station Of The British Broadcasting Company. History is made as RCA's relay station in Belfast, Maine receives an experimental longwave pickup of 2LO in London, and relays that fragile signal by shortwave to the network of WJZ in New York and WRC Washington — giving thousands of American listeners their first taste of Overseas Broadcasting. The technology is something of a dead end — longwave would prove too unreliable for long-term, long-distance use — but the broadcast is a vivid demonstration of how radio can truly bring the world into your home.

Fibber's closet opens for the first time 3/5/40

A gimmicky sound effect that becomes a national institution — and which for many symbolizes everything fun and innocent about "Old Time Radio."

Fibber McGee and Molly had plenty of running gags over the years, due largely to the always inventive scripting of Don Quinn: a writer who can impart fresh flavor to even the moldiest corn — but none have lingered longer in the public consciousness than that overstuffed hall closet.

"The Step on the Stair" 1926

Based on a story in "Radio Digest" magazine, this Old Dark House thriller is radio's first true mystery serial — heard over WLW, Cincinnati in a series of weekly installments adapted for radio by programme director Fred Smith (who is better known as the creator of "The March Of Time.") Smith is one of the most important unsung pioneers of radio — his 1923 play "When Love Wakens" may be the first American drama to be written especially for radio. Although "Step" is actually a rather crude bit of melodrama, it proves the thriller to be an ideal format for radio: so much so that the script is sold to other stations for local productions, and is still being heard as late as 1930.

Gracie Allen's Brother January/February 1933

It isn't radio's first running gag — but it's the most memorable of its time, as Gracie Allen begins popping up on programmes all over the schedule, asking for help in locating her enigmatic "missing brother." The bit grabs the national imagination during the most wretched of Depression winters — and vaults Burns and Allen to the front ranks of radio's comedy stars.

Report on Chain broadcasting reshapes the Industry 1941

It's not a radio programme — it's a small, paper-bound book. And between the government-issue-orange covers, there's a bombshell: the Federal Communications Commission rulings condemning monopolistic practices in broadcasting. Beginning in 1938, the FCC had been holding detailed hearings investigating the degree of control exercised over the broadcasting industry by NBC and CBS — and the Commission didn't like the picture that emerged: stiff, one-sided contracts that strangled local control of programming and which tended to concentrate the power of radio into the hands of two dominating corporations. The report sends a shock wave thru the industry, forcing the networks to revise their contractual ties to their affiliates — and forcing the National Broadcasting Company to divest itself of one of the two networks that it operated.

Rudy Vallee Refines the Variety Show Fall 1932

He's more important as an impresario than as a performer — and the "Fleischmann's Yeast Hour" is the reason why. Rudy Vallee had been on the air for Fleischmann since 1929, broadcasting an hour-long programme of dance music, broken up only by the appearance of a single guest star each week. But beginning in October 1932, Vallee and the staff at the J. Walter Thompson agency dramatically revise the programme format: de-emphasizing Vallee's performances and turning the spotlight on a continuing parade of guest artists. Big names, famous names, old names and new names — for the next seven years, the Vallee programme features the best that Broadway and Hollywood have to offer — and Vallee gains a reputation as radio's foremost talent scout. Whether he himself is actually entitled to that reputation is a question that can be debated: some claim he did run the show — and none claimed this more energetically than Vallee himself — while others say he was just a front man and embittered JWT staffers did all the work. The truth is probably somewhere in between — but the importance of the show itself is beyond question: it's the pace-setter for every variety series that would follow.

The Rise Of Major Bowes Spring/Summer 1935

As spinning goes that weekly wheel of fortune — round and round she goes and where she stops nobody knows — as the saponaceous Major Edward Bowes takes the nation by storm with his Sunday night new-talent showcase, moving a longstanding local New York feature to a high-profile Sunday night slot on NBC. Never mind that, as a Radio Guide expose reveals, elements of the show are rigged — the idea of young entertainers from Mudville USA getting their big break on the air ignites a craze for amateur entertainment that inspires a range of imitators. Few of the Bowes discoveries amount to anything — but there *are* a few who stand out, including a skinny singer from Hoboken who appears in September 1935 as a member of a pop quartet. His Bowes experience proves something of a dead end - but fate has other plans in store for Frank Sinatra.

The Music Licensing War 1940-41

The American Society of Composers Authors and Publishers doesn't much like the attitude of Network Radio — and radio likes ASCAP even less, as negotiations for a new contract allowing the use of ASCAP music break down during the last months of 1940. As the name-calling continues, it becomes evident that there will be no peaceful resolution, and the broadcasters form their own music licensing agency — Broadcast Music Incorporated, which quickly signs a roster of second-tier songwriters in anticipation of a long standoff. As of January 1st, 1941 all ASCAP-controlled music disappears from the network air, leaving only public domain and BMI compositions in their place. Longstanding theme songs abruptly vanish, bandleaders scramble to come up with workable arrangements, the broadcasters put up a brave front — but listeners quickly grow tired of "Jeannie With The Light Brown Hair" and "The Wise Old Owl." By mid-year, the networks and ASCAP have a new agreement — and the status quo resumes. However, BMI sticks around — cultivating new songwriting talent and evolving into a major force in the music business: remaining so to this day.

Paley's Financial Maneuverings Save CBS 1928-1929

William Paley perpetuated a lot of legends about his early years at CBS. Although he styled himself "Founding Chairman," Paley *didn't* found the network — George Coats and Arthur Judson did, with help from the Levy brothers of Philadelphia and Major J. Andrew White. Nor did the infusion of Paley's personal fortune completely turn the tide for the struggling company. But the real story of how Columbia survived the Depression is even more interesting - and says a great deal about Paley's remarkable ability as a businessman. The young son-of-a-cigarmaker manages to talk the cagey film mogul Adolph Zukor of Paramount Publix Corporation into a complicated stock swap in 1929, which gives the foundering network the boost it needs to stay afloat during the bad years ahead: even though Zukor's own company, ironically, ends up in receivership!

The 1923 World Series 10/23

Broadcasting of major league baseball's main event was early on a major attraction — but it's the 1923 Fall Classic between the New York Yankees and the New York Giants that makes the big impression, and for reasons unanticipated. Originally, plans call for the action to be described over WEAF by veteran sportswriter Grantland Rice — and he's to be assisted by a recently-recruited member of the station's announcing staff: a former concert singer by the name of Graham McNamee. For the first three games, McNamee provides what would eventually come to be called "colour commentary" - and his descriptions are so vivid, so enthusiastic that listeners deluge the station with phone calls and telegrams demanding to see more. And so it is that beginning with game four, McNamee takes over the full play-by-play job — and is launched on a career as the most important personality of radio's formative years. One can fault his accuracy, one can criticize his style — but none can deny his impact.

Premiere of the NBC Symphony 12/24/37

Arturo Toscanini had been a familiar personality to American radio listeners since the turn of the thirties thru his work with the New York Philharmonic — and had already come to personify the traditional image of the "glowering maestro." And so it is that NBC scores a major publicity coup in 1937 when it lures Toscanini back to the United States with the unprecedented offer of an orchestra constructed especially for him, designed to his specifications, and to be directed as he sees fit — and for nearly eighteen years, the NBC Symphony Orchestra under Toscanini's baton is one of radio's outstanding musical attractions.

Eddie Cantor Runs For President Winter 1931-Fall 1932

The Depression's darkest months fall in the middle of 1932: more 15 million are unemployed in the US, and more than 270 thousand families face imminent eviction from their homes. By September of that year, more than 34 million Americans are without any income whatsoever, and the nation has witnessed the grim spectacle of tanks rolling thru the streets of Washington DC against an army of unemployed veterans. Against this backdrop, Americans are desperate for escape, desperate for anything that will take their minds off the horror of the times. And they get it — in a pop-eyed, hyperkinetic Broadway clown. Eddie Cantor takes the nation by storm with his satirical run for the Presidency, setting an audience record never to be equaled by any other continuing radio series. Cantor's comedy is frenetic and flamboyant, with a strong undercurrent of contempt for authority — and, by extension, for those who have brought the nation to rock bottom. Small wonder the bouncing chant of "We Want Can-tor!" still echoes thru the memories of that era.

The Benny-Allen Feud January-March 1937

"The Bee," by Franz Schubert — a showy specialty composition for violin — becomes the most famous piece of music in the country as the question rages: can Jack Benny play it? It all begins, innocently enough, with a boy violinist named Stewart Canin, appearing on the "Town Hall Varieties" segment of Fred Allen's programme on 12/30/36. During the second show for the west coast, Allen comments on the boy's rendition of "The Bee" with a single, simple observation: "Jack Benny," he drawls in that inimitable snarling whine, "should be ashamed of himself." And out in Hollywood, Benny listens — and the following Sunday makes his response: "When I was ten years old, I could play "The Bee" too!" And the following Wednesday, Allen challenges this assertion — and from then on, every week marks an escalation of the "argument," until finally, on the night of 3/14/37, the combatants meet face to face in the Grand Ballroom of New York's Hotel Pierre to have it out once and for all. The results? Inconclusive. But for the next twelve years, Jack and Fred — in reality old-time friends from vaudeville — will snipe back and forth in radio's most memorable phony feud. And they don't forget the boy who started it all: in 1940, Benny and Allen jointly award Stewart Canin a scholarship to help cover the cost of his future musical education, helping him along the way to a distinguished adult career in classical music.

The Rise Of Syndication 1928-1932

When all is said and done, the invention of the syndication concept is without doubt the most important of Freeman Gosden's and Charles Correll's contributions to the broadcasting industry. The idea of distributing recorded programmes to individual stations begins with "Amos 'n' Andy" in 1928, and the two performers attempt to patent the concept, only to be told by their attorney that they can't. And so it is that before the end of 1928, the National Radio Advertising Company is selling recorded programming to national advertisers — and by the end of 1930, syndication is sweeping the industry, offering real competition to the wire-line networks in attracting major national sponsors like Chevrolet and major nationally-licensed properties like Edgar Rice Burroughs' "Tarzan." Syndication remains an essential element of both radio and television to this day: a billion-dollar industry that owes its existence to Gosden and Correll and their simple, ingenious idea for a "chainless chain."

WGY and the Birth of Radio Drama 9/22

You might not have heard of Kolin Hager, unless you're from Schenectady. He was the programme director and chief announcer at General Electric's station WGY in the early twenties — and he could well be considered the Father of Radio Drama. In September 1922, Hager gives a forty-minute weekly time slot on WGY to "The Masque," a troupe of community-theatre actors from nearby Troy, NY, headed by one Edward H. Smith. As the "WGY Players," Smith's company offers condensations of recent stage plays — forty-three of them in the first season — and gain national attention for their efforts: the first regular dramatic series ever broadcast on American radio. Among the members of the group - a former stage technician named Frank Oliver: radio's first true sound effects man. The WGY Players are a fixture at the station for more than a decade, and in 1928 perform another historic first: the first play ever to be televised.

The Second Louis-Schmeling Fight 6/22/38

He was called "The Brown Bomber," "The Tanned Titan," "The Sepia Superman," and, most embarrassingly, "Shufflin' Joe." But on a steaming June night at Yankee Stadium, all the condescending "credit to his race" talk is forgotten, as Joe Louis stands as the symbol of America — facing the equally-formidable symbol of "Aryan Superiority," German heavyweight Max Schmeling. Schmeling had defeated Louis in a prior bout — but not this time. Before NBC announcer Clem McCarthy has a chance to get warmed up, Louis gives Schmeling the beating of his life — and gives radio listeners a few quick minutes they will never forget.

NBC Takes Over 11/15/26

Not the first network broadcast, but the most heavily publicized. When the newly formed National Broadcasting Company takes over operation of the AT and T Red Network in November 1926, it's taking over a network that's already providing sixteen-hour-a-day service to seven stations, and varying hours of service to twelve others. NBC puts the whole operation on a full-time basis and with a four-hour gala from the Waldorf Astoria Hotel, announces to the whole nation (or at least the whole nation as far west as Kansas City) that the age of Big Time Radio has arrived.

London after Dark August/September 1940

Americans receive a jolting dose of reality when CBS begins a dramatic series of broadcasts from the heart of a city under siege. Airing as a joint venture of the BBC and the CBS London staff headed by Edward R. Murrow, "London After Dark" is a heart-stopping document of the Blitz. CBS correspondents Larry LeSeur, Eric Sevareid, Vincent Sheehan and author J. B. Priestly all contribute to the programme, but it's Murrow who makes the dominant impression in the initial broadcast of 8/24/40: his chilling account of defiant Londoners strolling casually to the air raid shelters — illustrated by the hollow sound of their footsteps —provides an audio picture that will echo forever in the annals of radio journalism. Less than a month later, on September 21st, Murrow tops this broadcast with an even more dramatic scene, as "London After Dark" presents a bomb-by-bomb description of another air raid, live from the rooftop of Broadcasting House. Similar broadcasts will be made by NBC's Fred Bate — who is nearly killed in a subsequent air raid — and by Mutual's Arthur Mann: but Murrow gets the credit for the idea, and for forcefully bringing the horrors of modern war into American homes.

Death and Funeral of FDR 4/12-15/45

For a generation of Americans, he was simply "the President." Millions loved him — millions hated him. But all Americans are stunned at his death, when on the afternoon of April 12th, childrens' adventure serials are interrupted by the sudden announcement of Franklin D. Roosevelt's passing. Radio helps express a nation's grief with detailed coverage of the funeral procession on all networks, including a memorably emotional description by CBS's Arthur Godfrey.

8XK Becomes KDKA 11/2/20

It wasn't the First Radio Broadcast — experimental stations had been on the air for over a decade. It wasn't the first Scheduled Broadcast: some of the experimenters had been operating on a scheduled basis before the first World War. It wasn't the First Radio Election Coverage — Lee deForest had offered detailed coverage of the 1916 returns over 2XG, New York (and got the results wrong). In other words, many of the "firsts" claimed for this famous broadcast have their basis in the Westinghouse publicity department, not in reality. So why is it important? Well, the Westinghouse publicists did a good job. A *very* good job. They make an essentially regional event into headline news all over the country — and in doing so help make Americans radio conscious. KDKA would go on to be an important laboratory for future radio developments — as would Westinghouse's second station, WJZ in Newark (later, in New York)

The 1924 Democratic National Convention June-July 1924

"Allllll-a-baaaaaaaama casssts twennnnnnty-four votes for Oscarrrrr W. Under-woooood!" That's the call, as delivered a total of one hundred and three times by Alabama Governor William Brandon during the Democratic National Convention, as broadcast June 24th thru July 9th, 1924. The eventual nomination goes to John Davis, who will of course be trounced by Coolidge in the general election that fall. Underwood was actually a pretty significant figure in politics at the time — he had been Senate Minority Leader, and went on to become Governor of Alabama. But all anyone remembers about him is that he got those 24 votes at the convention. Eighteen stations make up the AT and T network for this broadcast, extending as far west as Kansas City — and the RCA stations also join in. The broadcasters are Graham McNamee and Phillips Carlin for AT and T, and Major J. Andrew White and Norman Brokenshire for RCA, who together help to introduce millions of fascinated listeners to the intricacies of the political process — and also spawns a national catch phrase that echoes across playgrounds and city streets for much of the summer.

Crosby In The Can 1946

Actually, it should be Crosby in a paper sleeve — since Bing's first venture in to pre-recorded programming was done on disc, not tape. Excited by the potential for a flawless performance afforded by disc-editing techniques exploited during the war years by the Armed Forces Radio Service, the crooner finds himself a sponsor and a network willing to allow him to experiment with pre-recording his regular weekly series beginning in the fall of 1946 — and Philco Radio Time proves a success. Among those who notice is an Army veteran named Jack Mullin - who had become interested in the tape-recording systems used by the German radio during the war years, and who convinces Crosby to invest in his fledgling Ampex Corporation. The Crosby programme begins to be mastered on tape in 1947 —and with Crosby's support, Ampex becomes a major force in the development of broadcast recording technology, leading the way the in the early development of video tape in the 1950s. And Crosby's success in recorded form helps to bring down the unreasonable network barriers against the use of prerecorded programming — already compromised in many areas, the walls come tumbling down for good in 1949.

The Dempsey/Carpentier Fight 7/2/21

What the KDKA Harding-Cox Election Broadcast was in legend, the broadcast of the Jack Dempsey-Georges Carpentier Heavyweight Fight is in reality: the event which really makes the general public sit up and take notice of radio. While no more than a thousand hobbyists heard the KDKA Election Broadcast, advance publicity leads over two hundred thousand to hear the fight broadcast eight months later, and the resulting excitement draws many thousands of others into discovering what this new radio thing is all about. As was his custom, David Sarnoff greatly exaggerates his role in promoting this epoch-making broadcast — the real man behind the scenes — and behind the mike — is Major J. Andrew White: who would go on to be one of the major figures in the early years of CBS

The inauguration of Coolidge 3/4/25

For the first time, Americans from coast to coast listen in as the President takes the Oath of Office and delivers his inaugural address. AT and Ts Red Network and RCA's smaller Radio Group network broadcast all the pageantry as Calvin Coolidge begins his first full term — and proves himself to be an adept radio speaker, well-attuned to the demands of the microphone. An estimated fifteen million listeners follow the proceedings, with Graham McNamee at the microphone for the Telephone Group and Major J. Andrew White and Norman Brokenshire on hand for the RCA/Westinghouse stations.

The Dempsey/Tunney Long Count Fight 9/22/27

If the twenties were truly the "Golden Age Of Sport," the second heavyweight title fight between Gene Tunney and Jack Dempsey at Soldier Field in Chicago may be the high point of that age — and radio helps make it so. For the first time, all NBC's associated stations, Red, Blue and Pacific, are joined to broadcast a single event, with the exuberant Graham McNamee and Phillips Carlin at the mike. Was the final count improperly delayed? Debate still rages to this day.

McNamee, Carlin, Cross and Daniel broadcast the return of Lindbergh 6/11/27

It's the News Story Of The Decade — the moment which seems to epitomize the mystique of the "Roaring Twenties." And when the twenty-five year old newly-promoted-to-Colonel Charles A. Lindbergh returns to the United States courtesy of the U. S. Navy, a team of NBC's top announcers turn out for day-long coverage of his arrival — helping impress the moment forever on the national consciousness. And, to this day, recordings of the honest, overwhelming *thrill* in Graham McNamee's voice as he sees the aviator step down the gangplank capture the essence of that moment in a way the printed page never can.

Radio Transforms Itself 1931-33

Two factors change the face of radio programming during the lowest ebb of the Depression — a disastrous season on Broadway in 1931, and the desire of advertising agencies for better bang for their bucks. The collapse of the Live Theatre drives many of the top names of musical comedy and vaudeville into broadcasting — Eddie Cantor, Ed Wynn, Jack Benny, Fred Allen, Burns and Allen, and many others all turn to radio during these years, and in doing so, forever shift the emphasis in programming away from radio-grown talent and towards Big Names. Agency control of programme development builds on this trend — taking the responsibility for programme building away from the networks, and placing it under the control of sponsors: firms interested more in selling product than in encouraging real creativity. The result, from the mid-thirties forward: a compulsively cautious attitude towards innovation in programming that dominates the medium until the rise of television.

Andy sued for breach-of-promise by Madame Queen January-March 1931

Movie theatres really do interrupt their screenings to play "Amos 'n' Andy" over the sound systems. Department stores really do broadcast the show over their public address speakers. Water consumption really does take a drop for fifteen minutes, six nights a week. And when Andy Brown is taken to court by his beautician fiancee Madame Queen in early 1931 — the climactic event in a storyline that's been brewing for over a year — an estimated 40 million listeners hang on the outcome of each night's episode. For a weekly show, that would have been an unprecedented audience — but for a *nightly* show, it's a stunning accomplishment. The secret of the program's success is readily apparent to anyone who digs back into the early scripts: a gallery of finely-drawn, fully-realized, and all-too-human characters, and an instinctive, near-Dickensian grasp of serial storytelling technique. What also becomes apparent is that by and large, listeners don't tune in to *laugh at* the characters. They tune in because they truly *care* about what happens to Amos, Andy and their friends — fictional characters who are as real to Depression America as the people next door.

War Of The Worlds 10/30/38

Like a lot of legends, the story of Orson Welles and his Martian Invasion has grown with the telling. It's probable that no more than six million people heard the broadcast, and Professor Hadley Cantril in his landmark study of the "invasion" estimated that at most only about a million people were actually fooled — out of a total population of around 150 million, and compared to the 35 million Americans who went on blithely listening to Charlie McCarthy, unaware that anything was out of the ordinary. But the numbers, in the end, don't really matter.

What matters is that Welles and company provide a graphic demonstration of just how powerful the audio medium can be — and even more significant, the post-mortem public response to the broadcast reveals just how unprepared Americans really are for the brave new Media Age ahead.

FDR's First Inaugural 3/4/33

The winter of 1932-33 may have been the most grim in our nation's history. The economy was in ruins, the banking system was collapsing, tens of millions were hungry, with no money, no jobs, and no hope. But on a chilly March afternoon, a newly inaugurated President reaches out with his voice to calm the panic, to convince a terrified America that, indeed, the only thing it has to fear is fear itself.

The Hindenburg Description 5/8/37

Is there a living American who *hasn't* heard WLS staff announcer Herbert Morrison's sobbing account of the explosion of the legendary German dirigible? Without doubt the most famous actuality recording of all time, Morrison's description of the disaster is so vivid that it becomes the first notable exception to NBC's prohibition on the airing of recordings. It only aired twice over the network — and never in its entirety — but Morrison's recording has nonetheless transcended the original event to become one of the most familiar audio documents of the twentieth century.

FDR's first Fireside Chat 3/12/33

"My friends. I want to tell you what has been done in the last few days, why it has been done, and what the next steps are going to be." In a calm, reasoned, thirteen-minute talk, the new President outlines the steps taken to prevent a full-scale collapse of the nation's banking system — explaining the complexities of industrial economics in terms that any citizen can understand. This gentle, informal approach projects the atmosphere of a man talking to his neighbours by the fireside — and CBS-Washington manager Harry Butcher coins an enduring phrase to describe the style: a "fireside chat."

The European Crises: 9/38 and 8/39

Mounting tensions in Europe work to a peak over a year's time — beginning with the Sudetenland crisis in September 1938 and culminating in the dispute over control of the Polish Corridor and the free city of Danzig the following August. The Sudeten crisis proves to be the first great international challenge for radio news — still hamstrung by the terms of the 1933 Press-Radio Agreement. But the medium rises to the occasion, making household voices out of CBS's Ed Murrow and William Shirer, NBC's Max Jordan and Fred Bate, and Mutual's John Steele — and above all, CBS's H. V. Kaltenborn, who provides a continuing stream of concise and well-reasoned commentary as the crisis unfolds. Following the agreement at Munich — the "peace in our time" accord — radio documents the continuing deterioration of European peace, until the German invasion of Poland leads to the declaration of war. The tired voice of British Prime Minister Neville Chamberlain announcing that declaration early on the morning of September 3, 1939 is evidence of a terrible lesson, learned too late: if you sit down at table with Hitler, prepare to be the main course.

Farewell Speech of the former King Edward VIII 12/12/36

The "Love Story Of The Century" transcends national borders, as the American people join with all the rest of the English-speaking world in listening to the thin, weary voice of a man who gave up the throne of the world's most powerful empire for the woman he loves. The poignant broadcast by Edward, Duke of Windsor, is the single most-listened-to moment of the 1930s.

Pearl Harbour 12/7-8/41

A typical Sunday afternoon by the radio — light music, sustaining drama, public affairs programmes, pro football. But at 2:22 pm, a one-line bulletin flashes over the Associated Press wire, shattering the tranquility. Within minutes, the news of the Japanese attack on Pearl Harbour, Hawaii is being relayed by all four networks — and all the debate between Isolationists and Interventionists is suddenly and terribly rendered moot. Radio covers the story in depth — and perhaps the most chilling moment is the voice of an unnamed staff announcer at NBC's Honolulu affiliate, proclaiming "This is no joke! This is war!" The following day, record audiences tune in as President Roosevelt's message to a joint session of Congress sets the tone for the next four years.

The Rise of Toll Broadcasting 1922-23

Radio advertising didn't just suddenly spring into being one afternoon in August 1922 at WEAF. There's evidence to suggest paid commercials had aired on stations in Massachusetts and Washington state several months before the WEAF landmark, and barter advertising goes back at least as far as 1916 and Lee deForest's experimental station 2XG. But WEAF doesn't have to have been the birthplace of the commercial for it to have been the most important station in the evolution of modern broadcasting — for it was indisputably the first station to be established for the specific purpose of selling time to advertisers. WEAF's success leads in October 1924 to the formation of the first permanent radio network — and the concept of "toll broadcasting" proves to be the foundation on which the entire structure of American radio — and later, television — would be built.

End of the War 8/14/45

V-E Day on May 8th was just the beginning of the end — and the enthusiasm that greets the end of the war in Europe is tempered by the realization there's still a war to be won in the Pacific. But the use of atomic weapons against Japan changes the whole complexion of the conflict — and beginning with the dropping of the Nagasaki bomb on August 9th, radio listeners anxiously wait for word on Japan's imminent surrender. August 10th goes by - the 11th — the 12th — the 13th — all with a steady stream of bulletins, but no official statements. Unofficial reports come in early on the morning of the 14th — and at 4:18 that afternoon, NBC's Max Jordan reports from Berne, Switzerland with the first word confirming that the intermediaries have received a message from the Japanese Government. "I myself," announces Jordan in his distinctive clipped voice, "am going to a party of the American consulate here to celebrate V-J Day!" Shortly after 7 pm, official word is released by the White House — and the long-delayed celebration finally erupts. Radio paints an unforgettable sound picture of celebrations in Times Square, outside the White House, and in towns and cities all over the United States as the nightmare of the Second World War finally draws to a close.

D-Day 6/6/44

It is arguably the single most important news story of the 20th Century — the beginning of the Liberation of Europe from a regime which has come to embody modern evil. And radio covers it from beginning to end, in depth and in person. The highlights are many: Wright Bryan of NBC describing the disappointment of a paratrooper who failed to make his scheduled drop, Charles Collingwood of CBS making his way to a Normandy beach, George Hicks of the Blue Network describing the joy of Navy gunners bringing down their first Nazi plane. But perhaps the greatest thrill comes at 3:32 am on June 6th, as Colonel R. Ernest Dupuis reads the concise, understated communique the entire world awaited: "Under the command of General Eisenhower, Allied naval forces, supported by strong air forces, began landing Allied armies this morning on the Northern Coast of France." History in the making — and, for me, radio's finest moment.

RADIO BROADCASTING IN THE UNITED STATES

In 1906, an inventor from the General Electric Company (GEC) developed a device capable of transmitting human voice through radio waves. This technology was put to use in 1917 in a powerful station in New Jersey by Guglielmo Marconi, who represented his British company. This radio station was then taken over by the US government in 1917 to be used for communications during the World War I.

The great significance of the device was noted to be the ability of one nation to speak to another, and after the war US government was reluctant to give the technology back to the British company.Instead, the government offered its support to GEC, preferring state monopoly to the foreign one. The idea was to organize an American radio company powerful enough to withstand Marconi commercially, and GEC would become the nucleus of such enterprise. The American General Manager of the Marconi Company realized that state and public opinion were raging against his company, and was forced to give up his share of the market. Instead, the American Marconi Company merged with the newly formed Radio Corporation of America (RCA), opposing the monopoly of GEC. "RCA also allowed a limited measure of government influence in its affairs and the following provision appeared in its bye-laws:

The corporation may permit a representative of the Government of the United States the right of discussion and presentation in the board of the Government's views and interests concerning matters coming before the board."

Most American broadcasting stations of the late nineteen tens were run by amateurs, who viewed radio as a hobby. At that time, the broadcasts were still directed to a limited number of people, since "receiving a broadcast required a good bit of skill and perseverance."In 1916 a Westinghouse engineer began regular radio broadcasts, playing music during his programmes, apparently funded by a local store selling radio receivers. This idea was picked up by Westinghouse, that in 1920 established the first American commercial radio station, KDKA.18 By establishing such a station Westinghouse took an enormous step in radio development by realizing that the future of the radio lies in mass communications, and not in confidential radio conversations.

Commercial stations such as KDKA were funded by sales of radio receivers that were necessary for listening to their programmes. The new marketing strategy became very popular in nineteen twenties — 670 stations were licensed in the US by the end of 1922.

The main goal of these companies was the sale of equipment; broadcasting was simply a way to promote sales. But, as radio technology was becoming more popular, sales of radio sets were being affected by radio amateurs that assembled receivers from parts.

Radio companies were slowly realizing that the sales of radio receivers would not support their industry for long. A hit idea from AT and T, a partner of RCA, was to sell air time to businesses willing to advertise on the radio. The idea of advertisement on the radio was strongly opposed by the public, and has reached its crisis in 1927, "by which time the industry had discovered which side of its bread was buttered—there was no going back."

In 1926, a High Court judgement ruled that government regulations imposed on radio companies were too strict. The result of this decision was "chaos in the airwaves as the radio stations arbitrarily increased power, shifted frequency and started up without licenses." The American public demanded the return of government regulations, and in 1927 the Federal Radio Commission (FRC) was founded.

By monitoring and regulating the development of radio stations, FRC brought back the order into the radio business. An Act of 1934 clarified the function of the Commission, which included "studying new uses for radio, providing for experimental uses of frequencies and generally encouraging the larger and more effective use of radio in the public interest." The Act also spoke of broadcast licenses providing use of channels, "but not the ownership of thereof."

RADIO BROADCASTING IN BRITAIN

The first experimental broadcasts, from Marconi's factory in Chelmsford, began in 1920. Two years later, a consortium of radio manufacturers formed the British Broadcasting Company (BBC). This broadcast continued till its licence expired at the end of 1926. The company then became the British Broadcasting Corporation, a non-commercial organisation. Its governors are appointed by the government but they did not answer to it.

Lord Reith took a formative role in developing the BBC, especially in radio. Working as its first manager and Director-General, he promoted the philosophy of *public service broadcasting*, firmly grounded in the moral benefits of education and of uplifting entertainment, eschewing commercial influence and maintaining a maximum of independence from political control.

Commercial stations such as Radio Normandie and Radio Luxembourg broadcast into the UK from other European countries. This provided a very popular alternative to the rather austere BBC. These stations were closed during the War, and only Radio Luxembourg returned afterwards.

The British Broadcasting Corporation (BBC) is the largest broadcasting corporation in the world. It produces programmes and information services, broadcasting on television, radio, and the Internet. The motto of the BBC is *Nation Shall Speak Peace Unto Nation.*

The BBC is a public service broadcaster though not in the sense used in some other countries (in particular, the United States) of a producer expected to provide only programmes that commercial companies would not broadcast. On the contrary, many BBC programmes are expected to achieve high viewer ratings, not least as justification for the levying of the universal licence fee by which it is financed (BBC schedules do not include any advertising). The BBC produces, for example, dramas, game shows, often innovative comedies and soap operas, including the very popular *Eastenders*. Commercial broadcasters in the United Kingdom have, on the other hand, historically been required by the terms of their licences to produce a certain minimum amount of "minority-appeal" programming.

The original *British Broadcasting Company* was founded in 1922 by various private firms to broadcast experimental radio services. The first transmission was on 14 November of that year.

The Company, with John Reith as general manager, became the *British Broadcasting Corporation* in 1927 when it was granted a Royal Charter of incorporation and ceased to be privately owned.

The BBC has five major national stations, Radio 1 ("the best in new music"), Radio 2 (the UK's most listened to radio station, with 13.7 million weekly listeners), Radio 3 (specialist-interest music such as classical, world, arts, drama and jazz), Radio 4 (current affairs, drama and comedy), and Radio 5 Live (24 hour news, sports and talk).

There is also a network of local stations with a mixture of talk, news and music in England and the Channel Islands as well as national stations of BBC Radio Wales, BBC Radio Cymru (in Welsh), BBC Radio Scotland, BBC Radio nan Gaidheal (in Scots Gaelic), BBC Radio Ulster, and BBC Radio Foyle.

The BBC has been at the forefront of digital radio broadcasting with Five Live Sports Extra (a companion to Five Live for additional events coverage), 1Xtra (for black, urban and gospel music), BBC 6 Music (*alternative* genres of music), BBC7 (Comedy, Drama and Kids shows), Asian Network (Asian talk, music and news in many Asian languages), and World Service.

For a world-wide audience, the BBC produces the Foreign Office funded BBC World Service, which is broadcast worldwide on shortwave radio, and on DAB Digital Radio in the UK. The World Service can be received in 139 capital cities worldwide and is a major source of news and information programming for over 140 million listeners worldwide. The Service currently broadcasts in 43 languages and dialects (including English), though not all languages are broadcast in all areas.

Since 1943, the BBC has also provided radio programming to the British Forces Broadcasting Service, which broadcasts in countries where British troops are stationed.

All of the national BBC radio stations, as well as the BBC World Service, are available over the Internet in the RealAudio streaming format. The BBC has also recently experimented with the free, open source Ogg Vorbis streaming audio format and podcasting.

Radio Normandie: Captain Leonard F. Plugge (1889–1981) was a British Member of Parliament from 1935 to 1945 who created the International Broadcasting Company in 1931 as a commercial rival to the British Broadcasting Corporation by using buying airtime from European radio stations such as Radio Normandy in the 1931. Other stations IBC worked with were Toulouse, Ljubliana, Juan les Pins, Radio Paris, Post Parisien, Athlone, Barcelona,Madrid and Rome. IBC only worked indirectly with Luxembourg. Among other things Plugge invented the two-way car radiotelephone.

Radio Luxembourg (1933-1992) was an important forerunner of pirate radio and modern commercial radio in Europe. It was a cheap and effective way to advertise in the UK, France and (since 1957) in Germany by circumventing the broadcasting restrictions in place at the time. For many years complete English programmes were pre-recorded in London and flown to the tiny independent grand duchy of Luxembourg on mainland Europe. German programmes were produced in a studio in Luxembourg. A powerful transmitter enabled broadcasts to be received throughout northern Europe. Luxembourg was special, because while radio stations all over Europe were exclusively government-owned and operated well into the 1980s, Radio Luxembourg was right from the beginning privately owned. A radio amateur (Ham) managed to get a licence in 1924 and used the license to broadcast military music, too. French businessmen bought the license from the radio amateur in May 1929 and managed to get a broadcasting monopoly in Luxembourg in November 1929. In May 1931 the *Compagnie Luxembourgeoise de Radiodiffusion* was founded, which started to build the transmitters. Transmissions in French and English started in 1933.

The station was closed three weeks after the beginning of World War II, because the grand duchy of Luxembourg wanted to keep neutral. However, Luxembourg was occupied by Nazi-Germany, and the station became part of the Großdeutscher Rundfunk. The usual propaganda was broadcast, *e.g.* fabricated news stories delivered by William Joyce ('Lord Haw-Haw').

Luxembourg was occupied by American troops in September 1944. It was then used as Radio 1212, a black propaganda station aimed at undermining German morale. Between April to November 1945 the station transmitted the programming of the Voice of America. Radio Luxembourg produced and transmitted its own programming during this time, too. But not under the name "Radio Luxembourg", but as a "United Nations Station.

The station reached its peak in the 1950s after it switched its wavelength to 208 metres (1439 kHz, later 1440) the number with which it became synonymous, in 1951 ("”2-0-8 Power Play"). Its cultural influence in the UK was immense and it is rightly regarded as one of the main forces for the popularization of rock'n'roll in Britain; those who equate popular culture with politics argue that this is ironic for a station based in mainland Europe.

In the 1960s the station had to compete against the pirate radio stations located closer to the UK on ships or abandoned World War II sea forts, and was disadvantaged by its inability to broadcast by day. The tendency of its signal to keep fading in and out also put many listeners off. In the 1970s its audience continued to decline as BBC Radio 1, Capital Radio and other local radio stations competed for its audiences. At one point it became an all disco station. The station's 50th anniversary in 1983 was a rather low-key affair in the UK.

RADIO BROADCASTING IN INDIA

Radio broadcasting began in India in 1927, with two privately-owned transmitters at Mumbai and Calcutta. These were nationalised in 1930 and operated under the name Indian Broadcasting Service until 1936, when it was renamed All India Radio (AIR). Although officially renamed again to Akashwani in 1957, it is still popularly known as All India Radio All India Radio (AIR) is still the most popular media, considering the fact that it is assessible even in the remotest parts of our country where any other media like TV or newspapers cannot reach. When India attained Independence in 1947, AIR had a network of six stations and a complement of 18 transmitters. The coverage was 2.5 per cent of the area and just 11 per cent of the population. Rapid expansion of the network took place post Independence.

AIR today has a network of 223 broadcasting centres with 143 medium frequency(MW), 54 high frequency (SW) and 161 FM transmitters. The coverage is 91.42 per cent of the area , serving 99.13 per cent of the people in the largest democracy of the world. AIR covers 24 Languages and 146 dialects in home services. In Externel services, it covers 27 languages; 17 national and 10 foreign languages. Today there are all types of programmes braodcasted on AIR. Although there is tough competition with the new upcoming private channels, AIR has introduced new channels to offer options to listeners like music, news, drama, sports etc. In spite of recent penetration by other media such as Cable TV, AIR remains the most common means of gaining access to information and entertainment, as the radio receivers are relatively cheap and affordable. AIR has many different services each catering to different regions/languages across India. One of the most famous services of the AIR is the Vividh Bharati Seva (roughly translating to “Multi-Indian service”). This service is the most commercial of all and is popular in Mumbai and other cities of India. This service offers a wide range of programmes including news, film music, comedy shows, etc. The Vividh Bharti service operates on different MW band frequencies for each city.

Yuv-vani: Yuv-vani service of AIR provides an enriching and novel radio-experience by encouraging youth participation and experimenting with varied script ideas. With shows like “Mehfil”, “In the groove” and “The Roving Microphone” which have been around for more than three decades, Yuv-vani still holds a firm ground of its own.

Some of the big names on the Indian media scene began their journey with Yuv-vani. Some of the other names that have been associated with Yuv-vani in the past include Celebrity game show host Roshan Abbas, VJ Gaurav Kapoor, DJ Kaushal Khanna,Emcee Kshitij Sharma and DJ Pratham among others.

News-on-phone service: All India Radio, after launching the news-on-phone service on 25th February 1998 from New Delhi, is running the service from Chennai, Mumbai, Hyderabad, Patna and Bangalore also. The service is accessible through STD, ISD and local telephone calls. The service is going to be started from 9 more cities — Ahmedabad, Guwahati, Imphal, Jaipur, Kolkata, Lucknow, Raipur, Simla and Thiruvanthapuram shortly.

English and Hindi hourly news bulletins can be heard live on http://www.newsonair.com. The news in MP3 format can be directly played from the site. In the file name the hourly time of news is mentioned. Text of the English and Hindi bulletins can be read from http://www.newsonair.com/BulletinsInd.html.

AIR news bulletins are available in 9 regional languages (Tamil, Kannada,Gujarati, Bengali, Marathi, North East, Punjabi, Telugu, Urdu) from http://www.newsonair.com/regional.html.

News-on-phone access numbers in India are:

1. Chennai: 044-2467 1111/1258 (Tamil), 044-2467 2222/1258 (Tamil)
2. Delhi: 011-2332 4242/1258 (Hindi), 011-2332 4343/1259 (English)
3. Mumbai: 022-2281 7009/1259 (Marathi), 022-2281 5420/1258 (Hindi)
4. Hyderabad: 040-2324 4343/1259 (Telugu)
5. Patna: 0612-220 7621 (Hindi)
6. Bangalore: 080-22377525 / 1258 (Kannada), 080-22377530 / 1259 (English)

9

Impact of Television Advertising

Advertising to children has always provoked strong feelings and contradictory opinions. Some advocates of child-directed advertising believe that advertising has no or negligible negative effect on children, and that the consequences of advertising are rarely lasting. They argue that children are critical consumers who are capable of defending themselves against the possible harmful effects of advertising. According to other advocates, advertising provides children with valuable product information, so that they learn how to become consumers.

Many opponents of child-directed advertising, however, believe that commercials aimed at young children can have a profound impact on their beliefs, values, and moral norms. Critics fear that children, more than adults, are susceptible to the seductive influences of commercials because they do not have the necessary cognitive skills to protect themselves against the attractive and cleverly put advertising messages. According to these authors, advertising to children can

- Create materialistic attitudes;
- Result in conflicts in the family;
- Encourage bad eating habits.

Finally, opponents argue that advertising can make young children dissatisfied and unhappy because they are less able than adults to resist the temptations in advertisements. Since the mid 1970s, an impressive number of studies on the topic of children and advertising have been conducted. These studies have focused on three types of effects: cognitive, affective, and behavioural effects. Studies examining the cognitive effects of child advertising usually focus on children's ability to distinguish commercials from television programmes, and their ability to understand the persuasive nature and selling intent of advertising. Most of these studies have adopted Piaget's theory of cognitive development to guide their research.

Cognitive-effects studies have demonstrated that children who are at Piaget's preoperational stage (2-7 years) react differently to commercials than do children at the concrete operational stage (7-12 years). It has been shown, for example, that children in the concrete operational stage are progressively more able to distinguish commercials from television programmes, and show a better understanding of the persuasive intent of commercials.

Studies investigating the affective effects of advertising concentrate on children's liking of and trust in commercials. Affective-effects studies have documented, for instance, that children's responses towards commercials gradually become less favourable as they enter the concrete operational stage. As children get older, they are more likely to display irritation and skepticism while watching commercials. Finally, studies examining the behavioural effects of advertising focus on the extent to which children are persuaded by advertisements. Since young children usually do not have the means to purchase products, behavioural effects are usually measured by children's preferences for products, or by the requests they make in response to advertised products.

In behavioural-effects studies, children usually watch one or more commercials, after which they are given a choice from a series of products, which include the advertised brand. Researchers then often demonstrate that the advertising of a specific brand makes the child's subsequent choice of that brand more likely. A disadvantage of these studies is that the results that are found within a controlled laboratory setting may not be generalizable to more naturalistic contexts. A number of behavioural-effects studies have attempted to solve this problem by investigating advertising effects in a field setting. One type of field study has focused on the impact of advertising on children's purchase requests by surveying parents or children. Another, less intrusive, type of research has observed how parents and children in retail environments interact with each other regarding the product requests of children.

A third type of field studies has investigated to which extent children's Christmas gift ideas are determined by television commercials. These studies were conducted in the Christmas season, first because child-targeted advertising reaches a peak in this period, and second because children are generally eager to list their preferred Christmas present choices.

Despite the differences in methodology, both the laboratory and the field studies have yielded a number of consistent findings. First, it has been shown that television viewing is a major source of children's gift ideas, and that children who watch more television are more likely to ask for advertised products.

Second, it has been demonstrated that children's requests for advertised products decrease as they mature. Not only do children become more critical about and, thereby, less susceptible to media offerings in middle childhood, they also become more sensitive to peer influences. Research has found that conformity to the peer group peaks between the ages of 11 and 13 years. There is reason to assume that the norms and values that are created in particular peer groups function as a filter for other socializing forces, including advertising.

Finally, it has been suggested that gender plays a role in children's requests for advertised products. A number of studies have demonstrated that boys are more persistent in their requests for advertised products than girls are. This research finding is consistent with general theories on gender differences in parent-child interactions.

It has been shown that boys are on average less compliant than girls to the requests and demands of their parents. Boys also more often rely on forceful or demanding strategies when trying to persuade their parents to comply with them, whereas girls are more likely to rely on tact and polite suggestions. Gender and developmental level also have been shown to influence the types of gifts requested.

Boys tend to ask for activity-oriented items, like computer games, racecars, and action heroes, whereas girls prefer clothing, dolls, and jewelry. In addition, younger children--because of their early cognitive level--often ask for simple, friendly stuffed animals, dolls, and toys, which provide them with feelings of comfort and safety. As children become older, toys begin to lose importance, whereas products with a social function, like clothing and music equipment, take increasingly prominent places as favoured objects.

The aim of the present study was to provide an extension of the third type of field studies, which investigated how television commercials influence children's preferred Christmas gifts. This line of research needs extension for several reasons. First, studies of this type were all conducted in the 1970s.

As most western societies have become increasingly child- and consumer-oriented in the past two decades, there is a need to investigate whether the results of these early studies are still valid. Second, in previous studies the sources of children's ideas were measured by asking children directly where they had seen or heard about the presents that they mentioned (*e.g.*, television, catalogs, interpersonal influence). These studies have consistently found that television was the most dominant source of children's gift ideas. However, it is not certain whether the self-report measures that were used in these studies can be considered as valid indicators of young children's information sources of gift ideas.

In the present study we did not rely on children's self-reports to investigate the extent to which television is an information source of their gift ideas. Like the previous studies, we asked children to nominate their preferred Christmas gifts, but rather than asking children directly to list the source of their requests, we compared their requests to the commercials that were broadcast in the period leading up to Christmas.

We specially examined whether and to what extent the brand names children mentioned in their gift requests were identical to the brands that were advertised at the Christmas season. We also explored if and how children's gender and developmental level predict their requests for advertised products.

RESEARCH QUESTIONS AND HYPOTHESES:

In earlier studies, the percentages of children's requests that were determined by television advertising ranged from 25 per cent, to 49 per cent, and 78 per cent. In the present study, we investigated how these previous statistics compare to elementary school children sampled in 1997. Our first research question therefore was:

RQ.sub.1: To what extent are children's Christmas wishes influenced by television commercials shown in the period leading up to Christmas?

As argued above, several earlier studies have demonstrated that:

- Children who watch more commercial television are more likely to ask for advertised products;
- Children's requests for advertised products decrease as children mature;
- Boys are more persistent in their requests for advertised products than girls are.

We therefore investigated the following three hypotheses:

H.sub.1: Children who watch a lot of television commercials ask for advertised products more often than children who are less often exposed to commercials.

*H.sub.*2: Older children ask for advertised products less often than younger children do.

*H.sub.*3: Boys make requests for advertised products more often than girls do.

Finally, earlier studies suggested that the types of products children request depend on their gender and developmental level. Since research into the types of wishes of boys and girls in different age groups is too scarce to formulate hypotheses, our second research question asked:

*RQ.sub.*2: What types of products do boys and girls in different age groups request?

METHOD

SAMPLE

A total of 250 children between the ages of 7 and 12 participated in the study. The children were recruited from three elementary schools in Utrecht, an urban district in the Netherlands, which consisted primarily of Dutch students with various socioeconomic backgrounds. The sample consisted of 124 boys and 126 girls. The children were grouped into three age ranges: 7-8 (30.6 per cent), 9-10 (40.7 per cent), and 11-12 (28.6 per cent).

This trichotomy was chosen for three reasons. First, it provided us with the opportunity to investigate whether the observed trends in our sample were linear or curvilinear. Second, we wanted to investigate seven- and eight-year olds as a separate age group, because these children are still on the threshold of concrete operations, which qualify them as a separate subgroup. Third, we wanted to investigate 11- and 12-year-olds as a separate subgroup. As discussed earlier, children in this age group develop an interest in products with a social function and the influence of peers is at its peak in this age group. These developments may affect their interest in advertised products.

Procedure

Early in December 1997, children in each classroom were presented with a paper-and-pencil questionnaire. The questionnaire contained questions about children's gender and age, their television viewing behaviour, and their preferred Christmas wishes. Completing the questionnaire took about 20 minutes.

To investigate the number and types of commercials children were exposed to in the period leading up to Christmas, we taped the two most popular commercial children's networks, RTL-4 and Kindernet.

We recorded all commercials that were shown on these networks on Saturday mornings from 8.00 to 12.00 a.m. in the period from 8 November 1997 to 20 December 1997. In total, 876 commercials were sampled, 553 on RTL-4 and 323 on Kindernet. Almost 90 per cent of these commercials were about toys, and 80 per cent of them were shown on both channels.

RTL-4 and Kindernet have the highest viewing density among 6- to 12-year-olds. Both commercial networks were introduced at the end of the 1980s. We selected their Saturday morning programmes because these programmes have the highest ratings among elementary school children. The numbers of television commercials shown on RTL-4 ranged from 25 to 113 per four-hour time span, and those on Kindernet ranged from 13 to 78 over the same time period. Overall, RTL-4 showed 71 per cent more commercials than did Kindernet. This difference is due to the fact that RTL-4 has a larger market share (16 per cent) than Kindernet (10 per cent) in the target age group, with the result that advertisers are more interested in this network.

MEASURES

CHILDREN'S GIFT IDEAS

We asked the children to write down their two most favourite Christmas wishes. For each present mentioned, we determined whether an advertised brand was mentioned. In some cases this was easy. In other cases we were not sure whether the product was advertised. In these cases, the brand name was traced in the recorded advertisements.

Of course, gift ideas like"a doll,""a racecar""money," and"a teddy bear" were not considered as brand names. The intercoder-reliability based on a subsample of 25 per cent of the requests was 99 per cent.

TELEVISION VIEWING FREQUENCY

The children were presented a list of 12 popular children's programmes that were broadcast on RTL-4 and Kindernet. They were asked to indicate whether they always, often, sometimes, or never watched each of the programmes. This method of children's television exposure has proved to be the most valid one for elementary school children.

On the 12 items, we conducted a factor analysis with varimax rotation. This factor analysis yielded three factors, which explained 53.8 per cent of the variance. The first factor (4 items, Eigenvalue 2.01) represented the chi Idren's programmes that were broadcast on Kindernet, the second factor represented the children's programmes broadcast on RTL-4.

The third factor (3 items, Eigenvalue 1.1 8) represented programmes that were made for adults and broadcast in the evening hours.

Scales were constructed for each of the three factors by totaling the unweighted scores on the items that loaded on each factor. Cronbach's alpha values were.72 for the Kindernet scale.70 for the RTL-4 scale, and.51 for the programmes made for adults. Since the latter scale had an inadequate reliability, it was omitted from further analysis.

RESULTS

Our first research question asked to what extent children's Christmas wishes were influenced by commercials broadcast around Christmas. The analysis of children's Christmas wishes revealed that 51.6 per cent of the children specifically asked for at least one brand that was advertised at the time of the survey. The brands that were most frequently advertised also turned out to be the most wanted toys. K'nex, Nintendo, Lego, and Action Man were all in the top 10 of most frequently broadcast commercials. Three of these products, Nintendo, K'nex, and Lego, were also in the top five of most requested products in the whole sample. Action Man also occurred in the top 10 of wishes, but only for the youngest boys.

Barbie turned out to be the most advertised toy. The Barbie commercial represented almost 10 per cent of all the commercials that were broadcast during the period of analysis. Barbie occupied the ninth place in the top 10 gift requests for the whole sample. For the youngest girls, this toy was the second most wanted product.

CHILDREN'S REQUESTS FOR ADVERTISED PRODUCTS BY AGE, GENDER, AND TELEVISION VIEWING FREQUENCY

To investigate our three research hypotheses, which stated that younger children, boys, and children who are more often exposed to commercials ask for more advertised products, we conducted a multiple regression analysis, with the child's age, gender, and television viewing behaviour as independent variables. The dependent variable was the number of gift ideas mentioned by the children that corresponded to one of the commercials broadcast during the period of investigation. The number of children's toy wishes consistent with the brands in television commercials was predicted by exposure to RTL-4, the network that aired most commercials, and not by exposure to Kindernet.

Consistent with our second hypothesis, younger children asked for products advertised on television more often than older children did. Finally, contrary to our third hypothesis, the child's gender did not predict the number of advertised product requests. To investigate curvilinear patterns and possible interactions between age and gender, which would not be expressed in the regression coefficients, we investigated how many boys and girls in each of the three age groups requested advertised products.

Older children asked for advertised products less often than younger children did. Our cross tabulation revealed that the negative age effect that was found in the regression analysis only held for boys. Seventy-six per cent of the seven- and eight-year-old boys asked for at least one advertised product, whereas only 2 7.5 per cent of the 11- and 12-year-old boys requested at least one advertised product. For girls no significant age effect was found. Older girls asked for as many advertised products as younger girls did.

The cross tabulation yielded an interaction effect between gender and age. Among the seven- and eight-year-olds, boys asked for an advertised product more often than girls did, whereas, among the 11 - and 12-year-olds, girls asked for an advertised product more often than boys did.

THE TYPES OF PRODUCTS REQUESTED

Our final research question asked whether and how boys and girls differ in the types of Christmas wishes. To answer this question, we investigated the most popular product requests for boys and girls in the three age groups. All children, particularly the youngest, were quite brand conscious in their selection of toys. The most frequently requested Christmas present was Nintendo. Although Nintendo products were popular among all subgroups, boys in all age groups asked for Nintendo products more often than girls did.

Younger children asked for toys and games more often than older children did. For seven- and eight-year-old boys Nintendo, K'nex, and Lego accounted for 72 per cent of all Christmas wishes. The boys in the lower age group mostly requested activity-oriented toys (racetracks and racecars) and construction toys. For the youngest girls, stuffed animals, dolls, and real-life pets were the most frequently mentioned wishes.

Children in the middle age group more often asked for useful items, like school stationery and sports items. For these categories, children generally did not mention a specific brand name, but asked for"a ball" or"a school notebook." Also in this age group boys and girls differed significantly in their toy wishes. Boys mainly requested sports items, construction toys, computer games, and racecars, whereas girls showed a preference for Spice Girls merchandising, school stationery, stuffed animals, sports items, Fingernail Fun, and Barbie.

11- and 12-year-old children often mentioned products like music equipment and clothing, without mentioning a specific brand name. For the oldest girls, this type of product accounted for 58 per cent of all requests. Popular requests for boys in the highest age group were Nintendo, compact discs, clothing, and a personal computer. For girls of this age, merchandising related to their favourite pop groups, and items related to horses and horse riding were the most favourite gift requests. The main aim of this study was to investigate to what extent child-directed television advertising influences children's Christmas gift requests. Our findings revealed that in the overall sample more than half of the children (51.6 per cent) asked for at least one brand that had been advertised in the period of investigation. How do our Dutch findings compare to the American results obtained in the 1970s?

In the study by Frideres (1973), 78 per cent of the children reported that they saw their requested toys on television. At first sight this percentage may seem incomparable to the 52 per cent that we found. However, the sample in Frideres' study consisted of children in the ages of five and eight, which is younger than the age group that we investigated. When we compare our youngest age group (seven- and eight-year-olds) with those in Frideres' study, the results are more similar. In our study, 76 per cent of the boys and 57 per cent of the girls in the youngest age groups asked for at least one advertised product. The relative low percentage (25 per cent) of requests for advertised products found by Caron and Ward can also be explained in terms of differences in age groups between the studies, because their percentages were based on older children than the children in our sample. The 11- and 12-year-olds in our sample also less frequently asked for advertised products than did the younger children.

Finally, Robertson and Rossiter who used the same age groups as we did, found percentages of requests for advertised products (49 per cent) that were virtually equal to ours. In summary, our Dutch percentages are comparable to the American percentages that were found more than 20 years ago. One could argue that our percentages should have been higher because most societies have become more consumer-oriented over the past two decades. An explanation for this unexpected lack of difference could be that media in the Netherlands have only recently been commercialized. Until the end of the 1980s, Dutch children's programming was limited to public television on Wednesday afternoons and Saturdays.

However, since the introduction of commercial television in 1989, children can watch children's programmes every day and all day long. While the Dutch public broadcasters have always been reserved with child-targeted advertising, today's children's programmes aired by commercial networks are usually loaded with more than 25 child-targeted commercials per hour.

Our first hypothesis predicted that children who watch a lot of television commercials ask for advertised products more frequently than children who view little or no commercials. To investigate this hypothesis we asked children how often they watched a number of programmes on the two most popular commercial networks, RTL-4 and Kindernet.

Children who more often watched RTL-4, the network with most commercials, nominated significantly more advertised products as favourite gifts than did children who less frequently watched this channel. No significant differences were found for Kindernet, the network that showed fewer commercials. Our results are in line with prior research.

In these studies, it was also shown that children who watch more commercial television have more favourable attitudes towards commercials, and are more inclined to believe the advertising messages, which in turn make them more susceptible to advertising influences.

Our second hypothesis that older children ask for advertised products less often than younger children do also received support. We found that two-thirds of the seven- to eight-year-olds nominated an advertised brand product as their favourite Christmas gift, whereas only one-third of the 11- to 12-year-old children did so. One explanation for this finding could be that the needs and preferences of younger children were more similar to the types of commercials that were included in our sample of commercials. We recorded all commercials that were shown during two Saturday morning children's programmes. We found that 90 per cent of these commercials were toy commercials.

Since younger children are more interested in toys than older children, the commercials that were taped might have been more congruent with the preferences of younger children than with those of older children, resulting in more younger children asking for these advertised brands.

Another explanation for our finding that younger children asked for more advertised brands than did older children could be that the younger children in our study are in a transition period with respect to their cognitive and affective reactions to commercials.

As children enter the concrete operational stage (7-8 years), their abilities to understand the selling intent of advertising rapidly increases. They then also become more skeptical towards commercials, and less susceptible to advertising effects. Since the younger children in our sample were only on the threshold of the level of concrete operations, they might have been more vulnerable to the toy advertising campaigns during Christmas than the older children.

Our third hypothesis, that boys would make more requests for advertised products than girls, received support only in the youngest age group. Gender differences were not found among 9- to 10-year olds, whereas for the 11- to 12-year-olds, girls asked for advertised brands more often than boys did.

An explanation for the finding that younger boys are more affected by television commercials than younger girls could be that the commercials in the Christmas period were more appealing to younger boys than to younger girls. Our results showed that for the youngest boys, Nintendo, K'nex, and Lego accounted for no less than 72 per cent of all Christmas gift requests in this age group. The youngest girls asked most often for a nameless stuffed animal.

Our finding that 11- and 12-year-old girls tend to ask for more brand name gifts than did boys in this age group could be because they often requested merchandising related to pop groups, which inherently includes a brand name. Boys in this age group were more interested in items like clothes, personal computers, and stereos, items for which no specific brand name was mentioned.

Both gender and age played an important role in the types of products children requested. Consistent with Kamptner's findings, younger girls preferred stuffed animals, pets, and dolls, whereas younger boys mainly requested activity-oriented toys and construction toys.

In accordance with earlier findings, children in the middle age group start to attach more value to the usefulness of products.

For instance, they frequently asked for school stationery, electronic organizers, and sports equipment. Although the older children in our sample were only 11 and 12 years old, their product preferences resembled Kamptner's findings among adolescents. Boys and girls in the highest age groups requested products with a strong social function (*e.g.*, clothing), and products that facilitate social ties and the expression of aspects of the self (*e.g.*, music, jewelry).

STRENGTHS AND LIMITATIONS OF THE STUDY

This field study, conducted in a naturalistic setting, was designed to investigate to which extent television advertising plays a role in the Christmas gift ideas of school-aged children. We asked children to nominate their favourite Christmas wishes.

We then compared their requests to the commercials broadcast on the two most popular Saturday morning children's networks in the Netherlands.

The methodology of combining a two-pronged approach--the content analysis and the subsequent survey--is in certain ways similar to agenda setting methodology. Traditionally, the theory of agenda setting assumes that public judgements of the importance of certain issues are a result of the prominence of those issues in the media. Agenda setting theory claims that the media determine what the audience thinks and talks about.

Although agenda setting theory has traditionally focused on the realm of news and issue salience, this theory might have broader applications to contexts in which a mass medium could influence what an audience perceives as important. In this study we compared the content of children's commercial media environment with their gift wishes.

We found that the brands that most often appeared on children's wish lists, were exactly the ones that were most frequently advertised. To speak in agenda-setting terms, we found a striking similarity between the agenda of advertisers and that of children.

Although we think that this study has made an important contribution to the literature on behavioural effects of advertising, several limitations do exist. First, our study failed to investigate some alternative sources of children's preferred Christmas wishes.

For instance, children could have seen the toy in a store or got the idea from a friend. Second, some toys, such as Barbie, might be popular, irrespective of advertising, because they perfectly connect to the fantasies of young elementary school girls.

Over the years, manufacturers of children's products have developed a diverse spectrum of highly sophisticated research techniques to investigate children's preferences during the product development cycle.

As a result, children have increasingly added their voices to newly developed toys. The extensive research into children's likes and dislikes, together with the wealth of commercial messages meticulously targeted to specific child segments, has made it difficult for researchers to determine whether toy manufacturers set the agenda for children's ideas and wishes, or whether children dominate the dynamics of toy development.

The two basic tasks of marketing communications are message creation and message dissemination. Media planning supports message dissemination.

Media planning helps you determine which media to use--be it television programmes, newspapers, bus-stop posters, in-store displays, banner ads on the Web, or a flyer on Facebook. It also tells you when and where to use media in order to reach your desired audience.

Simply put, media planning refers to the process of selecting media time and space to disseminate advertising messages in order to accomplish marketing objectives.

When advertisers run commercials during the Super Bowl game at more than $2.5 million per thirty-second spot, for example, media planners are involved in the negotiation and placement.

Media planners often see their role from a brand contact perspective. Instead of focusing solely on what medium is used for message dissemination, media planners also pay attention to how to create and manage brand contact.

Brand contact is any planned and unplanned form of exposure to and interaction with a product or service. For example, when you see an ad for Volkswagen on TV, hear a Mazda's "zoom zoom" slogan on the radio, are told by a friend that her iPod is the greatest invention, or sample a a new flavour of

Piranha energy drink at the grocery store, you are having a brand contact. Television commercials, radio ads, and product sampling are planned forms of brand contact.

Word of mouth is an unplanned brand contact -- advertisers normally do not plan for word of mouth. From the consumer's perspective, however, unplanned forms of brand contact may be more influential because they are less suspicious compared to advertising. The brand contact perspective shows how the role of media planners has expanded.

First, media planners have moved from focusing only on traditional media to integrating traditional media and new media. New media -- cable and satellite television, satellite radio, business-to-business e-media, consumer Internet, movie screen advertising and videogame advertising -- is playing an increasingly significant role. Spending on new advertising media is forecast to grow at a compound annual rate of 16.9 per cent from 2005-2009, reaching $68.62 billion by 2009, while traditional media advertising is expected to rise only 4.2 per cent on a compound annual basis during the same period to $192.28 billion. Second, media planners are making more use of product placements now, in lieu of advertising insertions.

Advertising insertions, like print ads or television commercials, are made separately from the content and are inserted into it.

The ads are distinct from the articles or TV programmes, not a part of them. As a result, the ads seem intrusive. In contrast, product placement (also called brand placement or branded entertainment) blends product information with the content itself.

Whether content is a television programme, movie, video game or other form of entertainment, product placement puts the brand message into the entertainment content. For example, in the movie E.T., the extraterrestrial eats Reese's Pieces candy. The candy was authentically integrated into the movie ?and sales of Reese's Pieces soared 80 per cent after the movie, catapulting the new product to mainstream status.

On the other hand, inappropriate or excessive product placements may do more harm than good to the brand. Finally, the role of media planners has expanded as media planners have moved beyond planned messages to take advantage of unplanned messages as well.

Whereas planned messages are what advertisers initiate -- like an ad, press release or sales promotion -- unplanned messages are often initiated by people and organizations other than advertisers themselves.

Word of mouth, both online and offline, is one form of unplanned message. Although advertisers have little direct control over the flow of unplanned messages, they can facilitate such a flow.

For example, advertising agency Crispin Porter + Bogusky (CP+B) created a viral marketing mascot, the Subservient Chicken, for Burger King to illustrate its slogan "Have It Your Way." Visitors to the www. subservientchicken.com site can ask the chicken to make a move, such as jump, dance or lay an egg. In the first two weeks after the site's launch, the Subservient Chicken story appeared on 63 broadcast segments, including five separate segments in television shows unplanned success.

Within months, the site had generated 426 million hits from 15 million unique visitors averaging six minutes per session. Many visitors learned about the site through word of mouth, both online and offline. More recently, specialized agencies have started to hire word of mouth agents to work for advertisers on a fee basis.

Initial research suggests that many consumers react positively to this kind of word of mouth communication. For example, Rock Bottom brew pub chain, reported a 76 per cent jump in 2003 revenues after hired gun Bzz-Agent launched a 13-week word of mouth campaign employing 1,073 of its "agents" to get the word out.

These new approaches have altered how media planning works in the advertising process. "Seven years ago media was the last five minutes of the presentation. Now it's reversed," said Rishad Tobaccowala of Publicis Groupe Media, whose fast-growing Starcom division helps clients buy and measure interactive, mobile, and gaming ads. Media planners are playing an increasingly important role in today's advertising industry because of the continuing proliferation of new media options and the increased complexity of media and audience research.

How is a media plan developed? Media planning is a four-step process which consists of

- Setting media objectives in light of marketing and advertising objectives,
- Developing a media strategy for implementing media objectives,
- Designing media tactics for realizing media strategy, and
- Proposing procedures for evaluating the effectiveness of the media plan.

Let's take a look at the planning process through an example: P and G's launch of the Gillette Fusion shaving system for men in early 2006. First, P and G's media objectives called for a $200 million media blitz to reach men in the U.S. Second, P and G's strategy included a mix of national media to introduce the brands. For example, television advertising, such as a $5 million Super Bowl ad campaign, portrayed Fusion as an advanced technology found in a secret government UFO lab.

The TV ads also established the brand's signature orange and blue colour scheme. In store aisles, 180,000 display units promoted Fusion, using the brand's colours to catch consumers' attention. "We're trying to put the product wherever men shop," said Pauline Munroe, marketing director for blades and razors in P and G's Gillette business unit. Third, P and G's media tactics -- such as a Father's Day sweepstakes, an episode of NBC's The Apprentice in which the show's teams competed to promote the razor, and sponsorship of competitive surfing -- helped the company reach men of all ages.

"Fusion will get so much attention that it will drive a lot of men to try these grooming products," said Gary Stibel of New England Consulting Group. Finally, P and G used sales and market share targets to assess the effectiveness of the media plan. P and G expects sales of Fusion to reach $1 billion in sales by year three. P and G knows that the brand has already achieved 25 per cent market share in the U.S. Thus, although $200 million seems like a lot to spend on advertising a new product, it represents a sound financial investment towards the tremendous future profit that P and G will gain from the new shaving system.

Now, let's take a deeper look into the media planning process. Media planning, such as planning the marketing communications for the launch of the Fusion new shaving system, starts with setting media objectives.

Media objectives usually consist of two key components: target audience and communication goals. The target audience component of the media objectives defines who is the intended target of the campaign. For example, P and G's target audience objective for its Fusion shaving system was men 18-40 years old. The communications goals component of the media objectives defines how many of the audience the campaign intends to reach and how many times it will reach them. In short, media objectives are a series of statements that specify what exactly the media plan intends to accomplish.

The objectives represent the most important goals of brand message dissemination, and they are the concrete steps to accomplish marketing objectives. You'll learn about sources of data to use to identify your target audience. You'll also learn how to quantify communication plans. The first objective of a media plan is to select the target audience: the people whom the media plan attempts to influence through various forms of brand contact.

Because media objectives are subordinate to marketing and advertising objectives, it is essential to understand how the target audience is defined in the marketing and advertising objectives.

The definition may or may not be exactly the same, depending on the marketing and advertising objectives and strategies. A common marketing objective is to increase sales by a specific amount. But this marketing objective does not specify a target audience, which is why the media objective is needed.

Consider Kellogg's Corn Flakes and all the different strategies the advertiser could use to increase sales among different target audiences. For example, one target audience might be current customers -- encouraging people who eat one bowl a day to also "munch" the cereal as a snack.

Or, the advertiser might target competitors' customers, encouraging them to switch brands. Or, the advertiser might target young adults who are shifting from high sugar "kids cereals" to more adult breakfast fare. Finally, the advertiser could target a broader lower-income demographic.

The point is that each campaign could increase sales via a different target audience. Marketers analyse the market situation to identify the potential avenues for boosting sales increase and consider how advertising might achieve those aims. If the advertiser chooses to attract competitors' customers -- like what Sprint does to attract users of other wireless services -- the media plan will need to define the target audience to be brand switchers and will then identify reasons to give those potential switchers to switch, such as greater convenience, lower cost, or additional plan features. For example, in 2006 Sprint Nextel ran an ad campaign urging consumers to switch to Sprint because "no one has a more powerful network."

THE IMPACT OF INTERMEDIA AND NEWSPAPER COMPETITION ON ADVERTISING

A truism of the media industry is that newspapers face increasingly complex and competitive markets for advertising. The growth of other media during the past few decades has been remarkable. The number of radio stations in the United States almost doubled between 1970 and 1996, and the number of television stations increased from 872 in 19703 to 1,576 in 1998. Daily newspapers' share of total advertising revenues declined from 26.4 per cent in 1986 to 22.5 per cent only ten years later.

As the number of media outlets increases, there is a potential for advertising in a greater number of outlets and a greater diversity of media. However, the degree and nature of intermedia advertising competition's impact on newspapers remain unclear. On the one hand, newspaper managers argue they face an extremely competitive advertising market where they fight with other media to survive. Media economics scholars, on the other hand, maintain that the print and electronic media are not good substitutes for all types of advertising. The nature of intermedia competition with newspapers has gained importance as the newspaper industry becomes more concentrated. The 1990s has seen an increase in groups buying independent newspapers and other groups. One force behind this concentration process is the practice of clustering, a business strategy in which a group buys several newspapers in close proximity. Clustering allows a group to share printing and distribution costs and to provide regional advertising. Although clustering makes good business sense, there is some evidence that it can reduce competition for readers, which in turn can affect newsrooms budgets" and news coverage.

However, the potential impact of group clustering on regional competition has led to little action by the Justice Department with one exception. Observers have suggested that the lack of antitrust activity reflects the recognition that newspapers compete with a variety of media for advertising. However, this assumption has received little empirical testing. This study examines this assumption and the nature and degree of intermedia competition for newspapers by using a convenience sample of forty daily newspapers. More specifically, it explores the connection between the availability of other media outlets in a county and number of advertising lines in the daily newspapers.

Competition occurs among products when buyers are willing to substitute these products for each other. A standard way of defining the degree of substitutability is price cross-elasticity of demand, which is the change in demand for a product when the price of a substitute changes. The greater the change (elasticity), the better substitutes the products are for each other. Of course, demand also can be elastic with respect to other variables, such as quality.

The degree of substitutability reflects the similarity of products. In perfect competition markets, products are homogeneous and, therefore, perfect substitutes. However, in monopolistic competitive markets, products are heterogeneous to varying degrees and substitutability varies.

Monopolistic competition was developed as a reaction to the limitations of monopoly and perfect competition theories because most markets do not fit the assumptions of these types of theories.

Chamberlin's theory states that in monopolistic competitive markets, products compete through advertising and the nature of the products, as well as price, which is the primary variable affecting demand in perfectly competitive markets. Chamberlin concludes that in markets with heterogeneous products, firms tend to develop market segments through advertising and product characteristics in which they have monopoly power. This allows firms to increase prices above perfectly competitive levels. However, these segments are not perfectly monopolistic either because higher prices will push people towards imperfect but acceptable substitutes, or higher prices can induce other marginally competitive firms to produce products more like the one that dominates a market segment.

Lacy and Simon state that advertising markets, when defined as all media, are monopolisticly competitive rather than perfectly competitive because print and broadcast by their nature result in a degree of product differentiation. Although broadcast and print advertising can be substituted for one another, the degree of substitutability varies with the function and nature of the advertising. According to Picard, different media are not completely interchangeable for advertisers because they provide different types of access to audiences. Their audiences vary in how they use the medium and in the nature of the audiences delivered to the advertisers.

Busterna goes even further, saying,"To some degree, broadcast stations also compete with daily newspapers for advertising dollars. In practice, however, most advertisers do not see the different media types as good substitutes for each other." Niche theory has been applied to media competition for advertising. This theory, however, has not been used to compare pairs of media in local markets.

In summary, theory about newspaper competition does not support a strong assumption that other media are always good substitutes for newspaper advertising in all markets. Theory suggests that the degree of substitutability of television and radio for newspapers varies by type of advertising and possibly by market. However, theory should be tested empirically.

If broadcast advertising is an acceptable substitute for newspaper advertising, all other factors being equal, theory suggests two results:

- The amount of advertising in a newspaper would be lower as the number of media outlets in a market increases, and
- Newspaper advertising prices would be lower with more non-newspaper media in the market, but they would not be as low as with more direct newspaper competition.

The first occurs because acceptable substitutes will siphon off some advertising revenue from newspapers, reducing linage, and the second occurs because, if newspapers do not lower ad prices, advertisers will move some advertising dollars to lowercost-per-thousand broadcasting.

Previous research into competition and advertising has concentrated on advertising price as the dependent variable while ignoring the impact of competition on linage. The former is more problematic because the price a newspaper charges for ad space represents a variety of variables besides demand. Production costs, the skills of sales personnel, and managers' perceptions of demand, as well as competition, can play a role in advertising prices. Prices are decisions made by managers that reflect perceptions of the marketplace, whereas linage purchases represent direct decisions by advertisers. This implies that level of newspaper linage is a good measure for studying advertising competition in local markets.

Theory suggests that non-print forms of advertising are imperfect substitutes for newspapers advertising.

However, being an acceptable substitute for another product is a matter of degree. Imperfect substitutes can result in competition if enough buyers accept them as substitutes. The nature of newspaper and intermedia advertising competition has been examined empirically in a variety of ways.

NEWSPAPER COMPETITION AND ADVERTISING

A series of studies during the 1960s and 1970s examined intracity daily newspaper and intermedia advertising competition with mixed results. The studies differed in their dependent variables (line rate versus cost-per-thousand), and the independent variable for competition was often a dummy variable, which may be an inadequate measure for competition. Overall, studies that used the costper-thousand rate as the dependent variable found increased competition was related to price decreases. A similar pattern for use of open-line and cost-per-thousand rates was uncovered with weekly competition. Blankenburg concluded that competition had no relationship with the open line rate in Wisconsin weeklies.

Lacy and Dravis replicated and extended the study with Michigan weeklies and found that when cost-per-thousand was used as the dependent variable, a relationship was discovered. Matthews found that some ad prices in competitive markets were lower than those in monopoly markets. In a further test, she noted that the results were the same regardless of whether the open line rate or average line rate was used.

BROADCAST COMPETITION AND ADVERTISING

Just as with intracity newspaper advertising competition, most studies of intermedia competition have looked at the impact on advertising rates. A series of studies examining the relationship between newspaper and television joint ownership found that when cost-per-thousand was used, joint ownership resulted in higher rates.

Ferguson examined 815 newspapers and found markets with more radio and television stations had lower national and run-of-the-paper (ROP) cost-per-thousand. He also concluded that cross-ownership of radio and newspapers did not affect the cost-per-thousand rate, but cross-ownership between television and newspapers did.

Busterna, however, examined the elasticity of demand for daily national advertising from 1971 to 1981 and reported no significant relationship between ad prices and other media. He did not use the cost-per-thousand rate.

Looking at intermedia competition for advertising in six small daily markets, Smith concluded that advertisers were largely uninformed about the advertising conditions in their particular markets, but that the majority of advertisers believed the small dailies competed with other media for advertising dollars. However, many advertisers were unable to say which media choices were best for which purposes or the relative cost-per-thousand rate for the available and competing media.

This is consistent with Sentman's study that found heavy newspaper advertisers in three metropolitan markets did not know the duplication in consumers among media, particularly for newspapers, nor were they certain which of the media they used was best for reaching their own target audiences in the most cost efficient manner.

The study also found that given a change in availability of newspaper outlets in a metropolitan market, the majority of advertisers would switch the allocation for advertising to other print media (suburban or a surviving daily). Fewer than 20 per cent of those surveyed stated they would move the money to radio, television, or direct mail.

ADVERTISERS' PERCEPTIONS AND COMPETITION

A few studies have examined factors affecting advertiser satisfaction. Otnes and Faber examined 200 retailers across five business categories to discern reasons for media choices among local advertising options. They concluded that both product category and advertising budget were significant predictors in this type of decision.

A study by Frederick-Collins extended the Otnes and Faber work by asking about the service component and quality of the relationship with sales representatives. She found that a relationship with the sales representative was a factor in making decisions. Perhaps more importantly, this study considered value a factor in the relationship between price and effectiveness and stated that the advertiser is interested in achieving goals in a cost-effective method. This suggests that advertisers are more interested in the cost-per-thousand rate than absolute rates. A similar result was found by Cameron, Nowak, and Krugman, who looked at two mid-sized cities and concluded that the ability to reach target audiences and cost effectiveness were important factors in placing advertising. Shaver, in a study of advertiser perceptions in a metropolitan area, found that advertisers ranked cost effectiveness above actual cost as a means of making advertising choices among available media. Advertisers defined this effectiveness as a combination of actual cost and perceived efficiency in reaching the desired target audience.

Smith studied advertisers in six smaller cities and concluded:"The vast majority of local decision makers are not sophisticated when it comes to advertising. They select media based on a diverse number of factors, with return (italics in original) being the factor cited most frequently in this study." The Shaver and Smith studies taken together suggest that advertisers vary greatly as to the factors that affect their buying decision.

HYPOTHESES

Theory and research suggest that electronic media are at least imperfect substitutes for daily newspapers in some markets, but that competition will not have as great an impact as competition among newspapers themselves. The strength of the relationship between competition and advertiser behaviours can vary from market to market, and advertisers may lack knowledge as to the relative price and effectiveness of advertising in the various media.

Missing from the literature is evidence that intermedia competition affects the distribution of advertising space and time among media outlets in local markets. If advertisers substitute broadcast media for newspapers, it would seem that an increase in the number of broadcast outlets would increase the likelihood that advertisers would reallocate their advertising dollars away from newspapers towards these increased broadcast outlets. Economic theory predicts that increased sellers of advertising space and time will result in lower prices, and lower prices result in lower cost-per-thousand. Chamberlin said lower prices can result in movement of dollars from higher price sellers to lower price sellers when buyers perceive the two products as being acceptable substitutes.

On the basis of this reasoning, this study tests the following hypotheses:

H1: As the number of TV stations per 1,000 households in a daily's market increases, total ad lines will decrease.

H2: As the number of TV stations per 1,000 households in a daily's market increases, run-of-the-paper ad lines will decrease.

If television is considered a substitute for dailies by a sufficient number of advertisers, an increase in the number of outlets in a market would likely result in the movement of advertising dollars from newspapers to television.

H3: As the number of radio stations per 1,000 households in a daily's market increases, the daily's total ad lines will decrease.

H4: As the number of radio stations per 1,000 households in a daily's market increases, the daily's run-of-the-paper ad lines will decrease.

The same logic underlying H1 and H2 applies here. Increases in substitutable outlets should lead to a decline in ad linage at newspapers.

H5: As the penetration of other dailies in a daily's market increases, the daily's total ad lines will decrease.

H6: As the penetration of other dailies in a daily's market increases, the daily's run-of-the-paper ad lines will decrease.

As other dailies in a market gain penetration, they will become better substitutes for a competing newspaper. This reflects the role of penetration as a measure of advertising quality at a newspaper.

H7: As the penetration of weeklies in a daily's market increases, the daily's total ad lines will decrease.

H8: As the penetration of weeklies in a daily's market increases, the daily's run-of-the-paper lines will decrease.

Theory and research suggest that one daily is the best substitute for another daily from an advertiser's perspective. However, one study found a negative relationship exists between weekly and daily penetration within a county.

This indicates that these two forms of newspapers are substitutes for readers in some markets, so the relationship in the advertising market should be tested. Although the hypotheses are written as bivariate relationships, each assumes that the relationship will hold even after controlling for other independent variables. Multiple regression is used to provide this control.

METHOD

Lack of access to advertising linage data has always created problems in studying the impact of competition on ad lines. Most newspapers do not make this information available, which explains the lack of published research using this dependent variable. However, the compilation of linage given voluntarily to Editor and Publisher, the source of data for this study, is available.

Data were taken from 40 newspapers that reported their advertising linage in Editor and Publisher during 1994. They represent a wide range of geographic distribution, ownership patterns, and circulation size. This year was chosen because it was the latest year for which all the other desired market statistics were available. The number of run-of-the-paper (ROP) ad lines was selected as one dependent variable because local retail ads make up more than half of a newspaper's advertising. Total ad lines were selected as a dependent variable because that figure represents the newspaper's overall success at selling advertising. Other forms of advertising lines, inserts and classified ad lines, were not studied separately (but they were part of total ads) because these data were missing for many cases.

This study controlled for advertising price by using the open-line, cost-per-thousand rate. The cost-per-thousand was calculated using ABC circulation figures and open line rate reported in the Editor and Publisher International Year Book. It may appear that using the open rate as a price control for total ad lines is problematic because inserts and classified advertising have different prices. The researchers could think of no way to create a combined price for all forms of advertising. However, using the open rate for all hypotheses was acceptable because the Pearson's product moment correlation between the open line rate and classified rates equaled. and the Pearson's r between the open line rate and insert rates equaled. These high correlations suggest that the measurement error created by using the open line rate would not be large enough to alter the conclusions.

Measures for radio and television competition were based on the number of stations per 1,000 households. Such a measure was used because of the strong correlation between market population and number of radio and television stations. Weekly and daily newspaper competition was measured by using the penetration of all other dailies and all weeklies in the county in which a daily was located. Penetration levels came from Circulation.

The penetration of competing newspapers as a competition measure rests on the assumption that an increase in a competitors' penetration makes them better substitutes for the daily being studied. Newspapers vary in their geographic markets, and no one political boundary will describe all accurately. However, most dailies aim to circulate widely in their county, and the county has been used in previous studies as a geographic basis for defining the market.

Using the county also allowed the collection of data from a variety of sources for the same geographic area. Classical economic theory states that income plays a role in demand. The appropriate measure of income would be the advertising budgets for all firms in a daily's market that advertise.

However, because these data are proprietary and unavailable, this study used the effective buying income (EBI) of the county. The assumption is that business (advertiser) revenue is related to the income of consumers in a market, and that advertising expenditures are related to business revenues.

The total local ROP lines and all advertising total lines for 1994 were used to measure the dependent variable, in twelve months from 19 March 1994 to 18 February 1995. These editions yielded 50 newspapers.

However, because of missing data, the actual number of papers used in the total linage regression was 40, and the number used in the ROP analysis was 31. These dailies are not a random sample. Therefore, no sampling error is present and statistical significance was not used to interpret the regression analysis. The test for hypothesis support was a part correlation squared of.04 or higher. This indicates that 4 per cent of the variance in the dependent variable is shared with an independent variable. This cut-off point for degree of relationship is arbitrary, but it was selected because it represents a part correlation of.16 or higher rather than the.09 associated with a part correlation squared of.03. A higher standard would increase the chance of type II error, which should be avoided at this stage of research because this is an under-researched topic. Hierarchical multiple regression was used, and the hypotheses were evaluated using beta weights, change in R-square and regression coefficients. The data were tested to see if they fit the assumptions of regression analysis. One or two outliers (defined as plus or minus three standard deviations from the mean) were found with cost-per-thousand, EBI, radio stations per 1,000 households, total ROP lines, and TV stations per 1,000 households. The outliers were reassigned the value of three standard deviations from the mean, which reduces the extreme impact of the outlier and retains the case.

The standardized residuals were plotted against the standardized predicted values to see if the linearity assumption was violated. The distribution of the cases was random, which indicates the assumption of linearity was appropriate.

Residuals were examined for violation of homoscedasticity. Only minor violations of normality were found, which most likely reflect the small size of the sample. Also, no evidence of multicollinearity was found. The variable to case ratio for the total ad linage was 1 to 6.66 and 1 to 5 for ROP linage. While this is below the optimal ratio, the ratio here is acceptable in exploratory studies such as this.

RESULTS

The most notable observation about the data, and therefore the 40 markets, is the great variability. The standard deviations for all variables are high relative to the means. For three variables--penetration of dailies in the county, television stations per 1,000 households, and effective buying income--the standard deviations are actually larger than the means. This large variation reflects two characteristics of the data. First, the markets vary greatly in size; and second, the sample is not large enough to reduce the impact of this large range. H1 states that as the number of TV stations per 1,000 households increases, the total ad lines will decrease. It is supported. The regression estimated that for every additional television station per thousand households the daily loses 279,810 ad lines a year. This variable had a part correlation squared of.087, which exceeded the.04 cut-off point. Similarly, the daily loses 454,257 ad lines for each radio station per 1,000 households. This variable had a part correlation squared of.064, which indicates H3 is supported.

H5 states that as the penetration of other dailies increases, the total ad lines will decrease. This hypothesis is supported. For each increase of 1 per cent penetration by other dailies, a daily loses 22,241 ad lines per year. The part correlation squared for this relationship is.214, which exceeds the.04 cut-off point. H7, which states that daily ad lines are negatively related to the penetration of weeklies, was not supported. The part correlation squared was.003, and the daily loses only 5,893 lines a year for each percentage point increase in weekly penetration. An interesting phenomenon is the wide variation among the cases in all four measures of competition. The standard error of the television regression coefficient is 7.8 times larger than the regression coefficient, while the standard error of the radio coefficient is 1.68 times the regression coefficient. The standard error of the weekly penetration coefficient is almost three times the coefficient, and the standard error of the daily penetration coefficient is only slightly smaller than the coefficient itself.

The wide variation in the impact of weekly penetration on daily ad lines may explain why H7 was not supported. Had the standard error been much smaller for weekly penetration, the relationship identified by the equation would have been stronger. The great variation in cases, which represents the small sample and the great variation among cases, resulted in small beta weights because standardization involves dividing values by the standard error; large standard error, relative to a coefficient, results in small beta weights. This is why the part correlation squared was used to evaluate the hypotheses. The two control variables, cost-per-thousand households and effective buying income, accounted for 18.9 per cent of the variation in total ad lines. Total variance accounted for by all variables equaled 55.8 per cent.

Data address the even numbered hypotheses, which concern the relationship of competition with lines of run-of-the-paper advertising. The total variance accounted for in the regression equation is higher than that accounted for by the regression equation, but at least part of this reflects the decreased number of cases. The adjusted R-squared is.717, compared to the reported R-squared of.774. H2 states that as the number of TV stations per 1,000 households increases, the number of ROP lines will decrease. This hypothesis is supported. The part correlation squared for this variable equals.224, which indicates 22.4 per cent of variance in ROP lines is associated with TV stations per 1,000 households. For each increase of one TV station per 1,000 households, the daily lost 46,000 ROP lines. H4 states that as the number of radio stations per 1,000 households increases, the number of ROP lines will decrease. The part correlation squared equals.158, which exceeds the cut-off point. The equation indicates that for each increase in one radio station per 1,000, the daily lost 165,070 ROP lines. H6 states that an increase in the penetration of other dailies will be negatively related to the number of ROP lines. This hypothesis is supported. The part correlation squared of.058 exceeds the cut off. For each increase of one percentage point of penetration of other dailies, the daily lost 4,972 ROP lines. H8 states that as the penetration of weeklies increases, the ROP lines will decrease. This hypothesis was not supported. Even though the relationship was negative, the part correlation squared only equaled.011, which did not exceed the cut-off point.

The same wide ranging variation among the independent variables found with total ad lines also was present for ROP lines. The standard error of coefficients was much greater than the coefficient for TV stations per 1,000 households, radio stations per 1,000 households, and weeklies' penetration. The standard error of the coefficient for dailies' penetration was only slightly less than the coefficient itself.

Effective buying power explained a large amount of the variation in ROP advertising, accounting for 32.7 per cent of the variation. This is even higher than the percentage for total ad lines. The purpose of this study was to test whether radio and television are acceptable substitutes for people and organizations seeking to advertise in newspapers. The data in this limited sample reveal a notable negative relationship between number of broadcast outlets and lines of newspaper advertising.

Because this is consistent with economic theory and because other potential explanatory variables have been controlled for, a logical inference is that at least some advertisers are substituting advertisements on television and radio for ROP newspaper advertising in at least some markets. However, other dailies continue to be much better substitutes for total ad lines.

This probably reflects the inclusion of classified and inserts advertising in these figures. Television and radio currently are not good substitutes for these types of advertising. These results are consistent with traditional economic theory and with statements by Picards and Lacy and Simon. In addition, they are consistent with research by Ferguson that radio and TV competition are negatively related to the ROP cost-per-thousand rate.

It appears the intermedia advertising market is monopolistic competitive with some media being better at some types of advertising than others. The markets used here also tend to vary greatly in the level of substitution. This variation is consistent with the existing body of literature that shows advertisers tend to be uninformed about advertising conditions in their markets and the importance of sales representatives in selling advertising. The conclusions must be tempered by the limitations of this study. The sample was small and not representative of anything other than the dailies examined. In addition, the mean level of penetration by competing dailies and weeklies was low on average.

A sample with more extensive penetration by dailies and weeklies might show a stronger impact on print competition on ROP lines. It may be that TV and radio become attractive ROP substitutes when no other newspaper has enough household penetration in the county to act as an acceptable substitute.

However, the consistency of these results with theory and research and the strength of the relationships suggest that these findings should be pursued with replications. Furthermore, the use of ad lines instead of price to study competition looks promising because it sidesteps the argument about whether to measure the dependent variable price as a set rate or as the cost-per-thousand rate. Future studies should include larger samples, and the role of non-economic variables, such as advertisers' knowledge of the advertising market and the role of sales representative, should be incorporated into studies of advertising competition. The development of online advertising also needs inclusion in the future. Electronic classified advertising and online merchandising could offer better substitutes for some forms of newspaper advertising than currently exist.

This study holds policy implications as well. There is some justification for assuming daily newspapers compete with other media for advertising, but that level of competition varies by type of advertising and from market to market. Because one justification for lack of antitrust actions in recent newspaper group acquisitions is that newspapers compete with other media, these results have interesting implications. The variations in television's and radio's impact on daily linage found here suggest the Justice Department cannot assume that intermedia competition in every market reduces a daily's monopoly power in all advertising submarkets.

This finding should be pursued as newspaper companies increasingly reduce competition through clustering. The Justice Department should expect adequate evidence from ownership that acquisition of newspapers to promote clustering will not have anticompetitive effects in the advertising market as well as in the circulation market. The need to study the impact of clustering is urgent because the pace of newspaper groups acquiring other groups and single newspapers is expected to continue if not increase61 and the recreating of competition after it disappears is extremely difficult.

JOURNALISTIC RESPONSIBILITY AND POLITICAL ADVERTISING

In modern political campaigns voters must rely on the mass media for most of their information about political candidates and issues. Candidates, of course, seek to maximize the advantages of this reliance for their own campaigns by providing voters with information the candidate can control directly, usually in the form of televised political advertising. As advertising has become more and more dominant in campaigns and as new media technologies have provided campaigns with new ways to manipulate media messages, journalists have recognized the importance of providing voters with independent information about such advertising messages.

In fact, Washington Post columnist David Broder issued a call for journalists to improve their efforts to verify claims made in candidate spots. Political consultant Roger Aries characterized news coverage of candidate spots as follows:"... journalists, who had begun to feel ignored, decided to go on the offensive. They vowed to protect the American people and formed, as Michael Oreskes of the New York Times termed it, a self-appointed journalistic `police force' to clean up campaign advertising".

Researchers noticed the increased attention given to political spots and began to investigate journalistic coverage of candidate advertising. However, most of the research focused on journalistic coverage of political advertising has been done on presidential campaign coverage on national television networks or prestige press print outlets, ignoring state and local elections and journalistic reporting for state and local newspaper and television media.

This neglect is particularly significant since survey evidence indicates that less than half (42 per cent) of the American public regularly watch one of the network news broadcasts while 650/0 say they watch their local news. This study seeks to address this deficiency in existing literature by examining both print and local broadcast analysis at both the presidential and non-presidential level during the 1996 campaign.

JOURNALISTIC COVERAGE OF POLITICAL ADVERTISING

The media's role in this relationship is usually highlighted by its responsibility to provide citizens with information needed to make informed and rational decisions (often labeled the social responsibility theory of the press). Among the tenets articulated by the Commission on the Freedom of the Press in 1947, social responsibility theory of the press instructs that media should"represent all hues of the social spectrum," take responsibility for the quality of their programming, and"inject truth in advertising".

Although there may be many applications of these tenets to media coverage of political campaigns, the"truth in advertising" responsibility is particularly relevant here, especially since a regulatory agency for political advertisements does not exist. As Patterson and Wilkins in their popular textbook on media and ethics point out, this journalistic responsibility is a challenging one in modern campaigns because candidates now have so many capabilities for manipulation.

In the late 1980's journalists began to recognize how significant television advertising had become in the voter decision-making process and to see the need to provide another viewpoint or interpretive mode for this type of direct, unmediated form of candidate to voter communication. Journalists subsequently adopted a new strategy for covering campaigns, the"adwatch."

Adwatches can be defined as"media critiques of candidate ads designed to inform the public about truthful or misleading advertising claims". As described by West adwatches "review the content of prominent commercials and discuss their accuracy and effectiveness".

At the national level, at least, there has been a tremendous increase in recent years in news coverage of political television spots. Scholars have presented numerous possibilities that may explain media coverage of candidate ads, such as the drama of a close election campaign. Kaid et al. argued that candidate ads have received more attention in recent years because ads provide an easily transferable format for news reports, ads fit the horse-race nature of political reporting, and ads serve as a platform for campaign discourse.

Furthermore, Jamieson asserted that journalistic attention to candidate spots enables the spot to shape the news. Given the fact that the media may use spots as springboards or lead-ins to other campaign coverage, coverage of political advertising may not always be labeled as a formal"adwatch."

Content analyses of journalistic coverage of political advertising, despite focusing on presidential campaigns, show some important patterns. For example, the percentage of adwatches that address negative and issue ads is relatively stable across election years. More critically, research shows that print and televised adwatches are not always fair, neutral, or sufficiently critical.

For example, as Tedesco et al. report, Perot ads were the dominant focus of 43 per cent of network adwatches in 1992, whereas Bush and Clinton ads were much less likely to receive scrutiny (21 per cent and 7 per cent, respectively). Thus, despite the fact that the 19 short spots Perot produced and aired in 1992 were far fewer than the 39 spots aired by Clinton or the 32 shown by Bush, Perot's ads were far more likely to receive media attention.

In addition, content analyses show that presidential adwatches are given high priority in television news segments and in newspapers by appearing mostly within the first 10-minutes of the news broadcast or the first section of the newspaper. Researchers have concluded from the few studies that have been done on adwatches, either in print or broadcast media, that the journalists doing the adwatches have tended:

- To focus primly on television ads in presidential campaigns
- To analyse negative ads much more than positive ads from campaigns.

This approach may have left ads in state and local races less covered, ignoring positive ads in which candidates can make as many false and misleading claims as in negative advertising.

Another disturbing trend in political ad coverage, particularly in the national network coverage of political spots, is the lack of in-depth interpretation and analysis of the ads. According to Jamieson, only 1.7 per cent of the content of coverage about ads dealt with the accuracy of the ad claims. In her comparison of print and broadcast adwatches from 1992 and 1996, Bennett indicates that the percentages of advertising reports with in-depth analysis of spots dropped 68 per cent for the networks and 20 per cent for print sources from 1992 to 1996. To address some of the criticisms of media adwatches, several scholars have offered suggestions for more systematic and effective results. For example, Jamieson developed a critique framework that incorporates previewing (setting up), distancing (setting off) disclaiming (labeling), displacing (interrupting), and recapping (summarizing) the ad under analysis. Furthermore, suggestions were made to extend the analysis of the ad claims to broader patterns and more concrete audiovisual and narrative frameworks.

Although Richardson acknowledges the constraints hindering analysis of long-term candidate policy stances and major argument premises, he argues that current practices of isolating specific claims,"rather than patterns of behaviour and record, moreover, may contribute to the alienation among voters that some scholars have attributed to adwatch journalism".

Yet adwatches can be an important tool in pointing up manipulative and deceptive ads. For instance, in the 1996 Virginia race for U.S. Senate, incumbent Senator John Warner ran a television ad in which the head of his opponent Mark Warner was substituted for the head of Virginia's other Senator, Chuck Robb, in a picture designed to show that Mark Warner was a liberal associating with other"known liberals" like President Clinton and former Virginia governor Wilder. If news reporters had not spotted the manipulation, voters might never have been informed about it. John Warner was forced to fire his advertising consultant and apologize for the deception, although he did go on to win re-election. Indeed, how adwatches affect voter interpretations of ads is not completely clear. According to Cappella and Jamieson, how a reporter frames a political adwatch may affect voters' attitudes towards the ad itself, the perceived fairness of the ad, and the perceived importance of the ad. Cappella and Jamieson's research shows that well-constructed adwatches accomplish their goal and inform voters about the deceptive appeals made in candidate spots.

However, such effects do not always have the effects journalists intend. In fact, because the advertisement appears in a credible news environment, it may actually benefit the political campaign. The majority of research shows that adwatches may produce a boomerang effect, further enhancing the ad itself.

Likewise, Jamieson found that viewers in focus group, s recalled the ad itself better than the corrections made by the media commentator. These findings suggest that journalists must develop new and compelling ways to analyse spots or they risk failure in their attempts to provide voters with better decision-making tools. This background on prior research on adwatches suggests that very little is known about how journalists cover advertising below the national level. The research reported here addresses this question by considering the following research questions about the 1996 campaign:

- How much coverage of political advertising do state and local media outlets give to presidential versus non-presidential races?
- When state and local media outlets cover political advertising, are there differences in the types of ads (negative versus positive) and in the party (Republican vs. Democrat), gender (male vs. female), or position (incumbent vs. challenger) of the candidate?
- Are there differences between television and print outlets in the nature of their coverage of political advertising?

METHOD

The study relied on content analysis to determine the characteristics of adwatches in state and local media outlets. The sample of newspaper and television coverage came from a database of materials collected by the Political Communication Centre (PCC) at the University of Oklahoma during the 1996 campaign.

As part of a larger study on the campaigns, the PCC coordinated an election study in cooperation with 16 locations around the United States, balanced for regional diversity. At these t6 sites, the researchers working with the PCC collected local newspapers and recorded local television newscasts for the eight weeks from Labour Day through election day in 1996. A list of the newspaper and television station sites is included at the end of this chapter.

All television stations are, of course, generally local ones, although many have statewide reach in their areas. In addition to a mixture of large and small city daily newspapers, we also included USA Today in our newspaper sample because, while it is in some ways a national newspaper, it is also a paper that makes an attempt to cover major competitive races below the presidential level. In the case of newspapers, the first edition of the day, as distributed to subscribers, was chosen, and the television station recorded in each market was the one with the highest viewership ratings in the fall of 1996. The first step in the project involved going through all newspapers and all local television newscasts for these eight weeks and identifying the stories in which campaign spots were analysed. Thus, each story identified in the newspapers or the local television news broadcasts was a unit of analysis. Since our goal was to identify and analyse all types of coverage given to political spot advertising, a story did not have to be identified as a formal"adwatch" or use that term specifically in order to fall into the sample of stories analysed.

Indeed, most of the stories were a type of"adwatch," but media outlets, both print and broadcast, have many different ways of incorporating spot coverage into their stories, and we wanted to get a broad and comprehensive look at the treatment of television spots.

A series of categories were developed, derived from prior work on adwatches described above, and applied to each story or unit of analysis.

This would include such standard categories as:

- Story placement (quadrant location for newspapers, location in first, second, and third part of newscast for television stories),
- Length of story (in column inches for newspapers; in minutes and seconds for television,
- Type of story (campaign news report, advertising feature, candidate profile, issue report, etc.),
- Level of race covered,
- Type of ad analysed (negative ad/positive ad);
- Candidate and political party,
- How the ad is analysed (verbal content, visual content),
- Whether misleading verbal or visual techniques are identified,
- Reproduction of ad (for instance, is part of the ad played on television or shown in picture frames for newspapers?),
- Use of experts for criticism (are other analysts quoted or consulted in critiquing the ad?), and several additional categories.

Coders also determined if the advertising discussed in the story received in-depth analysis by marking if the ad received any specific commentary by the reporter, beyond mere description, about its content or campaign context. Coders specifically marked if the story attempted to label the ad as misleading, false, untrue, wrong, unfair, or some other evaluative characterization.

A written codesheet for these categories was developed, along with a written codebook defining each category. One graduate student and one undergraduate student were trained in the use of the codesheet and did the actual coding. Intercoder reliability was computed on a sample of the print and newspaper stories and averaged across the categories reported here. Individual category reliability was also high, ranging from a low of.88 for how video content was analysed to a high of 1.00 for several categories such as identification of party and level of race covered.

The sample described above yielded a total of 190 adwatches; 143 of these were in newspapers and 47 were on local television stations. This differential between newspapers and television is partly accounted for by the larger number of adwatches undertaken by the larger dailies in the sample. For instance, of the 143 newspaper adwatches, 28 (20 per cent) were done by the New York Times.

The Washington Post and USA Today printed 18 (13 per cent) adwatches each, and the Boston Globe contributed 17 (12 per cent) to the newspaper sample. Thus, well over half of the newspaper stories were done by these three large dailies. Of the less well-known papers, The Oregonian did 15 adwatches, the St. Louis Post-Dispatch printed 10, and the Sacramento Bee provided 9. Only one newspaper in our sample, The Indianapolis Star, failed to write any adwatch stories during the time frame of the sample.

In the television sample (n = 47), the distribution among outlets was more even. No local station carried the national obligations of the large city dailies. The largest number of adwatches on television came from KVAL in Eugene, Oregon, and WTVD in Raleigh, North Carolina (7 each; 15 per cent each of the total sample), followed by KARE in Minneapolis and WCJB in Gainesville, Florida (6 each; 13 per cent of the total sample). Several stations undertook no adwatches at all.

COMPARISON OF PRESIDENTIAL AND NON-PRESIDENTIAL COVERAGE

An important reason for looking at ad coverage from more local sources is to determine, as our first research question suggested, the amount of coverage that advertising receives for races below the presidential level. In the newspaper sample of 143 adwatches, 80 per cent of the candidates covered in the ads were presidential candidates. Of course, as in the overall numbers of adwatches, the largest numbers of these adwatches for presidential candidates came from the prestige dailies. Of the 114 (80 per cent) newspaper adwatches covering presidential candidates, 20 presidential adwatches came from the New York Times, 18 came from USA Today, and the Washington Post was the source of another 16. However, it is clear that many smaller dailies also gave their attention to the presidential race.

Even the television stations, which were all local stations, focused their attention on presidential races; 36 per cent of the local television adwatch stories were on presidential candidates.

While we have no way of knowing if, in fact, all Congressional candidates aired political spots, with the growth of political advertising on state and local levels, we feel safe in our assumption that spot ads were featured in these races yet ignored by state and local media. In the 16 states represented by our various newspapers and television news stations, nine of the states (or 56.25 per cent) featured a U. S. Senate race, and three states (18.75 per cent) had gubernatorial races.

TYPES OF CANDIDATES AND ADS COVERED

Our second research question concerned the types of candidates and ads that received coverage. The first thing to notice is that party affiliation of the candidate does make a difference; Republican candidates receive the most adwatch scrutiny. Both newspapers and television give Republican candidates three times as much advertising coverage as they give Democrats. An interesting finding, however, is the large amount of coverage received in 1996 by Independent and Reform Party candidates in television adwatches. One reason for this attention was the fact that Reform Party candidate Ross Perot chose television ads as a way to highlight his exclusion from the presidential debates, and many television stations chose to use analysis of these ads as a way of airing this issue.

For example, the local news in Gainesville, FL (WCJB), after reporting that Republican nominee Bob Dole narrowly trailed Bill Clinton in Florida polls, next noted that Ross Perot's support was low in that state and that he had been excluded from the upcoming presidential debate. This campaign news report then went on to highlight Sunday morning interviews in which Perot blamed Bob Dole for excluding him from the debates,"he [Dole] has been rude and arrogant... I guess he's desperate." Next, a Perot ad was featured which claimed Perot"won the debates" in 1992, that"76 per cent of voters" wanted Perot in the 1996 debates, and concluded with"let Ross speak, the truth never hurt anyone."

The news report in no way attempted to analyse the claims made by the Perot ad, but rather was an analysis of campaign strategy. The ad received flee media exposure because it conveniently helped to tell the story of Perot vs. Dole and Perot's debate plight.

Another ad sponsored by an independent candidate that garnered considerable media attention was that of Taxpayer Party candidate Chad Koppie who was seeking the U. S. Senate seat in Illinois. Koppie's ad, which deals with the abortion issue, opens with a choir of young children singing the words,"How long must the killing go on?

How long must the blood be on our hands?" The ad then fades from the chorus of children to show an adult hand holding the remains of a bloody fetus.

The local TV news programme that reported on the ad began their segment by showing the candidate in their studio viewing his own ad. The news report then featured a few seconds of the actual ad but blurred the screen when the fetus appeared. Finally, the candidate was allowed to comment on his ad.

The use of candidate commentary was noted often in our analysis of television news' reporting of local races and candidate ads. Frequently, when a station would highlight a local candidate's ad, and often these ads would be of some controversial nature, the station would then invite the candidate him or herself to explain or justify their own ad. Thus, not only would the ad receive free media exposure through its airing on the local news broadcast, but the candidate would also receive exposure on the local news to further comment on what they were saying in the paid advertising messages.

The controversial Koppie ad described above also received national attention when the New York Times reported that Koppie was a little-known candidate in Illinois until he began running his controversial abortion advertisement featuring the remains of dead fetuses. The Times article did not examine the actual ad, but rather focused on the dilemma faced by the two Chicago TV stations from which Koppie had purchased time to run his ads.

The stations had received many complaints and requests to stop broadcasting the"graphic" spot as many viewers were"horrified... that young children [were] watching." The article reported that the TV stations, due to a recent Federal court ruling, had"no choice but to broadcast it, and to do so when children are likely to be watching, because the commercial advocates the election of a candidate for the United States Senate."

As Kahn has shown, female candidates often do not receive their fair share of news coverage, and clearly this extends to coverage of their ads. In 1996 in this sample no woman candidate received individual coverage of her ads in newspapers or on television.

In fact, 90 per cent of newspaper adwatches and 70 per cent of television ones focused on male candidates. Even when featured with male candidates, women candidates could not hope for much coverage. The lack of coverage for female candidates' spots may actually be a feature of the type of ads covered by the media. As discussed in the previous section, advertising in U. S. Congressional races was among the most neglected, the very campaigns that most often featured female candidates.

In fact, of the 16 states represented by our media sample, all but one state (Oklahoma) featured female candidates vying for U. S. Congressional seats. While there were no female Senate candidates in the nine Senate races from our 16 states, two of the three states from our 16-state sample with an active race for Governor (Indiana and Missouri) did feature female Gubernatorial candidates. Again, Gubernatorial campaigns received the least amount of coverage in both print and broadcast media.

In considering the disparity of whose ads receive attention by the news media, one may question the advantages and disadvantages of having one's spot ads the focus of media analysis and commentary. Clearly, existing evidence suggests that lack of attention to one's ads, even as part of news critique and commentary, places a candidate in a disadvantageous position.

First, as the current study has found, most often the attention paid to ads in state and local media is devoid of critical assessment and, particularly in television coverage, provides a free airing of at least a portion of an ad, and furthermore, may often serve as an opportunity for the candidate to provide their own analysis of their ad message. Also, as discussed in our review of literature, a growing body of adwatch research has shown that the credible environment of news reporting may actually enhance an ad's effectiveness.

One of the very few female-candidate sponsored ads that received news attention was that of Connie McBurney, Democratic challenger for a congressional seat in Iowa. McBurney first aired a spot dealing with the issue of abortion, which was followed by a response ad from her opponent, the incumbent Republican member of Congress, Greg Ganske. The two ads were the focus of a report by the local Des Moines, IA (KCCI) evening news programme.

The news anchor announced that both candidates had just"unveiled new TV ads about abortion," and clips from both candidates' ads were then shown, set off in a TV screen and clearly labeled"advertisement." The challenger, Connie McBurney, who supports abortion rights, revealed in her ad that"We were excited about having a baby, but something went wrong and she died only six days old. I thought I would have more children, but I didn't. Now Greg Ganske says I want to kill children.

That's indecent." Next, a segment from the Ganske ad was shown which featured a head-shot of the candidate stating,"and we can only have compassion for the loss of Connie McBurney's new born baby, but I have never accused Connie McBurney of wanting to kill children."

The TV report then featured an interview with candidate Ganske who called McBurney's ad a"media ploy," and he concluded the news report by stating"I really think that probably the McBurney campaign feels that they need to try to do something dramatic in the last few days to try to turn this campaign around." Interesting in this news segment is the fact that while both candidates' ads were featured, only the male incumbent Ganske was interviewed and allowed to comment on his opponent's ad. Another finding that stands out is that challengers are much more likely to receive adwatch attention than are incumbents. On both television and in newspapers, 2 out of every 5 adwatch stories (38 per cent) were on challenger ads, double the amount for incumbents in newspapers and triple the coverage for incumbents on television.

As with previous research on adwatches at the national level, this study shows that negative ads are the most likely type of ad to be analysed in an adwatch. Negative ads were the dominant focus of 50 per cent of the newspaper stories and 60 per cent of the television stories.

COMPARISON OF PRINT AND BROADCAST COVERAGE CHARACTERISTICS

In addition to looking at what types of candidates and ads were the focus of adwatches, our third research question focused on the characteristics of the adwatches themselves in print and broadcast outlets. Here there were some clear differences between newspapers and local television stations. The ads themselves were the main focus of the newspaper adwatches (88 per cent of the time for newspapers but only 36 per cent of the time for television stations). This finding may substantiate the fact that television stations often use ads and analyse them as a supplement to other stories and as a way of providing video or dramatic visuals for general campaign news stories.

Table: Characteristics of Adwatches in Newspapers and on Local Television

Newspaper Local TV n = 143 n = 47 Advertising main Focus	88 %	36%
Use of Experts		
Independent consultant	3	4
Campaign consultant	8	0
Campaign official	42	11
Candidate	27	19
Media	11	38
Academic expert	10	2
Picture or Video Shown	32	98

Often, the story that ads help local television stations tell is of a negative campaign with"nasty" attack ads that only succeed in alienating voters. For example, the Minneapolis, Minnesota station led with a story on the Paul Wellstone/Rudy Boschwitz U. S. Senate race that blamed candidate ads for turning voters off.

The anchors began this story by proclaiming,"Nasty sums up the advertising war between Paul Wellstone and Rudy Boschwitz... what the negative ads have done are anger the voting public."

The local correspondent introduced the report by noting,"If you're like many Minnesotans, you've seen a lot of this..." which was followed by clips of three uninterrupted ads, labeled"adwatch."

Following the three ad clips, the correspondent concluded,"And if you're like many Minnesotans, you're not happy about it." Next, a citizen on the street is interviewed, and offers his assessment:"I think they suck... it's all kinda `B.S.' You know, they're not looking at issues, they're just sniping at each other."

More segments from ads are shown, and the news story ends with yet another citizen proclaiming,"It makes me not want to really vote, or not have too much faith in either one of the candidates."

A similar story of negative ads and voter alienation appeared on the Des Moines, Iowa (KCCI/Channel 8) news, as its lead segment was introduced with the following question,"They're getting a lot of air play these days, but are the politicians getting all the mileage they want from all those commercials you've been seeing running just these days before the election?"

The second anchor picks up the introduction with"Election day will be a day of ending-an ending to some political careers and to all political campaign commercials... we want to go ahead and show you just how tired people have been getting of all the political campaign commercials here in Central Iowa."

The local news correspondent first revealed that 71 paid political campaign ads would be aired on their station that day alone, and the report then goes to a local shopping mall to find a citizen who laments,"That's all that's on television." Next, this story features uninterrupted clips from three different ads, labeled"advertisement", with each of the three ads focusing on the abortion issue. Following the three ads, it's back to the shopping mall where one citizen proclaims,"Oh, I'm pretty well burned out on them. You learn to filter them out."

As these examples illustrate, quite often when local television stations do feature candidate ads as part of their campaign reporting, they do so not to analyse the content of ads, but rather to use ads as convenient material to help them tell their story of a negative campaign. While the ads' claims and counter claims go unanalysed by the local journalists, citizens are provided with frequent reminders of just how nasty the campaigns have become.

Further reinforcement of the importance the television stations place on the visuals is provided by the fact that 98 per cent of all television adwatches use a video clip of one or more spots in their stories.

On the other hand, although it would be quite easy to reproduce a picture or still frame image from a spot in print, newspapers use pictures of ads to support their analyses only one-third as often as television stations do.

It is also clear that newspapers often rely more on experts to assist in the analysis of spots. While local television stations find their own or other media experts, or as noted earlier, use the candidates themselves, to be the best source of opinions on spots, newspaper are more ready to consult other experts, frequently tapping into campaign consultants and officials and even academic experts. Even more significant than the simple content characteristics of ad coverage may be the approach that is taken to analysis of the ad.

As mentioned in the introduction, other research, particularly on national television networks and large daily newspaper adwatches, has suggested that the media are often not sufficiently analytical in their scrutiny of ads and perhaps do not provide voters with sufficient information to judge the flaws in political spots. This study suggests that these earlier findings provide continuing cause for concern. Local television stations in particular are not providing much in-depth analysis of the spots they analyse.

Fewer than one-third (28 per cent) of television adwatch stories attempt any in-depth analysis of the spots they examine. Based on our category definitions this means that the media outlet coverage was basically descriptive and did not make any attempt to analyse the ads being covered, to evaluate them or characterize them in any way that would provide voters with a cue as to the truthfulness or fairness of the claims in the ad.

The failure to provide in-depth analysis may leave voters confused by competing, and often contradictory, claims that go unexplained or clarified. Such journalistic coverage of ads was most apparent in local television newscasts, as campaign reporting would often feature candidates' response ads as a convenient way to develop the narrative of a negative or nasty campaign, while ignoring the actual claims made in the ads.

An example of unexamined competing claims is illustrated in a lead segment of the local news programme of WISH (Channel 8-Indianapolis) on the Indiana gubernatorial campaign. The 1996 Indiana governor's race featured Democrat Frank O'Bannon and Republican Steve Goldsmith. This local newscast began with one of the anchors announcing"We start with the race for Governor today as the negative tone of the campaign is growing harsher." The second anchor concluded the introduction with"This time Frank O'Bannon has a new attack ad on the air."

The anchors then go to their correspondent who introduces the story by noting,"Steve Goldsmith launched a television volley on Friday, and today Frank O'Bannon answered." The report next features an uninterrupted portion of the O'Bannon ad, labeled"counterattack," that stated"How low can Frank O'Bannon go? He knows Steve Goldsmith never raised a tax-never!"

The journalist continues to tell the story of candidate attack and counterattack by informing viewers that"The latest ad war surrounds Frank O'Bannon's claim that taxes in Indianapolis have gone up under Steve Goldsmith. A Goldsmith ad refutes this claim and Republicans on the city/county council today called the O'Bannon ad `quote' false." Next, a Goldsmith campaign representative is interviewed, stating"The taxes went down, they did not go up. Very simply, Steve Goldsmith has not increased taxes... and we demand that he [O'Bannon] take the ads off the air." The local journalist continues the story of dueling ads and competing claims,"But not only is O'Bannon refusing to apologize, his campaign unveiled a new ad today that repeats the claim while attacking Goldsmith."

Viewers are then shown an uninterrupted portion of the ad that states"Steve Goldsmith has resorted to negative attacks the press calls sleazy, deceptive, not true." The ad clip is followed by an O'Bannon campaign spokesperson who comments"anyone who's got property tax bills for'95 and'96 can see that their property taxes went up."

As this news story is constructed, its primary focus is to demonstrate to voters that their gubernatorial candidates were attacking one another over the issue of taxes in their most recent ads, yet the reporting does nothing to examine the competing claims made by the candidates and their ads. In fact, the correspondent leaves the voters to figure things out for themselves when he concludes the report with,"Democrats points to higher property tax assessments, while Republicans point to a lower rate. It's become a game of he said/he said." While fewer than one-half of newspaper stories also performed in-depth analysis (43 per cent) in their ad watches, newspapers sometimes were more substantive than television in giving voters independent information needed to evaluate competing candidate claims. For instance, The Oregonian, in a series of adwatches called"Analyzing the ADS," often engaged the actual content of ads and pointed up correct and incorrect information.

The paper did exactly that in a September 24 story assessing one of Perot's ads complaining about his exclusion from the presidential debates. In the spot, Perot claims that support"seventy per cent of Americans want Ross Perot in the debates." The adwatch report tells voters that this is a bit misleading since that figure was from an early September poll, and that now the percentage who want Perot included has dropped to only 52 per cent. Other statistics are evaluated as well, and thus, the newspaper provides the reader with more information to evaluate the claims made in the ad.

While newspapers analyse the audio content of spots in 89 per cent of their stories, television stations actually engage and analyse the audio content in only 40 per cent of their adwatch stories. Neither television nor newspapers give as much consideration as may be justified to the video content of spots. Only just over half of all newspaper stories (55 per cent) address the video content of an ad, and only 13 per cent of television analyses do so.

In addition, most stories about spots are"neutral" in their focus, providing neither a negative nor a positive focus most of the time. Only 13 per cent of newspaper stories and 4 per cent of television stories actually critique ads as misleading, and fewer provide sufficient judgemental information to suggest that any ad is false or untruthful. Only about one in seven stories (13 per cent for newspapers and 15 per cent for television) make any mention in their analyses of suspect technological maneuvers in the spots.

That is, the analysis do not call to the attention of the voter any use of special effects, video editing, digital alterations, colour or shaded video, altered sound effects or any other technique that might be designed to mislead or create false impressions for viewers.

While statistics for ads in the same races covered here are not available, recent research on presidential elections suggests that 42-43 per cent of television spots from the 1992 and 1996 campaigns had identifiable distortions, far more than the percentages identified by the media coverage.

Some political observers have feared that showing political spots on television without setting them off in some way or labeling them may actually serve to reinforce the effect of the ad, rather than to point up its faults. This study shows that most television news stories now take note of this concern.

When candidate spots are shown as part of an analysis, 83 per cent of television stories label the ad or set it off in some way, and 87 per cent provide a journalist or other voice-over that further serves to interrupt and break-up the ad's flow. Only 21 per cent of the stories analysed in this study allowed political spots to run"full screen" in original form without offsetting or labeling.

The conclusions from this study begin to provide a clearer picture of the media coverage of candidate advertising below the presidential level. First, as our analysis reveals, congressional and state-wide races are often ignored even by local media. Quite often, and particularly with local TV news programmes, the local media will feature analysis of the presidential candidates' ads provided by their network affiliates. With such"news" material easily available to the local stations, it appears that these news organizations may not be willing to invest the time and resources needed to analyse the advertisements that are featured by their local and state-wide candidates.

With more and more candidates at all levels increasingly turning to advertising as their primary way to communicate with voters, local media must begin to devote the resources needed to help readers and viewers understand the messages of their local and state-wide candidates.

Another troubling conclusion that can be drawn from this study is the lack of in-depth analysis provided by local media. Here, local TV, as opposed to print media, is even more negligent in analyzing the actual content of candidate advertising. As illustrated above, often an ad is featured in a broadcast news report to help tell a larger campaign story; and the story told is most often that of campaign strategy-particularly how candidates are engaged in attacking one another. In reporting candidate attacks made through their advertising spots, very rarely would the reporter/journalist analyse the often competing claims made in the ads, providing voters with an assessment of those ads and claims that might be misleading, false, or unfair.

While the current study provides a more in-depth picture of ad coverage at the state and local level than previously available, our findings point to several additional questions for future analysis. For example, why would Republican candidates receive three times as much advertising coverage as Democrats? Is this level of coverage in any way equivalent to the proportion of Republican vs. Democratic ads that appear? National trends have shown that Republican candidates are often better funded than their Democratic counterparts.

Perhaps a greater number of Republican ads appear at the state and local level and thus receive greater media coverage. While it is much easier to determine the numbers of ads produced and broadcast by presidential candidates, one might also be able to monitor ads that appear on local stations and then compare the frequency of these ads to the coverage and analysis of ads provided by local news media.

While newspaper coverage and analysis of advertising is most often based on televised ads, with the exception of a small number of print ads, the coverage of televised ads by local news organizations raises several interesting questions. For example, in terms of the actual ads that are selected for analysis or commentary in local news broadcasts, what relationship, if any, is there between the advertising that appears on (and generates revenue for) a local station, and that which is given critical assessment by the local news operation?

The influence of money in political campaigns, and advertising in particular, has emerged as a major concern in the electoral process. A more complete understanding of the role of money, political advertising at the state and local level, and critical assessment of such ad messages by media organizations require a closer look at the candidate ads that are broadcast by local stations and that receive analysis by these same stations.

Our analysis describes the differing amounts of ad coverage based on level of race, party and status of candidate, as well as candidate gender, with those races that most often feature female candidates receiving the least amount of attention. In addition to these factors, other features of a campaign may also influence the coverage afforded particular ads and candidates.

For example, do more ad watches appear in highly contested races? Does the coverage of ads, and particularly the type of critical analysis or commentary of ads, differ for successful vs. unsuccessful candidates? Such questions would require monitoring the development and outcome of particular races combined with the type of content analytic analysis provided by the current study.

In failing to provide in-depth analysis or to point up potential ethical abuses, journalists may be failing in their responsibilities to provide voters with the information they need to make good voting decisions. As interpreters of the candidates and their campaign messages, journalists must realise the extent to which voters rely on them to help us make sense of the many and often conflicting messages. As political communication scholars, it is imperative that we continue to investigate how the media establishment is fulfilling, or abdicating, this"watchdog" role.

10

Impact of Journalism in a Computer World

In a computer-generated world called Second Life, the bodies that defined me as the interviewer and her as the interviewee (our avatars) sat in a lounge rendered on my computer screen at my desk in New York City, and on her computer, wherever she was. Second Life looks like a video game but isn't. It's more of a meeting place, a hangout, some would say an alternative reality.

Pixeleen Mistral, red-haired and stylish in a black jacket and miniskirt, sat with her legs crossed. I didn't even know how to cpross my legs. When she typed to me, her avatar remained seated and suave."I got an animation override," she told me when I acknowledged the obvious fact that I was a foreigner in her land."Most girls get them so they don't walk like complete dorks."

She pointed out another sign of her form-fitting comfort in this world: her boots. Second Life is streamed to the computers of the thousands of people who"live" and work there, or just visit, by the servers of a company in San Francisco. Mistral said her boots--also black, with metal buckles and studs--were so complex that they sometimes crashed one of Second Life's servers if she walked into the wrong place.

Her boots, though, aren't Mistral's most compelling feature. She is the managing editor of the most popular in-world newspaper, The Second Life Herald. She, like a handful of other pioneering Second Life reporters, covers the virtual beat, one keyboard-driven step at a time. We met in this lounge so that she could tell me what it's like to do this, and how the dozens--maybe hundreds--of mainstream media reporters who have been stomping through the world of late, wearing boots that are decidedly less cool than hers, have been getting the story wrong.

But first, I should tell you that journalism has defined the four-year-old land of Second Life as it has few places that exist on real soil. In the early days, Second Life reporters were stars of an experimental online culture, the Web-based town criers of a place where every innovation--the first gun, the first hug, the first recreation of Hiroshima as it was minutes after the bomb--was worth writing about. Those journalists wrote mostly for digital newspapers and blogs created specifically to cover Second Life, and although some also wrote for mainstream publications, they bought into the experimental and evolving nature of this virtual world and attempted to cover Second Life as a distinct, self-contained place, even when it meant jettisoning real-world journalistic conventions. In a second phase that began about a year ago, a new wave of reporters, representing big media outlets and with a somewhat different agenda from the pioneers, came in. They shined a spotlight, asked for real names, and were generally more interested in the phenomenon of Second Life--in the wow factor and the growing number of ways it mimicked real life--rather than the liberating possibilities of building a world from scratch.

In October 2006, this new wave of media attention helped draw Second Life its one-millionth new virtual resident--even though the actual import of that is a matter of some debate--then its second, third, fourth, and fifth-millionth, all by the end of February. To the reporters who were there at the start, this new wave wasn't exactly welcome, and the clash of journalistic styles raises interesting questions about why we do what we do, and about what's important-journalistically--in a place that isn't quite real, but where what happens can have real-world consequences. I've reported in this other world during both phases. This spring I spoke with many of the Second Life reporters who have worked the hardest to define journalism in their virtual land. I've been told, as I think about Second Life and what is happening here, not to get distracted by the wrong weirdness. I've been told why real names don't matter here and why understanding someone's virtual self does.

I've been told to think clearly about a place where the government is also the god, the maker of the land upon which we walk, and a private company. I've been told not to witness the virtual beat through eyes that see a proliferation of obscuring masks, but those that see an abundance of revealing truths about how people might live if they got a chance to start over. I've been told this in a place where you can fly to a story with the flap of your butterfly wings, and I've been told that's a liberating thing.

Beyond the journalists who have set out to cover this virtual world as a beat, Second Life has been"explained" in dozens of articles. It was a 2006 cover story in Business Week and has been featured in at least eight stories in The New York Times and dozens more in other major papers.

Second Life has been profiled on CBS'S Sunday Morning and serves as an occasional host location for NPR'S The Infinite Mind. This little, virtual place gets a lot of shine. I'll take some of the blame for that-and it is blame I hear in the rising backlash against this world from reporters who cover it and virtual world-watchers who think it's all a bit much.

I wrote the first of those Times stories and I've covered Second Life online and on air for MTV News, where I write about video games. But Second Life isn't a game. It just looks like one because, like the worlds of Grand Theft Auto or Super Mario 64, it's a digital place rendered on a screen. The ways Second

Life differs from a game are what propel all this interest. Launched in 2003, Second Life is the product of Linden Lab, a San Francisco company, and its blond, wide-eyed CEO, Philip Rosedale, a former chief technical officer at RealNetworks who as a teenager tried to build a hovercraft powered by lawnmower blades. He never saw Second Life as a game, but as an extension of real life.

"We were trying to create a living space that you could just go into and it would be real," he told me recently. His new world would provide people who communicated through the Internet with something more vivid than an e-mail address or chat-room nickname: a virtual body. A new user of Second Life would customise an avatar, and maybe what you created as a representation of your RL self would say something about who you are--or who you want to be.

Users or residents-pointedly not"players"--could build themselves a house or a tower or a car or anything else they could alchemize from the Second Life tools of creation. Linden Lab added land as more people moved in. The rest of Genesis would be the work of the residents.

Eventually, they were able to create new physical movement for the world's bodies and objects. Someone invented hugging. Someone else invented a Native American war dance. Somebody made motorcycles that worked. There was no high score to be won, no competition. People could just socialize and work and explore. Some built games--casinos and areas for adventure--but they also built book clubs and places for virtual romantic liaisons (a lot of the latter, actually). Perhaps more important, there is an actual economy in Second Life, and people are making real-world money. But I'm getting ahead of myself.

From the start, Rosedale envisioned people creating golf courses and shopping malls (which they have). He expected reporting, too."The big strategy was always that it would be emergent like everything else, and, in fact, as journalism in Second Life emerged it would be a sign to us that we were doing something right," Rosedale says.

Though he saw journalism as an inevitability, and a useful way for this new world to be explained to its residents, he worried that Second Life's early population was too small to produce a good reporter."We had to make calibrated bets early on that were sometimes risky," he says,"where we would try to do something to be a seed kernel for something that we hoped would happen." So he made journalism happen. He tapped a freelance tech reporter named Wagner James Au to be the Adam of Second Life journalism--paid on Rosedale's Linden Lab government dime.

On April 22, 2003, writing as Hamlet Linden for the New World Notes blog on Second Life's Web site, Au introduced himself."For the next few months, Linden Lab has invited me to set aside my journalist cap, and instead, don the digital beanie of their in-house virtual correspondent." He wasn't paid to keep it positive. He wrote about builders and eccentrics, but then in August of that year, he reported on a tax revolt against Linden Lab (a complaint about the fees it charges users who build stuff) led by a resident whose avatar was a big cat. It was a great beat. "Being in Second Life is sort of like underwater lucid dreaming," Au told me recently. "It's got this weird silence to it, like being underwater. And the dreaming part is just everything happens at the same time and has no internal logic" A reporter can fly through his beat or teleport instantly to any public quadrant of Second Life's ever-expanding map, and report on anything interesting that he encounters. (One of the first times I entered Second Life, I flew through a Hiroshima awareness exhibit, met people at a virtual casino, explored a chamber designed to simulate the medically recorded symptoms of schizophrenia, and climbed a giant half-open refrigerator that made me feel the size of a mouse.)

Reporters can hold office hours, as some do in their virtual headquarters, and welcome a colourful parade of residents who come to tell them what they're up to. There is much to explore: a castle, a cluster of people re-enacting a war, a popular nightclub, or a recreation of the United Nations' General Assembly room floating in the virtual sky. "It's kind of one strange wonderful thing after the other, at its best," says Au. "I just realized that's the experience, so I have to write it with a straight face."

Au wasn't alone on the beat for long. Before I fluttered into Second Life in late 2004 to describe for readers of the Times a world that had at the time just 15,000 residents, Peter Ludlow, a University of Michigan philosophy professor, had jumped in to practice his brand of journalism.

He'd already been in the Times himself, featured in a front-page article in January 2004 for having been booted out of another virtual world, The Sims Online, for either violating the terms of service of operating in that world—which is what Electronic Arts, the company that controls The Sims Online, claims—or, as Ludlow contends, for raking a little too much muck about in-world scams and cybersex through his Web-based newspaper, The Alphaville Herald. After his eviction, Ludlow brought his avatar, Urizenus Sklar, and his newspaper, now renamed the Second Life Herald, to Philip Rosedale's world.

The paper remains a chronicle of the more ribald and ingenious creations of Second Life residents—those often being innovations in avatar-to-avatar or avatar-to-object sex. It also continues to take on the "government." "The big issue in these worlds is always how is the corporation managing the world? What are the conflicts between the user and the management?" Ludlow told me recently. "Inevitably you end up writing about that. And if you're not writing about that you're not writing about the world."

In late April and early May, the Herald published a story about an open letter signed by more than 4,000 Second Life residents addressed to Linden Lab, detailing a laundry list of administrative complaints, and a series of op-eds attacking Linden Lab's new identity verification systems. zhe paper also reported on the supposed inefficacy of Linden Lab's recent effort to run offusers who participated in "ageplay," or sexualized encounters involving avatars that look like children.

In 2003, Daniel Terdiman, a tech reporter then freelancing for Wired, heard about Au's work and began trying to convince editors at Wired, and later C-Net, to let him cover Second Life. Last October, Terdiman engineered the creation of a C-Net bureau in Second Life, where he used his avatar to conduct town-hall-like interviews with Second Life newsmakers in front of an avatar audience. At one point, this oh-so-modern endeavor was interrupted by an audience member who mischievously triggered a rain of virtual male genitals, a protest against Terdiman's controversial interview subject, an in-world real-estate mogul who had made a lot of money and a lot of enemies.

Then, in early 2005, the Brooklyn-based freelancer Mark Wallace was tired of reporting about equity markets in the Persian Gulf and about millionaires for Details. He wanted a new beat. He logged on to Second Life, discovered an ad for a job at Ludlow's Herald, and signed on as Walker Spaight, Urizenus Sklar's reporting partner.

Susie Davis, a copy editor in Connecticut, also jumped into Second Life. She started reporting there in April 2006. She could have been anything in that world, which she visited outside her eight-hour copy-editing shifts. She thought she'd join a Second Life book club. "The book club I picked hadn't met in six months," Davis told me. She could have spent her Second Life time dancing in discos, but, she said, "If you're going to dance you might as well dance for real." Reporting seemed the most interesting.

"The art of chasing a story is what kept me in Second Life," she says. By the middle of 2006, her avatar, Ute Hicks, was hired as editor of the Second Life Business Magazine, a monthly publication that lasted roughly six months, until its publisher shut it down (according to Davis, the publisher was wrapping up a stint as a defence contractor in Afghanistan, and returning to America where he would have less free time to log on to Second Life). Davis had a fallback though, because while Ute Hicks was editing the business magazine, another avatar that Davis used, one Marvel Ousley, was helping to start the Second Life News Network, a contender to take on the world's dominant media outlet, The Second Life Herald.

Those were the small engagements. Then Reuters got involved, and phase two of journalism's evolution in Second Life was firmly under way. Last summer, Philip Rosedale met the Reuters CEO, Tom Glocer, at the elite Allen and Company media and technology conference in Sun Valley, Idaho. Glocer heard Rosedale speak about Second Life, and, according to Rosedale, the two brainstormed over lunch about having a Reuters reporter enter that world full-time. One rationale for Reuters was the business angle of Second Life. There was an economy in there. The Linden dollar, the currency of Second Life, was freely transferable to U.S. dollars (as of June 13, the exchange rate was 266 Lindens to every U.S. dollar).

A resident who built cool virtual motorcycles could sell them to other residents for Lindens. Then Linden Lab would transfer that "fake" money into real money in the resident's credit card account. (Money can be transferred either way). As in the real-world economy, someone who makes things that people want or need could turn a profit. People were trying to make careers in this world. (Of the more than 12 million transactions in May in Second Life, some two hundred were for upwards of $2,000.)

Glocer bit, and in August 2006 Adam Pasick, a London-based reporter for Reuters, was assigned the Second Life beat, with a virtual Reuters building and a special feed on Reuters' Web site to showcase his efforts. "Honestly, it sounded like a career killer," Pasick told me.

"The whole idea sounded faintly ludicrous that we're going to cover this world that doesn't quite exist." The bureau opened in October and Pasick quickly warmed to the concept, finding rich material in the crackdown on casino advertising, profiles of entrepreneurial builders, and protests against the invention that allowed users to copy anything they encountered in the virtual world (Second Life's own copyright infringement problem).

"The more I got used to things in Second Life," he says, "the more it just felt like another reporting job" This infusion of journalists was just one of the migrations altering the Second Life landscape. Businesses were coming, too.

Pontiac and BMW bought land and opened virtual shops. Major League Baseball built a stadium where you can sit and watch the M1-Star game home-run derby on a giant in-world screen. Sundance Channel built a movie theater that shows the occasional film free. Last summer, I flew into Second Life to sneak through an American Apparel store that was a day away from its grand opening but already well publicized by the clothing company's PR folks, who were eager to promote this new way of buying virtual versions of the company's clothing as well as the real-life inspirations.

The spill of real-life brands into Second Life became a major technology/ pop culture story of 2006. The New York Times, usa Today, Time, and more than a dozen other major news outlets, including MTV News, found it worthy of coverage. But to Wagner James Au and the other resident journalists in Second Life, this incursion of real-life commercialism and the attendant media attention were a distortion of what is significant in the world. In December 2006, the tech blogger Clay Shirky gave voice to this backlash, first in a post titled "A story too good to check," and a follow-up called "Naming names: the tech reporters who flack for Second Life."

In the latter, he charged journalists from CNN, Fortune, The New York Times, and usa Today with a willful or sloppy tendency to misread the population count of residents posted on SecondLife.com (then topping one million) as a measure of the number of people actually using the world. In the interest of selling editors or readers on the relevance of something—anything—happening in Second Life, he wrote, these reporters failed to mention that the number of residents was arrived at by counting avatars, not the people who have avatars. So Ute Hicks and Marvel Ousley were being counted as two residents, for example, even though both are controlled by Susie Davis. Second Life wasn't quite as popular as the multimillion statistic suggested.

Shirky had a right to be skeptical. Log on to Second Life today, when the official resident number exceeds five million, and the population of people actually in the world at any given time is only about 20,000 to 30,000. Rosedale estimates that there are about 180,000 unique users of Second Life each day, and says that of the five-million-plus people who log on at some point, only about 10 per cent return after one month.

Reporting about this world for MTV News, I wasn't susceptible to the numbers hype. Our young TV audience and Web readership don't need dazzling statistics to sell them on the relevance of online worlds. But what I was susceptible to was corporate-driven novelty. For every homegrown Second Life tribute band that I discovered, I was pitched pieces on banks or brands coming to the virtual world. But after doing stories on American Apparel and Universal Music's exhibition space, I decided that was enough. Some of this corporate innovation/invasion had no more novelty than the dairy industry's creation in the late 1990s of an official Web site for milk. I'm not the only one for whom 2006 was the year to get both excited and jaded about media attention to the influx of companies coming to Second Life.

Listen to Philip Rosedale: "Is it totally irrelevant that big brands are in Second Life? No. It's a sea change. They weren't around a year ago and now they're here. That tells us something. It especially tells us something because I didn't do those deals. We don't do any deals. We didn't ask them to come. Personally, I wish people would write more about education [several universities offer classes in Second Life]. I really wish that people would write more about the life-changing stuffgoing on, write more about that oppression support group that meets on this island every couple of days and sits on prayer cushions and talks about themselves. That's a big deal. Do I wish people would just write about that? Sure. But I also wish everybody would read every night."

But the criticism of this second-wave journalism's treatment of Second Life is more fundamental than just hype and factual disputes. Au believes that journalists who come into the virtual world thinking the hot story is how the real world is planting a footprint here miss stories that are just as good, maybe even better, but don't hinge on a connection between the real and the virtual. He's one of several influential Second Life reporters who think that the real-life media's obsession with the "real" dismisses the importance of what is happening wholly on a virtual plane. "People go here to create an alternate identity that a lot of times will be totally different than who they are in real life," he says. Respect that spirit and embrace it, is his philosophy. So Au typically doesn't even ask the people he interviews in-world to give him their real names. It's the best way he knows to capture what is going in the world.

Au's attitude invites an immediate howl from us real-world reporters. Doesn't the full truth matter, even in a place where so many real-world conventions are irrelevant? On April 17, I wrote a story for MTV News about a Second Life memorial for the previous day's shootings at Virginia Tech. The piece was potent because the resident I met at the memorial was a teacher at the university. He said he'd been on campus that awful Monday.

Au has interviewed residents who claim to be veterans of America's current wars in Afghanistan and Iraq. If our interviewees are lying to us, we're in trouble. I fact-checked the teacher by getting his real name and confirming his status with Virginia Tech. Au has mostly relied on instinct to confirm the veracity of what his sources say about their real life.

Reporting on the puppet without observing the person pulling the strings can seem like a willful dismissal of an important part of a story, an invitation to be duped. To the extent that what happens in Second Life has real-world consequences—such as comments by a faculty member about an all-too-real shooting at his school, or the opportunities to make real money—it seems risky, and potentially irresponsible, to dismiss the broadly agreed-upon journalistic convention of verification. The counter-argument I heard from Second Life journalists is that in real life, many articles do not describe what their flesh-and-blood subjects do when they are not in the mode that made them a topic for, or character in, a story.

Peter Ludlow maintains that people role-play and use avatars in real life, anyway, that there are masks on us all. "If I get in front of class, I'm in a sense presenting an avatar," he says. "I dress a certain way and I present myself in a certain way." This happens in real-life reporting, too. "I think it's probably the case when Christiane Amanpour is in front of the camera she's probably presenting a different side of herself than when she's, I don't know, chilling out at the bar."

And in fairness, Au and the others tend to write about people's lives in Second Life, rather than their lives outside it. (Au told me that in writing his forthcoming book about Second Life, he had to fact-check one of the vets he wrote about, and the story held up.) Second Life reporters ignore the artificiality of the artifice on their computer screens.

Without noting their subjects' real-life names, they confidently report on residents who are at war with each other, on residents who have flooded an area with virtual water to make a statement about global warming, on residents who have built virtual pot plants, and so many other activities that just seem interesting on their own merits. This is a new society forming here in Second

Life, they argue. Can't incoming reporters just focus on what's being done in this new world? No one I met in Second Life challenged my own reluctance to ignore the real world and unquestioningly accept the virtual one more than Pixeleen Mistral, the reporter with the server-crashing boots. I'm not the first person she has vexed.

A year ago, when Mistral sought work at the Herald, Mark Wallace interviewed her for the job. He preferred to pay Herald reporters in U.S. dollars transferred to them online. For that to happen, Mistral would have to surrender some real information about herself.

She asked to be paid in Linden dollars instead. She would convert them into real money herself. Wallace balked. Mistral started reporting--and reporting well--for the Herald anyway, for free. Wallace relented. Mistral got her Linden bucks, and Wallace never found out who was behind the avatar. These days, Wallace says he doesn't mind. Her virtual self is real enough. She gets the job done. Which is Mistral's point, exactly."You RL journalists always want to get RL verification, but if this is its own world, in-world verification here is what matters," she typed to me when we met virtual face to virtual face in the Herald's Second Life office."The people reporting from the outside miss most of the nuance and assume that recreating RL in SL is a good thing."

Her goal is to be a"gonzo Maureen Dowd" in Second Life. (For a taste of what that means, check out her April story in the Herald, for which she profiled an in-world casino developer who also ran an automated sex school, which Mistral suspected was his real money-maker.

As Mistral chatted her way through the interview, she simultaneously took a, urn, lesson.) What does it matter who she or anyone else is or wants to be in the flesh? She and I chatted in the Herald offices for over an hour. Only once did I push for identification. I asked if she'd tell me her age, her gender, or even her hometown."St. Paul, Minnesota," she wrote back."I think it is fair to know time zones. It's snowing here by the way." It wasn't in Second Life.

Editing the Herald has invited attention, and Mistral says she regrets the loss of privacy that has resulted from her work in Second Life. Some of that attention comes in monthly virtual fire-bombings of land she owns in Second Life--done sometimes as a demand for attention in the paper. Virtual paparazzi stalk her."I was sitting in a hot tub with a friend with my top off and they were taking pictures," she said of the screenshots the paparazzi took.

One threatened to publish them if she didn't put a specific number of words in one of her leads. She ignored it. The threats went away. She also misses sailing in Second Life. She misses free time. Do these details accurately represent the person who created Mistral? More importantly, does it matter? I think she's a dedicated reporter. She could be a reporter-hating, spurned politician or PR flack in real life. I don't know. I felt I learned enough to take her seriously.

It's worth noting, too, that not every avatar is camouflage."There's not a whole lot of distance between Adam Reuters and Adam Pasick," Pasick said, referring to the bylines his stories carry when they appear on the Second Life Reuters feed and the main, real-life Reuters feed, respectively. (His bosses bought the reality of his virtual beat only up to a point--on the Second Life Reuters site his pieces are datelined Second Life; on the main Reuters site they're datelined London or New York, wherever Pasick was sitting when he filed.) But the opportunity for metaphor and role-play is so rich that some Second Life reporters can't help but blur the lines. Mistral is adamant that she's a real reporter ("I'm trying to report as if SL was a self-contained world"), but Peter Ludlow says that sometimes in Second Life he's a reporter, and sometimes he's just playing one.

"If I feel like my writing is getting too serious I'll write something kind of silly," he told me,"or I'll do a report on some sort of ridiculous mafia war inside of Second Life or something." He likes playing up the tabloid shtick."If the deal is partly to role-play it's way more fun to role-play as a tabloid reporter than a New York Times reporter," he adds.

When should his readers think he's straight and when is it a put-on?"I think when we're at our best is when we're right on the edge, when people aren't really sure if we're playing a reporter or if we're being serious reporters.

And people hate that. They want to know.'What are you doing? Are you being serious or pretending? Let us know.' The answer is we're not going to let you know. We're trying to transcend that boundary." He wants to spark debate. He wants to entertain. These are the tools he uses, he says, to get readers to pay attention.

That's an extreme way of handling Second Life's blurring of truth and artifice. None of the other reporters interviewed for this story went quite so far. But for all the potential for slipperiness, for hamming up the reporters' voice or overlooking the inability to touch or smell these things and people manifested in a virtual place, for all the chances to miss the true motivations of the puppet masters behind the puppets, the virtual world has also proven to be a laboratory for an unusual form of accountability.

In a land where conversation is typed chat, and chat can be saved in Microsoft Word, the reporter has little room to misquote and not be busted-there is a transcript of every interview. In real life, a reporter in a far-flung bureau can tell the readers back home what he sees and hears, and the readers have little choice but to accept the journalist's account.

In Second Life, the places I write about--that American Apparel store, the Herald office, the casino, the sex shop, the virtual UN--can be visited by any reader who cares to check my story.

Outside of Second Life, the reporter who sweats about having blogs and online comment sections and other creations of the digital age undermining and second-guessing his work certainly understands how all this can both strengthen and aggravate the reporting process.

In early 2006 Linden Lab and Au parted ways. Au was focused on writing a book and could make more money not working for Linden Lab. Rosedale saw enough reporting elsewhere in his world that he was content to let Au go. Both told me the split was amicable. Au has continued reporting about Second Life through his New World Notes blog. Linden Lab gave him a parcel of land and rights to his old articles. He had to drop the Linden last name and now reports as Hamlet Au. He estimates he has 25,000 to 50,000 unique visitors to his site a month. His book will tell the history of Second Life and will be published by Harper Collins later this year. Terdiman is also writing a book, on how to succeed in Second Life as an entrepreneur. Ludlow and Wallace are crafting a history of The Alphaville Herald and The Second Life Herald. Mistral wants to write a book, too, but only when she's done with Linden Lab's world."What I would write would get me in trouble with the Linden's [terms of service] and get me banned," she says.

Undeterred by the limited financial rewards, people keep applying to become reporters in Second Life. Despite offering only about $3 a story, Mistral says she is inundated with applicants seeking to write for Second Life Herald. So, too, is Susie Davis of the Second Life News Network, who says good help for her volunteer outlet is hard to find. (Au pays the most, $25 apiece to contributors to his blog.)

Some reporting ambitions have changed. The in-world Wired, C-Net, and Reuters bureaus--places that Second Life experts say cost thousands of dollars to build--do not get much traffic."We had an idea that it would be all about getting people to the [Reuters bureau] island," Pasick says."It was a foot-traffic game."

Aside from big interview events, like his virtual sit-down with Arianna Huffington during last year's G8 summit, however, the place is anything but packed. The bigger marketing success has been the advent of free in-world gadgets that residents can install in their virtual homes or just have hover over their view of the virtual world. These gizmos flash an alert when a new Pasick story arrives, and provide links to his pieces.

Nevertheless, rumors abound that other big media outlets are coming in. Mistral considers the reporters who are in Second Life for the long term to be the"village storytellers." They are the small-town press, the people who understand the locals better than the national media that rumble into town only when there's a sensation, dragging along their stereotypes and biases and preconceptions. A lot of sensation has been happening in the virtual world lately.

It's a sensational place. Connecting people from around the world, it's a new community--a new city--with new possibilities as well as plenty of chances for the archetypal stories of life, love, and dreams to be chronicled. The avatars may lie. They may offer valuable insights. The numbers may confuse. The controls that move the avatars through this world may confound. You've got to breathe it deeply to get it. And you've got to answer this question for yourself'. In a brand-new world inextricably tied to, and simultaneously free of, the one we were born in, what truly matters?

THEORIZING AND MEASURING THE CONTENT AND STRUCTURES OF STATION WEB SITES

To examine the station Web sites as the consequence of some antecedent consumer and organizational context," the authors will first review the theoretical link between the antecedent conditions and the communication content to be analysed. Specifically, the authors will examine the assumed antecedent, the desire of an organization to maximize its Web site effectiveness, and the implications on its Web structure and content.

Using mostly a uses and gratification approach, various scholars have studied the functions of the Internet from a consumer's perspective. Many have concluded that information, communication, entertainment, transaction, and sociability are the most sought-after gratification items for online users. Accordingly, when visiting a station Web site, an audience may attempt to gratify one or more of these needs. As the expectation of media gratifications is influenced by individual predispositions and environmental factors, what an audience expects to derive from the use of a station Web site would logically be based on his/her previous TV consumption experience and the anticipated Internet utilities (*e.g.*, immediate information delivery).

Since the traditional product for broadcast TV is programming (including news), the audience Web users will likely expect to obtain gratifications from Internet-enhanced news and other programming related content from a station Web site, at least initially.

Thus, the authors proposed that the degree of relevancy between a station's on-air and online content and the inclusion of the structure/content that address the gratification items discussed earlier will largely determine a station site's attractiveness from the consumer's perspective.

Furthermore, as a Web surfer attempts to evaluate the value of a site based on his/her initial assessment of the gratification items that he/she may derive from the visit, it's plausible that the content components available on the"homepage" of a Web site will have the biggest impact on that impression.

Most Web sites in existence subscribe to a structural model that follows a newspaper design metaphor, using"front page" as the entry point to the site, relying on headlines to tell users what items are most important, and employing division into sections similar to the sections of a large metropolitan newspaper.

Accordingly, the effectiveness of a TV station Web site will be influenced by its ability to demonstrate to its target users (*i.e.*, broadcast TV audiences), on the"front page," that it has the utilities he/she is searching for. Assuming that an audience is active and goal-oriented, a perceived discrepancy between the expectation and the content on the front page will likely result in the user's leaving the site. Also from the consumer's perspective, research has shown that an Internet content provider that is associated with journalism was perceived as more credible. Editorial content and advertising placed in a journalistic product on the Web are seen as more credible. The overall perceived credibility of the content provider determined the perceived credibility of the stories and the ads in the online news service.

Moving towards an organizational context, the authors will review the issue of Web site effectiveness from the stations' perspective. There are few established criteria for judging the success of Web sites and little common ground for comparative purposes. Nel et al. proposed that before judging the effect of a Web site, he/she needs to classify the site in the context of whether a company is established already, or whether it is created solely to do business on the Internet because the two would have very different purposes for their Web sites.

They argued that the established company model, such as in the case of broadcast TV stations, would have an information-to-transaction content progression pattern. Specifically, to build an effective site, an established company would start a Web site with image/product information to existing customers, evolve to collect market information, offer better customer/internal support, and finally develop transactional capacity.

It is expected that the station Web sites will follow a similar process of development; however, as broadcasters are in the business of serving dual customers (*i.e.*, offering programming to audiences and access to audiences to advertisers), the customer support stage would probably involve two different goals, one aiming at attracting audiences and one aiming at serving advertisers.

In addition, because of the"relevancy" consideration, the authors believe that"transaction" will not be the ultimate stage of Web development for the broadcasters, but will become a complementing function for"serving" audiences and possibly advertisers. Since broadcast TV stations are local entities operated under modest organizational complexity (except for those stations located in top markets), the authors also do not anticipate a stage of internal services provided by the station Web sites.

According to an online report published by Editor and Publisher Co., Inc., three components, balanced content, proper user measurement, and savvy marketing, are critical to the profitability of a media Web site.

As for the specific online activities that contribute to Web site profitability, the same research found that a Web site is likely to be more profitable if it develops original editorial content; provides advertisers demographic measurement of users, click through data, and page view data; offers online surveys from users for content development; uses online traffic usage reports;

has voluntary registration; and provides secure electronic transactions of products or services.

It seems that a Web design mechanism that combines appropriate content with marketing and consumer information collection tools is critical in evaluating the effectiveness of a station Web site from the organization's perspective.

In regards to the antecedent market factors that might affect the different approaches in station Web site structures and content, industrial economists have long advocated that elements of"market structure" make up the economic environment of firms in an industry and induce these firms to behave in a certain way. One of the significant elements to surface in the discussion of market structure is"ownership concentration."

It is assumed that economic benefits such as scale economies, better bargaining power, and shared group know-how are more likely to be available to firms under multiple ownership.

The strategic importance of"size" also holds true in regards to audience market share. Since broadcast TV stations are in the market of selling access to audiences to advertisers, the higher the ratings (*i.e.*, access to more audiences) a station generates, the more revenues and resources are available to the station.

The"size" factor may be extended to the concept of geographical market. It is likely that the economic value of"size," in forms of market size, market ranking, and multiple ownership will contribute to the differences in TV stations' Internet strategies.

As the TV programming market becomes more and more fragmented with a proliferation of channels, broadcast TV networks have begun"branding" their images and programming, attempting to differentiate themselves from their competitors.

It is plausible that different broadcast networks will approach the Internet with different strategies that reinforce their branded positions. Subsequently, stations with different network affiliations may opt for different Web structures and content.

The purpose of this study is to describe the TV stations' application of the Web features that presumably would contribute to the effectiveness of their Web sites from both the organization's and consumer's perspectives. The authors also want to explore whether the market factors discussed are associated with the availability of these features.

Accordingly, the authors address the following research questions:

*RQ*1: What is the major content on broadcast TV stations' web sites, both overall and on the front pages? Is a TV station's online content relevant to its on-air content?

*RQ*2: To what degree have broadcast TV stations incorporated a structure for information (especially news), communication, entertainment, sociability, and transaction on their Web sites? To what degree have they used the Web sites for marketing and consumer data collection purposes?

*RQ*3: Do the broadcast Web sites follow the established company's"information to transaction" Web content development model?

*RQ*4: Are there any relationships between the content and structure of a broadcast TV station's web site and its market characteristics such as affiliation, market ranking, market size, and ownership?

SAMPLE AND PROCEDURE

The general methodology involved a content analysis of stations' web sites. A sample of 300 broadcast TV stations' web sites was analysed in this study. Riffe, Lacy, and Fico have discussed the difficulty of sampling Internet content. Since a complete station list for sampling frame is available, a proportionate stratified sampling method using DMA rankings (1 – 10, 11 – 25, 26 – 50, 51 – 100, 101 – 150, 150+) as the stratification variable was used to derive a representative sample with respect to market sizes.

Two coders, both graduate students, were employed to perform the coding tasks after receiving extensive training on both coding category systems and procedures. The coders also practiced coding a sample of 20 station web sites, applying the coding schemes independently to access the initial intercoder reliability. After the practice segment, disagreements were discussed with the principal investigator to improve reliability.

The web site HTML files were collected between I November through 31 December 1998. All sampled web sites were saved on a computer for coding purposes. The final overall inter-coder reliability using Scott's pi formula on all 300 Web sites was.82. It seems that the coders had most problems coding sponsorship-related items.

The difficulty was somewhat anticipated, as these categories require careful reading of the Web content to identify the presence of sponsorship, a less intrusive and thus evident advertising method. Bakeman and Gottman have indicated.70 as an informal criterion for good reliability figures. More than 90 per cent of the variables in the present study had reliabilities that exceeded this minimum.

MEASURES AND CODING SCHEME

The unit of analysis in this study was a station's complete web site, defined as all HTML pages that are included in a broadcast TV station's root web. The content of a station's "home page" was analysed separately as it is instrumental in forming a user's impression of gratification potentials. In examining the effectiveness of a Web site from the aspect of "design" as perceived by Web users, Abels, White, and Hahn identified a set of user-based criteria for establishing a well-designed, useful Web site. They concluded the factors of "appearance," "content," "linkage," "special feature," "structure," and 11 use" to be most influential in the surfers' decisions to use certain Web sites. Specifically, "use" (*i.e.*, ease of use, ease of navigation, and ability to get overview of structure) was found to be most important, followed by "content" (*i.e.*, usefulness of information, currency of information, concise, unique, and non-repetitive information). In regards to Web site interactivity, Ghose and Dou argued that the greater the degree of interactive design, the more likely it is for the site to be considered a top site by popular Internet portals. They also believed such a recognition will attract more new visitors and affirm current visitors' of its appeals. Accordingly, three sets of coding schemes were developed for the present study: front page (home page) content, overall Web content, and overall Web structure.

MARKET CHARACTERISTICS

To investigate the relationships between a station's market characteristics with the content and structures of its web site, the authors examined the sampled stations' network affiliations, DMA rankings, ownership, and market rankings. Two ownership measurements were used.

The first ownership variable was measured by the number of broadcast TV stations the owner of the sampled station owns.

Since such a measurement does not take into account the size of audience each station may reach, a second measurement was used to classify sampled stations into three types of stations: a station that is owned by one of the top 25 station groups as measured by the total number of households reached; a station that is a part of a station group but not one of the top 25 station groups; and a single-owned station. Because of the limited reports accessible, only the ratings records of the stations that were in DMA markets 1-100 by the end of 1997 were reviewed (172 stations).

Two-way contingency table analyses using cross-tabs were used to evaluate whether statistical relationships exist between the market variables and the web content and structure variables. Chi-square statistics were performed to assess the statistical significance of the variable relationships and were reported at.01 and.05 levels. Cramer's V, a measure of association based on chi-square with values range between 0 and A were reported.

Of the 300 stations coded, more than 60 per cent were affiliated with the three major networks, followed by Fox (12 per cent), PBS (9.7 per cent), WB (59 per cent), and UPN (4.3 per cent). Almost 7 per cent of the stations were independent stations. As for market sizes, close to 30 per cent were in the top 25 DMA markets (compared to 28 per cent in real station population), 21 per cent in markets 26 to 75 (compared to 27 per cent in population), 33 per cent in markets 76 to 150 (compared to 30 per cent in population), and 16 per cent in markets ranked over 150 (compared to 15 per cent in population). In terms of group ownership, about 28 per cent were single-owned stations, resembling the actual proportion of single-owned stations in the United States (25.2 per cent). Major Web Site Content and On-Air to Online Content Relevancy. "Front Page" News. Headline news content appeared to be an important part of a station's home page as more than three-quarters of the sampled web sites offered top stories of the day, however, these stories were presented mostly in simple text format with only 16 per cent of the stations incorporating news photos in these reports. The presence of weather reports was more limited (26 per cent) and was mainly in text format with a mere 3.3 per cent of the sites offering some kind of weather images. Apparently, web-casting of news is still in its infancy as less than 4 per cent of the stations offered web-casting of local news from their home pages.

"Front Page" Advertising and Promotion. Fewer than half of the stations used their front pages as an advertising outlet as banner ads (placed by advertisers) appeared on 44 per cent of these pages.35 Some 26 per cent of the local stations aggressively placed ads promoting their local news and anchor teams on the home pages (8.3 of the 26 per cent contained both local and network news ads). Slightly fewer than one fifth of the stations specifically promoted their local news anchor teams on the entryway to their web sites. Some stations also promoted their non-news programmes on home pages (27 per cent). "Front Page" Network Presence. Affiliated stations seemed to recognize the importance of capitalizing their network brands as they overwhelmingly placed their network logos on home pages (83.9 per cent). Also, 60 per cent of the sampled affiliates linked to their networks' web sites on the front pages. Only 18 per cent of the stations advertised their affiliated networks' news programmes on these pages.

"OVERALL" GENERAL STATION INFORMATION

Contrary to other typical company sites, which often provide detailed corporate information to visitors, only slightly more than half of the stations offered online station or personnel information through out their web sites. Furthermore, only 27 per cent of the stations provided additional personnel contact information.

"OVERALL" PROGRAMMING-RELATED CONTENT

The most popular online programming-related content seemed to be programme schedules (79 per cent), followed by general programme content information (58 per cent) and specific programme content information on upcoming episodes (51.7 per cent). Web-casting of TV programmes is practically non-existent (1.3 per cent; 4 stations).

"OVERALL" NON-PROGRAMMING CONTENT

Except for the list of useful links (66.7 per cent), which is relatively easy to construct, sampled stations seemed to concentrate more on "relevant" programming than "irrelevant" non-programming content. Local information was moderately present as fewer than half of the station sites contained local content. Among all local information content, job listing was most popular (48.7 per cent), followed by business/market information (41.7 per cent), local life guide (40.3 per cent), yellow pages (40 per cent), event calendar (24.7 per cent), and significantly less, public service announcement (15). As for other lifestyle interest content, lotto results were posted in about 22, of the station sites, while horoscope was present in only 4.3 per cent of the sites. A, interactive games are one of the main activities that attract many Internet users, TV stations apparently do not regard the offering of online games or game software as one of their site functions. Fewer than 15 per cent of the sites provided game-related content.

"OVERALL" NEWS/SPORTS/WEATHER CONTENT

Top stories/headline news were very common among station sites, while in-depth feature stories (45.3 per cent), business news (42.7 per cent), and consumer news (41 per cent) were less widespread. Only 7.3 per cent (audio only: 3 per cent) of the stations web-cast their local news. In fact, most of the limited number of stations that had video streaming capability offered news rather than non-news programmes. Most of the sports content was devoted to professional sports news, fewer than 25 per cent of the sites offered news on local sports events (*e.g.*, high school footballs). Local weather information was present in 73 per cent of station sites, while weather images (*e.g.*, Doppler, radar, satellite, and UV index) were in 63.3 per cent of sites.

"OVERALL" PROMOTIONAL/ADVERTISING CONTENT

In regards to promotional content targeted at Web users from TV stations, programming banner ads were most popular (47.3 per cent), followed by news banner ads (36.3 per cent), online contests and sweepstakes (11.4 per cent), and rarely the announcement of station promotional events (7.39 per cent).

A comparison of programming and. news ads on front pages and overall webs revealed that stations tend to place the majority of their news ads on home pages, while advertising their other non-news programmes throughout the sites. The front-page news advertising approach reflects most TV stations' preference in transferring online its most visible on air content, news.

As for advertising content from advertisers to Web users, banner ads were the most prevalent format on stations webs (63 per cent), followed by classified ads (22.3 per cent), online coupons (16.7 per cent), and surprisingly unpopular sponsorship (5.7 per cent). Only 18.3 per cent of the station sites provide advertising sales information for potential advertisers.

"OVERALL" LINKS TO OUTSIDE RESOURCES

Few stations made an effort to link to popular local port sites (12 per cent). Affiliates were aggressive in linking to their network sites (77.5 per cent), especially network news webs (43.9 per cent). Only 10 per cent of the stations utilized their programme suppliers' web sites to provide their web users with more programming information. MSNBC.com (16.7 per cent) and CNN.com (15 per cent) were the two most popular cable sites that stations linked to. Major Structures of Station Web Sites: The Application of Communication, Entertainment, Sociability, and Transaction Mechanisms.

In regards to the communication factor, most of the stations did not provide their Web users with a more interactive communication mechanism as fewer than 10 per cent of the sites offered discussion forums/bulletins or chat rooms and approximately 35 per cent of the stations had feedback forms on sites. Only 8 per cent11 of the stations did online polling on specific issues. Some 6.3 per cent of the stations used their web sites to generate news tips, while a mere 4.3 per cent of the stations conducted any forms of online surveys of the web users. There seems to be limited interactive communication mechanism (*e.g.*, chat rooms and online forum) present in these Web sites. The lack of online meeting points (*e.g.*, chat rooms) and club/membership system also indicates a limited sociability structure. The same holds true for the entertainment structure as the content analysed revealed an informational focus with very little entertainment component. In fact, web-casting of non-news programming appeared in fewer than 2 per cent of the stations sampled. Nevertheless, the entertainment structure may become more important as the speed and quality of video-streaming continue to improve.

As for electronic commerce (transaction), though research has shown that electronic commerce increases profitability of media web sites, only 20 per cent of the stations offered some form of shopping opportunities on their web sites (only 11.7 per cent had true online order processing). Most of the products available online were station promotional items. Transactional structure, while continuing to develop, is not currently a widespread component in these station Web sites. A very limited number of stations actively collect web user data online. In the area of membership and registration mechanisms, only 14 per cent of the sites provided a membership system that offered content and/or online activity privileges for the users who signed up as members by giving certain personal information to the Web administrators. Very few stations (4 per cent) actually designed a registration system to gather more user information. It seems that most of the station Web sites were not very sophisticated in its design of interactive structures. Only 2.3 per cent of the sites offered some form of push technology that delivers content to Web users. Video streaming (8.3 per cent) and online audio (15.3 per cent) were used by few stations. Online assistance structures such as online database search (42.7 per cent), help functions (23 per cent), FAQs (12.3 per cent) were still applied by fewer than half of the stations. As for other design factors, many stations used animations to create moving effects (68 per cent), while counters (9 per cent) and moving news headlines (17 per cent) were used sparingly. Fewer than half of the sites utilized the frame format (47.3 per cent). Fewer than 10 per cent of the sites incorporated live camera views via the Internet. Of all stations that set up live camera views, simple scenery views were most prevalent, followed by traffic (6 per cent), and marketplace (0.3 per cent).

Most of the stations seemed to view their web sites as an important tool in extending their stations' reach and promoting their stations' brands Almost 93 per cent of the stations set up their own distinctive sites and 850/, managed to use an URL identical to their station IDs. While many affiliates placed links to their networks and readily put network logos on their front pages, most preferred to retain their identifies without network IDs as a part of their URLs (88.2 per cent).

BROADCAST TV WEB SITES' DEVELOPMENTAL STAGES

Information appeared to be the most prevalent content provided by the sampled station Web sites with many stations concentrating their online efforts on supplying information related to local news and weather, programming schedules, professional sports news, useful links for web users, and station/ station personnel. While a limited number of stations attempted to collect audience information for market research purposes, many have used their Web sites as a marketing and promotional tool aiming at TV audiences.

It seems that broadcast TV stations have not completely followed the Web Content Progression Model for an Established Company.

The Web sites appeared to offer product/image information; however, the content analysis also revealed that, contrary to the authors' expectation, these stations have neglected the important information collection stage and moved to the customer support stage with a marketing emphasis primarily on TV audiences. Largely ignoring the data collection capacity of the Internet, the stations seemed to be using the same promotional strategies that they have learned from promoting their programming on-air. The content analysis also depicted the existence of a transactional system that reinforces the marketing function of the Web sites by selling mostly station promotional items.

MARKET CHARACTERISTICS AND THE CONTENT AND STRUCTURES OF STATION WEB SITES

Different network affiliates applied different online strategies as affiliation appeared to be the most significant variable consistently across most design and content variables. In regards to the "front-page" content, except for specific features such as weather images, local news web-casting, and local news team ads, affiliation was significantly related to all other news-related, advertising and promotion, and network presence variables. The relationship between affiliation and the presence of network log is especially strong with a Cramer's

V of.574. Specifically, CBS affiliates seemed to be most aggressively in linking to their network sites (79 per cent of the sampled CBS affiliates) from their "home pages," while WB network was the least active (13 per cent).

When it comes to placing network logo on the "front page," UPN affiliates were most aggressive (100 per cent), while PBS affiliates preferred establishing local images with only 38 per cent of the stations incorporating PBS logo on their "home pages."

UPN and CBS affiliates' web sites contained the most banner ads from advertisers (71 per centand 62 per cent) on their "home pages." Interestingly, the non-majors, WB affiliates (73 per cent), UPN (54 per cent), and PBS affiliates (52 per cent) were most aggressive in promoting their programming on "front pages." CBS affiliates were also most active in promoting their news (local and network) and including top story news content (text: 51 per cent; photos: 49 per cent) and weather (text: 65 per cent) on their "home pages."

As for the "overall" web site content, affiliation was significantly related to most content variables except for personnel contact information, web-casting variables, and specific content such as horoscope and public service announcement. There seem to be strong relationships between affiliation and the content of top stories (V=.601), local weather (V=.625), and local market/ business information (V=.582). Specifically, while PBS affiliates were most active in providing general station information to their web users (82 per cent), NBC and ABC (both 68 per cent) were most likely to provide station personnel information on the web. Most affiliates were offering programming schedules online except for CBS affiliates which lagged behind with only about half of them incorporating such information on their web sites. Nevertheless, CBS affiliates did lead in providing programming content information throughout their web sites. Except for offering local job listings, with which NBC affiliates were most active (74 per cent), CBS affiliates seemed to include the most local life and business information, averaging 73 per cent. Nevertheless, NBC was most active in linking to local port sites.

In regards to news-related content throughout the web sites, CBS affiliates were most likely to incorporate news content (averaging 84 per centio), professional sports news (90 per cent), and local weather news (95'ia>). ABC affiliates were mot active in linking to their network news site (71 per cent), while PBS affiliates were the least likely to link to their network news site (10 per cent). Again, CBS affiliates were most active in carrying banner ads (89 per cent), while ABC affiliates provided most classified ads (48 per cent). Interestingly, CBS affiliates, whose "front pages" were the least likely to contain programming ads, promoted their programming and news heavily throughout their sites (76 per cent and 71 per cent). Affiliation was somewhat related to Web structures with the exception of online data collection variables. Strong correlations seem to exist between affiliation and mechanisms such as clubs/

membership structure (V=.636), help function (V=.636), and online shopping of station promotional items (V=.551). CBS affiliates were most active in offering communication mechanism such as feedback forms (78 per cent). They were also most aggressive in exploring electronic commerce opportunities (32 per cent) with mostly station promotional items. CBS affiliates were also most likely to offer user-friendly web tools such as help (75 per cent) and search function (76 per cent). As for URL strategies, many UPN affiliates incorporated "UPN" as part of their web addresses (46 per cent), while hone of the PBS affiliates chose to do so. Among the big four networks, Fox affiliates were most likely to include "Fox" in their URLs (25 per cent).

MARKET SIZE

Market size was the least relevant to all variables investigated. Only programming ads on front pages were more significantly related to market sizes at.01 level. Variables such as links to professional sports sites, links to affiliated network sites, programming banner ads, classified ads, chat room structure, and online shopping were related to market sizes at.05 level.

MARKET RANKING

Though not as prevalent as affiliation, market rankings were also widely related to many variables investigated. It seems like the more successful (*i.e.*, viewed by more audiences) a station is, the more likely it is to link to its network site (V=.445), include network logos (V=.479), offer top story and weather, and place programming ads (V=.356) on its front page. Local news leaders were even more aggressive in providing weather news and adding news ads on these pages. A station's market ranking also had a significantly positive relationship with variables such as personnel information, programme schedule, general programme content information, local life/job/business content, most news-related content, links to professional sport news, weather news, programming and news banner ads, banner and classified, and links to network webs and network news webs. In sum, leading stations were most likely to offer local information, news and weather, ads, programming information, and links to affiliated network sites. However, market rankings were not particularly related to the structure variables.

The few significant co-relations suggested that the more successful a station was, the more likely it was to be involved with mechanisms such as electronic commerce (V=.436), membership system (V=.418), and various design features.

OWNERSHIP

Ownership (in terms of ownership size) was related to fewer variables than market rankings. It seems like the larger a station owner was, the more likely it was to offer banners ads, and to some degree weather, top story news, network logo, links to network sites, and programming ads on its front page. As for overall content, ownership was most related to news, weather, local information, news and programming banner ads, banner ads, and to some degree station/personnel information, classified ads, links to network news sites, programmers' sites, and contests/sweepstakes/promos.

Again, larger station groups were more likely to offer this content. By the same token, larger station owners were somewhat more likely to include communication mechanisms, membership systems, and transactional features.

DISCUSSION AND CONCLUSIONS

Overall, local stations seem to capitalize on their news and programming strength in their online content, using the Internet as a tool to provide text-oriented headline news and programming information.

The role of headline news/top stories is especially important for the "front pages" of these Web sites, presenting an obvious relevancy between a local station's onair and online content emphasis.

Slightly fewer than half of the stations continue to establish themselves as local content hubs with community information such as local job listings and yellow pages. The Web content seemed to indicate that TV stations have been using their Web sites mainly to serve the "audience" rather than the "advertiser" segment of the dual customer base.

This study revealed the important role news-related content played on broadcast station Web sites and the stations' transfer of their relevant on-air product to the online system. Overall, broadcast stations offered an online presence that is predominantly informational, with limited communication and transactional structures and rare entertainment and sociability opportunities.

In other words, while broadcast stations have diligently transferred their news expertise online and possibly established credibility, they have not capitalized on the essence of the Internet medium, progressing from information provision to audience data collection to harvest the value of the Web for developing customer and internal support and even transactional services.

To a certain degree, a TV station that has acquired a competitive audience share and/or is owned by a larger station group is well positioned to take advantage of the strategic value of the Internet as the results of this study indicated a relationship between such market characteristics and the provision of local information, electronic commerce, communication mechanisms, and data collection systems. Television broadcasters seem to follow a somewhat different Web development approach than the one generally adopted by established companies. The broadcasters have transferred their on-air assets in informational content to the online platform. It's plausible to conclude that the stations are following a safer route of expansion into this new medium by re-assembling and re-purposing their distinctive existing products for online delivery. The emphasis on news-oriented content presents a less risky business approach because a station will be able to minimize costs by re-formatting the content it already owns and provide the utility currently sought by most audience Web users. As the Net grows and the delivery technology improves, the TV broadcasters will eventually enter a stage of Web development that requires more product differentiation. Stations may then develop Web sites that incorporate gratifying experiences in communication, entertainment, transaction, and/or sociability. Such a progression in Web development will require the broadcasters to create Web-specific original content and to capitalize on the interactivity and personalization characteristics of the Internet.

Future research in broadcasters' Web strategies may focus on the development of such original Web content, the application of interactive features that enhance the delivery of such content, and the audience usage of these content and structures.

MAJOR COMMERCIAL ONLINE SERVICES

Which commercial databases at the national level are the best to use for news research or other information gathering purposes? It depends on who is asked. Different information professionals, such as news researchers, prefer different combinations of sources for each unique situation. Of course, much depends on what the services offer.

There are different classes of online database services. The three major types that Paul identified are data superstores, boutique database services, and hybrid services. For beginners just learning about online services, the hybrid services are the best place to start. For more sophisticated researchers and computer-comfortable users, the data superstores and boutique services are the electronic sources of choice.

"Most professional database searchers we know automatically turn to specific databases when asked for news information. Nexis... DataTimes, Dow Jones, NewsNet, and, increasingly, Dialog, certainly are logical places to do comprehensive, retrospective searches for newspaper and news wire coverage," wrote *National Geographic* Assistant Library Director Ellen Briscoe and former Washington Post News Research Centre Chief of Research Catherine Wall.

"What marks the good researcher from the rest of us is knowing what paper is pertinent, how to get it, how to understand it,", wrote information consultant and investigative reporter John Ullman. "Databases, of course, are a great playing field leveler, making information equally available to those with mega resources and those with meagre." The World Wide Web and the Internet became the most popular online databases and information sources in newsrooms by 1995. The national studies conducted at the University of Miami from 1994 to 1997 show the rapid growth of the Web as the database tool of choice for journalists. Data show the most popular online database resources in newspaper newsrooms over a 4-year period. Use of the Web grew fastest among all major services used, jumping from 25 per cent to 92 per cent during the period ending in early 1997. It is increasingly rare to find a news organization not using at least minimal access to the World Wide Web.

Some city and county government databases that are available online continue to use older bulletin board system technology, but many have moved to the Web or have been originally created for the Web. State and federal government online sites are also valuable to journalists, the data show. Two of the most widely used federal online database services are fredWorld and PACER, the federal court information service.

Commercially available services remain popular. The largest number of online database tools is commercial in nature. Most are highly specialized in the types of information available (*e.g.*, science, law, or public records). The most popular commercial database service that does not appeal to general computer users is Lexis/Nexis. Its use has remained steady — from 26 per cent to 29 per cent of newspapers in the studies — despite its high cost to users. America Online (AOL), not a specialized service in any way, provides basic Web access, E-mail, and other general online resources that put online information in the hands of the smallest news organizations. AOL was used by 43 per cent of newsrooms in 1997 and is one of the fastest growing tools. CompuServe, which was acquired in 1997 by AOL in a three-way sale, was used by one quarter of newspapers.

These services are popular for several reasons, among them the ISP role and their affordability for smaller news organizations. Not all databases or database services used in news research are described in the following sections — there are far too many — but there are some that have risen to the top in terms of their value to reporters, editors, and news researchers. The services here are the major ones used in news organization libraries and in newsrooms today.

BROADCAST AND GOVERNMENT TRANSCRIPT DATABASES

There are other online sources of broadcast news and other types of transcripts in addition to Burrelle's Broadcast Database which is part of Burrelle's Information Services. Not only are broadcast news programmes on many of the major television networks — ABC, CBS, NBC, and CNBC — available through online databases, but so are government press briefings, press conferences, and speeches by leading government officials, such as the president, vice president, and cabinet members, and congressional hearings.

The service is updated daily within hours of broadcast. The database dates back to 1989. Lexis/Nexis offers full-text transcripts of ABC News, the British Broadcasting Corporation Summary World Broadcast, Burrelle's, Cable News

Network, and CNBC News as part of its News Library. The Federal News Service, a part of Federal Information Systems in Washington, DC, has been providing transcriptions of major federal government events for a decade. Press briefings and speeches, for example, from the White House, State Department, and Defence Department are staples of this daily updated database. The service also offers translations from selected events such as press conferences in Moscow. The Reuters Transcript Report has been provided by the Reuters international news agency since 1989. Similar to the Federal News Service, this database offers transcriptions of press conferences and speeches from major executive branch sources in the federal government in Washington. Reuters also offers international access to selected transcribed world-level news events such as press conferences or speeches by world leaders.

Despite the obvious advantages to finding something that was said by a newsmaker on the air, there are problems unique to broadcast news and public event transcription databases. Marydee Ojala, an information consultant, said the foremost problem Is the visual component of television news.

It is seldom represented and, when it is, users find only brief parenthetical material supplied. She also said live interviews are a search challenge: "People interrupt each other. They talk over each other. A sentence might begin far away from where it ends", she warned.

The shorter, more conversational writing style might also cause search problems not encountered in print-oriented databases. Repeated stories in newscasts are also a minor concern. The major future area for development of these broadcast news databases will be major market local news stations.

ONLINE CREDIT RECORDS AND DATA

Private commercial credit reporting services are another major source of online information. Credit records are maintained for a variety of reasons on just about every adult in the country.

Credit records, because of the personal nature of their information, are highly restricted databases. Typical customers of these services are retail businesses, banks, and financial institutions that extend credit or take other risks of substantial value.

The federal Fair Credit Reporting Act sets the rules for disclosure of this information. Usually a user must submit specific legitimate reasons for seeking information such as employment, loan applications, and other credit situations. Credit service managers claim they have worked hard to self-regulate themselves to follow the letter of the law, if not also the spirit of the law. These businesses provide limited forms of their credit reports for more general public consumption that do not violate the federal credit information reporting law.

Even in stripped, or restricted, form, these files can be a tremendous asset for reporters or news researchers involved in "people finding" or searching for background information about individuals or businesses. The most common information available to the general user in a credit history will be the full name, current and former residential addresses, gender, birth date and place information, Social Security number, name of spouse, and employment history.

The three major national online credit network services are as follows:

- *Equyifax*: This Atlanta company is the largest consumer credit information service in the United States, and largest consumer and business credit source in Canada and the United Kingdom. The Consumer Centre provides profiles of individuals in the database. Overall, Equifax has 10,000 employees and operates in 17 nations.
- *Experian information services*: This service was created when businesses formerly known as TRW Information Systems and Services and CCN Group were combined in 1996. With 7,000 employees and close to $1 billion in sales, Experian is one of the largest consumer and business credit information suppliers. In North America, Experian is based in Orange, California.
- *Trans union credit information*: Located in Chicago, Trans Union provides consumer credit history reports at a national level. The Trans Union consumer database held about 300 GB of information in 1997.

In addition to the three leaders, the National Credit Information (NCI) Network, based in Ohio, links consumer credit information from more than 1,000 credit bureaus providing 250 million consumer credit and commercial credit reports on businesses for qualified users. Each of these services maintains hundreds of millions of credit records in numerous databases. However, as with other online databases, caution is necessary in using the credit databases because of errors and because of legal concerns involving privacy laws. Consumers Union, publisher of Consumer Reports, says there are numerous errors, some serious in nature, in these reports. Error rates may run as high as 43 per cent to 48 per cent of the records, including some errors in 19 per cent of the records that could cause credit application rejections.

Using this type of information for facts in a story may be risky, if not an outright bad idea. Instead, as many reporters and news librarians do, the information should be used to locate additional personal information and people from other sources. Then the two sets of information can be used to verify facts through more conventional reporting strategies such as interviewing and firsthand observation. Another growing set of concerns involves the unethical, and often illegal, access to information contained in credit reports. Credit services sell certain basic information, such as names, addresses, and telephone numbers, to the general public for a search fee. Other financial records are not supposed to be sold by the services to the general public, including journalists.

Some news organizations have been accused of using access to credit databases improperly to obtain credit ratings, credit card balances, mortgage balances, and related personal data that are protected by state and federal laws. Even in cases where access is legitimate, there is growing concern about public access to this information and the conflict with privacy interests.

GROWTH IN CD-ROM AND OTHER PORTABLE DATABASES

The number of news organizations and individuals using CD-ROM drives and CD-ROMs is growing rapidly. Similarly, the number of CD-ROM-based databases available to the public is growing as fast or even more quickly. There were nearly 3,000 CD-ROM databases -- about 26 per cent of the more than 11,300 databases published -- that were placed on the market in 1996. The number of businesses producing CD-ROMs has grown as well. In 1997 there were more than 1,800 CD-ROM vendors. This is 18 times the approximately 100 vendors in business in 1975.

Results from the CAR studies conducted at the University of Miami from 1994 to 1997, show that the amount of use of CD-ROM resources is increasing.

The number of newsrooms with CD-ROM drives has grown. In 1997, 70 per cent of the nation's newspapers had CD-ROM drives for use in newsrooms. Of that total, 42 per cent had more than one CD-ROM in the newsroom.

Three years earlier, usage was scant — only 43 per cent total-because CD-ROM drives were not part of the basic desktop or notebook PC hardware configuration. Only 40 per cent had a single CD-ROM drive and just 3 per cent had more than one available for newsroom access. Use, it appears, will continue to increase. Many newspapers that did not have CD-ROM drives indicated plans to acquire them in the near future. CD-ROM storage differs from floppy disk storage in that most floppy disk drives can both write data to the disk and read data from it. CD-ROM technology exists to do both as well, of course, and the cost of drives that read and write has dropped in recent years. However, although some major daily newspapers and other large news organizations are producing their own CDs, the lower cost has not resulted in any major change in use in newsrooms in 1997. It has led to increased distribution of data by some businesses that might have selected other media in the past.

CD-ROM drives are quite inexpensive by comparison and are installed in many off-the-shelf personal computer systems, especially those designed for multimedia software. The best single advantage of a CD-ROM is its high capacity of data storage. A CD-ROM can store about 650 MB of information. This compares to 1.44 MB of storage on a conventional 3.5-inch double density diskette. The CD-ROM's capacity makes it ideal for large databases that do not require updating, such as census data or large full-text databases.

CD-ROM technology is the current standard for data distribution. It is well established in the computer industry, in government, and in other sectors dealing with data and information. CD-ROM will remain in place and in wide use for the short term only, however. Its most common replacement, digital video disk-read only memory or digital versatile disk (DVD-ROM), began public use in 1997 and continued in 1998.

DVD-ROM can be used much like CD-ROMs are used for most PC users — simply for a wide range of types of data transfer. DVD-ROM and its related digital video disk-random access memory or digital versatile disk-random access memory (DVD-RAM) and digital video disk+rewritable or digital versatile disk+rewritable (DVD+RW) technologies — the latest optical disc formats — will ultimately replace CDs for several reasons.

Perhaps the most significant is the storage capacity of DVD. A first-generation DVD can store about 4.7 GB of information and later generations are expected to hold as much as 17 GB of data. Because most of the computer industry uses CD-ROM and it is still mainstream, the focus here remains on CD-ROM. DVD, however, will be useful for databases, but should have a significant impact on music audio data and video data as well.

CD-ROM drives work by use of laser optic technology rather than magnetic storage that is used in conventional diskettes. These units are often rated by access speed time in milliseconds. CD-ROM drives used for loading software or reading databases can also be used by PCs to play music or other audio and video if the computer system is equipped for multimedia.

For a home system, especially, the capabilities of CD-ROM give the drive additional use for the single investment. There are also devices, called optical CD-R (compact disc-recordable) devices that permit writing to the disc only one time, but allow unlimited readings from the disc. For several years, PC and Macintosh manufacturers have included multimedia tools with the base set-up of a computer. In addition to high-speed CD drives, computers also have sound cards, faster video cards, and speakers to take maximum advantage of CD content. For journalists, this means most recent desktop computers installed in newsrooms have CD capability or, if not at their workstations, there are more PCs around the newsroom with CDs and more convenient access to data on CDs. Some newsrooms have gone much further, however. With networked PCs and Macs, some newsrooms have purchased CD "Jukeboxes" that store a large number of CDs for use on demand from a single server. CD jukeboxes function in a manner similar to an old-fashioned record jukebox. For example, a set of telephone number databases or a encyclopaedia or reference book set on CD would be accessible at any desk through the database's search software on the server and the CD jukebox.

Bibliography

T Rajsekhar: *Modern Media and Television Journalism*, Sonali Publications, 2007.

Vandana Jyotirmayee: *Television Journalism and Programme Formatting*, Kanishka, 2013.

Vamsee Juluri: *Becoming a Global Audience : Longing and Belonging in Indian Music Television*, Orient Longman, 2004.

Nalin Mehta: *Behind a Billion Screens: What Television Tells Us About Modern India*, Harper Collins, 2015 .

Biswarup Sen and Abhijit Roy: *Channeling Cultures: Television Studies from India* , Oxford University Press, 2014.

Victor Sunderaj: *Children and Television*, Authorspress, 2006.

Anirudh Deshpande: *Class, Power and Consciousness in Indian Cinema and Television*, Primus, 2009.

M. Husain: *Distance Education Through Television*: , Anmol, 2004.

K.V. Joseph: *Economics of Culture Industry : Television in India*, Shipra Pub, 2010.

N. Usha Rani: *Educational Television in India : Challenges and Issues*, Discovery, 2006.

S Shukla: *Handbook of Journalism and Mass Communication*, Rajat Publication, Delhi, 2008.

A.S. Shukla: *Journalism Today : Concepts and Practices*, Rajat Publications, Delhi, 2010.

Adarsh Kumar Varma: *Advanced Journalism*, Har-anand Publications, Delhi, 2010.

Ajay Das: *Journalism : Editing and Reporting*, Omega Publication, Delhi, 2010.

Ajay Dash: *Basic Concept of Journalism*, Discovery Publishing House, Delhi, 2007.

Ajay Dash: *Broadcasting Journalism*, Discovery Publishing House, Delhi, 2007.

Ajay Kumar Sharma: *Journalism Laws*, Random Publications, Delhi, 2012.

Anant Chauhan Vishwendra: *Crime Journalism*, Random Publications, Delhi, 2012.

Anil K. Rai 'Ankit' and Shekhawat Hussain: *Community Journalism*, Shree Publication, Delhi, 2007.

Anurag Singh: *Journalism and Democracy*, Prateeksha Publications, Delhi, 2011.

Arnold S. De Beer and John C. Merrill: *Global Journalism : Topical Issues and Media Systems*, PHI Learning, Delhi, 2011.

Arun Bhatia: *Impact of Internet on Journalism*, Akansha Publication, Delhi, 2005.

Arun K Goel: *Encyclopaedia of Journalism and Mass Communication (2 Vols-Set)*, Saurabh Publishing House, Delhi, 2008.

B. S. Rao: *Emerging Trends in Media Journalism and Communication*, Enkay Publishing House, Delhi, 2012.

B. S. Rao: *Handbook of Photo Journalism in the Digital Age*, Enkay Publishing House, Delhi, 2013.

B.L. Jana: *Agricultural Journalism*, Agrotech Publishing Academy, Delhi, 2014.

B.N. Tripathi: *Handbook of Journalism and Mass Media*, Saurabh Publishing House, Delhi, 2001.

Balai Lal Jana and Kanai Prasad Mitra: *Farm Journalism*, Agrotech Publishing Academy, Delhi, 2013.

Barbie Zelizer and Stuart Allan: *Keywords in News and Journalism Studies*, Tata McGraw Hill, Delhi, 2010.

Bhanu Pratap Singh: *Communication Management in Journalism*, Anmol Publication, Delhi, 2011.

C Bhaskaran; R Prakash and N Kishore Kumar: *Farm Journalism and Media Management*, Agrotech Publication, Delhi, 2008.

C.S. Shrivastava and R.K. Parekh: *Broadcast Journalism*, Crescent Publishing Corporation, Delhi, 2012.

Carole Fleming, Emma Hemmingway, Gillian Moore and Dave Welford: *An Introduction to Journalism*, Vistaar Publications, Delhi, 2006.

D N Kapoor: *Broadcast Journalism*, Mohit Publication, Delhi, 2006.

D S Verma: *History of Journalism*, Pearl Books, Delhi, 2007.

D V R Murthy: *Development Journalism: What Next? : An Agenda for the Press*, Kanishka Publication, Delhi, 2006.

D. G. Gupta: *Development of Journalism Management*, Pearl Books, Delhi, 2012.

D.D. Arora: *Business Journalism*, Saloni Publication, Delhi, 2003.

D.V.R. Murthy and Y.D. Ramdas: *Gandhi and Journalism*, Kanishka Publication, Delhi, 2013.

D.V.R. Murthy: *Developmental Journalism*, Dominant Publication, Delhi, 2012.

Index